D0309972

Dr Harold Shukman is University Lecturer in Modern
Russian History at Oxford and Fellow of St Antony's
College, where from 1981 to 1991 he was also Director
of the Russian and East European Centre. His trans-
lations include Anatoly Rybakov's *Heavy Sand* and
Children of the Arbat, the memoirs of Andrei Gromyko,
and Dmitri Volkogonov's monumental trilogy *Stalin*,
Lenin, and *Trotsky*. He is currently translating
Volkogonov's *Seven Leaders*. His books include *Lenin
and the Russian Revolution*, *The Blackwell Encyclopedia
of the Russian Revolution* and a forthcoming study of
Rasputin.

STALIN'S GENERALS

EDITED BY
Harold Shukman

A PHOENIX GIANT PAPERBACK

First published in Great Britain
by Weidenfeld and Nicolson in 1993
This paperback edition published in 1997
by Phoenix, a division of Orion Books Ltd,
Orion House, 5 Upper St Martin's Lane,
London WC2H 9EA

Copyright © Weidenfeld and Nicolson, 1993

The right of Harold Shukman to be identified as the editor
of this work has been asserted by him in accordance with
the Copyright, Designs and Patents Act 1988.

All rights reserved. No part of this publication may be
reproduced, stored in a retrieval system, or transmitted,
in any form or by any means, electronic, mechanical,
photocopying, recording or otherwise, without the prior
permission of the copyright owner.

A CIP catalogue record for this book is available
from the British Library.

ISBN: 0 75380 002 0

Printed and bound in Great Britain by
Butler & Tanner Ltd, Frome and London

CONTENTS

v

MAPS

CONTRIBUTORS

CATHERINE ANDREYEV is a Student (Fellow) of Christ Church and a Lecturer in Modern European History at the University of Oxford. Her book *Vlasov and the Russian Liberation Movement* was published by Cambridge University Press in 1987 and appeared in a Russian and a Polish translation in 1990. She is currently working on the history of the Russian émigrés between the two world wars.

VIKTOR ANFILOV graduated from the Frunze Military Academy and General Staff Academy and served from 1941 to 1945 at the front. From 1957 to 1964 he conducted research at the General Staff Military History Department. He was a Senior Lecturer in the General Staff Academy until 1970, when he became a Professor at the Moscow State Institute of International Relations. He is a member of the Executive Council of the Russian Historians' Second World War Association. Among his many books (in Russian) are *The Outbreak of the Great Patriotic War* (1962), *The Approach and Opening Phase of the War* (1971), *The Failure of the Blitzkrieg* (1974), *1941* (1982), and the *Collapse of Hitler's March on Moscow* (1989).

JOHN ERICKSON is Director of Defence Studies at Edinburgh University, specializing in Russian and Soviet military history and military organization. He is the author of *The Soviet High Command 1918–1941* (1962, 1984); a two-volume history of the Soviet-German war, *The Road to Stalingrad* (1975) and *The Road to Berlin* (1983); and a study of the Soviet Army, *Soviet Ground Forces: An Operational Assessment* (with Lynn Hansen and Wm. Schneider) (1986). He is presently completing a study of the Soviet war effort 1941–1945 entitled *Blood, Bread and Steel*, initially delivered as a series of lectures in the Department of History, Yale University.

COLONEL DAVID M. GLANTZ, Director, Foreign Military Studies Office, Combined Arms Command, Fort Leavenworth, Kansas, holds a degree from the Virginia Military Institute and the University of North Carolina at Chapel Hill. He is the author of numerous articles on Soviet military affairs and books on Soviet strategy, military operations, deception and intelligence in the Second World War. His book on Soviet military strategy was published in 1992, and an expanded history of Soviet airborne forces and operations during the initial period of war (June–August 1941) will appear in 1993.

GABRIEL GORODETSKY is a Professor of History at Tel Aviv University. He has been the Director of the Cummings Center for Russian Studies at the University since 1990, and the Academic Adviser to the Staff College of the Israeli Defence Forces since 1986. Professor Gorodetsky is the author of *The Precarious Truce: Anglo-Soviet Relations, 1924–27* (Cambridge, 1977), and *Stafford Cripps' Mission to Moscow, 1940–42* (Cambridge, 1984), and editor of *Soviet Foreign Policy, 1917–1991: A retrospective* (London, 1992). He has published numerous articles on Soviet foreign policy and the history of the Second World War and is now writing a new history of the Grand Alliance in the Second World War.

GEOFFREY JUKES is a Senior Fellow in the Department of International Relations at the Australian National University, and has been there since 1967, following fourteen years in the British Civil Service (Ministry of Defence, Foreign and Colonial Office). He has specialized in Russian/ Soviet defence and foreign policies since leaving Oxford in 1953, with particular reference to the two World Wars, and his previous writings on military history include two books on the Battle of Stalingrad, one each on those of Moscow and Kursk, and one on the Russian offensive of 1916, as well as a number of articles. He is currently engaged in research on Russian/Soviet military policy in the Far East, and is writing a book on Stalin's wartime leadership.

BRIGADIER-GENERAL SHIMON NAVEH is a Senior Research Fellow of the Cummings Center for Russian Studies at Tel Aviv University. For 26 years he served in the paratroops of the Israeli Defence Forces. From 1988 until his retirement in 1992 he commanded a division. He graduated from the Royal College of Defence Studies in 1987, and received his MA in history from Tel Aviv University in 1990. His expertise is in Soviet military doctrine and he is currently completing a Ph.D. at King's College, London, on the Evolution of Operational Theory.

OLEG RZHESHEVSKY is Head of the Department of Military History in the Moscow Institute of World History. He graduated from aviation school and military institute and served as a Red Air Force pilot from 1942 to 1948.

His books include *War and History* (1976, 1984), *The Second World War: Myths and Realities* (1984) and *Europe 1939: Was War Inevitable?* (1989). He is the Russian editor of *The Grand Strategy* by Michael Howard, *The History of the Second World War* by B. Liddell Hart, *Crusade in Europe* by David Eisenhower and *The Rise and Fall of the Third Reich* by William Shirer.

HAROLD SHUKMAN (Editor) is a University Lecturer in Modern Russian History at Oxford and a Fellow of St Antony's College, where from 1981 to 1991 he was Director of the Russian and East European Centre. His books include *Lenin and the Russian Revolution* (1966, 1977), *A History of World Communism* (1975 with F. W. Deakin and H. T. Willetts), (Ed.) *The Blackwell Encyclopedia of the Russian Revolution* (1988) and a study of Rasputin (forthcoming). He is General Editor of *Longman's History of Russia* and has translated plays by Shvarts and Babel, Rybakov's *Children of the Arbat*, the memoirs of Andrei Gromyko and Dmitri Volkogonov's trilogy of *Stalin*, *Lenin*, and *Trotsky*. He is writing a study of the Russian emigration during the First World War, and translating Volkogonov's *Seven Leaders*.

COLONEL-GENERAL DMITRI VOLKOGONOV was Defence Adviser to President Yeltsin. He graduated from the Military-Political Academy and occupied various posts. He reached the rank of Colonel-General and also held doctorates in philosophy and history. In 1986 he became Director of the Institute of Military History, leaving it in June 1991 when he was attacked by the senior military, including former Defence Minister Yazov, for the line he took in editing a new history of the Second World War, publication of which is now unlikely. His study of Stalin, based on unpublished documents, was published in the West in 1991, followed by publication in Russia of his portraits of Trotsky and Lenin, also based on unpublished materials. These were published internationally in 1994 and 1995. He died in December 1995.

RICHARD WOFF qualified as a Russian linguist and served in the King's (Liverpool) Regiment and Intelligence Corps from 1951 to 1955. He worked in banking and industry from 1955 to 1958, when he entered London University, taking his degree in Russian and East European Studies in 1961. Between 1961 and 1987 he served in the Diplomatic Service. From 1987 until 1991 he edited *Jane's High Command* and *Warsaw Pact*. Since 1991 he has been a senior researcher at the Soviet Studies Research Centre, Royal Military Academy Sandhurst. He is the editor of *CIS and National Armed Forces of the Former Soviet Union*.

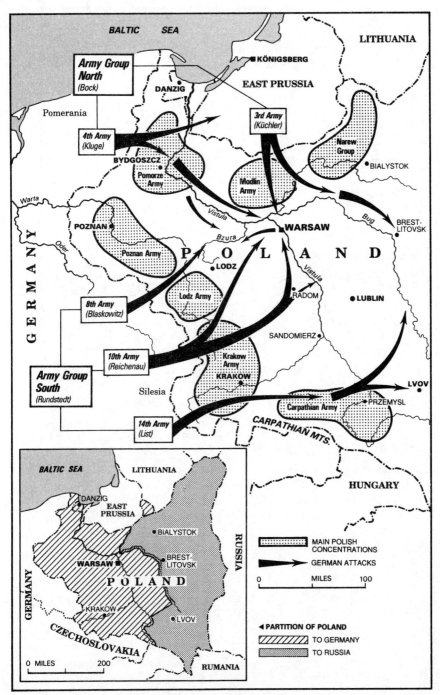

The invasion of Poland, September 1939

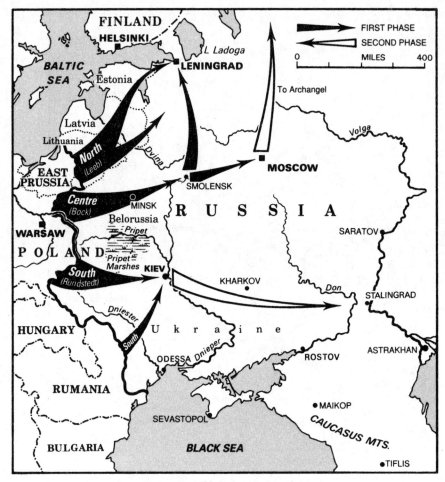

'Barbarossa': Hitler's invasion plan

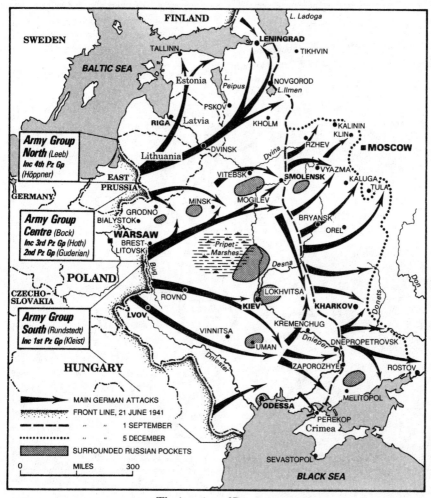

The invasion of Russia, 1941

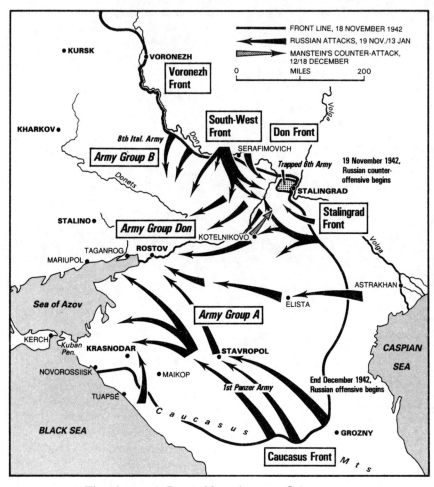

The tide turns in Russia, November 1942–January 1943

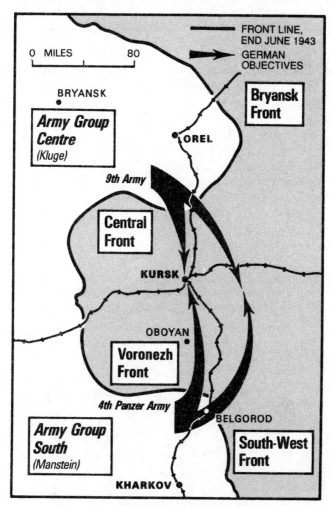

Operation 'Citadel' and the Kursk salient

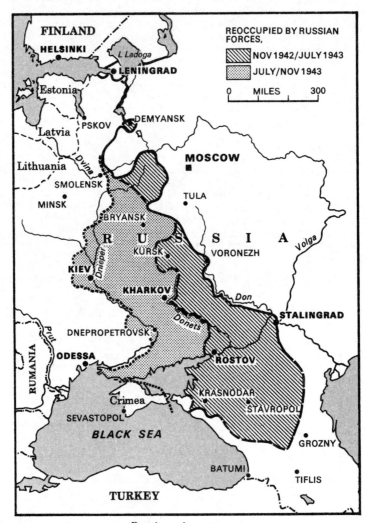

Russian gains, 1942–43

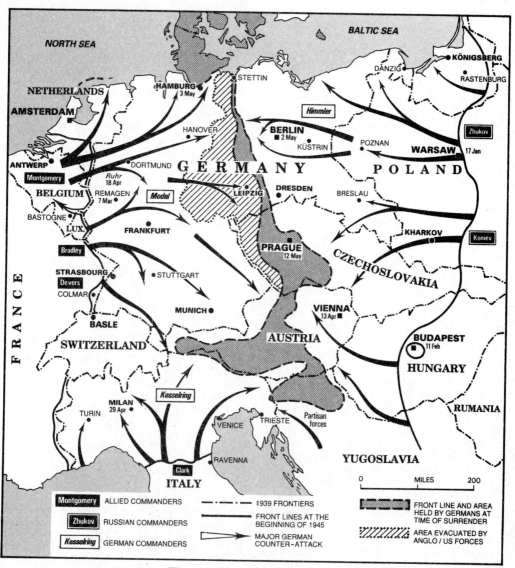

The end of the Third Reich, 1945

INTRODUCTION

HAROLD SHUKMAN

It was not self-evident in the ideology of the new Soviet state founded by Lenin that this was to be a militaristic or even well-armed society. The World Revolution, though it might proceed through violent clashes, was understood as the natural and inevitable outcome of the economic incompatibility of Capital and Labour. In practice, the Russian revolution quickly turned into a bloody and prolonged civil war, and in the course of it many figures surprisingly emerged as men of military bent and skill. Least likely as the founder of the Workers' and Peasants' Red Army was a fiery orator and intense intellectual, a 'professional revolutionary', a striking figure with black hair, a pointed beard and pince-nez whose name, Leon Trotsky, would soon become as well known as that of Lenin. Like Stalin, his arch-rival, and his nemesis, he had not seen a day's service in any army, but was none the less to be responsible for commanding fronts and armies and planning strategy.

The origins of the Red Army, in other words, lay in the efforts of amateurs who were improvising in order to keep their régime in being. While Semen Budenny achieved great success in 1919–20 with his 1st Cavalry Army, Viktor Anfilov shows that he was mentally fixed in those events, and though he remained in favour and high office, he was unable to meet the demands of modern warfare when they arose. Even more spectacular was the rise to supreme state office of the legendary hero of the Civil War, Kliment Voroshilov, described by Dmitri Volkogonov as 'the most mediocre, faceless, intellectually dim' of individuals, who was to play a truly evil part in determining the fate of his fellow officers in the 1930s. To a great extent the first generation of Red Army commanders had real military men to thank for their eventual success, for Trotsky saw early on that only by recruiting the talents of experienced and battle-hardened former tsarist officers, who might otherwise go to the other side, could the Soviets hope to field trained and properly commanded troops, and he had Lenin's approval for this policy. Political commissars with military experience were appointed to watch for ideologically dangerous moves by these 'bourgeois experts', but, as John

Erickson has shown in his *The Soviet High Command*, many of the latter saw an opportunity to pursue a promising military career that had been cut off by the disintegration of the tsarist army. Among our subjects, the most outstanding 'experts' were Vasilevsky and Shaposhnikov, who remained as indispensable advisers to Stalin throughout the 1930s and the war.

Indeed, expediency became the hallmark of the new régime very much at the expense of ideology. By the early 1930s, in a world that was proving both stubbornly resistant to Communism and increasingly polarized by the rise of Fascism, the Soviet Union had become a militarized power with a highly defensive outlook. Its armaments industry was developing fast, the army was an honoured and respectable profession, and technical and strategic innovation were becoming recognizable features of this great section of state activity. Promising commanders studied tactics and strategy at the Frunze Military Academy in Moscow until 1936, when the General Staff Academy was established and became the indispensable springboard to senior command status. In the mid-1930s Western military observers watched as the Red Army displayed state-of-the-art tactics and operational originality. The combined operations that gave the Second World War its characteristic features – great battles involving the co-ordinated use of vast tank armies, infantry, aircraft and airborne forces – were highly developed by the Soviets. The USSR had by the middle of the 1930s become a major military power.

And at the peak of its achievement its command structure was torn down, physically destroyed, traumatized by accusations of treason, forced by torture and brain-washing to spread the damage far and wide by implicating others, equally innocent. Stalin's purge of the officer corps swept through the upper ranks from Marshal down to Major or below. These were not courts martial conducted with the customary decorum and soldierly honour expected by a military caste. Soviet officers, like hundreds of thousands of ordinary Party members and plain citizens, were simply arrested, stripped of their documents and flung into gaol or deported to Siberian exile. Only those, as in all other walks of life, whose 'testimony' was required to establish the guilt of others, or who were to be exploited as an example, would be arraigned in a court. Commonly, their 'trial' would be preceded by interrogation and torture and, equally commonly, they would then be shot. Out of some 40,000 officers (36,761 army and 3,000 navy) who were arrested, about one third, or nearly 15,000 were executed, the rest serving sentences of varied lengths and most of them returning to the army, still as officers, in time to fight in the Great Patriotic War. One of the most distinguished survivors of this ordeal was the future Marshal Rokossovsky, who rebutted the evidence at his 'trial', as Richard Woff writes, by reminding the court that its source had been dead seventeen years. Rokossovsky was one of the few officers who survived the ordeal, was miraculously saved by a three-year prison sentence, rejoined the forces and rose to the highest rank with full honours. Similar stories are recounted by Richard Woff in his article on 'Stalin's Ghosts'.

By the time the purge had subsided to a lower key – arrests never ceased, continuing even at the height of the war – Stalin had disposed of all the vestiges of the Red Army's revolutionary origins, and along with them its best trained and most highly educated echelons. The removal of all military district commanders, 90 per cent of district chiefs of staff, 80 per cent of corps and divisional commanders, 90 per cent of staff officers and chiefs of staff, also drastically reduced the intellectual quality of the army leadership. As Dmitri Volkogonov has shown in his *Stalin*, by the beginning of 1941 only 7.1 per cent of officers had a higher military education, while 55.9 per cent had secondary education, 24.6 per cent had been put through accelerated officer training, and 12 per cent of both military and political cadres had no military education at all.

Like so many diplomats, Party functionaries, industrial managers, academics and state officials, so an entire generation of lower-ranking officers who had escaped the meatgrinder found themselves rocketed into higher rank and greater responsibility. Most of the Red Army generals we deal with here (plus two Air Marshals and an Admiral of the Fleet), and, it is safe to assume, a large majority of the Red Army's 3,000 generals (in 1941) whom we have omitted, were born in the last decade of the nineteenth century, making them at least ten years younger than their English counterparts. But it would be wrong to assume that they had leapt up the rungs of the ladder to replace older men who had been disposed of: the purged had been of closely similar ages to those who stepped into their boots. Volkogonov's analysis of intellectual quality tells us that it was the most able whom Stalin most feared, a fact underlined by Shimon Naveh's discussion of the Tukhachevsky affair. It is also significant in our selection of senior generals that almost all of them were among the 7.1 per cent who had been through higher military training. In other words, at the very top, one élite was replaced by another. Stalin was, David Glantz explains in his article on Batov, relatively more tolerant of failure among these, the survivors; he actually permitted these generals to make mistakes and to learn from them.

However, the threatening, punitive atmosphere that persisted for so much of the army's history expressed itself on many levels. A particular tragedy of the purge, not recorded in this collection, is that infant sons of 'repressed' officers were taken into military schools and brought up and trained as professional soldiers themselves. But in order to prevent the emergence of a 'vengeful' generation, their names were changed, so that today in Russia and other republics there are thousands of middle-aged army men who may never know their true name or who their father was. In the conduct of the war itself, the threat of arrest and execution was ever-present. A number of commanders who suffered defeat at the hands of the Germans were then faced by the rigours of an NKVD tribunal and shot. Terror was even applied in the conduct of operations, as in the use of penal battalions – *shtrafbats*. These were army units dating officially from 1942, and copied from the tsarist past and the German Army. They were of two types, battalions for senior and middle-grade commanders and companies for junior officers and other ranks. Echoing long-established Imperial Russian Army practice, the wartime penal, or disciplinary, battalions came with the July 1942 order 'Not a step back!' Like the units formed of Gulag prisoners, it was the fate of these battalions to go in front of the tanks as forward infantry, knowing they would be shot in the back by their own side if they tried to escape or surrender to the Germans. Terror in the interests of stiffening the fighting spirit was even used outside the army: Order No. 270 of October 1941, as Oleg Rzheshevsky shows here, sanctioned the arrest of a serviceman's family if he deserted to the rear or surrendered. Given the number of Soviet prisoners-of-war – the staggering figure of 5,475,000 is now officially accepted – one can imagine the state of mind and the anguish of the civilian population which had this to bear, as well as all the other appalling privations visited on the country by the German invasion (see 'Shaposhnikov').

If Hitler's generals were largely of noble origin and Churchill's mostly from gentry families with a military tradition, Stalin's were overwhelmingly of peasant stock. At Potsdam in 1945, he told Churchill's interpreter, 'We have good generals in the Soviet Army, but so have you and the Americans. Only ours lack breeding and their manners are bad. Our people have a long way to go!' These generals were men who as children had laboured on a family smallholding, often in conditions of dire poverty. Setting aside native intelligence and fortunate timing as reasons for their advancement, what can be the qualities of a peasant upbringing that will emerge in generalship – leadership, initiative, imagination and flair? Are these qualities, indeed, typical of the Russian peasant? The Russian peasant, almost for as long as we have been aware of him in history, has not figured among the country's most creative, autonomous forces. For centuries enserfed as chattels to noblemen who could deal with them much as they chose, the bulk of Russia's peasantry was emancipated only in 1861, just four years before America's black slaves were freed. And emancipation had brought with it indebtedness, inadequate land and capital, and mounting poverty and a sense of having been cheated by the state in all but a handful. Also, under the tsars, it had been the peasants who had provided most of the recruits in the annual levy for the Empire's army of well over one million men in peacetime. Before the military reform of 1874, a recruit served twelve years, with the possibility of rising to NCO status and the chance to exercise the same brutal authority over the lower orders that he had himself suffered. Officers traditionally came from the landed gentry, often the titled aristocracy. After the 1874 reform, all subjects were theoretically liable to military service, now reduced first to six, then to four years, but in practice, the educated classes retained certain privileges of exemption or status, while, again, it was from the rural masses that the main body of the army continued to be drawn.

Given this deeply entrenched tradition, the high incidence of peasants among the Red Army officers corps may simply be an accident of continuity, a simple extension into the new era of the socially acceptable class of the old army, that is, the proletarian's new ally, the peasant. This would seem to be reinforced by the fact that so few commanders of note came from the working class, the new 'ruling class', who might have been expected to figure large in the 'Workers' and Peasants' Red Army'. Excluding Antonov, Bagramyan, Golikov, Rokossovsky, Tukhachevsky, Vasilevsky and Voroshilov, only one of whom (Bagramyan) was of truly working-class origin, all the generals portrayed here were of peasant background, and even Rokossovsky's alleged proletarian origins are seriously in doubt.

It would seem to be self-evident that individual military leaders in wartime make a unique contribution, or commit particular mistakes, either of which may affect the outcome of the conflict. The training, experience and personality of a general and the nature of his relations with his peers and his political leaders are legitimate aspects of military history, going well beyond Tolstoy's musings about the possible effects of Napoleon's cold in the head. In the case of the Soviet Union under Stalin, however, the question is overshadowed by the thought that, since Stalin was the omnipotent dictator, and since 'mistakes' were usually punished by irreversible sanctions, it is also legitimate to ask whether individual commanders could be expected to carve out a place of their own in the history books. Were they not automata, desperate to carry out the Leader's orders without question? Was there sufficient variety of background, education and experience to create a choice from which Stalin could appoint his commanders? Did any of them, especially following the bloodletting of the officers corps in the 1930s, have the guts and the commitment to stand up to the dictator when a military controversy arose? And if there were such qualities to be found among the most outstanding of the Soviet *generalitet*, how might it add to our understanding of Stalin?

Four basic phases, I believe, define the history of the Soviet Army during the period touching the generals in this collection. First, the creation of the Red Army during the Civil War of 1918–21; second, the mass purge of the officer corps in 1937–8 (while not forgetting that arrest, interrogation, camp or execution were sanctions used against the army throughout the Stalin period: 1937–8 was a period of mass trauma, a shock device intended to alter once and for all the outlook of officers); third, the Second World War (called in Soviet terminology the Great Patriotic or Fatherland War, but since we also encompass the campaigns against the Japanese in Mongolia in the 1930s, and the Finnish War of 1939–40, we here refer to the more general title); and fourth, the restructuring of the army in the light of the USSR's enhanced rôle in world politics after the Second World War. The centre of gravity of most of the articles in this collection is, however, the Second World War.

The arrangement of subjects in this collection reflects to some extent the unique character of the Red Army. While it would be possible to group a small number of generals whose careers were spent almost exclusively at staff level and close to Stalin (the *genshabisty*), and a similarly small group of those who are known only as theatre or army commanders (the *polkovodtsy*), so many of our characters divided their lives between staff appointments and field commands at different levels, that I decided only the alphabetical ordering of their biographies made sense.

Choosing which generals to include and which to leave out presented few problems. Apart from the 'pillars' of Soviet military historiography, such as Zhukov and Konev and Rokossovsky, we have included men who represent different branches of the service, whose actions affected a particular field, whether in the theory or practice of war, and about whom there was sufficient biographical material to make writing studies of them a feasible proposition. With one exception, all the subjects of this book were active before Stalin came to power, during his rule and following it. The intention in choosing this category of general was to show the degree to which individual character and military personality were affected by the political climate of the time, or how, if at all, senior military men balanced their military and political judgements. The single exception is that of Marshal Mikhail Tukhachevsky, who was executed in 1937. Tukhachevsky, however, could not be omitted. He was the focus of the 1937–8 purge. The entire thrust of his theoretical innovations was aimed against the automatic response to orders. He structured initiative and creative response into his operational theorems. His army was not one that could easily coexist with a Stalin in command. And yet his execution did not extinguish his influence as an innovator. Indeed, as Shimon Naveh shows, in the summer of 1942 Stalin resurrected Isserson, the sole surviving exponent of Tukhachevsky's deep operation theory, miraculously alive, and put him to work helping to plan the battle of Stalingrad.

Whether it was the spirit of Tukhachevsky or native character, during the war we find numerous occasions when a commander exercised his own judgement. The initiative shown by Admiral Kuznetsov, for example, in bringing naval shore installations up to war-readiness, as Geoffrey Jukes shows, while it earned a rebuke from the ever-nervous Stalin, meant the Red Navy was able to defend itself from heavy damage during the German attack. Elsewhere, a self-willed commander might manage to keep his favourite staff officers with him, despite orders from Supreme Headquarters (Stavka), and there were even some who argued with Stalin in terms which for others brought the almost inevitable consequences of incarceration and worse. But their action showed that the purge and the terror had not cowed the best of the army leadership. Nevertheless, none was capable of shifting Stalin in his determination 'not to provoke' Hitler in 1941, when most of Europe was already in German hands and the Wehrmacht was deploying in ever greater numbers on the Soviet border. Despite the fact that, like Churchill, he was insisting on seeing the most important intelligence material, the shock of the invasion on 22 June 1941 paralysed Stalin. His judgement, as Gabriel Gorodetsky shows in his article on Golikov, was seriously hampered by a pathological suspicion that Germany and Britain might close ranks and mount a crusade against Russia, a suspicion dating back to the Allied intervention during the Civil War, the Locarno Treaty in 1925 and the Munich Agreement of September 1938.

He soon took charge of the situation, however, and even so unforgiving a critic of Stalin as Dmitri Volkogonov admits that, while Stalin's rôle as military leader has been exaggerated in Soviet historiography, by the middle of the war he had acquired a good deal of strategic skill. At least he was now capable of listening to intelligent voices, well informed army men like Antonov, Shaposhnikov and Vasilevsky, who had the ability and the nerve to lay before him their frank assessment of the situation and to recommend what course of action he should adopt.

The war, however much drama and suffering and national pride it generated, did nothing to dilute the vengeful and sadistic nature of the Leader and his chief henchman, Beria. The category of 'repeaters' was invented: anyone who had been in prison or Gulag before the war and had been released into the forces, would, on returning home, even if covered in glory, be sent straight back to the camp. They were soon joined by hundreds of thousands of Red Army men who had been released from German prisoner-of-war camps – where, incidentally, their presence had been denied by Stalin, thus depriving them of Red Cross relief. Also flooding back into the Gulags were soldiers who had found themselves encircled by the Germans or under German occupation before making their way home.

Even more breathtaking in its sheer cynicism was Stalin's assault on the very military leaders who had made the victory possible. A number of generals went home bedecked with foreign medals and honorary knighthoods, as well as the highest Soviet honours awarded on the eve of the victory, only to find themselves, like their brothers-in-arms of a previous generation, accused of plotting with foreign governments or seeking power for themselves. The full vigour of late Stalinist paranoia thus struck at this section of society that had just brought Russia her most famous victory. In 1946, Chief of the Air Force Novikov, Admiral of the Fleet Kuznetsov and Marshal Zhukov were only the best known names of many to be arraigned and disgraced, some serving long and bitter years in prison, others

7

'mercifully' permitted to go to undistinguished postings to rot. Any wartime notion that the Party and state would relax their grip on society, when the Soviet Union stood on an equal footing with the West as the conqueror of Nazi Germany, was thus quickly nipped in the bud. Stalin made it plain that he rejected the dictum, 'the victors shall not be judged'.

The opening up of Soviet history by the *glasnost* of the Gorbachev era exposed virtually all aspects of the last seventy or so years to public scrutiny. Even so uncomfortable a subject as possible Red Army collaboration with the Germans, exemplified by General Vlasov, has been tentatively aired, and Catherine Andreyev reports suggestions that a statue might even be erected in Russia in his memory. History in the last few years has become the means whereby ordinary folk might rationalize their rejection of an entire period. But by labelling everything that occurred since 1917 as 'Bolshevik' in origin, or since the late 1920s as 'Stalinist', the Russians have risked creating a new historical wasteland, as devoid of heroes and heroism as Soviet historiography had depicted Russian history before 1917. All the signs in the early 1990s are that they are looking back to the achievements of the tsarist era, as they perceive them, in the search for moral inspiration and national rebirth. Paradoxically, it was the most cynical of Stalin's initiatives in the late 1930s, but particularly during the Second World War, that first revived Russian nationalism as a means of uniting the nation against Fascism. By restoring in 1943 a small degree of freedom of action to the Orthodox Church, and abolishing Comintern, he hoped both to rally the people and to allay any doubts his Western Allies might be harbouring about his post-war intentions: Russia, he wanted to suggest, had its own domestic agenda, its own path, and should not be seen as a threat to the post-war world order.

In the post-Soviet era, the Russians seem unable to move forward without first recovering the lost baggage of the pre-1917 period. As they cast about for new heroes, settling now on Witte, the prime minister of 1905, now on his successor, the more decisive Stolypin, and even on Nicholas II himself, they have no time to reflect on those figures of the 'Stalin era', the military leaders of the Second World War who, even if they saved Stalin and his appalling régime, also saved the Russians from the rule of a madman whose very philosophy would have enslaved them as 'sub-humans'. The war, and the part played in it by the men we depict here, may temporarily go out of focus, as the Russians concentrate their attention on other matters, but on the global scale it will remain one of the most devastating and heroic chapters of world history.

EDITORIAL NOTES

1. Soviet Supreme Headquarters is commonly referred to by its Russian name, Stavka, and sometimes, for added clarity, as GHQ.
2. The term 'Direction', e.g. Moscow Direction, may be ambiguous in general English usage. It signifies an area extending from a front but having no particular shape (as might be suggested by 'sector'), but aiming in a particular direction, or along a line towards a target. We have chosen the alternative term 'Axis' as more accessible to the general reader.
3. The term 'Front' generally denotes what it suggests, i.e. the forward area of combat. 'Front' in Russian may also signify an Army Group, i.e. the full panoply of forces – ground, armoured, air – under a general commander. We describe such Groups as 'Fronts', e.g. 1st Belorussian Front, thus distinguishing them from their German equivalents, e.g. Army Group Centre.
4. Also to avoid ambiguity, Roman numerals are used for German units, e.g. XVII Corps, VI Army.
5. Wholly consistent transliteration of Russian words and names is impossible without recourse to specialized glossaries. Therefore, the most easily recognized forms have been used in the text, e.g. Rokossovsky, Alexander, Kharkov, while in the bibliographies, for the sake of accurate reference, such names appear as Rokossovskii, Aleksandr, Khar'kov.

Alexei Innokentievich
ANTONOV

RICHARD WOFF

In his relationship with the Red Army High Command Stalin revealed a number of contradictions in his character. Capable of capricious cruelty, and possessed by vindictive megalomania, he thought nothing of sending lifelong friends to their death. Distinguished commanders, like Zhukov, could be banished with callous contempt. He learnt, none the less, to respect the professional ability and judgement of some of his closest military advisors. While he regarded them as tools to be exploited in order to embellish his own reputation as a leader and 'greatest strategist in history', he was prepared to listen to, and take, their advice. This was the basis of his relationship with the ex-tsarist staff officer Marshal Boris Shaposhnikov. In the case of other younger members of the Red Army General Staff, it suited Stalin's ego to further the careers of 'favourites', such as Colonel Sergei Shtemenko. One officer, however, who gradually won Stalin's confidence by sheer ability alone was Alexei Innokentievich Antonov. A member of Stalin's entourage of advisors from 1943 until the end of the Second World War, American and British officials with whom he came into contact expressed varying opinions regarding his character. All, however, agree with President Truman's impression of Antonov as 'a highly efficient staff officer and administrator'.

A rising young officer in the late 1930s, following an unpromising start to his wartime career, the fortunes of the 44-year-old Antonov underwent a radical transformation on appointment in December 1942 as a Deputy to the Chief of the General Staff, Army General Vasilevsky. Chief of the Operations Directorate, First Deputy Chief of the General Staff (May 1943), and Chief of the General Staff (February 1945) in turn, Antonov was to be at the centre of events for the remainder of the war, as the strategic initiative gradually slipped from the grasp of the German High Command and the scale of Red Army operations widened. During Vasilevsky's frequent absences at the front Antonov was *de facto* Chief of the General Staff and Stalin's senior advisor in operational matters. With the final phase of the war determined by the degree to which the Allied leaders could co-ordinate their actions, Antonov was destined to play a rôle in Allied military diplomacy at Stalin's side during his meeting with Churchill in Moscow, and later Yalta and Potsdam, plotting Allied strategy and ultimately the fate of post-war Europe.

While professional friendships and a justifiable measure of good luck had a hand in shaping Antonov's career, success was due in equal measure to physical and intellectual stamina, outstanding professional ability and a seemingly inexhaustible capacity for mastering the details of the most complicated brief. None the less, while respected for ability, Antonov was not accorded due recognition in his own lifetime. He was probably the only senior figure in the wartime Red Army High Command not promoted Marshal of the Soviet Union or created a Hero of the Soviet Union. He published no memoirs, although he kept a diary and corresponded regularly with his wife, sister and close friends. His epitaph is inscribed in the numerous Soviet accounts of the rôle of the wartime Soviet General Staff, and in the memoirs of former comrades, above all Vasilevsky and Shtemenko. All agree on Antonov's crucial rôle, along with Vasilevsky and Zhukov, as a member of the Stavka triumvirate: planning, co-ordinating, executing and monitoring the major Red Army strategic operations. In Shtemenko's words, Antonov 'devoted himself completely and without hesitation to the service of the nation . . . shouldering the burden of responsibility for solving the most difficult missions during the armed struggle.'

Family background predestined Antonov for a military career. His father, like his father before him, was an artillery officer. While serving in Siberia he met and married Tereza Ksavertevna, a Polish lady whose father had been banished to Siberia by Alexander II for his part in the Polish insurrection of 1863–4. The family moved frequently from one provincial garrison to another. The second of three children, Alexei Antonov was born on 9 September 1896 in the Belorussian garrison town of Grodno. According to Antonov's elder sister, Lyudmila, the parents instilled in their children instincts of self-improvement, discipline and love of the homeland. From his earliest years Antonov learnt to speak fluent Polish, good German, French and English, an invaluable asset in later years enabling him to become acquainted with some of the seminal studies on the revolution in strategy and tactics. While at the local gymnasium he also excelled in history, geography and literature. At the same time his father encouraged his interest in military history, with visits to nearby battlefields and the garrison summer camp. Inevitably, Antonov was soon expressing a desire to follow his grandfather's and father's footsteps. These hopes were jeopardized, first by the death of his father in 1908, followed in 1915 by the death of his mother in Petrograd, where the family had lived since 1914. His education completed, in order to support the family and earn money to study at the university he started work at a factory. With financial support from his fellow workers, he was able to register at the Physics and Mathematics Faculty of Petrograd University.

Inevitably, by 1916 wartime events were to affect Antonov's life. Called up for military service, he was sent to the Petrograd Pavlovsky Military School for a six-month course, at the end of which he was posted to a Life Guards Light Infantry Regiment, the beginning of a military career spanning almost forty-five years. By early 1917 Antonov's regiment had joined the 8th Army on the Southwestern Front, commanded at the time by the legendary General Alexei Brusilov. Given the rank of senior NCO, Antonov spent six months at the front, time enough to gain his first battle experience and take part in the last Russian offensive of June 1917. Initially the attack on the 8th Army sector was successful, advancing some 40 miles to occupy Kalush by 28 June. On 16 July the Germans launched the counter-attack, and in the ensuing Russian retreat Antonov was wounded in the head. For bravery he was awarded his first medal. By August 1917 the Russians had been driven out of Galicia and Bukovina.

In August Antonov was evacuated to a military hospital in Petrograd. In the intervening months the political situation in the capital had changed irreversibly following the February Revolution, the abdication of the Tsar and the establishment of the Provisional Government under Kerensky. With the final collapse of the Russian Army, throughout August and September Kerensky's authority crumbled. Released from hospital on the eve of the October Revolution, Antonov rejoined a Guards Chasseur Regiment in time to participate in the operation to put down the Kornilov uprising against the Provisional Government in early September. For the time being this was to be Antonov's last action; in early 1918 the regiment was disbanded. For a short time he studied at the Petrograd Forestry Institute, working in his spare time on the Petrograd Food Committee. Before long, however, he could not resist the call to defend the new Soviet state, now embroiled with the invading Allied expeditionary forces, and in September he enrolled in the Moscow Workers' Division. His first action was in December as Assistant Chief of Staff of the 3rd Brigade on the Southern Front near Lugansk in Ukraine, fighting against the White Cossack volunteer formations. In the words of a senior officer he was 'modest and responsive', demonstrating 'ability, and a profound grasp of military affairs'. He was always ready to assist a comrade. At times he was also called upon to organize brief field training courses for raw recruits. The first period of the Civil War gave Antonov his first experience of 'staff work' and command and control. Throughout the final stages of the Civil War he served in the Inzensky Rifle Division, taking part in the campaign against General Wrangel on the lower Don, the Kuban, the North Caucasus, and the capture of Novorossiisk on the Black Sea in March

1920. Of abiding interest for the future were Antonov's fleeting meetings with Tukhachevsky and Frunze. By this time he was Chief of Staff of the 45th Rifle Brigade, 15th Rifle Division.

With the end of the Civil War, like thousands of other junior officers Antonov faced a period of uncertainty as the new Bolshevik leaders debated the rôle of the professional army in Soviet society. Inevitably, the period following the Civil War was an anti-climax, and Antonov spent part of the time compiling a study of the rôle of the staff in the field based on his wartime experiences as a brigade staff officer. While accounts of this period of his career stress his popularity with the rank and file, and his dedication to the new state, Antonov was first and foremost devoted to his chosen career, and had ambition. Despite combat experience, however, apart from the three months spent at the Military School in 1916, he lacked any formal military education. To a certain extent this deficiency was more than compensated by the advice and guidance he received from Tona Yakir, the Commander of Ukraine Military District. The year 1928, therefore, was to prove to be a watershed in his career: he joined the Communist Party, by the late 1920s the indispensable passport to promotion, and entered the Frunze Military Academy. Subsequently, between 1928 and 1940 he was to spend no less than nine years either as a student or lecturer in both the Frunze and General Staff Academy in turn.

The Frunze Military Academy offered Antonov the first opportunity to widen his view and deepen his grasp of operational art, studying new ideas and the influence of the 'technological revolution', while his linguistic ability in German, English and French enabled him to study the latest foreign literature on military theory. He also met other promising officers, such as Konstantin Rokossovsky and Matvei Zakharov.

On graduating in 1931, Antonov was appointed Chief of Staff of the 46th Rifle Division located at Korosten in Ukraine Military District. The division was about to receive some of the latest equipment, including artillery and prototype tanks, and was one of the first in the Red Army to be reorganized in accordance with new operational concepts. Within a year, however, Antonov returned to the Frunze Academy for a six-month course at the recently established Operations Faculty. Not only did he meet some of the leading military theorists, he renewed his acquaintance with the group of junior officers destined to achieve supreme command, including Zakharov and Vatutin. He also studied the works of Boris Shaposhnikov, including his *Brains of the Army*, developing ideas on the rôle of the staff.

On passing out of the Academy Antonov was commended as 'an excellent operations staff worker', competent to control a front-level staff, and recommended eventually for the General Staff. Initially, however, he returned to his former post before being promoted Head of the Operations Department of Kharkov Military District in August 1935. A month later he took part in a two-party exercise involving the recently established Kharkov and Kiev Military Districts. The 'Kiev Manoeuvres' of 1935 were probably the most important held by the Red Army before 1941. A total of 65,000 men took part, with some 1,000 tanks and 600 aircraft, on a front of 250 kilometres and a depth of 200 kilometres, under the direct control of Yakir, now Commander of Kiev Military District. Practically the whole of the Red Army High Command attended, including Voroshilov, Budenny, Tukhachevsky and Yegorov. Apart from the widespread use made of some of the latest technology, the object of the exercise was to put the theory of the 'deep operation' to the test. The highlight of the exercise was an airborne drop by a regiment numbering 1,188 men. Inevitably, the respective district staffs had to face the stiffest test, planning and co-ordinating operations involving all arms. As Head of the Operations Department of Kharkov Military District, Antonov played a leading part and was commended by Voroshilov and Yakir.

This in effect was a recommendation for Antonov to attend the first course at the General Staff Academy in 1936, joining other younger officers destined for high command. As planned by Shaposhnikov, the course was designed to instil in students a deeper grasp of military art, enabling them to exercise command and control at front level and above. Students were expected to demonstrate ability for supreme command, taking part in exercises both within the Academy and outside. Reports of the first course single out Antonov, along with Zakharov and Govorov, as the three outstanding students. Antonov, furthermore, made an impression on senior lecturers, such as Isserson, who commended his 'incisive intellect, erudition, energy, and all-round ability'. Apart from the future Marshal Zakharov, another student with whom Antonov established a warm relationship was Alexander Vasilevsky, the wartime Chief of the General Staff and ultimately Antonov's mentor.

Originally, the course was scheduled to last eighteen months. Within a year, however, some of the brighter students were being posted as replacements for Stalin's purge victims. Consequently, in summer 1937 Antonov was appointed Chief of Staff of Moscow Military District, commanded at the time by Budenny, one of Stalin's closest associates. Now a Brigade Commander, much of Antonov's time was occupied in advising on the establishment and structure of the new formations, drawing up training schedules and preparing for the big annual manoeuvres. His stay in Moscow, however, was to be comparatively brief. In December 1938 he was replaced by Vasili Sokolovsky on his return to the Frunze Academy as lecturer in the General Tactics Faculty. The move was part of a shake-up in the senior Red Army academies occasioned by the need to replace the large number of officers 'liquidated' in the purges, and to improve the general level of instruction for regimental commanders. Much of the instruction was based on the first lessons of the Spanish Civil War, and Antonov himself helped to draw up two manuals which were to remain in the Academy curriculum down to 1941, one on tank and mechanized formations and the other on German army tactics. A senior lecturer from February 1940, in January 1941 he was promoted Deputy Head of the Faculty, and a senior examiner of the State Commission responsible for vetting works on military theory. In early 1941, despite a promising record, it looked as if Antonov was condemned to spend the rest of his career in the Academy as a respected lecturer in tactics.

On 14 June 1941 *Izvestiya* dismissed 'rumours of Germany's intention to break the [Soviet-German] Pact and begin an attack on the USSR' as 'devoid of all foundation', and talk of Soviet preparations for war with Germany as 'lies and provocations'. None the less, a mood of nervousness in Moscow regarding German intentions had set in even before the German occupation of Norway and Denmark, the Low Countries, and finally the fall of France in June 1940. Indeed, the 1938 Munich Agreement had been the first shock, followed by a restructuring of Soviet strategic defences along the Western frontier throughout 1938–40. As early as May 1939 reports from contacts in the German Foreign Office to the Red Army Intelligence Directorate spoke of an impending German attack on Poland, to be followed by 'a military campaign in the East'. By early 1940 there were signs that Stalin was turning his attention towards pulling the Red Army High Command back into shape, restoring some of the prestige and freedom of action jettisoned during the purges. In early May 1940 Voroshilov was replaced as Defence Commissar by the man of the hour, Timoshenko. Some days later Timoshenko, Shaposhnikov – who had missed out on the 1935 promotions – and the windy nonentity Kulik were created Marshals of the Soviet Union. This was followed by the restoration of the old tsarist ranks of General and Admiral, involving the promotion of some 1,000 officers, including Zhukov, promoted Army General (four-star). After the promotions to Colonel-General (a three-star rank that had not existed in the tsarist army) and Lieutenant-General, it was the turn of the Major-Generals. On 4 June 1940 some 479 officers were promoted to the rank, including Vasilevsky, Rokossovsky, Zakharov and Antonov.

Antonov's promotion was the first sign that he was destined to play an important rôle in the event of a German invasion of the Soviet Union. Some months were to pass, however, before he was extricated from the frustrating existence of Academy lecturer. In January 1941, after a brief interview with Timoshenko, he departed for Kiev Special Military District on appointment as Deputy Chief of Staff, replacing Major-General German Malandin. Some indication of his excitement can be seen in a letter to his sister before he left Leningrad, speaking of 'the great and serious mission ahead'.

As Head of the Organization-Mobilization Department Antonov worked closely with Colonel Ivan Bagramyan, a fellow graduate of the General Staff Academy of 1937, now Head of the Operations Department. The first task was to draw up a plan for deploying 5th, 6th, 26th and 12th Armies of the District to cover the southwestern strategic approaches to the Soviet Union, some 1,000 kilometres long. The Antonov/Bagramyan plan of operations, supported by District Chief of Staff Lieutenant-General Purkayev, focused on 5th Army, commanded by Major-General M. I. Potapov, deployed on the Lutsk–Rovno axis on a front of 176 kilometres. Clearly the two were soon able to establish an excellent working relationship, and Bagramyan has described Antonov's 'unique ability to get to the root of the problem in a flash', adding that 'he was a great support in every respect'.

Unfortunately, the plan as finally sanctioned by the General Staff was dictated not by the logic of strategic defence, but by the assumed need not to 'provoke' the German High Command. As a result all the major formations took up defensive locations too far back from the frontier, there was no co-ordinated command and control structure, and – with the sole exception of Rokossovsky's 9th Mechanized Corps – the artillery was separated from its organic command. Antonov's main responsibility was the mobilization of reserves, civil labour, and transport for military purposes. The problem of manning was particularly acute, with many formations merely 60–70 per cent of normal strength as late as May 1941.

Kiev Special Military District lay on the main axis of advance of the German Army Group South, poised to seize control of the rich economic resources of Ukraine before pressing on to the Caucasus. Consequently, the German High Command had assembled an impressive force: VI, XVII and XI Field Armies; First Tank Group; III and IV Romanian Armies; and the VIII Hungarian Corps. In all Army Group South, commanded by Field Marshal Gerd von Rundstedt, comprised 57 Divisions, and 13 Brigades; 16,000 pieces of artillery and mortars; 850 tanks; and 1,300 aircraft. In numbers, the Soviet force assembled in Kiev District, some 50 rifle divisions, was equal to the opposing force. There were, however, fatal flaws: lack of mobile armoured formations to match the massed German tank divisions, and the inability of senior Red Army commanders to match the scale and mobility of the German offensive. But the most damaging factor was complacency in Moscow, and passive indifference on the ground. The senior political officer, Khrushchev, would describe Colonel-General Mikhail Kirponos, the District Commander, as an outstanding commander in the Finnish War, but out of his depth in a war of armour and manoeuvre across the vast Ukrainian steppes. Rokossovsky was even more caustic, doubting Kirponos's ability for such a key command, being 'unequal to the burden of responsibility'. None the less, Kirponos was to prove a resourceful and brave commander in the first weeks of the German offensive, frequently fighting his way out of Rundstedt's traps until his gallant death in September while defending the beleaguered Kiev. Indeed, the tragic case of Kirponos illustrates Stalin's impulse on occasion to promote outstandingly successful divisional commanders to key posts for which they were ill-suited on intellectual grounds, lack of professional ability and experience.

For Antonov the fifteen months following the German invasion were to be the most desperate of his whole career. The hard-earned rare moments of triumph were frequently overshadowed by tragedy, in a succession of posts, with the German offensive rolling on over Ukraine to the foothills of the Caucasus. For a short time he was Chief of Staff of Kiev Special Military District in succession to Purkayev, mobilizing men and junior commanders for reserve formations. At the end of August Antonov was appointed Chief of Staff of the Southern Front, preoccupied with the defence of the Dnieper. By early October Kleist's First Tank Group had broken through Soviet defences, and by late October had reached the Don. Here the German offensive suffered a temporary reverse in late November with a spirited Red Army counter-attack and the liberation of Rostov. For his part in the Rostov operation, on 27 December 1941 Antonov – who had studied Kleist's writings on armoured warfare while at the Academy – was promoted Lieutenant-General. The temporary respite had important re-percussions for the German High Command, with Rundstedt's dismissal following a telephone confrontation with Hitler involving the strategic implications. Antonov, meanwhile, remained in good heart, writing to his wife that he derived much encouragement serving alongside former comrades, singling out Timoshenko and Bagramyan.

In July 1942 Antonov was appointed Chief of Staff of the North Caucasus Front, serving once more under Budenny. Established some days earlier with the fusion of the Southern and North Caucasus commands, the move was symptomatic of the mood of desperation which once again hung over High Command in the summer of 1942, as the Germans, having vaulted over the Don, mustered for a final push to roll up the Red Army's southern strategic flank based on the North Caucasus. The battle for the Caucasus had commenced, the climax of which was the Tuapse defensive operation of the Black Sea Operational Group (25 September–20 December 1942). As Chief of Staff of the Black Sea Operational Group, commanded since October by the intrepid Lieutenant-General Ivan Petrov, Antonov played a major rôle in planning the defence of the Black Sea littoral, in co-ordination with the Black Sea Fleet. The operation ended with the virtual emasculation of the German forces in late December, and the Red Army retaining a perilous grip on the North Caucasus and eastern Black Sea.

There are two other aspects of the Transcaucasus operations which deserve attention, affecting as they did Antonov's career in the early post-war years. A classic example of combined operations, based on local command of the sea, and illuminated by intermittent epic episodes, in the post-war decades the Transcaucasus was subsequently relegated to the status of a 'sideshow', overshadowed by Stalingrad and subsequent events elsewhere on the Soviet–German front. None the less, in the 1960s and 1970s there were those who staked a reputation on their part in the Battle for the Caucasus: Marshal Grechko; Admiral Gorshkov; Marshal of Aviation Vershinin; Colonel-General Petr Yefimov; and Marshal Leonid Brezhnev – former 'fighting commissar' of the 'immortal Eighteenth' (18th Army), and 'the Hero of glorious Malaya Zemlya'.

The second aspect was the inherent instability and suspect anti-Soviet mood of the north Caucasian nationalities, many of Turkic origin: Chechens, Ingushes, Crimean Tartars, Karachai, Balkars, Kalmyks and Volga Germans. In order to 'cleanse the situation' in late August 1942, Beria was dispatched as Stavka Representative, bringing with him a team of 'special assistants': in essence a parallel NKVD command structure for the 'defence' of the North Caucasus. Beria at times virtually controlled the Transcaucasus Front, intimidating in turn most of the senior commanders, including Tyulenov (Front Commander), Malinovsky (Commander of the Don Operational Group), and Antonov. Worse still, Beria ordered the 'repression' of many 'national units' – Azerbaijanis, Armenians, Georgians, Chechens and Kuban Cossacks, regarding their loyalty as suspect and fighting qualities questionable. Many of these 'national divisions' had been raised at Antonov's initiative. It was a tragic episode Antonov was never to forget, subsequently spurning Beria's blandishments in the early post-war years, and as a consequence blocking any chances of senior promotion.

By the time the Tuapse defensive operation was approaching the decisive stages in November 1942 Antonov had been transferred yet again, replacing Lieutenant-General P. I. Boldin (not to be confused with I. V. Boldin) as Chief of Staff of the Transcaucasus Front following his death the previous week. In the event, Antonov's tenure of the new post was brief. None the less, his Front Commander, Tyulenev, vividly recalled him, pencil in hand, hunched over the operations map for hours on end, 'always one step ahead in the Battle for the Caucasus'.

In early December 1942 Vasilevsky paid a routine visit to the Transcaucasus Front to be briefed by Antonov on the operational situation. Impressed, as always, by Antonov's characteristically accurate and brief presentation of the situation, on departing later the same day Vasilevsky offered his old classmate the post of Chief of the Operations Directorate of the General Staff. Initially overwhelmed at the honour, and daunting challenge, the over-cautious Antonov requested time for consideration. The following day Vasilevsky telephoned a reluctant Antonov to confirm that 'the Supreme Commander-in-Chief' had agreed.

On 11 December Antonov departed for Moscow, where he was met by Shtemenko, Deputy Chief of the Operations Directorate. It was the beginning of an indissoluble partnership. The appointment of Antonov to this key post within the General Staff inevitably prompted some scepticism. Moreover, with the rapid turnover since early 1942 many old hands such as Major-General Bokov forecast that Antonov would not survive Stalin's first summons. In fact, Antonov's reputation was already high with Stalin, who, moreover, trusted Vasilevsky's judgement in such matters. Antonov himself had yet to overcome his initial doubts, while anxious to justify Vasilevsky's trust in his ability. On taking up his appointment he spent a week familiarizing himself with the overall strategic situation, the work and organization of the Operations Directorate. Consequently, when Antonov finally presented himself at Stavka he survived the first searching test with honour.

Antonov had joined the General Staff at a portentous moment in early 1943, with the tide about to turn following Stalingrad. The senior direction in the prosecution of the war was also beginning to switch into top gear, with the General Staff Operations Directorate functioning as Stavka's 'work horse', directing the activity of its Representatives, hand-picked officers from the General Staff and arms of service monitoring the activity of the Front staffs, at times much to the latter's disgust. Within a short time Antonov had established his hold on the Operations Directorate, introducing a rigid routine on a 24-hour basis, and dispersing responsibilities among his senior deputies. Each day Stalin received three reports from the General Staff: between 1000 and 1100 hours (Shtemenko); 1600–1700 hours (Antonov); finally, the 'night report' by Antonov, based on a 1:200.000 scale map presentation down to divisional level, assisted by Shtemenko.

Initially, however, much of Antonov's time was spent visiting the front, first in early January as Stavka Representative to the Bryansk Front, then to the Voronezh and Central Fronts to assist Vasilevsky and prepare recommendations for Stavka concerning future operations.

The first major strategic operation in which Antonov was involved was the battle of Kursk, the planning for which had commenced in early April. Much of the workload fell on Antonov's shoulders, preparing daily briefings with Stalin following strenuous meetings with Vasilevsky and Zhukov. The latter in particular appreciated 'the utmost clarity and conviction' with which Antonov presented his assessments. In order to co-ordinate planning within the General Staff the Main Organization Directorate was established in mid-1943, and the rôle of the Intelligence Directorate widened. As the scale of Red Army operations expanded Antonov was fortunate in having in Shtemenko, A. A. Gryzlov and N. A. Lomov, able deputies with whom he had worked in the past. One further sign that Antonov had gained Stalin's confidence was promotion to Colonel-General on 4 April 1943. In May he handed over control of the Operations Directorate to Shtemenko on appointment as First Deputy Chief of the General Staff, enabling him to concentrate exclusively on planning strategic operations.

Throughout the battle of Kursk in July–August 1943 Antonov remained mostly in Moscow, reporting to and advising Stalin and visiting the front only when necessary or at Stalin's bidding. The final defeat of the German strategic operation ('Citadel') created optimum conditions for a strategic counter-attack, the planning for which was to be based on the work of Antonov and his staff in assessing the 'condition of the German Army' in late 1943, and the options facing the German High Command. Meanwhile, in accordance with his increasing responsibilities, on 27 August 1943 Antonov was promoted Army General.

With the strategic initiative now passing to the Red Army, the two immediate tasks were to complete the liberation in turn of Belorussia and Ukraine. With these missions accomplished ahead lay the liberation of Eastern Europe throughout 1944–5, and the final assault on Berlin. As the hub of Red Army operations moved west the General Staff took on the task of co-ordinating strategic operations with Moscow's British and American Allies. This was particularly important as the date approached for launching the 'Second Front' ('Overlord'), an option first raised by Stalin in August 1941, and repeated with growing impatience at the first meeting with Churchill in Moscow August 1942 as the Red Army was bracing itself for the German assault on the Caucasus.

The main channel for liaison with the Allies were the British and US Military Missions in Moscow, headed respectively by Lieutenant-General Burrows and Major-General Deane. It was from the Missions that Antonov received the Anglo–US notification of the likely date for 'Overlord', coinciding with Soviet planning for the summer 1944 campaign ('Bagration') dealing a final blow to the remaining German forces on Soviet soil. In October the same year Churchill paid a second visit to Moscow, in the course of which Antonov briefed Field Marshal Lord Alanbrooke on the situation on the Red Army front, for Antonov somewhat of an experience, and a foretaste of the next high-level meeting with the Allies – the Yalta Conference of February 1945. For Antonov the highlight of the Conference was his briefing of the three Allied leaders on 4 February about the situation on the Eastern Front. The previous day he had already urged the British and American Chiefs of Staff to step up the Allied air offensive on German communications 'to prevent the enemy from transferring his troops to the East from the Western front, Norway and Italy'. In the 4 February briefing he went further, painting a sombre picture of the situation on the Soviet–German Front, finally reiterating his plea for increased Anglo–US air support. When speaking of some 31 German divisions being transferred to the Eastern Front, as Churchill's biographer points out, Antonov was grossly exaggerating the actual situation. None the less, Churchill was sufficiently moved, and on his return to London he altered previously agreed Allied bombing plans and ordered 'Bomber' Harris to step up the air offensive on the German Army's lines of communication in the Berlin–Dresden–Leipzig region.

On 18 February 1945 Army General Chernyakhovsky, the 39-year-old Commander of the 1st Baltic Front, was killed in East Prussia. Within hours of receiving the news Stalin signed a Stavka Order appointing Vasilevsky as the new Front Commander. The same day Antonov took over as Chief of the General Staff. For the remainder of the war in Europe Antonov was preoccupied in planning and monitoring the Berlin operation. He also had to adjudicate regarding the competing aspirations of Zhukov, now Commander of the 1st Belorussian Front, and Konev, Commander of the 1st Ukrainian Front, as they raced for the German capital.

With the defeat of Nazi Germany the victorious Allied leaders met in Potsdam in July 1945 in order to plan the new order in Europe and the future of Germany. The Soviet military delegation was headed by Antonov, assisted by Admiral Kuznetsov. One of the crucial issues discussed was the coming Soviet offensive against Japan. The post of Deputy Chief of General Staff for Far East operations had already been set up in 1942, and from 1943 was headed by Lomov. General Staff planning commenced in earnest in September 1944, and when Churchill visited Moscow in October Antonov was able to brief Alanbrooke on the plan of operations. The final planning draft document was agreed at a Stavka conference in mid-June 1945, together with the creation of a Far East High Command under Vasilevsky.

With Vasilevsky in the Far East, Antonov was in control of the General Staff until early 1946, his main task now to draw up plans for the demobilization of over 5 million men and their reintegration into the shattered Soviet economy. There were also major structural changes, with the abolition in September of the State Committee of Defence and Stavka, both of which were replaced by a single organ – the Supreme Military Council, of which Antonov was a Deputy Chairman. A reshuffle of senior personnel followed in March 1946. Vasilevsky returned as Chief of the General Staff, and Antonov reverted to being his First Deputy with responsibility for mobilization and organization.

By 1948 the first stage in the demobilization process of the Soviet Armed Forces was complete and in November of that year in order to 'acquire command experience' Antonov returned to Transcaucasus Military District, initially as First Deputy Commander, and from 1949 as Commander, replacing Marshal Tolbukhin. In terms of advancement, the move to the Transcaucasus was a step down and indicates that in the early post-war years Antonov was bereft of a rôle comparable to that which he had exercised with such skill in the latter half of the war. The Georgian capital, Tbilisi, was, however, far removed from the chilling and repressive atmosphere of Moscow of the late 1940s, and the attentions of Beria directed towards creating a 'military clique' in Stalin's declining years. The return to the Caucasus, where Antonov had spent much of his earlier career, appears to have given him and his wife a renewed lease of life, and when not on one of his frequent visits to units in the field, the Antonovs liked nothing better than a relaxing evening at the Georgian National Theatre.

In 1954 Antonov returned to the General Staff on appointment as a First Deputy Chief, the prelude to his nomination in May 1955 as Chief of Staff of the Warsaw Pact. For the first decade of its existence the Warsaw Pact was more important as a tool of Soviet diplomacy in Eastern Europe, and until the early 1970s most Western observers generally discounted its military clout. None the less, Antonov was invaluable in helping to put the Alliance back on course in the aftermath of the 1956 uprising in Poland, followed in November by the Soviet invasion of Hungary. He also played a leading part in joint Pact exercise activity, aligning command and control procedures, imbuing the disparate members with an element of combat efficiency, and a coherent military doctrine.

As the correspondence with his wife and sister shows, Antonov had had a punishing war, frequently driving himself to the very limit of physical and mental endurance. On several occasions he had had to receive medical attention, possibly for a heart condition, and in 1945 on his return from the Potsdam Conference he suffered a serious heart attack. In 1955 his wife, Mariya Dmitrievna, died, and in 1956 he re-married, with Olga Vasilievna Lepeshinsky, a People's Artiste of the USSR. She was to prove an invaluable companion as Antonov's health rapidly declined. He died on 16 June 1962 following a final heart attack in his office.

BIBLIOGRAPHY

Bagramyan, I. Kh., *Tak nachalas' voina*, Kiev, 1975.
Gaglov, I. I., *Army General A. I. Antonov*, 2nd edn, Moscow, 1987.
Gilbert, M., *Winston S. Churchill: The Road to Victory*, vol. VII, London, 1986.
Kievskii Krasnoznamennyi, Moscow, 1974.
Voenno-istoricheskii Zhurnal, no. 8, 1966; no. 5, 1989.
Volkogonov, Dmitri, *Triumf i tragediya*, book II, part 1, Moscow, 1989; in English *Stalin: Triumph and Tragedy*, ed. and trans. Harold Shukman, Weidenfeld & Nicolson, London, 1991.
Zhukov, G. K., *Vospominaniya i razmyshleniya*, vol. I, 10th edn, Novosti, Moscow, 1992.

Ivan Khristoforovich

BAGRAMYAN

GEOFFREY JUKES

The Red Army was as multi-ethnic as the Soviet Union, but its generals were overwhelmingly Russian. Very few non-Slavs reached high rank, and the highest proportion of those who did were Armenians, from the smallest Soviet Republic in area and second smallest in population. Two of them (Bagramyan and Babadzhanyan) reached the highest rank.

Ivan Khristoforovich Bagramyan, son of a railway employee, was born in Azerbaijan in 1897, volunteered for the Russian Army in 1915, and was a junior officer by 1917. He made the Red Army his career, though unusually for a senior officer he joined the Communist Party only in 1939.

In June 1940 he was a 44-year-old Colonel, not long returned to unit service after four years as a lecturer at the General Staff Academy. A former cavalryman, he had seen coevals such as Zhukov and Yeremenko rising fast in the command vacuum created by Stalin's purges, while he remained sidelined. So when Zhukov, already a four-star General, became commander of Kiev Special Military District early in 1940, he wrote to him offering to serve in any capacity. Zhukov responded favourably, and at once invoked his assistance in preparing a paper for the December meeting of Heads of Military Districts. This paper ('Conducting a Contemporary Offensive Operation') enhanced Zhukov's already high standing, and Bagramyan's contribution to it helped ensure Zhukov's future benevolence.

After the paper was completed, Bagramyan became Head of Operations of 12th Army, in recently-annexed Western Ukraine, but within three months was recalled to Kiev to become Deputy Chief of Staff of the District. He assumed duty in late December 1940, but Zhukov had already left on appointment as Chief of General Staff. Even before the German invasion the new Commander, Colonel-General M. P. Kirponos, abruptly elevated from a divisional command in the Finnish War to a post previously held only by senior generals, with four armies and 535 miles of frontiers, was at odds with his principal staff officers, General Purkayev and Colonel Bagramyan, over defence of the frontiers. He favoured only a light defence, arguing that the main forces would be able to counter-attack and destroy invaders quickly, whereas they argued unavailingly that the German campaigns of 1939–40 indicated they would attack fast and forcefully, and the frontiers would have to be defended strongly if main force units were not to be overrun before they were fully mobilized. When the Germans did invade, Kirponos's unquestioning efforts to carry out Stavka's unrealistic orders increased tensions between him and Purkayev, who was replaced after five weeks. During August it became clear that the entire Front would be encircled if it did not abandon Kiev. However, Stalin would not countenance withdrawal, and when Kirponos's superior, Timoshenko, sent Bagramyan, by then a Major-General, to him with an oral order to retreat, he refused to move without written instructions. In consequence the whole Front was encircled and destroyed. Bagramyan led his operations staff out on foot, but Kirponos was killed, several other generals killed or captured, and 665,000 prisoners were taken.

Timoshenko appointed Bagramyan to his staff, then controlling both the Southwestern and Southern Fronts. In October the German advance towards Moscow created a massive eastward bulge in the front line, threatening the southern forces with a repetition of the Kiev disaster. Stavka granted Timoshenko the permission to retreat it had denied Kirponos. Bagramyan noted 'the commander's authority means a lot', and that the orderly withdrawal, contrasted with the chaos of the early weeks, showed the Red Army was learning quickly. In October Stalin took two cavalry divisions to reinforce Moscow; Bagramyan observed that he persuaded rather than ordered Timoshenko to release them, and showed openness to argument, which Bagramyan would later exploit.

Having helped to plan two successful counter-offensives, in December Bagramyan was assigned by Timoshenko to form and head the staff of an operational group to control three Army Groups (the Southern and Southwestern Fronts, and a re-established Bryansk Front). He was promoted to Lieutenant-General and worked closely with Timoshenko and Khrushchev, then Timoshenko's chief political officer. He accompanied them to Moscow in late March to discuss with Stavka the summer campaign plan which he had drafted, and was surprised to find that he, not Timoshenko, was to present the plan to Stalin. They met for the first time on 27 March 1942 and Stalin deeply impressed Bagramyan; but clearly Timoshenko intended Bagramyan to impress Stalin, and subsequent events suggest he did.

The plan, for the recapture of Kharkov, was approved, and on 8 April

Bagramyan was appointed Chief of Staff of the Southwestern Front, then on 4 May Chief of Staff of the Direction (Axis) as well. He appeared set on a staff career. But the plan contained a fatal flaw, in that the offensive was to start from the Barvenkovo salient, which the Germans were about to eliminate. The Southwestern Front attacked on 12 May and recaptured Kharkov, but the trap was closing behind them. Bagramyan soon realized the danger, and on 18 May first unsuccessfully urged Timoshenko to change the plan, then took the bold step of asking Khrushchev to approach Stalin in the hope that he would act. Stalin declined to interfere; Kharkov was lost and three armies (6th, 9th and 57th) destroyed, gravely weakening the Southwestern Front just before the main German offensive began on 28 June.

On 26 June Stavka relieved Bagramyan of his post. Believing this to be punishment for the disaster, he again wrote a letter, this time to Stalin, offering to serve at the front in any capacity, however modest. But his belief that he was in disgrace was mistaken. On 28 June he was posted as Deputy Commander to 61st Army of the Western Front. His stay there was brief; Zhukov was the Front Commander and on 15 July, with Stavka's approval, he appointed Bagramyan to command 16th Army.

This was a major vote of confidence for Zhukov and Stalin to give an officer who had never commanded a division, and had commanded nothing at all during the previous seven years. But 16th Army was an easy one to take over; it was in good condition and needed a new commander only because the previous incumbent, Rokossovsky, had been promoted to command a Front. With a new headquarters to set up he had taken several of his senior staff officers with him, but Bagramyan's own staff experience would help him to surmount that problem.

His first test came soon. On 30 July two armies of the Western and two of the Kalinin Front began the Rzhev-Sychev operation to expel German forces from north of the Volga and east of the Vazuza rivers, where they were dangerously close to Moscow. The offensive began well, but on 11 August the Germans attacked the two southernmost armies of the Western Front – not involved in the operation – achieved surprise, and advanced 15 miles through 61st Army, isolating three of its divisions and threatening 16th Army's left flank. Bagramyan acted quickly to block the threat. By 9 September the attacks had subsided, and 16th Army prepared for its next tasks. Both Soviet and German efforts were centred on Stalingrad and the Caucasus, so most other sectors remained fairly quiet until February 1943. Bagramyan was required to attack on 22 February in support of the Bryansk and Central Fronts' offensive at Bryansk, and was given reinforcements which increased 16th Army from 4 divisions and 1 brigade of infantry to 6 divisions and 2 brigades, a tank corps, 4 tank brigades, and several artillery regiments – a large force for an inexperienced army commander to handle. But its performance earned it elevation to become 11th Guards Army, and be assigned an important task in the impending Kursk battle. To avoid attracting German attention its elevation was temporarily kept secret.

Stavka intended it to breach the German defences south of Kozelsk and advance due south towards Khotinets to meet a northwestward thrust from the Kursk salient by Central Front. The gap was about 75 miles, and closing it would cut off all German forces north of the salient (IX Army and part of II Panzer Army). The army would be enlarged to 3 rifle and 2 tank corps, totalling 15 divisions, with commensurate artillery and air support.

Bagramyan objected that the assignment was too ambitious. It would be difficult to protect his flanks, Central Front forces would be too busy fighting in the salient to play the part assigned to them, and the distance he had to cover was excessive. Stavka, he argued, was overinfluenced by the experience of closing a 125-mile gap in three days at Stalingrad, and had overlooked that he would have to break through prepared defences and fight forces which were themselves preparing to attack, a scenario more like Barvenkovo than Stalingrad. He advocated a more modest joint operation with 61st Army (now in the Bryansk Front) to destroy the German force at Bolkhov which covered IX Army against attack from the north. His Front Commander (now Sokolovsky) rejected the proposal, as did the Bryansk Front's Commander (M. A. Reyter). But when both Front and both Army Commanders were summoned to Stavka at the end of April, he seized his chance. When Stalin asked for comments, he put his arguments against the plan. Sokolovsky and Reyter attempted to refute him, but Stalin approved his counter-proposal.

The German offensive at Kursk opened on 5 July. Bagramyan attacked on the 12th, advancing 45 miles in six days, and this operation, concluded successfully on 28 July, earned him promotion to Colonel-General. His army then joined in the general pursuit that followed Kursk, and in October 1943 was redeployed to the newly established 2nd Baltic Front on the borders of Belorussia. In mid-November Stalin offered him command of 2nd Baltic's southern neighbour, the 1st Baltic Front, which was notoriously lagging behind other Fronts' rates of advance. Stalin told him he could take 11th Guards with him, and proposed Colonel-General N. E. Chibisov to command it. Bagramyan hesitated, said that Chibisov's having been a Lieutenant-General when he was still a Colonel might affect their relationship, and instead proposed Lieutenant-General K. N. Galitsky. Stalin grasped that the real problem was Chibisov's current rank, the same as Bagramyan's, and there and then promoted Bagramyan and Govorov, the two lowest-rank Front Commanders, to Army General. He also accepted Bagramyan's nomination of Galitsky, and his request for the 2nd Baltic Front to return a tank corps and infantry division which it had removed from 11th Guards. Bagramyan thus took command of four Armies (4th Shock, 43rd, 39th and 11th Guards), poised to advance through southern Belorussia to the Baltic states.

By this time the Red Army's numerical superiority in men, tanks, guns and aircraft was crushing, and final victory clearly only a matter of time. However, German forces could still punish carelessness severely, and a Front Commander who performed less well than his peers would soon lose Stalin's favour, as had Bagramyan's predecessor, Yeremenko (though he would soon regain it).

Bagramyan's first operation was a modest one, to capture the important communications centre of Gorodok. The attack, by 11th Guards Army and one tank corps, had to be postponed when an untimely thaw turned the dirt roads to mud, but finally got under way on 13th December. Despite weather and supply problems, a large area was liberated, four German divisions were mauled, and Gorodok fell on 24 December, earning the Front its first gun salute in Moscow. But subsequent repeated attempts to advance took more toll of his troops than of their opponents, and by March they stood in sore need of a rest. Bagramyan decided to ask Stalin for a breathing space, and sought support from Sokolovsky, his neighbour at the Western Front, who agreed that the troops were exhausted but declined to appeal to Stavka, so Bagramyan went ahead on his own, and on 2 April Stalin ordered the 1st Baltic Front on to the defensive.

However, not all the troops could rest, as the Germans exploited the lull to mount a major sweep ('Spring Festival') against the Belorussian partisans. Bagramyan's staff arranged communications, air attacks on German units, airdrops of ammunition and food, and evacuation of wounded, while a reinforced corps of 4th Shock Army was alerted to mount a diversionary attack if necessary. With this aid the partisans fought back, and most of them escaped through the German cordon. The diversion was not needed, but the corps assigned for it was used on 29 April to open a corridor for a group attempting to escape across the front line. The partisans would repay Bagramyan's aid later in the year.

The large Soviet advances in the northern Baltics and Ukraine left the four armies of Army Group Centre (III Panzer, II, IV and IX) in a large eastward-jutting salient (the 'Belorussian Balcony'), and Stavka set its elimination (Operation 'Bagration') as the main task for 1944. To keep the secret from the Germans, it was also kept from the Front Commanders, who received instructions to prepare elaborate defensive positions and belts up to 25 miles in depth. Not till early May was Bagramyan summoned to Moscow to be told his rôle in 'Bagration'.

Four Fronts (from south to north the 1st, 2nd, 3rd Belorussian, 1st Baltic) were to surround and eliminate the 'Balcony' and Army Group Centre. Bagramyan was to attack with all four armies and one corps each of tanks and cavalry, cross the western Dvina and form the northern prong of a pincer movement (the 3rd Belorussian Front would provide the southern prong) to encircle and wipe out the Germans in the Vitebsk area. Though the plan in general pleased him, he was concerned about his northern flank; the 2nd Baltic Front would not attack until later, and until it did German Army Group North would be free to attack him. He therefore proposed that after the Vitebsk operation his Front should drive due West to help destroy III Panzer Army and cut Army Group North in two. Zhukov and Vasilevsky favoured his proposal, Stalin approved it at a meeting on 23 May, and the directive arrived on 31 May.

Like all Red Army commanders in the later part of the war, Bagramyan accepted casualty levels which both enemies and allies thought unnecessarily high, but he did pay attention to reducing casualties by achieving surprise, and a subordinate of his has provided an example of his methods. In planning the Vitebsk operation he ordered 43rd Army to mount its main blow from its right flank, through open and marshy terrain. When its commander, General A. P. Beloborodov, argued that the terrain before his centre was more suitable, Bagramyan replied that that was logical, therefore just what the Germans would think, and confirmed his order. After the successful attack in June a captured German general told Beloborodov that the direction from which it came had been totally unexpected.

The Belorussian partisans repaid Bagramyan's help by providing intelligence on the bridges, ferries and fords over the western Dvina, listing sites suitable for airfields, and impeding German movements by attacking roads and railways. The main offensive opened on 22 June 1944, third anniversary of the invasion. Bagramyan's westward thrust went like clockwork, but as his northern flank lengthened he became increasingly anxious at the 2nd Baltic Front's inaction. Stalin gave him an extra corps, urged him to capture Polotsk to hamper Army Group North's communications and open the route to the central Baltic, but confirmed the 2nd Baltic Front's inability to attack soon. By 3 July his troops were in Polotsk and all tasks set in the directive had been carried out. His operating area was moved southwards by a transfer of northernmost armies, his (4th Shock) to the 2nd Baltic and 3rd Belorussian's (39th) to him. He also received 51st and 2nd Guards Armies from the Stavka Reserve Front, so now had six armies, and a bigger task. His Front and the 3rd Belorussian Front must advance as fast as possible to the East Prussian frontier to prevent Army Group North retreating to Germany.

Here Stavka's logic and Bagramyan's intuition parted company. Military logic had Army Group North hastening towards Germany so as not to be cut off; intuition argued (with only slight exaggeration) that the Germans had never voluntarily abandoned any Soviet territory for tactical or strategic advantage, and that Hitler's arbitrary will, not General Staff reasoning, dictated German actions. Logic pointed Bagramyan's troops to Kaunas, intuition to the Latvian capital, Riga. Vasilevsky, controlling the 3rd Belorussian and both (later three) Baltic Fronts from Bagramyan's headquarters, said the plan could be changed if Bagramyan proved right.

He pushed on west, even though granted a pause till 9 July, and with his fears of a flank attack beginning to be confirmed. Friesner, the new commander of Army Group North, was moving forces to Daugavpils, the most convenient starting point for a drive to link up with Army Group Centre. However, Yeremenko at last started the 2nd Baltic moving on 10 July, and Friesner thereafter had little to spare for southward attacks, though his efforts to reconcile Hitler's incompatible orders both to hold the Baltic states and to restore the link with Army Group Centre obscured his intentions for a few more days.

Vasilevsky, believing he would try to do both, attempted to persuade Stalin to redirect Bagramyan's main thrust from Kaunas to Shyaulyay and Daugavpils; failing in that he changed its direction on his own responsibility from southwest to northwest. A renewed offensive on 20 July captured both towns within a week, opening the road to the coast – and Riga.

On 23 July Hitler dismissed Friesner and put the fanatical Schörner in his place. The Germans would stay and fight. Bagramyan and intuition were right, Stavka and logic wrong. Vasilevsky activated the Riga option. The war still had almost ten months to go, but there would be only one setback, a German attack on 16 August which it took ten days to stop. On 23 September the 1st Baltic Front stood only 12 miles from Riga. Next day Stavka changed its task, ordering it to regroup and drive from Shyaulyay to Memel (Klaypeda), starting in six days' time and capturing it within another eleven. It could not regroup in the time; Bagramyan asked for two more days, was given six, and moved out on 5 October. His troops reached the outskirts of Memel and the sea north and south of it on 10 October, half the allotted time. The town itself proved too hard a nut to crack then, but the strategic objective was achieved. Army Group North was definitively sealed in; it would play no part in the final battles in Germany. That made up for having to leave Riga to the 2nd and 3rd Baltic Fronts, which entered it on 12 October. Schörner withdrew to the Courland peninsula, Army Group North became Army Group Courland, and Stavka began planning to attack it.

Whether it needed to is debatable. Stavka insisted that if the pressure was relaxed, the force would go by sea to Germany and prolong the final battles there. This is unconvincing, since the Soviets had command of the sea and air. And Bagramyan's list of the equipment Army Group Courland surrendered on 9 May 1945 (158 usable aircraft, 500 tanks and assault guns, under 3,500 guns and mortars, 18,000 vehicles and 675 tractors/transporters) hardly suggests much effect on the outcome, even if it had reached Germany intact. Bagramyan himself rejected an alternative argument, that it could have been destroyed, mainly by referring to the massive transfers of Soviet army and air units from the Baltic to the Fronts about to invade Germany. But he and the other Baltic commanders got the worst of both worlds, by persisting in storming fortresses which could have been besieged and left until starvation or Germany's final collapse compelled their surrender, as the Americans did with Cherbourg and the British with the Channel Islands. The heavy losses incurred in storming places such as Klaypeda, Königsberg – or Berlin – expressed an 'attack at all costs' mentality and rivalry between commanders, which Stalin fostered and exploited, rather than military necessity.

Bagramyan was the only non-Slav Front commander, and with the possible exception of Chernyakhovsky, the only one who was not already a general before the war. His intellectual capacity was recognized in 1935, when the General Staff Academy appointed him direct from pupil to lecturer, and his later sponsorship by Zhukov, Timoshenko and Stalin was obviously based on high regard for his abilities. His transfer from staff to command postings was an act either of faith or professional judgement bordering on genius. He was fortunate that the army he was given was already one of the best in the Red Army, but his performance in command of it was undoubtedly well above average. He was again fortunate in that by the time he became a Front commander the war was clearly won and both human and material resources were abundant, but he made good use of them and achieved impressive results. His empathy with Stalin may have owed something to their common Transcaucasian origins, but as both functioned within an overwhelmingly Russian milieu, it is more likely that Stalin saw the same qualities in him as did Zhukov, Timoshenko and numerous other senior officers. He reached Marshal's rank after the war, and died in 1982.

BIBLIOGRAPHY

Babadzhanyan, A. Kh. *et al.*, *Lyuki otkryli v Berline*, Voenizdat, Moscow, 1973.

Bagramyan, I. Kh., *Tak shli my k pobede* (combined volume), Voenizdat, Moscow, 1988.

Erickson, John, *The Soviet High Command*, Macmillan, London, 1962.

Erickson, John, *The Road to Berlin: Stalin's War with Germany*, vol. II, Weidenfeld & Nicolson, London, 1983.

Gurov, A., 'Boevye deistviya Sovietskikh voisk na yugo-zapadnom napravlenii v nachal'nom periode voiny', *Voenno-istoricheskii Zhurnal*, Moscow, nos 8 and 11/1988.

Moskalenko, K. S., *Na Yugo-zapadnom Napravlenii*, 2 vols, Nauka, Moscow, 1969 and 1972.

Vasilevskii, A. M., *Delo Vsey Zhizni*, 6th edn, 2 vols, Politizdat, Moscow, 1988.

Zhukov, G. K., *Vospominaniya i razmyshleniya*, 10th edn, Novosti, Moscow, 1992.

Pavel Ivanovich
BATOV

DAVID GLANTZ

Despite the devastating nature and effects of the military purges of the late 1930s, which destroyed the best and brightest of the Red Army leadership, a nucleus of talented junior officers survived, and largely because of the tremendous demands of modern war and the imperatives of national and personal survival, during wartime a new generation of talented officers emerged to lead the Red Army to victory. Although this volume focuses on those in high-level command, primarily Stavka (Supreme HQ), senior General Staff officers, and Front commanders, the growth and maturation of new officer talent at and beneath army level was a necessary precondition for the Soviet victory. The battlefield accomplishments of still largely unknown army, corps, division and brigade commanders, who rose to responsible command positions during the war, provided the grist upon which larger reputations were made.

No army commander better fits this mould than Pavel Ivanovich Batov, whose stint in army command uninterruptedly spanned seven years (three of them wartime), and whose accomplishments typified the stellar performance of tens of other successful army commanders. Born into a peasant family on 1 June 1897 in the village of Filisovo, Rybinsk region of Yaroslavl Province, Batov received his primary education while helping his family and working in a small commercial venture in the village. Aged 18, one year after the outbreak of the First World War, he enlisted in a student command and was sent to the Russo-German front. There he served as a scout in the 3rd Infantry Regiment of the Life Guards. Two St George Crosses and two other medals which he received attested to his apparent bravery. In 1917 Batov was wounded in combat and soon assigned to the NCO school in Petrograd, where he was converted to Bolshevism by the political agitator, A. Savkov.

He was in the Red Army for four years from August 1918, initially as a machine-gunner, and helped suppress White uprisings in his home province and elsewhere, serving simultaneously as assistant military chief of the Rybinsk Military Committee. Batov's career in the period immediately following the Civil War is unclear. He remained in the Red Army, rising to company command in 1926. During the same year, he was chosen to attend the Vystrel Officers' School, where among his classmates were many who would achieve high command or staff positions in the Great Patriotic War, including future Chief of General Staff A. M. Vasilevsky, army commanders M. I. Katukov (1st Guards Tank Army), N. P. Pukhov (13th Army), S. G. Trofimenko (27th Army), I. M. Chistyakov (6th Guards Army), and mechanized corps commander M. D. Solomatin (1st Mechanized Corps).

After completing the 'Vystrel' course, in 1927 Batov was appointed battalion commander in the newly formed (December 1926) and prestigious 1st Moscow Proletarian Rifle Division, a unit with which he would serve continuously for almost nine years. He joined the Communist Party in 1929 (rather late) and was appointed chief of staff of the Proletarian Rifle Division's 3rd Rifle Regiment. Four years later, in 1933, he rose to command the regiment. A fitness report of 20 November 1936 by his division commander, L. G. Petrovsky, amply revealed his value to the division. In the assessment Petrovsky wrote:

> Comrade Batov has commanded a regiment for more than three years. In the course of that time, the regiment has occupied first place in the division in all categories of combat and political training. In tactical training, the regiment stands out as superb; I always sent the regiment on the main axis. I have trust in the 3rd Rifle Regiment and confidence in its commander, Comrade Batov, that all will be done to fulfil the order.

For his combat skill and political acumen, in 1936 Batov was awarded the 'Sign of Honour' medal. Soon after, he also finished the Frunze Academy by correspondence course.

Batov was one of a chosen few promising commanders selected by the Soviet Defence Commissariat to 'volunteer' for service in the ideologically charged atmosphere of the Spanish Civil War. In 1936 the new volunteer was assigned, equipped with the code-name Fritz Pablo, to advise General Lukacz (the Hungarian Communist, Mate Zalka), whose 12th International Brigade was defending the approaches to Madrid. Batov was present at the evacuation of Madrid in October 1936 and, even later, as advisor on the Teruel front. Twice wounded in combat, for his service he earned the Orders of Lenin and Red Banner. He then fought with the 12th Brigade north of Madrid at Harama, where he served alongside A. I. Rodimtsev (twice Hero of the Soviet Union and famed wartime commander), and at Guadalajara, where the brigade won fame for repelling three heavy Fascist attacks. Later he was wounded on the Aragon front, and spent time recuperating in a Barcelona hospital.

After returning to the Soviet Union in December 1937, Batov was promoted to brigade commander and appointed commander of the 10th Rifle Corps, headquartered in Voronezh. At the same time, he was elected deputy of the Supreme Soviet from Voronezh district. Soon, more important duties required his presence in Moscow. After only several months in Voronezh, in early 1938 Batov assumed command of the 3rd Rifle Corps headquartered at Ivanovo Voznesensk in Moscow Military District. While serving as corps commander, on 29 July 1939 he was appointed member of a special commission, headed by Assistant Defence Commissar G. I. Kulik, formed to discuss and oversee the restructuring of Red Army motor-mechanized forces. The commission's controversial report, approved on 21 November 1939, included the ill-advised recommendation to abolish the army's four tank corps and to replace them with fifteen new, smaller motorized divisions. Although Batov's rôle in the proceedings is unclear, his and others' (especially D. G. Pavlov's) experiences in the Spanish Civil War prompted the recommendations.

As war clouds swept over Europe, Batov's 3rd Rifle Corps, which consisted of the 14th, 17th, 45th and 52nd Rifle Divisions, was mobilized and deployed to Belorussia in September 1939. The corps subsequently took part in the occupation of eastern Poland as part of the Belorussian Front. Immediately after the Polish operation, and after a short respite in Vilnius, Batov's 3rd Rifle Corps was transferred to the Finnish Front, where it took part in the second phase (February–March 1940) of the Russo-Finnish War by conducting operations in the Karelian sector under 13th Army. For his service in Finland, Batov earned another Order of Lenin and was promoted to Divisional Commander and then, in June 1940, to Lieutenant-General. Soon after, he was appointed Deputy Commander of Transcaucasia Military District and Chief of the Tbilisi garrison. Batov had been on exercise with district forces since 13 June, when on 17 June 1941 he was summoned to Moscow by Deputy Defence Commissar B. M. Shaposhnikov.

In Moscow, on 20 June Batov received command of the 9th Separate Rifle Corps stationed in the Crimea and all ground forces in the region. No sooner had he arrived at his new post than Operation 'Barbarossa' commenced. From his vantage point in the Crimea, Batov helped prepare the peninsula for defence and supported Soviet forces besieged in Odessa by German and Romanian forces. On 14 August, he was elevated to the position of assistant commander of the Southern Front's 51st Army and simultaneously became assistant commander of all ground forces in the Crimea.

As German forces raced across southern Ukraine in late August and September 1941, Batov was re-assigned to command an operational group tasked with defending the Sivash and Chongar sectors on the approaches into the Crimea. His three divisions (271st Rifle Division, 3rd Motorized Rifle Division, and 42nd Cavalry Division) were also designated as the principal Soviet counter-attack force. When the main German assault materialized on 12 September through the Perekop isthmus, Batov's forces had difficulty redeploying to meet it. After a futile defensive battle, on 26 September German forces succeeded in penetrating into the Crimean peninsula, and Batov's operational group conducted a fighting withdrawal into the fortress city of Sevastapol. Later, Batov travelled by sea to take command of Soviet forces (9th Rifle Corps) defending the Kerch peninsula in the extreme eastern Crimea. Despite his exertions, and in chaotic conditions, from 12 to 15 November Batov's forces were forced to evacuate Kerch and the Crimea. Once safely arrived in the Kuban region, Batov was given command of 51st Army.

Despite vicious recriminations over poor Red Army performance in the Crimean defence, Stalin exonerated Batov for his part in the disaster. On 27 December Batov again answered a summons to Moscow. At a meeting at 3 a.m. next day with Stalin and Shaposhnikov, both again excused Batov's part in the Crimean affair and appointed him to command 3rd Army of the Bryansk Front.

Batov later recounted some of the details of the Kremlin encounter. In the midst of the successful Soviet counter-attack around Moscow, Shaposhnikov, in their early-morning meeting, soberly assessed the Red Army's performance in this, its first successful offensive action. He confided to Batov that the army still had to go: 'We still need to master the experience of modern war. We threw the enemy back from the capital, but the outcome of the war will be decided neither here nor today. The crisis is far ahead.' At the subsequent Stavka session, Batov met Stalin, who personally informed him there were 'no complaints against him' regarding 51st Army's performance in the Crimea. Instead, Batov was to apply the fruits of his recent education to his new command on the Bryansk Front.

One could attribute this ready acceptance of failure on Stalin's part to his elation over the momentous victory unfolding around Moscow. Perhaps forgiveness was a product of Stalin's knowledge of Batov's long association with the Proletarian Division and his reputation as a loyal fighter. In any event, Batov's reputation would soon be put to the test, and Stalin's faith would be amply rewarded.

Batov served in the Bryansk Front from early January to 22 October 1942, first during January and February as 3rd Army Commander, and then, from February through October, as deputy Front Commander. K. K. Rokossovsky, who commanded the Front from mid-July 1942, praised Batov's work, later writing: 'My deputy, in charge of troop activation, was General P. I. Batov, a fine old combatant officer with a good organizing ability. From the outset, I saw that he was unhappy with his job. A man of such ebullient energy found it hard to lead the inactive life of a staff officer.' Rokossovsky soon acted on the basis of his keen appreciation of Batov's talent by recommending him for army command. A long association between the two commanders would ensue, and Rokossovsky would rely on Batov's as yet unproven talents in many subsequent operations.

During the culminating stages of the German Stalingrad offensive, after Soviet forces defending the distant approaches to the city had been defeated, Batov was reassigned literally into the centre of the action. On 22 October he was appointed to command 4th Tank Army after its defeat by German forces on the west bank of the River Don. The army was derisively referred to by its men as 'the four-tank army', since, by that time, that was the total number of tanks it possessed. Rokossovsky recalled the change in command: '[General Kryuchenkin's] place was taken by General P. I. Batov, a man of great combat experience and bold initiative with whom I had seen service on the Bryansk Front.' The remnants of Batov's new army fought on the approaches to the city of Stalingrad when, on 27 October 1942, the army was converted to a rifle army and renumbered the 65th. Batov would command 65th Army to war's end.

Batov led 65th Army (now reinforced) as the principal shock group of the Don Front during the Stalingrad strategic counter-offensive, which commenced on 19 November 1942. Batov played a key rôle in planning the operation, and his army was instrumental in destroying the German VI Army, encircled at Stalingrad. In a tense planning conference with Zhukov on 4 November, Batov provided critical intelligence information regarding the precise boundary between Romanian and German forces defending along the River Don northwest of Stalingrad. This information contributed in a major way to subsequent Soviet offensive success. Later, during Operation 'Koltso' ('Ring'), which was conducted to reduce the encircled German force, Batov developed tactical measures designed to surprise the enemy. His army's 10 January attack spearheaded operations to collapse the German encirclement. Rokossovsky, the Don Front commander, later wrote:

> P. I. Batov . . . displayed fine initiative with an improvised mobile task force. Assembling all the tanks he could, he mounted an infantry landing party on them and dispatched them to bypass enemy strongpoints. By striking at the enemy's flank and rear, the task force ensured the swift advance of the other units.

A. M. Vasilevsky, Stavka Representative for the Stalingrad operation, also had high praise for Batov's performance:

> Recalling my stay with 65th Army, I cannot fail to say several good words about the experienced combat commander, the most magnificent spirit, and the modesty of the man who was and is Pavel Ivanovich Batov. I was first acquainted with him in the 1930s, when I was working in the Military Training Directorate and he was a battalion commander in . . . the Moscow Proletarian Rifle division . . . . Batov was already seen

as an experienced, fine specialist and organizer and thoughtful commander, with a superb knowledge of his business. He had shown himself to be a magnificently trained combat commander in Spain, able to organize and control combined arms in battle. During the Great Patriotic War, Batov consistently and brilliantly performed the most responsible missions on the main axes of three Fronts. For most of the war he was assigned to serve under K. K. Rokossovsky, who loved, valued, and respected him very much. Supreme Headquarters also valued him highly.

Soon after the surrender of German VI Army, on 18 February 65th Army began regrouping northward to reinforce the Soviet Central Front, then advancing westward toward Kursk. Batov moved his headquarters, first to Yelets, then to Livny, and finally to just north of Kursk, where his army joined Rokossovsky's Central Front. From April through June, 65th Army operated in the Sevsk sector. Soon after, in July, Batov's army participated in the Central Front's defence at Kursk, though in a secondary sector.

When Soviet forces began their strategic offensive operations after the German defeat at Kursk, from 26 August into October 1943, Batov's army spearheaded Central Front's Chernigov-Pripet operation. 65th Army formed the main attack force and seized Sevsk and a bridgehead over the River Sev, through which 2nd Tank Army was committed. Batov's operations opened the way for the subsequent brilliant exploitation by Lieutenant-General I. D. Chernyakhovsky's 60th Army. Then, by 5 September, Batov's army raced forward 125 kilometres, crossed the river Desna, beat back repeated German counter-attacks, and advanced on Gomel on the river Sozh. On 20 September lead elements of 65th Army crossed the Sozh south of Gomel, while neighbouring 61st Army secured two small bridgeheads across the Dnieper. Only then did German resistance bring Batov's headlong advance to a temporary halt.

On 15 October 1943, after an extensive secret regrouping, Batov's army seized a bridgehead across the Dnieper near Loev. After another subsequent secret regrouping, Batov renewed his advance to enlarge the strategically significant bridgeheads. Both operations have since become prime examples of successful Soviet combat deception. From 10 to 30 November 1943, Batov's army played a key rôle in the Gomel-Rechitsa operation as part of the Belorussian Front. Batov became well known for his skilful expansion of the Dnieper bridgehead, for his continued successful employment of operational and tactical deception, and for his imaginative use of 1st Tank Corps to seize the city of Rechitsa, despite the difficult wooded and swampy terrain. Rokossovsky later noted that Batov 'had made good use of the high mobility of the tank and cavalry corps to pursue the enemy westward, through the forests and swamps of the Polesie country'. Batov's forces later participated in heavy fighting for the towns of Kalinkovichi and Mozyr, both of which fell to Soviet forces by mid-January 1944.

During the important Belorussian strategic offensive in June and July

1944, Batov's army participated in the Bobruisk operation as part of Rokossovsky's 1st Belorussian Front. Batov was successful in arranging for passage of 65th Army across the swampy regions southwest of Bobruisk and was the first to employ the 'double' artillery barrage to support a penetration operation. His forces subsequently encircled and destroyed German IX Army in Bobruisk. For his performance he was promoted to Colonel-General.

In later stages of the Belorussian operation, in July and August 1944, 65th Army took part in the Lublin-Brest operation of the 1st Belorussian Front. On 22 July 1944 his army secured crossings over the River Bug north of Belostok and, although cut off for a time, held the crossings against heavy German counter-attacks. Then, on 27 August, 65th Army began the final Front advance to the River Narew spearheaded by 1st Guards Tank Corps. The army secured crossings over the Narew by 4 September and subsequently held those crossings against heavy German counter-attacks for over two months.

In January 1945, during the winter campaign to clear German forces from Poland, Batov and 65th Army took part in the East Prussian operation under the 2nd Belorussian Front and ultimately secured crossings over the Vistula in early February. The Front commander, Rokossovsky, later noted: 'This meant that General Batov's 65th Army would be with us, which pleased me very much. I had been with 65th Army since Stalingrad and had had ample opportunity to observe the splendid combat qualities of its men, commanders, and, of course, above all, Pavel Batov, a brave and talented soldier.' Later in February 1945, Batov's army took part with the 3rd Belorussian Front in operations to clear German forces from Pomerania.

Finally, in April 1945, 65th Army forced the Oder in the Berlin operation as the principal shock group of the 3rd Belorussian Front. Rokossovsky is quoted as saying when he saw the river obstacle: 'Our men call it two Dniepers with a Pripet in between. Quite aptly, I think.' Despite the formidable river obstacle, Batov's forces prevailed and helped in the final reduction of Nazi Germany.

Batov continued his active military rôle after the war, both as a senior commander and as a prolific writer on military theory. In summer 1945 he was appointed to command 7th Mechanized Army of the Soviet Northern Group of Forces stationed in Poland. After Soviet force levels were reduced, and 7th Mechanized Army was redeployed to Belorussia (as 7th Tank Army), in 1947 Batov received command of Baltic Military District's 11th Guards Army, headquartered in Kaliningrad. His two years of service with the army was followed by appointment in 1949 as First Deputy Commander of Group of Soviet Forces, Germany. His brief service there preceded his attendance during 1949–50 at the Voroshilov General Staff Academy.

After his graduation from the Academy, Batov was assigned a command in Belorussia Military District, probably of 7th Tank Army at Borisov (1951–2) and later as a member of the military district staff. This prepared him for his subsequent assignment in March 1955 as commander of Carpathia Military District, where in August the same year he headed a staff group of 100 senior officers who conducted a survey of Hungary's military districts. A year later, Batov's forces capitalized on that experience by participating in the suppression of the Hungarian revolt.

In July 1958, after serving three years in Carpathia Military District, Batov was transferred to command Baltic Military District, a position which he held until late 1959. Although his assignments during the ensuing two years are unclear, in June 1961 he escorted the visiting Indonesian Prime Minister on a trip to Tashkent and Simferopol.

In late 1961 Batov returned to serve in Eastern Europe as commander of the Soviet Southern Group of Forces in Hungary. Later, from September 1963 through 1965, he was appointed to the prestigious positions of Deputy Chief of Staff of the Soviet Army and Chief of Staff of Warsaw Pact Forces, replacing the deceased General A. I. Antonov. Entering virtual retirement in 1965, Batov remained active in the Defence Ministry Inspectorate and, from 1970 through 1981, as Chief of the Soviet Veterans Committee. Throughout his military career Batov was politically active in the ritualistic way appropriate to senior officers, serving as a delegate to seven Party Conferences and as a deputy of the USSR Supreme Soviet from 1937 to 1950 and from 1954 to 1966.

While in the Inspectorate, Batov wrote his memoirs and numerous works on military themes, including treatises on various kinds of operations, notably river crossings, obviously drawn from his own extensive experience. His work on river crossing operations has become a standard Soviet military text on the subject. Batov died in April 1985 and was buried in Moscow's prestigious Novodevichy Cemetery. His numerous decorations included Hero of the Soviet Union twice (one for operations along the Sozh and Dnieper and one for his rôle in the Berlin operation), seven Orders of Lenin, one Order of the October Revolution, three Red Banners, three Orders of Suvorov, 1st Class, one Order of Kutuzov, 1st Class, one Order of Bogdan Khmelnitsky, 1st Class, one order 'For Service to the Proletariat', 3rd Class, and two 'Signs of Honour'.

As an officer and a person, Batov has received great respect and praise from both friend and foe. Soviet memoir literature mentions him often and favourably. A collective judgement characterized him as 'inexhaustibly energetic, able to foresee developing events and to undertake correct and well-founded decisions'. Batov was fond of saying, 'One must beat the enemy artfully, and that means with little blood.' As a commander, Batov always trusted in his men and related to his subordinates with respect, and, as a consequence, they trusted in him. Above all, he was a teacher of his officers and men. Thus, according to one who served under him, 'It was his distinctive style of work which his subordinates imitated and which produced positive results.' A post-war Western intelligence assessment confirmed these judgements, adding:

> During World War II, Batov enjoyed much confidence and great respect from the troops because he was one of the few senior officers who went to the front lines during battles and conversed with the soldiers. He was much admired by the soldiers for this very fact. He proved himself a capable and talented military leader and teacher of troops during the war.

BIBLIOGRAPHY

Kuznetsov, P., 'V Moskovskoi Proletarskoi', *Voenno-istoricheskii Zhurnal*, no. 12, December 1966, pp. 66–70. Hereafter cited as *ViZh*.

For other articles devoted to Batov in *ViZh*, see Troyanovsky, P. in no. 5, 1967; Kraynyukov, K. in no. 12, 1971; Grebov, I. and Kuzovkov, I. in no. 12, 1975; no. 6, 1977; no. 5, 1985; Pakitsky, A. N. in no. 6, 1987. Also in *Sovetskaya voennaya entsiklopediya*, vol. 1, 1976.

Batov, P. I. *V pokhodakh i boyakh*, Voenizdat, Moscow, 1962.

Operatsiya Oder, Voenizdat, Moscow, 1965.

Polki idut na Zapad, Voenizdat, Moscow, 1964.

Dvesti ognennykh dnei, Voenizdat, Moscow, 1968.

Na udarnom napravlenii, Stalingradskaya epopeya, Nauka, Moscow, 1968.

Perekop 1941, Simferopol, 1970.

'65-aya v boyakh za Belorusiiu', *Osvobozhdenie Belorussii 1944*, Nauka, Moscow, 1974.

Forsirovanie rek, 1942–1945, Voenizdat, Moscow, 1986.

Ivan Vasilievich
BOLDIN

DAVID GLANTZ

In early January 1945, a small party of Red Army soldiers approached a blindage near the front lines just north of the battered Polish town of Osowiec. The party gathered in the blindage and peered out over the frozen wooded swampland to the north, which was torn and scarred with enemy trenches and barbed wire. In the centre of the reconnaissance party, dressed in the garb of a common soldier to avoid identification by the enemy, was the commander of Soviet 50th Army, I. V. Boldin. He must have felt strange, coming back to this ground after a long and harrowing absence of four years. An eternity ago, in the lush warmth of early summer 1941, he had walked over this same terrain, when a single fragile border post and wire barrier gently punctuated the beauty of the countryside. In 1941 the potential enemy was the same, the circumstances, however, were markedly different. Then the thought of war was but a remote fear. Now, in 1945, this same countryside, torn and crushed by implements of war, crudely symbolized for Boldin what had transpired since that summer day. He had endured seemingly endless suffering so that he might now look across this territory as commander of a conquering army, rather than a leader whose force was about to be vanquished and humiliated. Boldin was a fortunate man; he was a survivor, a man about to reap revenge for thousands of comrades who had been less fortunate than he and had perished. Ivan Vasilievich Boldin's wartime military career symbolized much of what the war was about and what it could do to a man. Boldin entered the war as a deputy Front commander and finished the war in the same capacity. His fate formed a unity with the wartime fate of the Soviet state.

Like most commanders of his age, Boldin's life began in the relative obscurity of Russian rural life. He was born on 15 August 1892 in the village of Vysokaya in the Insa region of Penza Province, an agricultural region west of Samara (renamed Kuibyshev until recently) on the Volga. Son of a landed peasant, he was fortunate to attend primary and two years of secondary school before going to work with his father. In early 1914 he moved to the village where he worked in grain processing and bread making.

Soon after the outbreak of the First World War, on 28 July 1914, Boldin was drafted. After several months of infantry training, his regiment, the 23rd Rifle Regiment, deployed to Sarakomysh on the Turkish front. In three years of service in the war against the Turks, he took part in operations around Erzurum and Kars and was fortunate enough to complete his secondary schooling. After the February Revolution of 1917, Boldin became politically active, serving as an elected member of his regimental and divisional revolutionary committee until his demobilization in December 1917, when he returned to Insa. Even in these early days, he established a pattern of political service which would characterize the remainder of his career in the military.

After the Bolshevik seizure of power, Boldin became active in local and regional politics. From 7 January to 14 March 1918, he served as assistant head of the Insa District Executive Committee, then chairing it until 7 January 1919. After joining the Communist Party in June 1918, he attended the 5th All-Russian Congress of Soviets in July as a delegate from Penza. On 5 January 1919 he became First Deputy Chairman and head of the Financial Section of the Penza provincial administration, a position which he held until 24 October 1919. Simultaneously, from June to September he was a member of the Penza Bolshevik Party Committee.

As Civil War spread across the face of Soviet Russia, in October 1919 Boldin volunteered for military service in a Red Army detachment and was made assistant chairman of the Provincial Executive Committee of the Red Army Political Directorate. At the height of the Civil War, he served as company commander fighting Finnish forces on the Karelian peninsula. After several months he was reassigned to the Western Front, where he first fought along the Estonian border and in the defence of Petrograd against General N. N. Yudenich's White forces and then against the Poles near Polotsk and Lepel in the Russo-Polish War. In April 1920 Boldin was appointed a battalion commander in the 492nd Rifle Regiment, and, in August, as commander of the 52nd Rifle Regiment, 6th Rifle Division, which he commanded during the ill-fated Warsaw and Grodno operations of Tukhachevsky's Western Front. Thereafter, his division helped restore order in central Belorussia before being transferred to Orel in late 1921 as part of the 10th Rifle Corps, headquartered in Kursk. In December 1921 Boldin apparently demonstrated enough military potential to be enrolled in the Vystrel Officer Rifle School at Novogireevo, near Kursk.

While attending the Vystrel course from December 1921 to September 1923, he established the first of several lifelong relationships with fellow officers. Future Army and Front Commander M. A. Purkayev was his roommate, and future Army General N. E. Berzarin was among his classmates. In autumn 1922 Boldin and the Vystrel course relocated to the old 1st Cadet Corps barracks at Lefortovo near Moscow.

Having completed his officers course in September 1923, Boldin was posted to Tula, where he commanded the 252nd Rifle Regiment of 84th Territorial Rifle Division (2nd Rifle Corps), a unit which he had to form from scratch. While forming the regiment and commanding it until November 1924, Boldin continued his political activity by serving as a member of the Tula city Soviet. The Red Army staff continued to exploit Boldin's abilities as a unit-builder by assigning him in November 1924 along with personnel from the Tula Regiment to form and command a special Separate Moscow Rifle Regiment, stationed in Moscow's Chernyshevsky Barracks. The newly formed regiment was used as an experimental base for testing new weaponry. Meanwhile, Boldin remained politically active, and, from 22 December 1924 to 15 December 1925, he served as a member of the Moscow Regional Bolshevik Committee and other local political-military organizations.

To sharpen his military and political skills, from November 1925 to October 1926, Boldin attended a special 'short course' at the Frunze Military Academy. There, he was elected delegate to the 27th Congress of Soviets of the RSFSR and the 3rd All-Union Congress of Soviets. Upon his graduation from Frunze in October 1926, Boldin was posted as assistant commander of the 19th 'Labour Red Banner' Territorial Rifle Division of 10th Rifle Corps, stationed in Voronezh under Chernikov. There he served until May 1930, while also a member of the Voronezh city Soviet.

Continuing this pattern of alternating political and military assignments, from 1 May to 1 August 1930 Boldin taught at the Lenin Military-Political Academy in Moscow, which trained commissars, and served as a member of the Academy's Party collective. Then, from 1 August 1930 to 27 April 1931, he served as chief and military commissar in the All-Union School for Retraining Command Cadres of Soviet Military Industry. There the politically reliable Boldin took an active, albeit positive, part in the earliest of the 'purges' of the industrial cadres as a part of Stalin's forced industrialization programme, conducted under the rubric of the 'New Socialist Offensive' and the first of many Five Year Plans. For his effective work, Boldin was rewarded by being assigned from 27 April to 1 June 1931 as a member of the Leningrad District Communist Party Committee and Executive Committee.

Boldin returned to military service on 30 April 1931, when he became commander and political commissar of the 12th Rifle Corps' 53rd Pugachev Territorial Rifle Division, stationed near Samara in Volga Military District. Once again, Boldin was called upon to form a new division. He served in this capacity until 29 December 1934 under the tutelage of two military district commanders, P. E. Dybenko and B. M. Shaposhnikov. The former perished in the purges and the latter became chief of the General Staff. While in command Boldin again served in a variety of political offices and in January 1934 was elected as delegate from Saratov to the XVII Party Congress.

In December 1934, probably again based upon his political reliability, Boldin was enrolled in a two-year 'special course' at the Frunze Academy, which also included Purkayev, Yeremenko and Konev, officers also known for their political reliability and activity and who would rise to Front Command. Boldin's special class at Frunze, in effect, was earmarked to replace those who perished in the military purges of 1937. Upon his graduation in early 1937, he received command of a new division formed during the wholesale expansion of the Red Army and its conversion from territorial to regular status.

Boldin commanded the 18th Rifle Division (of 19th or 33rd Rifle Corps), located in Petrozavodsk in Leningrad Military District, from 13 April 1937 to 1938. In 1938 he was awarded his first Order of Red Banner and received command of the 17th Rifle Corps located at Vinnitsa in Kiev Military District. Here he served under Timoshenko, Military District Commander, and Khrushchev as Military District Commissar. After Boldin had spent several months in corps command, on 28 July 1938 he was assigned as commander of the newly created Kalinin Military District. Here he was promoted corps commander on 9 February 1939, and he continued his political activities, serving as Kalinin city delegate to the XVIII Party Congress in March 1939.

As a new world war loomed in Europe, in September 1939 Boldin was selected to command a Cavalry-Mechanized Group in M. P. Kovalev's Special Western Military District. Boldin's group, consisting of two cavalry, one tank, one rifle corps and a separate tank brigade, led the advance of Kovalev's Belorussian Front into eastern Poland at 0540 hours on 17 September 1939. After the short undistinguished campaign and the subsequent incorporation of eastern Poland into the Soviet Union, in late September Boldin headed the military delegation which effected the Soviet occupation of Latvia, again as a probable reward for his unquestioned political reliability.

Boldin's meteoric rise in status continued unabated. On 22 October 1939 he was appointed commander of Odessa Military District, this time to participate in the invasion of Romanian Bessarabia. In June 1940 the Soviet High Command created a Southern Group of Forces to conduct the operation and gave command to General Zhukov, commander of Kiev Military District. Boldin assumed command of the bulk of Zhukov's forces, formed into Soviet 9th Army. Between 28 and 30 June, Zhukov's and Boldin's forces invaded Bessarabia and forcibly incorporated the territory into the Soviet Union. Simultaneously Boldin was promoted to the rank of

Lieutenant-General. For his services, in September 1940 he was appointed Deputy Commander of Special Western Military District.

On the eve of the German invasion Boldin, as deputy of the Military District Commander General D. G. Pavlov, watched increasingly convincing intelligence indicators of the impending attack (later recorded in his memoirs). Neither their warning to High Command nor those of other key officers in other border military districts were heeded by the Soviet leadership. As a result, on 22 June German forces achieved both political and military surprise in the initial stages of Operation 'Barbarossa'. Boldin later recorded in his memoirs the harrowing opening hours and days of hostilities.

After being prevented by Defence Commissar Timoshenko from taking prudent and timely counter-measures in the face of the devastating German assault, late on 22 June Pavlov ordered Boldin by telephone to implement pre-planned defensive operations. Boldin's mission was to mount a counter-attack against German forces advancing on Grodno with a cavalry-mechanized shock group composed of two mechanized corps (6th and 11th) and one cavalry corps (6th). His utterly unrealistic mission, given the reigning chaos, was 'to attack in the general direction of Bialystok, Lipsk, south of Grodno to destroy the enemy on the left bank of the River Neman and to prevent the arrival of enemy units in the Volkovysk region'.

Boldin flew in a light aircraft through heavy enemy fire to 10th Army's command post, where he landed on a dirt airstrip outside Bialystok. Dodging enemy bombs, which torched airfield installations, he drove through the chaotic burning city to 10th Army headquarters, where he met the 6th Mechanized Corps commander to plan the hasty and ill-fated counter-attack. Plagued by constant German aerial bombardment, interrupted communications, and scarcity of fuel and ammunition, Boldin's force launched repeated disjointed attacks, but was utterly unable to perform its mission. The 6th Mechanized Corps commander perished, and by 27 June the entire force, together with Soviet 3rd, 4th and 10th Armies, was encircled west of Minsk. Boldin, at the head of a small group, spent forty-five days fighting for survival behind German lines. Finally, on 10 August 1941, with 1,650 men in tow, his group broke through the Soviet lines near Smolensk. Stavka Order No. 270 praised the heroics of Boldin's 'division'.

Immediately after Boldin's escape, Timoshenko, Supreme Commander of the Western Strategic Axis (Direction), appointed him as deputy to his old friend, General Konev, now commanding the Western Front. No sooner had Boldin occupied his new position on 2 October than the Germans launched yet another offensive toward Moscow. During the ensuing Vyazma operation, Konev assigned Boldin to command a Front operational group of two tank brigades and three rifle divisions tasked with stopping the German advance. The counter-attack failed, and once again Boldin's force was encircled as the Germans pushed on towards Moscow. During a subsequent successful attempt to break out from encirclement, Boldin was wounded and hospitalized in Moscow.

After a short period of recuperation, in late November Chief of Red Army General Staff, Marshal Shaposhnikov, summoned Boldin to his Moscow headquarters and assigned him command of 50th Army, then defending the city of Tula against Guderian's II Panzer Army. Having waited for hours in the Kremlin, Boldin finally met Shaposhnikov in the small hours, prior to the Chief of Staff's usual early-morning session with Stalin and the Stavka. Despite the crisis atmosphere in Moscow, Shaposhnikov appeared calm. After recalling earlier meetings with Boldin and sharing family news, the Chief of Staff turned to the matter at hand, indicating the seriousness of their position: 'The enemy not only has not abandoned the seizure of Moscow, but has even strengthened his onslaught.' Pointing to the large operational map, he went on:

> Hitler has thrown crack units into the Tula region and occupied Yasnaya Polyana. Can you imagine, his vandals have dared to defile the people's holy of holies – the grave of Leo Tolstoy, they are destroying the home where he created his work of genius, *War and Peace*, pillaging his museum and ravaging his estate. Now the enemy . . . is firing on Tula from the area of the Kosogorsk metallurgical factory. His aim is to seize Tula and convert it into a bridgehead for an attack on Moscow.

Shaposhnikov offered Boldin command of 50th Army, which was defending on the city's outskirts, and enjoined him with the warning, 'I think that the mission is clear. Do not forget that Hitler has entrusted the rather experienced combat General Guderian with the seizure of Tula.' Boldin later admitted it was a challenging task to undertake.

Boldin arrived in Tula on 22 November and took part in the planning and conduct of operations which soon halted the German advance. In early December his forces co-operated with Soviet 10th Army in repelling Guderian's forces from the southern approaches to Moscow. On 8 January 50th Army opened the second phase of the Soviet Moscow counter-offensive with a surprise attack on German positions southeast of Tula. Boldin has received credit for successfully committing to combat on 18 January an army mobile group, which tore through German lines and forced the Germans to abandon the city of Kaluga. Boldin later shared much of the credit for those feats with other commanders and the 1st Guards Cavalry Corps, which had spearheaded the attack.

After this success, Boldin's 50th Army took part in the Rzhev-Vyazma and Yukhnov offensives of February–April 1942, and launched repeated, if increasingly futile, attempts to cut the Warsaw–Moscow highway and encircle German Army Group Centre. The growing frailty of Boldin's army and the frustration of his repeated failures are eloquently attested to in the numerous post-action reports of his by now woefully understrength army.

In a report of 22 April to Stavka and Western Front headquarters, Boldin wrote angrily that he was being slowed down by lack of ammunition, caused by the poor road conditions for wheeled transport: 'As an extreme measure, in some units the troops are carrying supplies by hand.' Total lack of air support also drove Boldin to distraction. As a result of these parlous conditions, his offensive expired in the spring mud.

During the remainder of 1942 and early 1943, while battle raged throughout southern Russia, the central sector of the Eastern Front remained relatively quiet. Boldin's army, now consisting of but four rifle divisions, took part in erecting formidable defences covering the approaches to Moscow and participated in the virtually bloodless Rzhev-Vyazma operation of March 1943, when the Germans abandoned the large Rzhev salient, which threatened Moscow, to establish more defensible lines further west.

As the central portion of the Eastern Front once again erupted in flames after the battle of Kursk in July 1943, Boldin's 50th Army was destined, with one notable exception, to play a clearly secondary rôle, probably a measure both of its reduced strength and Stavka's limited faith in Boldin's military capabilities. Shortly before the Kursk operation, Boldin gave up four of his army's five divisions and received in subordination four new rifle divisions, three rifle brigades and one tank brigade, with which he was ordered to prepare to take part in the offensive phase of the Kursk strategic offensive operation against German forces defending the Orel salient. Boldin's force had orders to launch a secondary attack and provide flank support for the 11th Guards Army, which made the main attack against the northern sector of the Orel salient. The offensive of 13 July 1943 ended with 50th Army locked in fierce fighting along the River Zhisdra north of Orel, after an advance of 50 kilometres, where the initial Soviet offensive finally stalled.

After a pause, while operations continued to the north, east of Smolensk and in the south near Kharkov, Boldin's army took part in the Bryansk offensive operation. There it conducted two successive secret regroupings to enable it to strike a weakly defended German flank position south of Kirov. In its ensuing attack on 8 September, 50th Army unhinged German defences and forced the Germans to abandon Bryansk. The performance of Boldin's forces in the operation was mixed. The Germans detected his first regroupment, but not his second, and Soviet accounts seem to accord the Bryansk Front commander, General M. M. Popov, with much of the credit for success in the operation.

In subsequent stages of the summer–autumn campaign of 1943, Boldin's army played a clearly subordinate rôle. During the Gomel-Rechitsa operation (October–November 1943), on two occasions 50th Army launched diversionary attacks, successfully distracting German attention from the main Front attack of 65th Army at a location further south.

After a period of relative quiet across the central sector of the Eastern Front, Boldin's force again went into action during the Belorussian offensive of 22 June–29 August 1944, as part of Zakharov's 2nd Belorussian Front. In both cases 50th Army occupied secondary sectors, but was responsible in part for the reduction of Mogilev, where it suffered inordinately heavy casualties, and in the destruction of encircled German IV Army east of Minsk. Thereafter, 50th Army took part in the slow, gruelling advance through Belorussia across the River Neman through Grodno to the approaches into East Prussia, which it reached in late August 1944. At this point, Boldin's four-year odyssey had come full circle to the very same terrain where he had first experienced war against the Germans in June 1941.

In early January 1945, after a month of reconnoitring and offensive preparations, the 2nd Belorussian Front, of which Boldin's force was part, commenced the large-scale East Prussian offensive operation, designed to drive the Germans from their heartland and into the Baltic Sea. Boldin's army was arrayed along the Front's extended right flank with orders to support the main Front attack further south by maintaining pressure on German forces. On 13 January the offensive began, and Soviet forces penetrated deep into the German rear area towards Gdansk and the Baltic. Boldin's army soon joined the attack, but not ardently enough or in timely enough fashion. For his army's lacklustre performance, Front chief Rokossovsky removed Boldin from command of the 50th Army, noting later that Boldin had failed to detect the German withdrawal in time and had continued to report to Front HQ that the enemy was still firmly entrenched: 'Only two days later a reconnaissance in force revealed that 50th Army was unopposed, and the last small Nazi groups were hastily withdrawing to the north. This was an unfortunate oversight on the part of the Army Commander, and General F. P. Ozerov, the Chief of Staff, was ordered to take over command.'

Boldin's own memoirs tail off in 1944 and he mentions the East Prussian offensive only in passing, noting that he wished he could have finished the war with his army. 50th Army's official history notes without comment that Ozerov took command on 5 February 1945. Several months later, in April 1945 Boldin was appointed Deputy Commander of the 3rd Ukrainian Front, in which capacity he took part in the Prague operation of May 1945 and finished his wartime service.

His postwar assignments were undistinguished and reflected the political realities of the time. In 1946, when Stalin 'exiled' Zhukov and other popular wartime marshals to minor positions in the military hierarchy, the politically reliable Boldin was appointed to command 8th Guards Army of the Soviet Group of Occupation Forces, Germany. In 1951 he commanded Eastern Siberian Military District and later was First Deputy Commander of Kiev

Military District. During the de-Stalinization and reform period after Stalin's death, in May 1958 Boldin went into virtual retirement as military consultant to the Defence Ministry Group of General Inspectors.

When Khrushchev initiated the first period of *glasnost* during the 'thaw' of 1960–1963, Boldin was permitted to write about his experiences in the opening days of the war. In 1961 he published his memoirs, entitled 'Pages of Life', and chapters about the initial days of the war and his part in the defence of Tula appeared in the military history journal, *Voenno-istoricheskii Zhurnal*.

Boldin died in Kiev on 28 March 1965. Among his many awards were two Orders of Lenin, three Red Banners, an Order of Suvorov, 1st Class, an Order of Kutuzov, 1st Class and two Red Stars.

It would not be unfair to label Boldin a political general, whose career owed as much to his political activity and reliability as it did to his military acumen. His pre-war biography amply demonstrates his record. He was known as an efficient troop organizer and was carefully groomed for higher command as one of the replacements for the thousands of officers purged between 1937 and 1941. He rose to prominence in the wake of the purges, but unlike, e.g. Vatutin or Konev, his military performance never eclipsed his political importance. His military feats were undistinguished, whether before the war in Poland and Bessarabia, or during the chaotic first days of the war, when he at least proved that he could survive. During the war he showed promise briefly in the defence of Tula and in the Bryansk operation of 1943. Otherwise, the secondary rôle and record of his army career vividly exemplified his service. Finally, in 1945, his superiors could no longer tolerate his lacklustre performance in even a secondary rôle, and he ended the war in the same position as he had begun it, a Deputy Front Commander.

Soviet military literature singularly lacks material about Boldin's rôle, his personality and character. 50th Army's official history barely mentions the name of its long-time commander. This is unusual and no doubt signifies his low popularity. Memoirs of key Red Army commanders are similarly silent about Boldin, with the exception of Rokossovsky's scathing denunciation of his performance in 1945. The same is true of the immense number of memoir writers who served with him. It is reasonable to assume from this that he was not popular and that others well understood that his military success reflected his political links with Stalin, and resented this. As a sign that his political reliability survived his master, it is noteworthy that he was the only Soviet delegate permitted to attend an international conference on wartime Resistance movements held at Oxford in 1960.

Boldin represented a class of Soviet general officer numbering perhaps half of the wartime total. These were politically reliable and militarily undistinguished officers who helped keep the Red Army an effective military tool against the Germans, and a reliable political tool of the Stalinist régime.

BIBLIOGRAPHY

Articles by and on Boldin in *Voenno-istoricheskii Zhurnal* no. 9, 1960; no. 4, 1961; no. 11, 1961; no. 1, 1989.
Boldin, I.V., *Stranitsy zhizni*, Voenizdat, Moscow, 1961.
Sokolovskii, V., 'O boevom tovarishche i druge', *Krasnaya Zvezda*, 31 March 1965.
Sovetskaya voennaya entsiklopediya, vol. 1, Voenizdat, Moscow, 1976.

Semen Mikhailovich
BUDENNY

VIKTOR ANFILOV

Budenny made his name as a military leader during the Civil War, but it was during the 1930s, in company with Voroshilov, that he achieved wide popularity, as historians and writers exaggerated the martial accomplishments of these two figures as they laboured to build up and inflate the part played by Stalin in Soviet history. Legends about Budenny were fabricated in countless books and songs, while little boys played in the streets at being 'Budenny's men'.

Semen Budenny was born into a peasant family on 25 April 1883 on a farm near Platovskaya on the Don. Conscripted for military service at the age of 20, he served in the Russo-Japanese war in the 46th Dragoon Regiment. He commanded a group with courage and, although wounded, remained with his regiment at Vladivostok to the end of the war. In the autumn of 1906 he had an opportunity to show the sort of initiative which would get him into a course of military studies, and to complete it successfully. His commanding officer asked him, 'Whom do you serve?' Budenny replied, 'Our little father, the Tsar, and the Fatherland, your excellency.' 'Have you heard about the revolution in St Petersburg?' 'How could I not, your excellency, nobody talks about anything else.' 'And what do you think about it?' 'My job is to serve, your excellency.' His commanding officer said, 'I like you, dragoon. We need reliable people like you. You'll go away to study some more.' The essence of Budenny's life is revealed in that little dialogue. Until 1917 he served the Tsar and the Fatherland in faith and truth, and from 1918 to the end of the Great Patriotic War he served Lenin, Stalin and the Motherland.

In January 1907 he was sent to the St Petersburg Cavalry School and when he completed it with the rank of sergeant he returned to his regiment and stayed on to do extra service. During the First World War, from September

1914 to October 1917, he served as a platoon sergeant in the Caucasus Cavalry Division. For bold and successful action he was decorated with four St George Crosses and became the proud wearer of the full ribbon of a St George Cavalryman, the highest distinction a soldier could achieve.

He went home to the farm when the October Revolution took place. Partisan groups began forming locally in the spring of 1918 and were engaging the White forces of General Krasnov who was supported by the Germans. The partisans eventually formed the 1st Socialist Regiment under B. M. Dumenko, and Budenny became his aide. The regiment soon grew into a brigade, and when it became the Special Cavalry Division Budenny was given a brigade to command. He showed himself to be a talented cavalry officer in the battles at Tsaritsyn in 10th Army under Voroshilov and was decorated with his first Order of the Red Banner.

When Dumenko fell ill Budenny took over the division. Voroshilov having been removed for poor leadership, in July the new commander, A. I. Yegorov, ordered the unification of Budenny's division with the 1st Stavropol Cavalry Division, thus forming the 1st Cavalry Corps of the Red Army, with Budenny as its commander. The corps was particularly successful in the autumn of 1919 against the forces of Generals Mamontov and Shkuro on the Southern Front at Voronezh. Having beaten the best of the White cavalry, Budenny became famous not only in Russia, but also abroad. He had himself photographed to commemorate the capture of Voronezh and sent a copy to Lenin. It can be seen to this day in Lenin's study in the Kremlin, a small, yellowing snapshot, with the inscription, 'To Comrade Lenin – from Cavalry Corps Commander Budenny, 28.X.' The following month, for his 'enormous services to the Republic and the Revolution', the national hero was awarded a gold sword decorated with the Order of the Red Banner.

Having witnessed the successes achieved by large mounted forces, Yegorov decided to form a Cavalry Army, and on 17 November Budenny was appointed its first commander, with Voroshilov and Shchadenko as members of his war council. In manoeuvrability and speed of attack, the Cavalry Army had no equal, and according to former German Chief of Staff, General Halder, its experience was not lost on the Wehrmacht.

From the moment of its inception, 1st Cavalry Army was for the most part successful. Its most brilliant conquest at the end of 1919 was the sudden capture of Rostov-on-Don, which was the main organizing centre of Denikin's Volunteer White Army. In January the Red Cavalry was transferred to the Caucasus Front under the command of V. I. Shorin, and it was there that Budenny, influenced by Voroshilov, who was chairman of the war council, refused to carry out the Front commander's orders. Although composed of peasants, and Cossacks who had their own political agenda, the Cavalry Army was ready to follow wherever Budenny led. Budenny and Voroshilov ignored Shorin and took their complaint straight to Stalin, leaving the army in a difficult position, made worse by fatigue and muddy conditions. On 15 February Shorin cabled the Commander-in-Chief, S. S. Kamenev, that Budenny and Voroshilov had abandoned the army and gone to Rostov, and that they had disobeyed his order to return. Budenny had objected to Shorin's plan to bring two divisions under his temporary command and, contrary to military discipline, had even refused to discuss the matter. Kamenev showed Shorin's cable to Lenin who replied on 17 February to I. T. Smilga and G. K. Ordzhonikidze, members of the war council, that he was extremely disturbed by the state of affairs on the Caucasus Front and 'the total disintegration' caused by Budenny. The two insubordinate commanders were called to order, but their slanders cost Shorin his job as Front Commander. He was replaced by Tukhachevsky. The latter received Budenny and Voroshilov for the first time aboard his armoured train at Bataisk on 13 March. He asked them sternly why they had sent troops into battle at their own discretion and not on the Front Commander's orders, and went on: 'Why did you overstep the mark? I value the initiative of any commander if it is for the good of the cause. But you complained about Shorin.' Tukhachevsky in his wildest dreams could not have imagined that only seventeen years later Voroshilov would sanction his arrest and execution and that Budenny would sit in judgement on him.

After defeating Denikin, beset by the spring thaw and the mud, lacking proper provisions and fodder, the cavalry made its famous 1,000-kilometre march from Maikop to the Ukrainian Southwestern Front, where Yegorov was commander and Stalin was a member of the war council. It attacked the butt of the Polish forces grouped at Kiev and Odessa, broke through the enemy front and raced forward 140 kilometres. The advance continued but the possibilities gradually dried up. There was a hitch near Lvov. Stubborn but fruitless battles in the southwest continued.

Meanwhile Tukhachevsky's Western Front was performing well. He requested the Commander-in-Chief to let him have the Cavalry Army to enable him to go on and capture Warsaw. Following Kamenev's orders, Yegorov instructed Budenny to put himself at Tukhachevsky's disposal from 14 August. This could not occur, however, because Stalin had insisted that they could break through to Warsaw via Lublin, and the Cavalry Army was therefore continuing its advance on Lvov. Hence, it was not until 20 August that Budenny began to transfer units from the Lvov sector, and his and Voroshilov's refusal to obey Tukhachevsky's orders was one reason for the defeat of Red forces on the Western Front.

In early October the Cavalry Army was transferred to the commander-in-chief's reserve. The end of the war with Poland permitted all Red Army forces, including the Cavalry, to be concentrated in the south to confront General Wrangel's combined White forces. On 4 October Lenin cabled the Revolutionary War Committee of the Cavalry Army: 'Extremely important to do everything to speed up the transfer of your army to the Southern Front. I ask you to take all measures for this, without pausing for heroics.'

Again they had to march several hundred kilometres through the autumn mud, fighting occasional White units on the way. On Frunze's orders, they carried out an operation at the Kakhovka bridgehead – virtually en route – thus cutting off one of Wrangel's groups from the Crimean peninsula and, together with other armies, delivered a decisive defeat on the enemy in northern Tauride. After the infantry had broken through across Sivash Bay, the cavalry made a forced march through the breach and chased the enemy to the southern shore of the Crimea. For his leadershp against the Poles and Wrangel, Budenny received the highest decoration then available, a Weapon of Honour, namely, a Mauser pistol decorated with the Order of the Red Banner.

When the civil war ended the Cavalry Army was transferred to North Caucasus Military District where Budenny doubled as Voroshilov's deputy. At the end of March 1922 Budenny arrived in Moscow for the XI Party Congress where in the military section he took part in discussion on the organization of the armed forces. Against the line taken by Trotsky and Tukhachevsky, he and Voroshilov argued for further developing the cavalry. He declared:

> They say it has been surpassed by the new equipment, that now there are tanks and aeroplanes . . . . But the methods for using the cavalry should be changed, it should be adapted to the latest equipment. When you're planning the outcome of an operation, you have to use manoeuvres that will bring success in the shortest possible time.

While Budenny's idea of using large mobile formations to enhance the success of an operation was sound, the proper vehicle was not the horse, but the tank, as Tukhachevsky pointed out.

On 3 April the Central Committee Plenum which created Stalin General Secretary took place. Having decided he must congratulate him, Budenny was received by Stalin the next day in the Kremlin. They exchanged views on military strategy and Stalin agreed that the cavalry was extremely necessary: 'You are the most competent man in this matter, let me have your proposals.'

The debate on whether or not to retain large cavalry units in the Red Army continued. On 10 June 1922 a conference took place under Trotsky's chairmanship at which Shaposhnikov, the chief of operations, proposed that, as the West was replacing horses with motor vehicles, the Red Cavalry be disbanded. Despite vehement protests from Budenny and Voroshilov, the Cavalry Army was duly disbanded, although some of its divisions were preserved.

In order to create a military faction in his struggle for power, Stalin took steps to get jobs for his supporters in Moscow. In September 1923 Budenny was appointed Deputy Commander-in-Chief of Cavalry Forces, and when this post was abolished early the following year he became Inspector of the Cavalry. At the same time, Voroshilov was transferred as Commander of Moscow Military District and a year later became Commissar of Military and Naval Affairs. From that time, together with Voroshilov, Budenny served Stalin body and soul, facilitating the rise of the Stalin cult. Even after Stalin's crimes had been exposed, Budenny continued to believe in his wisdom and infallibility. Shortly before his death in 1973 he wrote:

> The veterans of the revolution went through a great deal, they survived many a disaster, and stared death in the face more than once. But we suffered no worse misfortune than to see doubt cast on the revolutionary passion and revolutionary acts of the leader of our party, Lenin's true comrade-in-arms, I. V. Stalin. History belongs to our descendants, so let us hope it will not be a distorted mirror.

At the same time, Budenny and Voroshilov battled tirelessly to preserve the cavalry. In July 1929 Budenny was present at a Central Committee meeting at which Voroshilov reported on the state of technical reconstruction in the army. During the debate, he declared that the district commanders had neglected the cavalry on the grounds that war would henceforth be determined by machines and motors. 'But the cavalry has not outlived its usefulness, it could still show its paces in a future war, if it were equipped with armour and weaponry.' In his summing up, Stalin gave support to Voroshilov and Budenny when he declared that 'aircraft will not replace the cavalry'.

However much he cherished his beloved cavalry, Budenny nevertheless began to realize that the restructuring of the armed forces demanded not only respect for past experience but also new knowledge. He later recalled that it was 'above all, we, the senior officers, who needed to study'. At his insistence, and with Stalin's support, a special group was set up at the Frunze Military Academy, where senior officers could take time off to study. It opened in the autumn of 1930 and lasted for two years. As its senior member, Budenny set an example to his fellow students, of whom Shaposhnikov wrote, in *Krasnaya Zvezda* of 26 August 1932, that these heroes of the war were showing as much diligence in mastering the fields unfolding before them in the academy as they had in the heat of war.

Despite his relatively modest post as Cavalry Inspector, on 20 November 1935 Budenny was one of the five military leaders, including Voroshilov and Tukhachevsky, who were honoured by being made the first Marshals of the Soviet Union. At the end of May 1937, as the mass arrests began, Stalin appointed Budenny head of the Moscow Military District. 'I will try to justify your trust,' Budenny declared. He took up his post on 6 June and four days later, as if to 'justify your trust', as a member of the USSR Supreme Court Special Board, he condemned Tukhachevsky to death.

In his new job, Budenny did his best to raise the combat-readiness of the forces, but his outlook was dominated by outdated views on training and education. Major shortcomings among the troops of Moscow District were exposed during the Soviet–Finnish war, and at the Central Committee Plenum of March 1940 Budenny had to listen to harsh but justified criticism. Yet he refused to learn, and went on relying on his experience in the Civil War, as the following episode illustrates. In July 1940 the new Defence Commissar, Timoshenko, who had once been a divisional commander of the Cavalry Army, carried out an exercise in Moscow District. During a 'battle with the enemy' Budenny was informed that the tanks were going into action. In order to direct the attack himself, he jumped on to the leading tank. Its driver lost his head and the tank almost went into a ravine full of water. Timoshenko had been watching the whole scene. During the debriefing he said to Budenny: 'I wouldn't advise you to sit on a tank, but rather at the command post where you can control your forces. In the Civil War we used to gallop after you with our sabres drawn. But those days are long gone, and a tank is not a horse.'

Budenny was soon removed as District Commander and given instead the honorific title of Deputy Defence Commissar, and he was in this post when the German invasion began. The day before the war broke out, he was made commander of a group of armies that were being transferred from the interior to the Dnieper ridge, but then on 1 July they were transferred to the command of the Western Front.

On 10 July the State Defence Committee decided to form commands for three strategic sectors, and Budenny was appointed Commander-in-Chief of the Southwestern Axis, with control over the Southwestern and Southern Fronts, the Black Sea Fleet and the Dnieper Naval Flotilla. He remained in this post until 14 September. In view of the fact that, apart from his headquarters chief and a few officers, he had no other resources, he was not in a position to command troops. In addition, Supreme Headquarters (Stavka) as a rule issued orders directly to the Front Commanders, and a commander could take no important decision without its permission.

In this connection, during critical moments of the battle for Kiev, which Stalin ordered must be held at all costs, Budenny found himself at the command post of the Southwestern Front together with the commanding general, M. P. Kirponos, and he went out to look at the forward positions a number of times. Arriving on 7 August, he was extremely dissatisfied by the course of the battle for the Ukrainian capital. He listened to Kirponos's report and then exclaimed angrily: 'We shouldn't be defending ourselves, but beating the enemy.' 'The forces of Kiev Fortified District are replying to the enemy with continual counter-attacks,' the Commander attempted to explain. 'Forget about these pinpricks,' Budenny told him. 'Use a strong fist.' He sent his own reserves to reinforce the defenders of Kiev.

Having failed with a frontal attack, the Germans decided to encircle the Kiev forces with converging attacks by I and II Tank Groups. Assessing the position correctly, on 4 September Budenny in a special report drew Stalin's attention to the fact that the enemy had established a pincer position on the flanks of the Southwestern Front and was threatening to break through to the deep rear of his troops. He asked Stalin to strengthen the front with reserves and to halt the advance of Guderian's tank group by striking it in the flank with forces from the Bryansk Front. Stalin declined to provide reserves, but did promise to organize an attack on Guderian; it failed to provide the desired effect, however. The position grew more difficult by the day, but Budenny displayed obvious indecision, requesting permission from Stalin before making virtually any manoeuvre, an approach which was costly in time and effort.

By 10 September German tanks had managed to drive a powerful wedge from the north into the deep rear of the Southwestern Front. When Kirponos asked for help, Budenny had to reply that he had no reserves and could give none. Over their heads hung the Sword of Damocles: Stalin's severe warning not to surrender Kiev. Had the decision to move the Kiev group eastwards been his to make, Budenny would have made it at once, as he could see the hopelessness of their position. He therefore decided to send a cable to Stalin in the name of the sector war council, of which Khrushchev was a member: 'Given the present position, the war council of the Southwestern Front regards it as essential to order a general withdrawal to a rear ridge .... Delay may bring the loss of troops and a vast amount of matériel.'

In conversation with Kirponos next day, Budenny expressed confidence that his petition would soon be granted. Stalin's response, however, was to relieve Budenny of his command, to summon him to Moscow and to appoint him commander of the Reserve Front. He was replaced by Timoshenko, who came too late to avert the catastrophe.

Budenny had barely taken up his new post when the German Army Group Centre, which had begun its advance on Moscow on 30 September, unleashed an attack on the forces under his command. He lost control and could not organize an effective defence. The Reserve Front was given to General Zhukov on 10 October. At the end of that month Stalin gave Budenny the task of organizing the traditional 7 November parade on Red Square, like those he and Voroshilov had arranged together in the late 1930s. At 8 a.m. Budenny spurred his horse and galloped out of the Spassky Gate of the Kremlin on to the snow-covered square. He inspected the troops to greetings of 'Hurrah!' and mounted the Lenin Mausoleum. Stalin addressed the parade, an act which aroused a great patriotic upsurge in both army and nation. Many units were going straight from the parade to the front.

At the end of 1941 and beginning of 1942, Budenny carried out various functions for Stalin and the Stavka. In the spring the situation in the south worsened sharply. On 21 April a command was created for the North Caucasus Direction (or Axis) covering the Crimean Front, North Caucasus Military District and the Black Sea Fleet, including the Azov Sea Naval Flotilla. Budenny was named Commander-in-Chief. Before departing for the front he was received by Stalin who stressed the importance of the sector and demanded that they 'fight to the finish. Not a step backwards without permission from Stavka.' Budenny replied: 'Comrade Stalin, my task is clear.'

His hopes, however, were soon dashed. In early May, having begun to advance on the Kerch peninsula, the Germans soon smashed the Crimea Front and began to advance south. After a nine-month siege, Soviet troops were obliged to abandon Sevastopol. Simultaneously with their drive into the Crimea, the Germans raced into the Caucasus. Budenny showed courage during those days, often visiting the troops, but he was unable to alter the position. He was summoned to Moscow in January 1943. Seeing Zhukov, he said Stalin had summoned him for some reason. Zhukov grinned and said: 'No doubt you're going to have to lead the cavalry again.'

It was late at night when Stalin received Budenny. The recent victory at Stalingrad had put him in a good mood. 'The State Defence Committee has decided to create the post of Commander of the Red Army Cavalry. I have recommended you for the job. You understand the tasks the Party is placing on you?' 'I understand, Comrade Stalin. Thank you for your confidence. I will try to justify it,' Budenny rapped out in his customary way.

To make most effective use of the cavalry, in the spring Budenny with Stalin's permission held a meeting of all cavalry corps commanders, following which, at his suggestion, Supreme Headquarters created mounted armoured groups. Budenny made frequent visits to the front to help in the organization of operations, and he saw to it that his cavalrymen were given aerial cover.

He received the Order of Suvorov 1st Class for his services during the war, and was thrice made a Hero of the Soviet Union in the post-war years, and also received decorations on the anniversaries of the Civil War. He was 62 when the Second World War ended. To the best of his ability, he continued to occupy himself with problems of horse-breeding, both on behalf of the Defence Ministry and as Deputy Minister of Agriculture. In addition, he wrote his memoirs. He died at the age of ninety on 26 October 1973 and was buried with honours in the Kremlin wall alongside Stalin and Voroshilov.

Marshal Konev, who knew him well, remarked that the world war had exposed Budenny's fatigue and helplessness: 'He was a man with a past, but no future, a man who hardly progressed in his thinking beyond the Civil War. Like other cavalrymen he lived by outdated ideas.' Zhukov had a very similar view of him, although, taking his Civil War reputation into account, he spoke of him with respect. Recalling the difficult times they had experienced in the war together, he said that he and Budenny had remained good friends-in-arms. Many a time at the Stavka they had argued over the rôle of the cavalry. 'Even though he was hot-tempered,' Zhukov said, 'Budenny was always objective. As Deputy Supreme Commander-in-Chief, I often had to give him assignments, and, unlike some commanders, he always carried them out in good faith.'

However contradictory his life and service may have been, he remained a patriot, a brave man, a talented military leader of the Civil War, and a national hero.

BIBLIOGRAPHY

Anfilov, V. A., *Bessmertnyi podvig*, Moscow, 1971.
Bagramyan, I. Kh., *Gorod-voin na Dnepre*, Moscow, 1965.
Budenny, S. M., *Proidennyi put'*, Moscow, 1968.
Don, no. 4, 1972.
Simonov, K. M., *Glazami cheloveka moego pokoleniya*, Moscow, 1989.
Tyulenev, I., 'Narodnyi geroi grazhdanskoi voiny', *Voenno-istoricheskii zhurnal*, no. 4, 1973.

Vasily Ivanovich
CHUIKOV

RICHARD WOFF

February 1993 marked the fiftieth anniversary of the Red Army victory at Stalingrad. Throughout the last five decades Moscow portrayed the battle as an achievement of the 'multi-national Soviet state' and its armed forces, under the leadership of the Communist Party. The Soviet state, the Soviet Army, along with Communist rule, disappeared in December 1991. Consequently, throughout late 1992 and early 1993 the celebrations in all the independent states of the former Soviet Union focused above all on the individual national contribution to the epic victory. In the Russian Federation Stalingrad ranks alongside Borodino (1812) as an outstanding milestone in national military tradition, of which the Soviet period is regarded as the latest chapter.

Among the names of the great wartime commanders associated with the battle of Stalingrad – Zhukov, Rokossovsky, Vasilevsky – one has been especially prominent: Marshal Vasily Ivanovich Chuikov, commander of the 62nd ('Stalingrad') Army, whose stoic defence of the city provided the focal point of the epic battle. In his later years no one did more to establish the myth of 'the battle of the century' than Chuikov himself, elevated in his lifetime to the status of a national monument. In his memoirs Chuikov portrayed his unique contribution to the history of the Red Army: Civil War volunteer and much decorated regimental commander; three-times military advisor in China; recall to the front May 1942; Stalingrad; the liberation of Ukraine, Belorussia and Poland; and finally, the fall of the Third Reich itself. Despite the seemingly extraordinary record, and a solid professional approach to military affairs, Chuikov was not an outstanding strategist. Ambition and determination compensated for limited intellect. There were, moreover, 'blank spots' in the record, notably a dismal performance during the Finnish war. Dedicated and courageous, tough and determined, Chuikov more or less exemplified the traditional qualities of the Russian soldier. At times, his career on the brink of disaster, he was lucky to retrieve his fortunes and survive. Many abler contemporaries were less fortunate.

Chuikov was born on 12 February 1900 in Tula Province. His father was a peasant and, despite doing well in the village school, Chuikov might well have stayed on the land, or become a migrant worker, had the October Revolution not changed the course of his life. In November 1917 he joined the Red Guards, serving in a sapper training section at Kronshtadt. In early 1918 he transferred to a junior instructors' course, graduating in April in time to help suppress an insurrection in Moscow by the Left Socialist Revolutionaries. He was then posted to the Southern Front as assistant commander of a company in the 1st Ukrainian Brigade fighting the Cossacks. Promoted assistant commander 40th Rifle Regiment on the Eastern Front in early 1919, and later commander 43rd Rifle Regiment of 5th Rifle Division, Chuikov took part in the Bolshevik conquest of the Urals and Siberia, returning to European Russia with his regiment to take part in the abortive 1920 campaign in Poland.

With the end of the Civil War Chuikov continued to command 43rd Rifle Regiment, subsequently entering the Frunze Military Academy in 1923. Graduating in 1925, he served briefly in northern China as a 'diplomatic courier', returning to the Academy in late 1926 for a course in the Eastern Faculty, established in the early 1920s to train 'specialists' and 'advisors' for service in Mongolia and China. Between 1926 and 1942 Chuikov twice again served in China, first in 1927–9. He was subsequently attached to the staff of the Special Far East Army, under Blyukher, and took part in the punitive expedition to re-establish Soviet control over the Far Eastern (China) Railway in 1929. Chuikov remained a further two years on Blyukher's staff, returning to Moscow to command a senior officers' course 1932–5. There followed a senior command course at the Academy of Mechanization and Motorization, command of a mechanized brigade in late 1936, and 5th Rifle Corps in April 1938. At the time the High Command was embarking on a long-term plan to tighten defences in the west, and three months later Chuikov was appointed commander of the Bobruisk Army Group in Belorussian Special Military District. After a brief tenure, in 1939 he was promoted to command the ill-fated 4th Army, taking part subsequently in the 'liberation' of western Belorussia (eastern Poland) September–October 1939, and setting the seal of official approval on future promotion.

As a mark of the regard in which his professional abilities were held by Stalin, and with Moscow preparing the ground for the assault on Finland in late November 1939, Chuikov was appointed Commander 9th Army. This was to prove a disaster from the point of view of Red Army credibility and for Chuikov, whose career had advanced steadily through the 1920s and 1930s and was accelerated after 1938 due to the 'command vacuum' caused by the purges. Throughout 1938 and early 1939 Chuikov himself had replaced commanders removed from their posts and eventually shot. In December 1939 he in turn became one of the senior casualties in the initial Red Army débâcle at the hands of a resilient Finnish Army, relying on superior tactics, exploiting local terrain and extreme weather conditions.

The roots of the Soviet–Finnish conflict lay in Soviet concern at the proximity of the Finnish frontier to Leningrad. The bullying tactics of Molotov, Stalin's Foreign Commissar, merely steeled Finnish resistance to Soviet demands. With 'diplomacy' exhausted, the Red Army launched the assault on Finland 29 November, Leningrad Military District deploying five armies on a front stretching over 800 miles from the Gulf of Finland to the Arctic. The initial operational plan was fundamentally flawed, paralysed by sheer immobility and poor co-ordination by field commanders. Overweening confidence, poor preparation, incompetence and inept leadership dissipated Soviet preponderance over the Finns, and by late December the Red Army campaign had ground to a halt, impaled on the 'Mannerheim Line', in the severest winter for over 30 years. The cruellest blow fell on Chuikov's 9th Army, deployed on the frontier facing central Finland, astride an axis directed at the Gulf of Bothnia. With three rifle divisions, 9th Army was significantly stronger than the opposing Finns. None the less the Finnish commander, Colonel Siilasvuo, chose his time and ground well, striking on 9 December at the point of concentration of Chuikov's two advancing divisions, finally reducing them to a huddled and exhausted frozen mass. With his command post too far in the rear and served by poor communications, Chuikov had lost control of the battle. After the débâcle of Suomussalmi, 9th Army ceased to play any effective part in the campaign. The Red Army finally bludgeoned the Finns into submission and acceptance of Soviet territorial demands in the Peace of 12 March 1940.

Chuikov, however, faced a personal crisis from which he was lucky to escape with his life. Until recently, Soviet studies, while presenting an account of the Winter War generally favourable to the reputation of the Red Army and Timoshenko, remained silent regarding the catastrophe suffered by 9th Army. Promoted Lieutenant-General in June 1940, Chuikov's chances of ever holding a responsible command again none the less appeared remote, and in December 1940 he was dispatched to China as Soviet Military Attaché, replacing Pavel Rybalko.

Fourteen months passed before Chuikov was recalled to Moscow in March 1942, as Stalin sought to withdraw from the quagmire threatening to engulf Soviet diplomacy in the Far East following Japan's entry into the war. In the intervening period since 22 June 1941, Chuikov had repeatedly requested a command at the front, and on his return to Moscow there was still no prospect of returning to active service. None the less, he still had friends 'at court', and in May he was appointed Deputy Commander of a reserve army located near Tula, with responsibility for training. Bad luck, however, continued to pursue him. He was seriously injured in a car accident and it was over a year before he regained full use of his legs.

In July the reserve army was redesignated 64th Army and under Chuikov's 'temporary command' assigned to the Southern Front, now in the process of withdrawing to a triangle Stalingrad–Kalach–Kotelnikov between the Don and the Volga. Here Chuikov experienced his first battles with the advancing German VI Army. There may still have been lingering doubts regarding his aptitude for high command, and lack of experience, and in early August he was replaced by Major-General Mikhail Shumilov, and given command of a 'special operational group' consisting of 29th Rifle Division and 154th Naval Brigade, created by Shumilov to strengthen his left flank. In keeping with its crucial rôle of blocking the German advance on the southwestern approaches to Stalingrad, Chuikov's Group was subsequently reinforced by three rifle divisions, one tank brigade, and two regiments of artillery. A week later the Group was pulled back within the Stalingrad strategic defence zone to form 64th Army 'reserve'. In late August, with General von Wietersheim's XIV Tank Corps having already reached the Volga at several points, Stavka concern now focussed on the defence of Stalingrad itself, and on 8 September Chuikov was appointed Commander 62nd Army, Southeastern Front, replacing Major-General Nikolai Krylov, who took over as his Chief of Staff. Throughout the next four months Chuikov's Army was to play the crucial part in the defence of Stalingrad.

The battle for Stalingrad consisted of two phases: the 'defensive phase', 17 July–18 November 1942; and the 'offensive phase', 19 November 1942– 2 February 1943. While Chuikov's rôle in the opening stages of the 'defensive phase' was not outstanding, he gained valuable experience and time to adapt to a tactical environment which by early September was changing 'hourly'. He also worked alongside other leading personalities destined soon to play crucial parts: Colonel-General Andrei Yeremenko and Shumilov. Three weeks after Chuikov took command of 62nd Army, Rokossovsky and Zhukov arrived in Stalingrad. Appointed Commander Don Front on 30 September, Rokossovsky was ultimately to be entrusted with overall control of operations down to the surrender of von Paulus's VI Army. While they had both served on Blyukher's staff in the Far East in the late 1920s, Rokossovsky had not previously been closely associated with Chuikov, and they were not to meet until late December, by which time the fate of VI Army had been sealed.

In late September 62nd Army comprised eleven rifle divisions, seven rifle brigades, 23rd Tank Corps, a combined anti-tank brigade, twelve artillery and mortar regiments, together with control over 115th (Stalingrad) Fortified Region. The whole force, organized in two defensive echelons, by early October was boxed into a small area some 10 kilometres long and as little as 2 kilometres deep, resting on the right bank of the Volga. In all 90,000 defenders faced 170,000 German troops. Initially the Germans possessed air superiority, an air armada of 1,000 planes ranged against 389 Soviet aircraft. Chuikov's mission was simple: 'to hold the city at all costs'. It was a mission demanding physical and mental stamina on the part of the commander, and a determination to defend the position against daunting odds, a challenge eminently suited to Chuikov's character and style of command. Thrown on to his own resources, he extracted the highest devotion to duty, and encouraged those under his command to perform feats of bravery which rank alongside the most outstanding achievements in the history of the Russian Army. Inevitably, the most eloquent tributes are to be found in subsequent accounts by German officers at all levels. General Dörr speaks of 'every house, workshop, water tower, railway embankment, wall, cellar, and every pile of ruins' being turned into a battlefield, bitterly contested 'to the end'. It was a situation where 'the Russians surpassed the Germans in their use of terrain and camouflage'. Moreover, with the symbol of 'Stalingrad' gradually mesmerizing Hitler, VI Army was increasingly sucked into a murderous struggle for what remained of the city. Large-scale operations across the endless steppes had now been supplanted by a battle in which 'the mile was replaced by the yard as the measure of distance'. From late August to late November 1942 the map of Stalingrad reflected the respective fortunes of the Red Army and the Wehrmacht.

The battle for the city itself comprised three phases. The first, 13–26 September, was perhaps the most critical, with a German breakthrough to the Volga effectively cutting off 62nd Army. The Germans were denied their victory by the heroic resistance of the defenders, symbolized by 13th Guards Rifle Division, commanded by Major-General Alexander Rodimtsev, a hero of the Spanish Civil War. During the second phase, 27 September–8 October, the Germans switched tactics, attempting to outflank the city on a northern and southern axis in a desperate attempt to reach the Volga. The second phase coincided with a restructuring of the senior Red Army command: Stalingrad Front was redesignated Don Front under Rokossovsky; Southeastern Front was replaced by a new Stalingrad Front commanded by Yeremenko, assisted by Khrushchev as 'political supremo', and Major-General Ivan Varennikov as Chief of Staff. Throughout the third phase, 9 October–18 November, operations centred on German attempts to wipe out the defenders of three factories: Tractor, Barricades and Red October.

The defence of Stalingrad was part of the wider campaign involving five fronts. Its significance was that it tied down and forced the Germans to expend valuable reserves of men and material prior to the Red Army counter-attack of 19 November. The junction of the Southwestern and Stalingrad Fronts at Kalach on 23 November sealed the fate of VI Army;

Chuikov's historic mission had been accomplished. On 2 February 1943 Field Marshal von Paulus surrendered to Rokossovsky.

With the victorious conclusion of the battle of Stalingrad the next few months were an anti-climax. In the subsequent regrouping 62nd Army lost many of its Stalingrad formations in a process designed to 'disseminate battle experience'. Chuikov retained 39th (Major-General V. S. Gurev), 74th (Major-General V. P. Sokolov) and 79th (Major-General N. F. Batyuk) Guards Rifle Division. Other Stalingrad 'veterans' assigned to Chuikov's command were 27th (Major-General V. S. Glebov), 88th (Major-General V. Ya. Vladimirov), and 82nd (Major-General I. A. Makarenko) Guards Rifle Division. Chuikov had however to take leave of his Chief of Staff, Krylov, replaced by Vladimirov, and his senior political assistant, Major-General Ivan Vasiliev. Subsequently, Krylov was to achieve supreme command; Vasiliev was killed some months later by a German sniper.

Assigned to Malinovsky's Southwestern Front in March 1943, on 16 April 62nd Army was redesignated 8th Guards Army. Following a period of replenishment, throughout the latter half of 1943 and the first half of 1944 Chuikov took part in the liberation of Ukraine and Belorussia, a series of offensive operations demanding tactical skill against an enemy who until late 1943 was still able to achieve local superiority on land and in the air.

The Izyum-Barvenkov operation (17–27 July 1943) was Chuikov's first taste of offensive operations, providing support on the southern flank of the Voronezh Front during the battle of Kursk. This was followed by the Donbas operation (13 August–22 September 1943), and the Nikopol-Krivoi Rog operation (30 January–29 February 1944), the latter as part of Malinovsky's 3rd Ukrainian Front opening the way to the final liberation of southern Ukraine, the Crimea and Odessa. The Bereznegovato-Snigirev operation (6–18 March 1944), and Odessa operation (26 March–14 April 1944) in conjunction with Konev's 2nd Ukrainian Front and Admiral Oktyabrsky's Black Sea Fleet, completed the liberation of southern Ukraine, with the Red Army poised for the assault on the Balkans.

In mid-1944 8th Guards Army was transferred to Rokossovsky's 1st Belorussian Front and took part in the Belorussian operation and subsequent liberation of eastern Poland. The Vistula-Oder operation (12 January–3 February 1945) opened the way to Berlin itself, and Chuikov's rôle in the Berlin operation was fitting reward for his achievement at Stalingrad. Operating on the main axis of the 1st Belorussian Front, under Zhukov, Chuikov's 8th Guards Army spearheaded the Red Army advance on Hitler's beleaguered capital. In many respects the final days of bitter house-to-house fighting amid the rubble surrounding the Chancellery and Reichstag recalled the defence of Stalingrad by 62nd Army, Chuikov depicting 'every stone, the brick rubble, asphalt pavements of the squares and streets of the German capital stained with [his troops'] blood'. Finally, late on 30 April, the defenders contacted Chuikov's HQ, and on 2 May 8th Guards Army received the surrender of the Berlin Garrison on behalf of the Red Army High Command.

After the war Chuikov remained in Germany for eight years, serving in turn as Commander 8th Guards Army and Deputy Commander-in-Chief of Soviet Occupation Forces, First Deputy Commander-in-Chief, and finally Commander-in-Chief (1949–53), in which capacity he also functioned as Chief of the Soviet Military Administration, and, following Soviet recognition of East Germany in October 1949, Chief of the Soviet Control Commission. As a sign that he still retained Stalin's confidence, Chuikov was promoted Army General in 1949, one of a handful of senior officers rewarded in the chilling atmosphere which marked Stalin's relationship with the Soviet High Command in his last years.

Following Stalin's death in March 1953, Chuikov was succeeded by General Andrei Grechko, replacing the latter in turn as Commander of the prestigious Kiev Military District. Part of a shake-up of the Soviet High Command by Stalin's successors, Chuikov retained the favour of Khrushchev, his wartime comrade-in-arms, and along with other members of the 'Stalingrad group' in 1955 Chuikov was promoted Marshal. His last senior post was Commander-in-Chief Soviet Ground Forces – Deputy Minister of Defence, 1960–4, with responsibility for Civil Defence from 1961. Relinquishing command of the Ground Forces in 1964, he retained responsibility for Civil Defence until retirement in 1972.

In March 1982, some months before the fortieth anniversary of the Battle of Stalingrad, Chuikov died after a brief illness. As a mark of respect he was buried on 23 March 1982 at a special memorial site in Volgograd (Stalingrad), leading members of the Soviet High Command and Stalingrad veterans paying their last respects. Recently President Yeltsin signed a Decree reprieving 'the Stalingrad Army' – 8th Guards Army – due to be disbanded following its departure from Germany. In 1993 Chuikov's old army was incorporated into the Russian Armed Forces 'as a mark of national [Russian] respect for its outstanding and heroic rôle in the defeat of Nazi Germany'. Other prestigious wartime formations, such as 11th Guards Army (Rokossovsky's 16th Army), located in the Kaliningrad region, may not be so lucky following the Soviet withdrawal from Eastern Europe and the disintegration of the Soviet Army since late 1991.

From the late 1950s onwards Chuikov published a large number of books and articles covering his service since 1917. Many were devoted to the controversy of the late 1950s and early 1960s surrounding wartime events and former comrades-in-arms. In the bitter war of words Chuikov emerged as a protagonist of Khrushchev in his vendetta against Zhukov, accused together with Sokolovsky of having delayed taking Berlin for 'lack of skill and initiative', at the same time upgrading Konev's rôle in the Berlin operation.

The unseemly debate detracted from Chuikov's own unique contribution to the victory over Nazi Germany.

BIBLIOGRAPHY

Chuikov, V. I., *V boyakh za Ukrainu*, Kiev, 1972.
Chuikov, V. I., *Gvardeitsy Stalingrada idut na Zapad*, Moscow, 1972.
Chuikov, V. I., *Srazhenie veka*, Moscow, 1975.
Chuikov, V. I., *The End of the Third Reich*, 2nd edn, Progress Publishers, Moscow, 1985.
Rokossovsky, Marshal K. (ed.), *Velikaya pobeda na Volge*, Moscow, 1965.

Filip Ivanovich
GOLIKOV

GABRIEL GORODETSKY

The life of Filip Ivanovich Golikov, the director of Soviet Military Intelligence (GRU) in the earlier stages of the Second World War and the head of the first Soviet military missions to London and Washington in the wake of the German attack on Russia, is still shrouded in mystery. There is an immense gap between the various portraits of him. His peers depicted him as an amateur, a politically subservient general and dilettante in military affairs, if not a coward on the battlefield. One should remember, however, that this criticism was a broadside in the 'War of the Generals' which followed Khrushchev's de-Stalinization. It stands in sharp contrast to the hagiographical biographies which appeared during the Second World War and which were highly coloured by enthusiasm for the new Soviet ally. Few Soviet generals have enjoyed such fame in the West, with cover features in *Time Magazine*, *Newsweek* and *Life*. Golikov's missions were presented as brilliant successes, while his military setbacks were vindicated by 'objectively' adverse circumstances. Golikov's life story, whether a success or a failure, is perhaps a living monument to the deficiencies of a military system that was an uneasy partnership of political and professional components.

Golikov was born in 1900 to the family of a poor village paramedic in the Kurgan oblast. He was the oldest of three children. As an adolescent he was determined to follow in the footsteps of his father and become a doctor. After excelling in his studies at the village school, he won a scholarship to attend the regional gymnasium. The terms of the stipend meant that he had to gain top marks to secure its renewal; moreover, living away from home and under economic hardship, Golikov was forced to work while studying. Ambition, hard work and commitment became the major traits of his personality. It was during these years that he became acquainted with the socialist movement.

His father, who was an activist in the movement, was even sent to jail for his subversive activities.

Shortly after the October Revolution Golikov joined the Communist Party. In April 1918 he was already manager of the local *Izvestiya* and published a number of articles advocating world revolution. When not yet eighteen he lied about his age and joined a rifle regiment nicknamed 'Krasnye orly' ('Red Eagles'). During the Civil War Golikov engaged the White Guards in the Urals and the legion of Czech soldiers, who had found themselves trapped in Russia after the Revolution and fought their way to freedom at Vladivostok, assisting the Whites en route. He distinguished himself in battle but, perhaps more significantly, proved himself to be a tenacious Bolshevik. He was consequently rewarded with a scholarship to the newly formed Petrograd Military Academy.

The Soviet official biographies highlight Golikov's training in mechanized warfare at the Academy. This expertise, however, developed later. In the early days of 'war communism' the Academy was geared towards training agitators. The curriculum was based mostly on the works of Engels, Plekhanov and Lenin. After passing his examinations with distinction, Golikov was first sent to act as a political officer in 3rd Army; but he was soon attached to a Special Brigade which was rushed to the countryside to clamp down on the hostile peasantry. He then went on with political work in the army. In February 1931, Golikov received his first operational posting as commander of a rifle regiment and shortly afterwards was appointed a divisional commander.

By 1933 Golikov had graduated from the Frunze Military Academy through a correspondence course. After a short spell in the field he became the head of the political department of the Defence Commissariat. Though details of this period have been deliberately obscured, he apparently played a decisive part in the suppression of the Leningrad Opposition and probably in the purges of the Red Army in 1937.

His political loyalty being above suspicion, the great purge gave a boost to Golikov's career. As a political commissar he was appointed in September 1938 to serve in the Military Council of Belorussia Military District. Soon afterwards he was promoted to command the special army group of Kiev Military District. He thus found himself in September 1939 commanding 6th Army in the occupation of eastern Poland. By that time he had refreshed his expertise in armoured warfare. His theories were put to the test during the Winter War, in which he distinguished himself and received several decorations.

In July 1940 Golikov was unexpectedly appointed director of Soviet Military Intelligence (GRU). In this capacity he was fully responsible for the erroneous evaluation of German intentions on the eve of 'Barbarossa'. Historians have suggested that he failed either to interpret the signals correctly or to alert Stalin to this possibility. Marshal Zhukov was the first to level such accusations, though undoubtedly in an attempt to discredit Military Intelligence and rehabilitate the Army.

The fortuitous appointment of Golikov as head of GRU reflected the havoc prevailing in the armed forces in the wake of the purges. He owed the appointment entirely to his close association with Timoshenko, who had just been named as Defence Commissar. Golikov succeeded General Ivan Iosifovich Proskurov, a pilot who had fought gallantly in the Spanish Civil War and was Voroshilov's deputy at the Defence Commissariat. During the Winter War, Proskurov was sent by Voroshilov on a special mission to Leningrad to tighten up the Northern Front. Being a rather ambitious and arrogant young man, he openly expressed his dissatisfaction when Timoshenko, who was Commander-in-Chief of the region, failed to greet him in person. This infuriated Timoshenko, who henceforth bore a grudge against him. Whether for this reason, or because of Proskurov's opposition to the Ribbentrop–Molotov Pact, Timoshenko's first act after succeeding Voroshilov as Defence Commissar in July 1941 was to replace Proskurov and install the faithful Golikov as his deputy and head of the GRU. Proskurov was subsequently shot, without trial.

When Golikov took over, the authority of GRU had hit rock bottom. His lack of prior experience in intelligence work was a serious disadvantage. Moreover, Stalin, like Churchill, did not trust the 'collective wisdom' of his intelligence officers and insisted on inspecting personally the most important raw material. As war drew nearer he even took charge of the strategic department of the GRU which dealt with the evaluation of intelligence. Thus, as a matter of routine, the GRU submitted a monthly factual report for Stalin's examination. The report consisted of a thorough compilation of evidence accompanied by a very brief evaluation by the strategic department. These reports, which were distributed to the Army as well, cast doubt on Zhukov's claim that the Army was oblivious to the looming danger because it was not made privy to such information.

Much of the blame should indeed be laid on Stalin, though his failure to make the correct evaluation was not entirely illogical. Stalin's judgement was seriously hampered by a pathological suspicion that Germany and Britain might close ranks and mount a crusade against Russia. This fear had its roots in the Allied intervention during the Civil War and was reinforced by the Locarno Treaty in 1925 and the Munich Agreement of September 1938, which left Russia out in the cold. Such suspicions were a major factor in the Soviet decision to sign the Ribbentrop–Molotov Pact. The crushing defeat of Poland and France increased the fear of a separate Anglo-German peace. After the surrender of Marshal Pétain's France, Stalin was particularly alarmed by the continued inclusion in Churchill's Cabinet of the 'Men of Munich', who might tip the scale towards a peace with Germany. The reports of the Soviet Ambassador in London, Ivan Maisky, fuelled Stalin's fears, which became acute in spring 1941 owing to the German encroachment in the Balkans, the heavy defeats inflicted on Britain in Greece and North Africa and the mounting criticism in London of the government's conduct of the war. The fact that Britain even reached the brink of war with the Soviet Union during the Winter War in Finland, and was contemplating bombing the oil fields of the Caucasus in March 1941, did little to reassure him. Moreover, his options were limited in view of the damage inflicted on the army during the purges, and the poor state of the Soviet armaments industry compared to that of Germany which by now controlled most of Europe's industrial resources.

It was against this background that GRU, headed by Golikov, functioned. In mid-April 1941, Sir Stafford Cripps, the British Ambassador in Moscow, stoked Soviet suspicions when he made an unauthorized approach to Molotov in a last-ditch attempt to draw Russia into the Allied orbit. Alluding to the strong presence of appeasers in the Cabinet, he warned that Churchill might be forced to conclude a peace with Germany unless a breakthrough was achieved in negotiations with Moscow. Following these threats, Churchill's famous, though cryptic and brief, warning to Stalin intensified suspicions in the Kremlin that a desperate Britain was striving to embroil Russia in war. So strong was the suspicion that Stalin even dismissed Richard Sorge, Russia's master spy in Japan, as a British agent when he furnished the GRU with precise and detailed reports on German intentions and plans. Stalin firmly believed that the British were attempting a provocation and that the Germans would not attack without an ultimatum.

The very nature of his rule discouraged his entourage, intelligence circles and Golikov himself from openly challenging this interpretation. As early as mid-March 1941, Golikov submitted to Stalin evidence indicating an ominous change in the German deployment in the East. However, the compilation of the various reports was accompanied by a short note which conformed with Stalin's well-known conviction that the reports on German deployment and intentions were provocations. Golikov concluded with the assessment, also common in England at that time, that a German attack was unlikely before Hitler had either conquered or concluded peace with Great Britain. During April and May the German troop movements in Poland and in Finland were indeed closely monitored, and on 5 May Golikov informed Stalin that over 100 German divisions were massed near the Soviet frontier. However, the manner of presentation was highly slanted. Golikov continued to forward the material and evaluation in two different boxes under the headings 'from reliable sources' and 'from doubtful sources'. The 'reliable sources' were always those implying that the reports of an imminent war were provocations.

The extent to which suspicion influenced the Kremlin's evaluation is reflected in their reactions to the flight of Rudolf Hess, Hitler's deputy, to England on 12 May on a peace mission. The silence maintained by the British about the debriefing of Hess was perceived in Moscow as a sign that the British Cabinet was actually giving his peace offers serious consideration. Both Sorge and Maisky reinforced the evaluation that Hess's flight was a last-ditch attempt, sanctioned by Hitler, to negotiate a peace. The alarm was undoubtedly sounded in Golikov's office in early June when the British decided to 'exploit Hess mendaciously'. GRU was disinformed through covert channels that Hess's flight indicated a growing split over Hitler's policy of collaboration with the Soviet Union. The Russians were warned that if they did not make serious concessions to Britain they might be left 'to face Germany single-handed in a weakened state'.

A balanced judgement thus leads to the conclusion that Golikov was indeed fully aware of the German deployment and even kept Stalin abreast of it. However, the suspicion on the one hand, and the atmosphere of terror prevailing in the Kremlin on the other, deflected him from reporting the real danger lurking around the corner. Golikov tailored his evaluation to Stalin's preconceptions as a sort of insurance against his wrath, which could still be fatal. It is interesting to note that after the Germans invaded Russia Stalin did not bear a grudge against Golikov; on the contrary, the occasion served as a springboard for his promotion.

Golikov's mission to London and Washington in July–September 1941 was undoubtedly the pinnacle of his career. Soviet historians made great efforts to present it as a total fiasco: the Western Allies not only refused to open a second front but presented Russia merely with a token supply programme. In reality, Golikov succeeded in dismantling the barriers between the new allies, in committing the Americans to the Eastern Front, and in establishing the supply life-line to Russia.

Stalin's choice of Golikov, who was accountable for the disastrous defeats inflicted on the Red Army in the early days of the war, as his first envoy to the new allies is baffling. But the appointment should again be examined in light of the circumstances prevailing in the Kremlin during the first week of July. Stalin had just recovered from his brief nervous breakdown. He returned to Moscow from self-imposed retirement at his dacha, adding to his titles that of Supreme Commander. He was still under the terrifying impression that the German offensive was a result of negotiations with Britain which had misfired. 'All believed,' recalled Maxim Litvinov in Washington a few months later, 'that the British fleet was steaming up the North Sea for a joint attack, with Hitler, on Leningrad and Kronshtadt.' The British, expecting the Russians to collapse within a month, had sent General Noel Mason-MacFarlane, a prominent intelligence officer, as the head of their military mission. Their task was to brief London on the pace of the Russian collapse and organize the nucleus of resistance after the German occupation of

Moscow. Golikov, as head of GRU, was expected to assess the atmosphere in London. However, his brief was also to establish a common strategy with Britain if conditions proved suitable for co-operation. The significance attached to his mission is attested by the list of dignitaries who briefed him before his departure: Molotov, Foreign Commissar, A. I. Mikoyan, the Foreign Trade Commissar, Marshal Shaposhnikov, the Chief of General Staff, and his old patron Timoshenko, Defence Commissar. In a two-hour session Stalin laid before Golikov the foundations of his allied strategy, which attached prime significance to long-term collaboration.

A delegation, headed by Golikov and Rear Admiral N. Kharlamov of the Stalin Naval Staff, set out for Scotland (a 24-hour flight) in the British Catalinas which had brought Cripps and the British Military Mission to Moscow a few days earlier. The mission arrived in London on the evening of 8 July to a tumultuous reception of Soviet sympathizers. However, a cold shower was to follow. The German invasion of Russia had not altered the views of the War Office, which, as an astute observer witnessed, were 'coloured by political prejudice and by the fact that Stalin murdered most of his senior officers'. Moreover, the Germans were expected to cut through the Red Army like a knife through butter. The feigned cordiality of the Chiefs of Staff towards Golikov was therefore intended 'to encourage' the Red Army to hold out a little longer and to conceal the fact that Britain was 'not allied with Russia' and did 'not entirely trust that country'.

To counteract the tendency of the War Office 'to deprecate the arrival of the military mission', the Foreign Office recommended a display of at least an 'outwardly cordial treatment of the Russians. . . . In order to give an atmosphere of friendliness we should be as lavish as possible in entertaining this mission, and the luncheon given in their honour should be as large as possible.' As the Russians were 'extremely partial to alcoholic drink' the Chiefs of Staff were encouraged to throw frequent cocktail parties in honour of Golikov.

But even a semblance of decency was difficult to maintain. The language barrier, which was later to frustrate Churchill in his conversations with Stalin, was daunting. Since Soviet officers had been discouraged from going abroad or learning foreign languages which might brand them as 'cosmopolitans', the negotiations were conducted only through interpreters. Golikov's first meeting was with Captain David Margesson, the Secretary of War, who refused to shake hands with him and left him standing throughout the short encounter. Margesson clearly conveyed the feeling that he 'hardly believed in the Red Army's victory nor in the viability of the Soviet political system'. The meeting with the Chiefs of Staff went no better. Admiral Pound was evasive, resorting to Churchillian rhetoric such as expressing 'admiration . . . for the way in which the Russian forces were fighting'. Golikov was left with the impression that Pound was 'horrified' to be in his company, was in a rush, and had 'more significant issues to look after than negotiations on "hare-brained" schemes with Bolsheviks'.

Golikov made great efforts to restore confidence in the Russian military by soft-pedalling the demand for a 'second front', which would have implied a desperate situation on the Eastern Front. Churchill would later mislead his readers by claiming that the failure of the talks was a result of the absurd Russian demand for a second front. In fact, Golikov's main demand was for naval operations in the North Sea which would secure communication routes as a basis for a long-term and massive supply programme.

On 13 July Golikov was recalled by Stalin for consultations in Moscow. His impressions were vital for the Soviet appraisal of British strategy and for assessing the possibilities for laying sound foundations for a Grand Alliance. They indeed confirmed Stalin's hunch that he would have to pin his hopes on American assistance. Golikov impressed on Stalin that, while strategic co-ordination would be difficult to achieve, the British would be forced to concede on the issue of supply. Golikov correctly estimated that Churchill's decision to approve even limited assistance to the Soviet Union was affected by the forthcoming visit to England of Harry Hopkins, Roosevelt's powerful adviser. Golikov therefore pressed Stalin to assign primary importance to supply, in view of the favourable disposition of the Americans and their decreasing sympathy with the British.

The eradication of American suspicions and prejudices and paving the way for co-operation would soon be entrusted to Golikov. Although the State Department and the Army had displayed a critical and hostile attitude towards Russia on the eve of the war, General George Marshall, the American Chief of Staff, had succeeded in casting doubts in Roosevelt's mind about the soundness of British strategy in the Middle East. Consequently Roosevelt adopted an unexpectedly benign attitude to the Soviet request for assistance, though he made it conditional on British willingness to share the American contributions. Indeed, Hopkins, who was soon leaving for London, did not hesitate to state that the British would be 'sensible enough' to realize that the Soviet Union was entitled to a portion of American resources. Maisky's encounter with Hopkins on 19 July at Chequers, the Prime Minister's country house, further advanced the Americans to the Russian cause. Golikov was now rushed to London to participate in the negotiations with Hopkins and to further his impromptu trip to Moscow. Hopkins's meetings with Stalin at the end of the month were to lay the foundations for the Grand Alliance and the American commitment to the new Eastern Front.

On 26 July Golikov arrived at La Guardia airport and was whisked to Washington, where he held a series of meetings with State Department officials and with General Marshall. His task was to implement the Lend-Lease Programme to Russia worked out by Hopkins and Stalin in Moscow.

While Golikov encountered resentment in the different state agencies, Roosevelt was most forthcoming in their meeting in the White House on 31 July. The confidence in Russian military ability which Golikov displayed and his attractive personality helped to offset the abrasive character of Konstantin Umansky, the Soviet Ambassador in Washington, who would soon be replaced by Litvinov.

Golikov deserves credit for his conduct of these very delicate talks in London and Washington, which culminated in the establishment of a supply programme and a convoy system to Russia during the visit of Lord Beaverbrook and Averell Harriman to Moscow at the end of September. He succeeded in diverting American resources to the Eastern Front while securing continued British commitment to the war effort. However, he was obliged to concede reluctantly at the end of his mission that the onus of the actual fighting would fall on Russia.

With his military-diplomatic mission in Washington successfully concluded, Golikov returned to Moscow. His return coincided with a severe deterioration of the situation on the Western Front. On 7 September Colonel-General Heinz Guderian, the brilliant Panzer commander, succeeded in ripping apart the Russian defences of the Bryansk and Southeastern Fronts. A few days later Budenny, Commander-in-Chief of the forces in Ukraine, found himself trapped in the Kiev salient. On 18 September the city fell and the bulk of the Soviet army was either annihilated or captured. On 30 September Field Marshal Fedor von Bock renewed his advance on Moscow, capturing 600,000 prisoners en route in the battle of Vyazma. On 15 October Moscow was in the grip of panic; a massive evacuation, partly uncontrolled, took place and emergency rule was established. On 21 October Golikov, who had expressed a wish to go to the front, was summoned by Stalin to the Stavka (General Headquarters) and assigned command of 10th Reserve Army under Timoshenko and Zhukov.

Golikov had to forge an army from scratch. Arriving in the field, he was appalled by the means at his disposal. The reserves consisted of uneducated soldiers, deficient in training and equipment; the transport was poor and the chain of command shaky. Within a month he managed to mould nine competent divisions which participated in the successful counter-offensive at the gates of Moscow in early December 1941. Golikov excelled mostly at the administrative side of the command, in raising the morale of the troops and in tactical warfare, but the strategic success was entirely due to Zhukov and Timoshenko, who planned and commanded the operation.

By the spring of 1942, when the Germans renewed their offensive in the southern sector, Golikov had endeared himself to Stalin and was assigned the defence of the crucial Bryansk Front. Thus he became involved in one of the major controversies which engulfed the entire Soviet command in the summer of 1942. On 23 April Golikov was rushed to Stavka and instructed by

Stalin to mount a massive outflanking offensive against the Germans in Orel to coincide with Timoshenko's major assault on Kharkov, planned for 10 May. Golikov complained about major shortages in manpower and supply and was granted a postponement of a few days. Consequently the co-ordination between the two fronts, loose to start with, failed to materialize. Timoshenko's onslaught was further forestalled by Operation 'Fridericus', mounted by Field Marshal Friedrich von Paulus and his VI Army, which slashed into his formations and exposed his communication lines. Golikov was now instructed to abandon his offensive and turn to the south to reinforce Timoshenko. This belated move ended in chaos and confusion throughout the entire southern sector. It was followed by a calamity in the Crimea, where Field Marshal Erich von Manstein routed the army led by General-Commissar Lev Mekhlis and later went on to crush Sevastopol.

The Germans now proceeded to implement Operation 'Blau', the four-stage plan to eliminate the Red Army in the south. The initial move aimed at breaking through Voronezh, Golikov's headquarters, to clear the way to the Don and Stalingrad. Unaware of the German plan, the Stavka had in the meantime ordered the launch of the long-delayed offensive on Orel. The operation was temporarily abandoned on 19 June, when the Russians acquired a detailed plan of the first phase of Operation 'Blau' from the papers of a German intelligence officer whose plane had crash-landed in Golikov's sector. However, when the German offensive failed to materialize on 22 June, the day fixed in the captured documents. Golikov was summoned to make a personal report to Stalin. Stalin informed Golikov in no uncertain terms that he did not believe a word of Operation 'Blau'. Golikov was now instructed to launch the offensive on Orel without further delay.

Golikov had hardly returned to headquarters when he was confronted by the major German offensive, which had been delayed for some days. Although his armoured formations enjoyed numerical superiority, they had already been deployed offensively in the northern sector and could not oppose the spearhead of the ten Panzer divisions, which cut deep into Golikov's army. Stalin, in the Stavka, personally assumed command of the operation, controlling the situation in the field. Golikov, who attempted to regain command even to the extent of bypassing the Stavka, was reprimanded severely: 'You are to get a tight grip on [the tank corps] at once, assign them specific tasks suited to tank corps and demand absolutely that these orders are carried out.' From 2 July Golikov was entirely ignored and the Stavka took direct control of the battlefield. The subsequent collapse of the Voronezh front was followed by a search for scapegoats. Golikov's realistic appraisal in a telephone conversation with Stalin that he could not guarantee to hold on to Voronezh cost him his command.

In retrospect, Golikov was made a scapegoat by Khrushchev and the generals at Stavka for their own failure. His tendency to cater to Stalin's obsessions on the eve of the war was now used against him. There is little to suggest, however, that he 'proved himself incompetent as a field commander', as some historians have suggested since. A more likely explanation is that in an attempt to exonerate himself, Stalin ruthlessly sacrificed the reputation of Golikov, Marshal Ivan Bagramyan and other less prominent officers.

The mark of Cain was on Golikov for the rest of his short service in the field. In September he was posted for a short time to Stalingrad, though the precise nature of his assignment is not yet clear. In the 1970 version of his memoirs Khrushchev condemned Golikov for cowardly behaviour. He claimed that when Golikov was informed that he would have to remain in Stalingrad to liaise with General Vasily Chuikov, he turned 'white as a sheet' and begged Khrushchev not to abandon him. 'Stalingrad is doomed!' he begged. 'Don't leave me behind. Don't destroy me. Let me go with you.' The credibility of this story is somewhat dubious. Chuikov mentions Golikov several times in his memoirs in a positive light. Golikov, he attested, 'was constantly on the move, personally knew the position of all the armies on our front, always looked at the situation sensibly and expressed his views frankly about the progress of a battle and the fighting in general. In Stalingrad, too, Golikov gave me valuable information and advice.' Officers who participated in the defence of Stalingrad remembered Golikov as 'a highly self-disciplined and self-possessed officer capable of inspiring his soldiers with confidence in victory. Never shunning danger, he was often seen at the front lines. . . . He was always ready with useful advice on the organization of battle and with assistance as regards logistic support of the troops.'

After the regrouping of the army following the victory in Stalingrad, Golikov launched a relentless counter-offensive across the Don which by Christmas 1942 brought him to Katermirovka. A month later his troops liberated Volokonovka, a railway junction some 78 miles northeast of Kharkov, after routing seventeen Axis divisions. By 6 February Golikov had cleared the last Germans from Voronezh and had driven some 100 miles to the west. One of his major accomplishments was the encirclement of the German forces between the Don and the Moscow–Rostov railway. Two days later, Golikov's army pounded its way to within forty miles of Kharkov, and on 16 February he stormed and reconquered the city. Golikov's troops pushed steadily westward and in the first week of March had advanced almost 100 miles in their new drive towards Kiev, the Ukrainian capital.

A month later, however, the Germans launched a counter-offensive, recaptured Kharkov and held it until the summer. This time Golikov himself admitted that he had made an 'incorrect evaluation of the intent and capabilities of the enemy'. He consequently lost his command in the field and was again assigned political and administrative tasks. In April 1943 he returned to his position as Deputy Defence Commissar, but was responsible only for matters concerning personnel. In this capacity he took charge of the repatriation of Soviet citizens from Germany and the countries formerly occupied by it at the end of 1944 – a grim chapter in the history of the Red Army.

After the war General Golikov served for a while as the head of the Armoured Forces Academy. In January 1958 he reached the peak of his career when he was appointed Director of the Main Political Department of the Soviet Army and Navy, a position he held for over four years. Honours followed, and in 1961 he was made a Marshal of the Soviet Union and a member of the Central Committee of the Communist Party.

The final crisis in Golikov's post-war career occurred against the background of the Cuban Missile Crisis. In the process of de-Stalinization following the XXII Party Congress in October 1961, Golikov favoured the expulsion of Malenkov, Kaganovich and Molotov from the Party and became the target of growing criticism from Khrushchev, who had hitherto supported him. Golikov's rôle in the Cuban affair would have been to explain to the officers and men involved the reasons for this agonizing reappraisal of traditional Soviet policy with respect to foreign bases. It seems that in view of his previous futile attempts to reach a settlement over Berlin, Khrushchev exploited the shipment of the missiles to Cuba as a device to exert pressure on the United States to reopen negotiations. The issue was discussed during the Party Presidium meeting held during the session of the Supreme Soviet between 22 and 25 April. In all likelihood Golikov opposed the plan and either resigned of his own accord or was forced to do so. His dismissal seems to have been closely connected with Andrei Gromyko's trip to Yugoslavia in the second half of that month. Gromyko returned to Moscow together with Yepishev, hitherto Ambassador to Belgrade, who now took over Golikov's position as the head of the Political Directorate of the Army. On May Day Golikov's absence from the rally in the Red Square was explained on grounds of illness. The decree of his relief from his post, dated 11 May, was released by *Pravda* only on 21 May.

The end of Golikov's career was bleak. He bore the title of General Inspector in the Ministry of Defence, devoid of any real power or influence. He had few friends and until his death in 1980 failed, despite great efforts on his part, to rehabilitate himself or to find an appropriate position even in a research institute. The political commissar who had succeeded in penetrating the officer caste was shunned by his fellow Marshals.

BIBLIOGRAPHY

I would like to express my gratitude to Dr Petra Marquardt-Bigman and Dr Boris Morozov for their assistance in tracing rare biographical sources.

Public Record Office, London: Admiralty papers; British Chief of Staff papers; British Foreign Office papers.

Sovetsko-amerikanskie otnosheniya vo vremya velikoi otechestvennoi voiny, 1941–1945, I, Moscow, 1984.

Sovetsko-angliiskie otnosheniya vo vremya velikoi otechestvennoi voiny, 1941–1945, I, Moscow, 1984.

Chuikov, Vasily, *The Battle for Stalingrad*, New York, 1964.

Erickson, John, *The Road to Stalingrad: Stalin's War with Germany*, vol. I, London, 1975.

Erickson, John, *The Road to Berlin: Stalin's War with Germany*, vol. II, London, 1983.

Glantz, David M., *Soviet Military Intelligence in War*, London, 1990.

Golikov, F. I., *Krasnye orly (Iz dnevnikov 1918–1920 gg.)*, Moscow, 1959.

Golikov, F. I., 'Reservnaya armiya vstupaet v srazhenie yuzhnee Moskvy', *Voenno-istoricheskii Zhurnal*, no. 11, 1966.

Golikov, F. I., *V moskovskoi bitve: zapiski komandarma*, Moscow, 1967.

Golikov, F. I., '10-aya armiya v nastuplenii', in *Bitva za Moskvu*, Moscow, 1968.

Golikov, F. I., 'Nezabyvaemye vstrechi', in *Bitva za Stalingrad*, Volgograd, 1973.

Golikov, F. I., 'Sovetskaya voennaya missiya v Anglii i SShA v 1941 g', *Novaya i noveishaya istoriya*, nos 3 and 4, 1969.

Kharlamov, Admiral N., *Trudnaya missiya*, Moscow, 1983.

'Marshal Sovetskogo Soyuza F. I. Golikov (K 80-letiyu so dnya rozhdeniya)', *VIZh*, no. 7, 1980.

Roberts, Geoffrey, *The Unholy Alliance. Stalin's Pact with Hitler*, London, 1989.

Seaton, Albert, *The Russo-German War 1941–45*, New York, 1970.

Tatu, Michel, *Power in the Kremlin. From Khrushchev to Kosygin*, New York, 1969.

Ivan Stepanovich
KONEV

OLEG RZHESHEVSKY

It was summer 1941 and the Red Army was retreating on all fronts, from the Baltic to the Black Sea. A fierce battle was developing around Smolensk, some 350 kilometres from Moscow, and the fate of the Soviet capital itself hung on its outcome. Colonel-General Ivan Konev was commanding 19th Army, which consisted of three divisions and some reinforcement units, and which was considerably outnumbered by the enemy. One day, on his way in his staff car to meet General A. Yeremenko, deputy commander of the Western Front, Konev and his adjutant, Colonel Chernyshev, stumbled on a group of German tanks. Spotting an abandoned 45mm gun and some shells not far away, they managed to roll it into position. Their first shot put one tank out of action and, while the Germans were trying to recover from their confusion, Konev and Chernyshev made their escape, miraculously un-scathed, and by evening arrived at army headquarters. They were not expected, as a telephone message had just been received with the news that Konev had been killed. The precise orders Konev issued on hearing this restored the situation. Personal courage and energetic initiative in difficult circumstances were characteristic of Konev as a military leader throughout the war.

Ivan Stepanovich Konev was born on 28 December 1897 into a peasant family in the village of Lodeino, in the Nikolsk district of the province of Northern Dvina. His mother died at his birth. As the only other member of the poor family, he helped his father on the land and at the age of twelve left school to start work cutting timber. In 1913 he went to his uncle in Archangel where he got work as a navvy in Amosov's timber mill. Then for two years he lived and worked at home in the village, where he discovered in himself an interest in political literature which he obtained from a cousin who had studied at the agricultural institute in Vyatka. In April 1916 he was called up before his time for military service. He evidently did well, as he was sent to a training course and emerged as a junior NCO. The artillery division to which Konev was posted was kitted out with British-made uniforms, a fact which reminded him that Russia was not alone in the fight against the Central Powers. Konev served one year in the tsarist army, but took almost no part in any fighting. When the Imperial Army disintegrated and the October Revolution occurred, he went home to his village as a supporter of the new régime. In 1918, as one of the local Bolsheviks, he was made Military Commissar of the Nikolsk district. He was elected a delegate to the 5th All-Russian Congress of Soviets in 1921 and, together with other members of his delegation, he took part in suppressing the Kronshtadt uprising. [The Kronshtadt rising of March 1921 was begun by Left SRs with strong local Communist support as a protest against the widespread disorder in the country brought about by the Bolshevik policy of 'War Communism'. The peasants in particular were hostile to the policy of forced requisitions, or fixed deliveries to the state, and to the suppression of free trade. The uprising, in which the main armed force was supplied by the crews of the Baltic Fleet, was suppressed after bloody fighting carried out mainly by 7th Army under M. N. Tukhachevsky. Some 250 delegates from the Congress of Soviets took part, as did 300 delegates from the X Party Congress, then in progress.]

During the Civil War Konev was active mainly on the Eastern Front, where he fought against the forces of Admiral Kolchak, then Ataman Semenov and the Japanese intervention forces, rising from an ordinary Red Armyman to commissar of an armoured train. On the liberation of Vladivostok he became commissar of the 17th Maritime Corps in the town of Nikolsk-Ussuriisk, transferring with the Corps in early 1924 to the Ukraine. In late 1924/early 1925, he was commissar and chief of the political section of the 17th Rifle Division of Moscow Military District. He completed staff courses at the Frunze Military Academy in 1926 and was appointed regimental commander, then until 1932 served as commander of the 17th Rifle Division in Nizhni Novgorod. The courses he had taken in Moscow stood him in good stead. The instructors were all top-class specialists, including former officers of the tsarist army, such as Colonel A. A. Shkolin of the Imperial General Staff, A. A. Svechin, prominent military theorist and head of the information department of Nicholas II's General Staff, Professor A. I. Verkhovsky, former War Minister in the Provisional Government, as well as Tukhachevsky and other leading professionals. The students were divided into small groups. Konev's group was taught by Professor N. Langau, a German by origin and a considerable expert on infantry. Konev later wrote that he learnt in one year everything Langau could teach him. Konev was particularly taken with military history and throughout his life he regarded it as an integral component of success.

There is very little on Konev's early career in his personal file, and what there is is somewhat inconsistent. In the spring of 1932, A. Kork, commander of the 3rd Rifle Corps, which included Konev's 17th Division, and commander of Moscow Military District, gave a personal assessment of Konev as 'a proletarian commander who took the full weight of his post on himself and always led by personal example'. Striving constantly for self-improvement, 'like a good Bolshevik, he has overcome the shortcomings I and the Revolutionary Military Committee had found in him at the beginning of the period. . . . Conclusion: he completely corresponds to what a divisional commander/commissar should be.' Yet only six months later, in November 1932, Kork took a very different view, noting that Konev was 'nervous, irritable, hot-tempered. At times unrestrained even towards his seniors.' He was unsystematic in his dealings with those under him, made them work in spurts and often harrassed them. He lacked self-discipline, over-reacted to criticism, resorted too readily to rules and regulations. 'Despite much work, he achieved poor results in rifle training. . . . Has absolutely no idea how to use HQ as an organ of command. Is somewhat dismissive of HQ and its personnel and is therefore unable to function alone in combined [i.e. military and political] command during training and manoeuvres.' Commenting that Konev did not get on well with regimental commanders and that he did not enjoy the respect of his juniors, Kork concluded that he required further training at the Military Academy. These personal documents reflect some of the contradictory traits which Konev displayed throughout his life and career.

Kork's advice was heeded and Konev spent from 1932 to 1934 at the Frunze Academy under such luminaries as the future Chief of General Staff Shaposhnikov. He did well and following the course was posted as commander of Belorussia Military District. At the beginning of 1938 he was promoted to Mongolia as commander of the 57th Special Corps.

The political upheavals and the purges of the 1930s left their mark on Konev's career. In 1933, while in the Academy, he passed unscathed through a Party purge. The comments on him included: 'Well trained politically. Shows Bolshevik dynamism in his studies and work.' The repressions of military cadres which soon followed posed a grave threat to Konev, although he apparently was unaware of it to the end of his life. Speeches made in defence of Uborevich, commander of Belorussia Military District who was subsequently executed, incriminated Konev. In 1937, when Konev was put forward as a candidate for the Supreme Soviet of the USSR, a denunciation was received by the political section of Trans-Urals Military District, claiming that Konev had concealed his parents' true material circumstances and that the facts in his biography, as presented for his candidacy, were far from the truth. The political section requested information from the Archangel authorities and received the following note:

'Information on Citizen Konev Ivan Stepanovich . . . He was born into the family of a wealthy peasant. Before the 1917 revolution the household consisted of two houses, 2–3 horses, up to 5 cows, some livestock. They always used hired labour. Right up to 1917 his uncle, Konev Fedor Ivanovich, worked as a village constable, was arrested in 1929 by OGPU, wounded himself with a knife during the arrest, but was treated in hospital, then put in prison where he died. Konev's father had parted company with his brother before the revolution and was left with a house, which is now an infants' school, one horse, 2–3 cows, and he occasionally used hired labour.'

This information was sent in early 1938 to the head of the army's political section, L. Mekhlis, one of Stalin's closest advisers and well known for his 'revolutionary' attitude to the military cadres. But nothing came of it, the scale of arrests having by then diminished somewhat. Konev moreover had by now been appointed Deputy of the Supreme Soviet and was in Mongolia. Such recriminations about concealing parental property and the activities of one's relatives would normally have been severely punished, leading to expulsion from the Party and arrest.

When Konev was posted to Mongolia in 1937 as commander of the 57th Corps, the unit did not yet exist. The Japanese invasion of Manchuria was a threat to the Soviet border and required counter-measures. With the agreement of the Mongolian People's Republic, Soviet units were deployed to forestall the further incursion of Japanese forces. The large fully motorized Soviet units thus deployed were drawn from Transbaikal Military District and given the name 57th Special Corps. At the same time Konev became an adviser to the Mongolian army and, although he did not take part in the subsequent battles on the river Khalkin-Gol, his services in defence of Mongolia were not forgotten and in May 1971 he was made a Hero of the Mongolian People's Republic. From October 1938 to May 1941 Konev, recently only a divisional commander, rose to command 2nd Separate Red Banner Army in the Far Eastern, then Transbaikal and finally Northern Caucasus Military Districts. This rapid advance was typical for talented officers during the period of the purges.

In May 1941 he was summoned to Moscow and ordered to transfer 19th Army in secrecy to the district of Belaya Tserkov-Cherkassy in Ukraine. Defence Commissar Timoshenko told him: 'The army must be in complete battle-readiness, and should the enemy attack Kiev, you are to attack his flank and chase him into the Pripet marshes.' Konev was made commander of the army, while remaining commander of the Northern Caucasus until the outbreak of the war.

On 22 June 19th Army was ordered to move into Kiev District and then to the Moscow axis at Vitebsk. The deployment at Vitebsk was carried out hastily and haphazardly, under constant attack from German aircraft against which only feeble defence was mounted. Konev wrote in his memoirs of this time:

> We were met on the highway by a chaotic stream of vehicles, carts, horses, columns of refugees, among them many soldiers. They were all streaming towards Smolensk . . . . It was especially strange to see tanks of the latest design retreating. Three KVs were allegedly going for repair. Literally threatening them with our weapons, by thrusting our revolvers through their drivers' look-out slits, we made them halt . . . and took them over. By this means we managed by evening to collect about a battalion of infantry, an 85mm anti-aircraft battery and an artillery battery of 122mm guns.

19th Army succeeded in driving the Germans temporarily out of Vitebsk, but then retreated towards Smolensk where fierce fighting was taking place. In August it carried out a successful counter-attack against the German IX Army and was mentioned in orders by Marshal Timoshenko, Commander-in-Chief of the Western sector. The press exaggerated these important but limited successes of 'Commander Konev's units', even describing them as a 'general counter-offensive', and this at a time when he was abandoning Dnepropetrovsk, Novgorod, Tallinn, Gomel and other major cities, prompting Stalin to ban further mention of Konev's name in the press. On 12 September 1941, Konev himself was appointed commander of the Western Front with the object of defending Moscow in a battle that had already in effect begun. Terrible defeats ensued. Five Soviet armies were encircled in the region of Vyazma and the majority of their manpower, some 500,000 men, were taken prisoner. Moscow was under dire threat. Responsibility for the defeat at Vyazma lay, among others, personally with Stalin and Konev. The encirclement of such a large force could have been avoided.

Konev faced serious consequences. A commission headed by Molotov arrived at the Western Front HQ and on 10 October advised that the Western and Reserve Fronts be combined, with Zhukov as commander and Konev as his first deputy. Konev wrote in his memoirs that Stavka accepted this advice, although the truth is different. Up to this point, Stalin had decided to remove Konev from his post and to put him on trial by a military tribunal with the threat of execution. It was only Zhukov's strenuous efforts that saved Konev who was made his deputy and sent to handle defence on the far right flank of the Front at Kalinin. When Zhukov was in trouble after the war, Konev did not reciprocate the favour, as we shall see.

After arriving in Kalinin, Konev was unable to strengthen the front immediately and it proved impossible to hold the city, but he did manage to prevent the enemy from going further. The Kalinin Front was formed under Konev's command as a Colonel-General on 17 October, an important date in his life, for it showed, at least for the time being, that Stalin still had confidence in him. Fierce fighting continued on the Kalinin Front right up to the beginning of December with sporadic success. Then gradually the Soviet counter-attacks took their toll and the enemy's offensive force was exhausted, even though he retained superiority in tanks and automatic weapons.

On 5 December Konev's Front launched a counter-offensive that was part of a general plan to destroy the German forces engaged in the battle of Moscow. On 16 December, under threat of encirclement, the enemy was forced to abandon Kalinin. A week later, General Halder, Chief of General Staff German land forces, recorded in his diary: 'The IX Army front has begun to fall apart. A newly threatened zone is emerging on the northern flank at Torzhok and to the west, and we have no means of correcting the situation.' (The recently created Soviet 39th Army had begun its operations in the region.) The battle of Moscow ended in a crushing defeat of German forces. Thirty-eight divisions were either destroyed or disabled with the loss of more than 500,000 men. Although Soviet forces had suffered more than twice the enemy's losses, it was essentially the beginning of the end of the war on the Soviet-German front. Konev was awarded the recently created Order of Kutuzov 1st Class. It was during the Kalinin campaign that he met and married his wife.

In August 1942 Konev was again given command of the Western Front. In March 1943 he took over the Northwestern, and in June the Steppe Front. In the battle of the Kursk peninsula of 5 July to 23 August 1943, the biggest tank battle of the Second World War, the Steppe Front was made a strategic reserve with the role of preventing the enemy from penetrating the deep rear of the Soviet defence, and then of going on to the offensive together with other Fronts. A notable feature of the situation was that through its intelligence network in Switzerland, the so-called Lucy Ring, the Soviet High Command knew in advance of the German planned offensive. This information was analogous to that which was being obtained by British intelligence at Bletchley via its decoding machine, Enigma – a 'coincidence' still to be explained by historians. In the first week of the offensive, the enemy nevertheless succeeded in advancing up to 35 kilometres behind Soviet defences and Konev was compelled to bring large numbers of his forces into play in order to prevent further penetration. This task was accomplished. Konev was somewhat slow to go over to counter-offensive, but he made up for this omission in due course.

On 3 August the Voronezh and Steppe Fronts began to advance along the Belgorod–Kharkov Axis. The artillery bombardment was so intense – 230 guns per kilometre of front – that, according to German prisoners-of-war, many German soldiers went mad because of it. On 5 August the forces of Konev and Vatutin liberated Belgorod. On the same day Orel on the northern flank of the Kursk salient was liberated. In Moscow twelve salvoes from 120 guns marked these victories in a ceremony that was to become a tradition. The Steppe Front, later renamed the 2nd Ukrainian Front, was chiefly responsible for liberating Kharkov, Ukraine's second city, taking an active part later in the forced crossing of the Dnieper. By this time, Konev had recovered Stalin's firm confidence, a fact noted by Zhukov in his memoirs. Of Konev's later operations, those worthy of note took place at Korsun, the Vistula and Berlin, in which he commanded successively the 2nd and 1st Ukrainian Fronts. With the 1st Ukrainian Front he crossed the Polish border on 17 July 1944, and at the beginning of May 1945 he commanded the last major operation of the war in Europe, the liberation of Prague.

The Korsun operation was carried out in western Ukraine between 24 January and 17 February 1944 by forces of the 1st Ukrainian Front, commanded by General N. Vatutin, who died after being seriously wounded shortly after the campaign, and the 2nd Ukrainian Front. Its purpose was to encircle and destroy a group of about ten divisions, part of General von Manstein's Army Group South, deployed on a vulnerable salient at Kanev. The Group was surrounded on 28 January. The German command took desperate measures to liberate it, but the Soviet command, in its turn, established a second ring of encirclement to prevent this. Hitler made lavish promises. In a cable to Colonel-General Stemmermann, he said: 'You can rely on me as on a stone wall. You will be freed from the cauldron, but for the moment you must defend yourselves to the last bullet.' It proved impossible to unblock the German Group from outside. Konev later wrote that the scene on the following morning after the operation appalled him.

> I had never seen, and never again saw, such a vast number of corpses in such a small area. The Germans had made a hopeless attempt to extricate themselves from the cauldron during the night . . . . We had not planned a bloodbath; I had ordered the capture of the Group. But because General Stemmermann had ordered them to break out at any cost, we had to meet force with force.

This major defeat for the Germans had strategic consequences. As for Konev, he was created a Marshal of the Soviet Union.

This operation, which so benefitted his own career, revealed certain of Konev's personal characteristics. Describing in detail the unfolding of the fierce fighting, the outcome of which was being closely watched in Moscow and Berlin, Konev wrote that 'no one came out of the encirclement'. In fact, part of the German Group did manage to break out. Konev was determined that the victory should belong to his Front alone, and this complicated his relations with other commanders during the operation, in which he got Stalin's agreement to put part of the Voronezh Front under his command in order to annihilate the encircled Germans. This spoiled his relations with Vatutin, and later with Zhukov and a number of other marshals for the same reason. An atmosphere of rivalry had been created, the roots and negative consequences of which have been analysed by John Erickson in his book,

The Soviet High Command. The sharpest rivalry between Konev and Zhukov emerged during the Berlin campaign.

As Stalin's deputy, Zhukov had been appointed commander of the 1st Belorussian Front, on which rested the main burden of taking Berlin. General Rokossovsky, one of the most talented of senior officers, was unfairly moved to the 2nd Belorussian Front so that Zhukov could receive the laurels for this most prestigious of operations, as a reward for past services. At the same time, Konev's 1st Ukrainian Front was not given the precise task of taking Berlin. Before continuing with these events, however, we must return to the beginning of 1945 and the actions of the 1st Ukrainian Front in one of its most effective operations under Konev's command, namely, the Vistula campaign, which was carried out in combination with Zhukov's 1st Belorussian Front.

These two Fronts had the task of destroying German forces in Poland and establishing a bridgehead on the west bank of the Oder in immediate proximity to Berlin. To carry out this single offensive operation, the largest group of Soviet forces to be created in the course of the war was formed, with decisive superiority over the enemy: 2.2 million men, 33,000 guns and mortars, 7,000 tanks and assault weapons and just under 600 aircraft. On 9 January Moscow suddenly ordered that the start of the operation be brought forward from 20 to 12 January, giving the Soviet command a mere two and a half days to prepare instead of eleven, and placing the entire organization under great pressure, as Konev later recalled. This sudden change had been provoked by a request from Churchill to Stalin to relieve the pressure being caused by a German breakthrough in the Ardennes and Vosges.

The defeat of the Germans in Poland was inevitable, despite the dozens of divisions brought in from the West to support the retreating forces. Zhukov attacked along the Poznan–Lodz–Warsaw axis, while Konev attacked on that of Radom–Breslau. The German commander, General Mellenthin, later wrote that the Soviet advance developed with unprecedented force and speed:

> It was clear that their Supreme High Command had fully mastered the technique of organizing an offensive by vast mechanized armies. It is impossible to describe what happened between the Vistula and the Oder in the early months of 1945. Europe had known nothing like it since the fall of the Roman Empire.

By 3 February the operation was complete. On Konev's front, the Silesian industrial sector and the city of Cracow, with its Wawel Palace and other historic treasures, were liberated with minimal damage.

The Berlin operation, which began on 15 April, was preceded by the following events. On 1 April Churchill sent a message to Roosevelt which said in part:

The Russian armies will no doubt overrun all Austria and enter Vienna. If they also take Berlin will not their impression that they have been the overwhelming contributor to our common victory be unduly imprinted in their minds, and may this not lead them into a mood which will raise grave and formidable difficulties in the future? I therefore consider that from a political standpoint we should march as far east into Germany as possible, and that should Berlin be in our grasp we should certainly take it. This also appears sound on military grounds.

The same day, Zhukov and Konev were summoned to Moscow by Stalin who asked them: 'So, who is going to capture Berlin, we or the Allies?' Konev replied: 'We will capture Berlin.' For his part, Zhukov added that the forces of the 1st Belorussian Front were ready to take the German capital. Stalin's orders gave the task to the 1st Belorussian Front, while Konev was directed to go further to the south, towards Dresden and Leipzig, in order to assist in the capture of Berlin by cutting the German front in two and joining up with US forces at the Elbe. But no line demarcating Konev's right flank from Zhukov's left front was defined, indicating that the two commanders would have to use their discretion in the light of circumstances. And it was precisely these circumstances that Konev anticipated in the directives he issued on returning to his HQ from Moscow: 'Part of [our] right flank forces are to assist the 1st Belorussian Front in taking the city of Berlin.' He also aimed his tank armies towards Berlin. He plainly regarded his own direct participation in capturing Berlin as of fundamental importance. He wrote:

I pictured mentally the end of the operation in the southern and south-western outskirts of Berlin. Of course, it would have been premature to order the subsequent shift of [my] tank armies towards Berlin deep behind enemy defences, the conditions were not ripe for it, and it would have required permission of Supreme High Command. But I wanted both tank army commanders (Rybalko and Lelyushenko) to share my mood, to sense my confidence that this was precisely the perspective that was opening up before them.

In fact, Konev put his main effort into the advance on Berlin, rather than Dresden. 'I gave [the tank armies] my blessing', he wrote, 'for their bold foray into a broad operational space, separately from our main forces.' The delay in Zhukov's advance, caused by stubborn and costly resistance at Seele, led to agreement by the High Command that Konev's tank armies should attack the southern outskirts of Berlin. On 21 April his troops captured Wünsdorf, where the German Army Group Vistula had its command point, and where later Soviet forces in Germany, or the Western Group, would have its headquarters for some months.

Konev's success in attacking Berlin from the south led to changes in the demarcation line between his and Zhukov's Fronts. It now divided the city as it were into two parts, and it was in this way that Berlin was captured. Konev cabled Moscow on 2 May that after nine days of street fighting his troops had occupied the whole of the southwestern and central districts (within the demarcation line fixed for the Fronts), and that 'together with the forces of the 1st Belorussian Front, we have occupied the city of Berlin.' To the end of his days, Zhukov adamantly contested this interpretation of events. In a preface to E. Dolmatovsky's *Avtograf Pobedy* (1972), he wrote: 'You say in your first chapter that Berlin was taken by the 1st Belorussian Front and 1st Ukrainian Front. Really? Look at the Order of the Supreme Commander-in-Chief.' The order to which Zhukov always referred in this connection was that signed by Stalin, stating that it was the 1st Belorussian Front, *with the assistance* of the 1st Ukrainian Front under Konev, that did the job. Konev's forward units were 200 metres from the Reichstag.

These details might today seem of little importance. In my view, an understanding of the relations between Konev and Zhukov, which left much to be desired, may help to dispel the idealized images that have been built up of these two outstanding war leaders. Konev himself was quite categorical on this: 'During the war Marshal Zhukov and I had dealings more than once and we had several tasks we had to carry out together. By the end of the war, the butt of our two fronts, like most neighbours, had plenty of misunderstandings, most of which were caused by him.' A little later, Konev's forces were withdrawn from the districts they had occupied and were replaced by Zhukov's forces. The 1st Belorussian and 1st Ukrainian Fronts carried out the operation together. During the operation Konev led his forces confidently and strove firmly to achieve his goal, at times taking high risks, for instance, ordering his tanks to force the river Spree before the bridges had been secured.

It has to be said that the battle for Berlin was notable for its great ferocity, as the Germans fought with desperate determination. Both sides suffered huge losses. In some of Konev's units all the officers perished and only some privates survived. In the course of the battle his troops liberated many British, American and other Allied prisoners-of-war, as well as some prominent military and political leaders, such as former French Prime Minister Edouard Herriot, and they also saved the Dresden art gallery.

It was Stalin's unexpected question, while speaking to Konev on the government link, 'What do you think, who's going to take Prague?' that launched preparations for Konev's last operation of the war. By this time, the configuration of the Front offered favourable conditions to make a dash for the city, urged on by the fact that the population had staged a rising and were asking for help. The situation was made more intense by a letter of 4 May from Eisenhower to Chief of Staff Antonov, in which he stated that US forces were prepared to advance into Czechoslovakia up to the Rivers Vltava and Elbe, effectively bringing Prague into the US orbit of activity. But there was no conflict over this. Once US forces had liberated western Czechoslovakia they called a halt. No small part in this was played by the personal meetings

Konev had with the US commander, General Omar Bradley, a fact Konev frequently recalled with warmth in his memoirs. Prague was liberated on 9 May. The decisive force were the 1,600 tanks of the 1st Ukrainian Front. The war in Europe was over.

Konev had ended the war as one of the most talented Front Commanders. His primary gift as a military leader, which had emerged gradually and was confirmed on the field of battle, was his careful study of the enemy. He used information gleaned at every level – by his troops, by his aircraft, his secret intelligence and his officers. It is worth dwelling on this last element. He taught his subordinates that the enemy must be analysed not in the abstract but visually. Everything must be examined and stored away in the memory. Officers at all levels must not be afraid 'to crawl to the front line on their bellies'. More often perhaps than other commanders, Konev himself was often at the front line of the battle, studying the location and the enemy frequently under artillery and rifle fire, and as a rule he established his command posts at the most difficult, key spots of the fighting. The writer Boris Polevoy, finding himself at dawn on a river bank at Poltava in 1943 just before its forcing, overheard an excited soldier hoarsely convincing his superior officer, 'It was him, Comrade Major, I swear it. He was standing right where you are, scanning the opposite bank with his binoculars, he was.' Both officers and men were impressed by such behaviour on Konev's part.

Another major component of Konev's military arsenal was the artillery offensive, the use of artillery in concentrated masses. He told his officers while he was still commanding the Kalinin Front: 'When you know the enemy's defence network, it is better to launch a barrage from all your batteries that will stun him, paralyse him, even momentarily, with a mighty artillery attack, rather than to spare the ammunition and spread the attack over time and then to pay for it later with the lives of many soldiers.' And he practised what he preached. The artillery offensive at Sandomir was a good example. Using medium-calibre artillery, he destroyed the troops and weapons of the enemy's first line of defence while his forward units rushed to take over the ridge. The artillery fell silent. Then the enemy opened up a powerful barrage, thus revealing what weapons he had in his deep defence. Konev then opened the second and decisive phase of his artillery attack by throwing in everything he had in the shortest possible time and with the greatest possible intensity, and with aerial support. His blows rained down on the German rear where their men, weapons and transport resources were concentrated. The return fire was nevertheless intense, but the enemy's lines of command had plainly been disorganized, his communications destroyed, he had lost his former manoeuvrability, and this gave Konev the chance to break through his defences at full depth and with minimal losses to his own side. As for short-range artillery, its effectiveness was improved by the use of blank maps – usually small pieces of stiff paper – on which data gathered by intelligence was entered daily about gun positions, reinforcements, lines of communication, crossroads and possible locations of enemy concentrations. They were then given to each battery commander and supplemented by information received during the battle, a procedure that today would be automatically established by electronic means.

Tank raids with powerful air support deep into the enemy's rear were also regarded by Konev as one of the most decisive means for achieving success. A number of tank army operations between 1943 and 1945 illustrate this. Von Manstein later described Konev's command in the second half of 1943 as 'far more energetic', while K. Tipelskirch wrote that Konev's attack was so strong, it destroyed both the first echelon and significant reserve forces, too. Writing of the Vistula operation, Tipelskirch says: 'Konev's tank penetrations of the German front were so numerous that it was impossible to contain, let alone liquidate them. It was not surprising that Konev's favourites were the commanders of his tank armies.'

The pincer movement, which the Germans had used to such devastating effect, Konev perfected into his own 'arrangement'. In January 1945 General Rybalko told a journalist he was about to attack Silesia:

> 'More precisely, surround. Even more precisely make a by-passing manoeuvre. I don't think there'll be a full encirclement. We'll probably leave an outlet. What for? So the enemy can get out. No, no, you misheard me, so the enemy *can* get out. It may sound somewhat strange, but that is how the commander of the Front has planned the operation. What would have been left of the beautiful city of Cracow if the Germans hadn't been able to escape through the gap left for them? Stones, nothing but stones. You must have seen Cracow after the liberation, almost wholly intact . . . . To save the Silesian basin the commander ordered me not to encircle the enemy completely, but to surround him and then suddenly to turn my army towards Ratibor. It was a devilishly difficult manoeuvre to carry out, but we did it.'

For saving Cracow Konev was given the title of honorary citizen of the city, and a monument to him was erected in one of its squares.

A final aspect of Konev's military skills was the element of surprise, a classic example of which was the planned defence in 1943 by the Steppe Front in the battle for Kursk, followed by a counter-offensive which was in fact the concealed strategic aim of the operation. True, neither his plans nor their execution always brought success. In order to conceal the direction of his main attack in the Korsun operation, Konev decided to alter the position of one of his tank armies, providing an appropriate plan of disinformation for the occasion. Camouflage and disguise were maintained with strict discipline, and troops and weapons were moved to their new locations mostly at night. Their places were taken by seventeen areas of dummy tanks and artillery. Evidence of the continued 'presence' of the previous tank units was fabricated by powerful amplifiers and by the movement of tractors and haulage vehicles, while headquarters was impersonated by army radio stations. The enemy reacted with intensified reconnaissance, however, and three days before the offensive German intelligence reported that 'in the district of Kirovograd the main attack has been moved north, and more to the east in the district of Novy Mirgorod. When the offensive begins, therefore, we should expect the main thrust to come from there.' Having discovered the preparations for the attack in this new area, the Germans strengthened their defence with two tank divisions, thus making a Soviet breakthrough more difficult and causing many Soviet losses.

Konev was not a military theorist, nor did he claim to be one, but the way he carried out his principles of warfare invariably showed his great originality as a military commander. Keitel said that to command a Front was to be the conductor of a great orchestra and to answer for everyone. Even before completing the Prague operation, on 5 May Konev was appointed Commander-in-Chief of the Central Group of Forces, deployed mainly in eastern Austria and partly in Hungary. It was formally created on 10 June 1945 under the agreement reached by the Allies for the surrender of the Axis powers, of which Austria was one. In practice, the Central Group was formed on the basis of the field command of the 1st Ukrainian Front. Austria's political life was supervised by an Allied Control Commission staffed by supreme commissioners of the USSR, USA, Britain and France. It should be noted that Konev was given obvious preference over Marshal Malinovsky, whose forces had liberated Austria. And in due course, Konev would be given even more responsible tasks by Stalin as well as Khrushchev, attesting to the special trust the Soviet leadership of the period placed in him.

He spent less than a year in Austria, during which time he established businesslike relations with Chancellor Karl Renner, leader of the Austrian Social Democrats, and gave much assistance in the food and other material supply of the population. In April 1946 he was appointed Commander of Land Forces and, not by accident as it later emerged, Zhukov's deputy. Konev was present at the meeting of the Supreme Military Council and Politburo which examined the Zhukov 'affair' (described in greater detail elsewhere in this volume), and he adopted a two-sided, if not two-faced, position. He charged Zhukov with having a difficult personality, being quarrelsome, and guilty of inconsistency as a leader, but he swept aside accusations of Zhukov's political dishonesty, lack of respect for the Party and for Stalin, which Beria had cooked up and which had been 'corroborated' by Air Chief Marshal Novikov, who was already in the hands of Beria's men. In June Konev had Zhukov's job as Commander-in-Chief Land Forces and Deputy Armed Forces Minister, and then in March 1956 became First Deputy Defence Minister for general matters.

Between these two important years in Konev's life, 1946 and 1956, there are two other events of a state and personal nature that are noteworthy. From

18 to 23 December 1953 he served as chairman of a Special Judicial Board of the Supreme Court of the USSR in the case of Beria. The character of the trial had been made clear at a Central Committee Plenum on 2–7 July 1953 where the matter was discussed. Beria was charged with attempting to seize power, political intrigue and organizing illegal repressions. In the best tradition of the 1930s, he was also accused – by Khrushchev and Molotov – of being an agent of imperialism. As evidence, his proposal that Germany be united on a neutral basis was cited, a proposal, be it said, advanced the previous year by Stalin himself, and also that relations with Yugoslavia be normalized. By this time, Beria himself was a member of the Politburo, Minister of the Interior, Commissar General for State Security, First Deputy Chairman of the Council of Ministers of the USSR and a Marshal of the Soviet Union. In his hands he held the power of all the repressive organs in the land and his 'comrades-in-arms' had sufficient grounds to fear some sort of action against them from this master of the Gulag. The trial of Beria was part of the struggle for power which erupted inside the Politburo after Stalin's death and which ran on for decades, ultimately destroying the state. The charges entered by the court over which Konev presided accused Beria of 'treason against the Motherland', acting 'in the interests of foreign capital', 'secret links with foreign intelligence'. The proof either never existed or remains unknown. There could be only one sentence. Beria was shot on 24 December 1953. It is difficult to say what rôle Konev really played in bringing in the death sentence, since Beria's fate was already sealed.

A note appears in Konev's personal file for 1956: 'The Hungarian People's Republic – led Soviet forces during the period of struggle against counter-revolution.' The reference is to the crushing of the anti-Communist rising, as a result of which thousands of people were killed or injured. Konev by this time was Deputy Defence Minister and Commander-in-Chief of the united armed forces of the Warsaw Pact. He acted decisively and without mercy. Reports that Western secret services were engaged in incitement only strengthened Konev and his forces in their actions. He reported to Moscow:

> Despite the difficult political situation in Hungary and the efforts of the counter-revolution to disguise itself with revolutionary phrases, the soldiers, NCOs and officers have shown a high degree of political maturity, a deep understanding of their military duty and, as a rule without hesitation, have carried out the military task assigned to them . . . . This is explained above all by a deep belief in the justice of our mission, by the idea that the defence of the popular democratic structure in Hungary and the interests of the entire socialist camp was close to and understood by the personnel and inspired them in the struggle with the Fascist insurgents.

This account was typical of the time. In his report on the military action itself, Konev listed the inadequacies in ordnance, especially transport, radio communications, the lack of specially equipped commanders' vehicles, unsuitability of battle dress, and other shortcomings which were reported to the government.

The parallel career ambitions and resulting hostile relations between Konev and Zhukov, which in Konev's words were at times 'extremely sharp', were exploited by the political leadership. At the end of 1957 Konev was drawn into a new case against Zhukov, this time organized by Khrushchev, who was alarmed by Zhukov's growing power as a member of the Presidium (as the Politburo was called between 1952 and 1966) and as Defence Minister. Konev at this time was extremely popular both in the country at large and in the army, and after crushing the Hungarian revolt he was regarded by the Kremlin as virtually the most reliable, most effective and most professional figure in the army. He was now given an extremely important part in the Zhukov affair.

He wrote an article in *Pravda*, entitled 'The strength of the Soviet Army and Fleet is in the Party leadership and the unbroken link with the people'. In it he attacked Zhukov for failing to ensure the army's preparedness at the beginning of the war. He also criticized him as a strategist. Zhukov, according to Konev, had been given credit for military actions he had not performed, for instance, planning the counter-attack at Stalingrad, which, Konev claimed, properly belonged to Yeremenko, Vatutin and Rokossovsky, who commanded the Stalingrad, Southwestern and Don Fronts respectively, which had encircled and destroyed Paulus's VI Army. The article included a number of true facts, but it was biased, showed all the signs of having been written to order, and in general made a painful impression. The thirst for glory which had been so sharpened by circumstances, however, was accompanied by friendly personal relations and mutual respect between many military men of the period. Zhukov himself turned up at Konev's seventieth birthday party in Moscow, while earlier in the day – and it was 30 degrees below zero – Rokossovsky had brought a basket of lilacs.

In March 1960 Konev left his posts and was appointed a Chief Inspector of the defence ministry, in other words the appearance was given that he had retired at his own request. At the age of sixty-three, he was still in good health. There was no age limit for top-ranking marshals. Indirect evidence suggests he may have retired because he did not accept Khrushchev's hastily proposed reduction of the army. But he did not have to suffer his humiliation for long. In August 1961, just a few days before the Berlin Wall went up, Konev was appointed Commander-in-Chief of Soviet forces in Germany, as the need for an aggressive, experienced military leader became apparent. His arrival in Wünsdorf was meant to make an impression on Western public opinion.

The building of the Berlin Wall was the last attempt to hinder the economic advance of West Germany, which had demonstrated its superiority over East Germany in both standard of living and lifestyle, and to stem the flow of East Germans to the West. The wall was erected thanks to the stubborn efforts of Walter Ulbricht, and on 3 August the idea was given support by Khrushchev and other leaders of the Warsaw Pact countries, though not without resistance. Konev was presented to the meeting on 5 August as the new Soviet Commander-in-Chief in Germany who would replace General I. Yakubovsky for the duration of the crisis. There was a threat of armed conflict with the Western allies while the wall was being built, for each of the four armies had extra-territorial powers extending over the whole of Berlin. The decision was taken that, in the event of Western counter-measures, Soviet troops would withdraw 100 metres twice, but that on the third occasion they would take military action.

It seemed that there was a real threat of war that could destroy the whole of Europe. The German Politburo member responsible for security was Erich Honecker and at midnight on 12 August he informed the Defence Minister, General Heinz Hoffmann, that zero hour was 0100 hours on 13 August, and he said: 'You know what you have to do. Begin.' For his part, Konev put twenty divisions on alert. It is not generally known, however, that in informal consultations the USSR and USA had reached a conditional and secret understanding that, as President Kennedy had made clear to Khrushchev at their meeting in Vienna in June of that year, access to Berlin for Western forces must remain free. Konev told the commandants of the Western sectors of the city: 'Whatever happens in the immediate future, your rights will remain inviolate, no measures will be taken against West Berlin.' In virtually one night Berlin was divided by a concrete wall and metal railings 165 kilometres long. It was defended by watch-towers, escarpments and dogs. Eighty people lost their lives trying to overcome that monster of the Cold War, but it did not save the German Democratic Republic from eventual extinction.

Konev remained in command of Soviet forces in Germany until 1963 and then returned to being a Defence Ministry inspector in active retirement. He wrote his memoirs in later years, made frequent speeches in factories and army units, carried out some missions for the defence ministry and was generally listened to. He died of cancer in 1971 and was buried in the Kremlin wall. He was a member of the Central Committee, had been twice made a Hero of the Soviet Union, and bore many Soviet and foreign medals and decorations.

The author of this essay was warmly received by his widow, Antonina Vasilievna, whom he married in 1942 on the Kalinin Front, and who still thrives and has a good memory, and also by his daughter, Natalya, who teaches at the Military Institute, and as curator of her father's papers is an authority on his life. Part of his papers and other relics are kept in the Konev Museum in the house where he lived as a boy. I asked the family how it was that, among the Marshal's many foreign decorations there were American and French medals, but no British. I was told that in fact he had been created an Honorary Knight Commander of the Bath in 1945, but had declined to receive it after Churchill's speech at Fulton in 1946. [Unlike those awarded to Rokossovsky and Zhukov in Berlin in 1945 by Field Marshal Montgomery, Konev's came back to St James Palace in 1949, marked 'unable to present'. Either Konev was slow to react to Churchill's speech, or by 1949 and the height of the Cold War, he felt it prudent to make this gesture. – HS] He nevertheless managed to visit England, on the occasion of Churchill's funeral, and despite the sad occasion, he was received with honour and respect, a fact he often recalled warmly. In a television broadcast from Cracow, it was reported that the local authorities had decided to remove a monument to Konev. A cable was thrown round its neck and the statue was pulled off its pedestal. It was 1992.

BIBLIOGRAPHY

Churchill, W.S., *The Second World War*, vol. VI, Cassell, London, 1954.
Konev, I. S., *Sorok pyatyi*, 2nd edn, Moscow, 1970.
Konev, I. S., *Zapiski komanduyushchego frontom, 1943–1945*, 4th edn, Moscow, 1991.
'Lichnye dela trekh marshalov', *Izvestiya*, Moscow, 8 May 1992.
Polevoy, Boris, *Polkovodets*, 2nd edn, Moscow, 1983.

Nikolai Gerasimovich

KUZNETSOV

GEOFFREY JUKES

Nikolai Gerasimovich Kuznetsov was born in 1904 in a village near the northern city of Kotlas, joining the infant Soviet Navy at the age of fifteen (giving a false age of seventeen) as a volunteer in the North Dvina Flotilla, to fight the British forces then occupying Archangel. He saw no action then, but after the Flotilla was disbanded decided to make the navy his career, and was commissioned in 1926.

The tsarist navy had not fully replaced its losses of the 1904–5 war with Japan by the time the First World War broke out. Losses in that war were followed by more in the 1918–20 Civil War, in which the British sank some Baltic Fleet units, while in the Black Sea Lenin ordered many ships sunk to keep them out of White hands; then when the Whites fled Russia they took most of the remainder to France, where they were sold for scrap.

So the Soviet Navy in 1926 was skeletal. Apart from small vessels it had only three pre-war battleships and an obsolete cruiser in the Baltic, a cruiser and two destroyers in the Black Sea, and nothing in the North or Pacific. The top Naval Academy graduates of each year, of whom Kuznetsov was one, were permitted to choose where to serve, and most ambitious young officers sought postings to the battleships. Kuznetsov, however, aspired to command a ship as soon as possible, and opted for the Black Sea Fleet, which was completing some ships already under construction in 1917, and adding new destroyers. He was posted to the cruiser *Chervona Ukraina* ('Red Ukraine'), and served in it till 1929, when he returned to Leningrad for further Naval Academy training, supplementing the normal curriculum by learning French and German. In 1933 he returned to the Black Sea as Executive Officer of the cruiser *Krasnyi Kavkaz* ('Red Caucasus'), but before long went back to *Chervona Ukraina* as Captain.

In 1935 his ship was judged best-trained in the navy, and thereafter his rise was meteoric. He was sent to aid the Republican Government in the Spanish Civil War, serving for a year from August 1936 as Naval Attaché in Madrid. Relative to its size the Soviet Navy suffered most from Stalin's assault on the officer corps, with several successive Commanders-in-Chief and all Fleet Commanders arrested and shot. This brought very fast promotion to younger officers; Kuznetsov, recalled from Spain in August 1937, was appointed First Deputy Commander of the Pacific Fleet, and four months later succeeded to command of it, when his chief, Kireyev, was arrested. In February 1939, Stalin appointed him First Deputy Commander-in-Chief of the Navy, and in April promoted him to Commissar for the Navy. He was then two months short of his thirty-seventh birthday, and had been a naval officer for less than thirteen years.

While the navy was being rebuilt almost from scratch from the mid-1920s, there had inevitably been intense professional debate about the kind of navy it should be. A wide range of concepts had been canvassed, from defence of the coastlines to sea denial in adjacent high seas, and hence from a 'mosquito fleet' of small coastal defence ships to a 'high seas' navy with battleships, cruisers and aircraft carriers. Kuznetsov's middle-of-the-road view, that naval strategy must be part of an overall strategy, that the navy's prime wartime rôle was to defend the coastal flanks of the army, that a range of surface ships and submarines would be needed, but that the navy's demands on the economy should not be excessive, apparently convinced Stalin that he would make a tractable head for a navy then being structured and equipped according to Stalin's own aspirations to make the Soviet Union a major naval power over time. But Kuznetsov's headship was to prove stormy, and the Admiral a doughty fighter not only against the Germans but also against Stalin, Khrushchev, the Red Army's leading generals, and the Shipbuilding Commissariat, at the cost to himself of a career twice prematurely terminated.

Despite the intensity of intellectual debate, the Soviet Navy's practical standards were relatively low. In the Baltic, winter freezing of the Gulf of Finland compelled the fleet, based entirely at Kronshtadt and Leningrad until the Baltic states and Finland were coerced into providing bases in 1939–40, to forsake the sea and train on land for about five months in every year, and the Black Sea Fleet did the same until the mid-1930s, even though that sea does not freeze in winter. Kuznetsov could do little to affect Stalin's shipbuilding programme, beyond achieving some improvements in detailed design and armament, but he set out to improve the navy's use of what it already had, by raising standards of training and efficiency. This proved a wise move, because the navy, as 'junior service' (the air force was then regarded as part of the army) enjoyed low priority in resource allocation, especially after Hitler's lightning victories of 1939 and 1940 made a land attack on the Soviet Union his next likely undertaking. Work stopped on half-built battleships and cruisers, as the materials needed to complete them were reallocated to tank and artillery production; only destroyers, smaller ships and submarines continued to be built and the navy's resources in 1941 (3 battleships, 7 cruisers, 59 destroyers and 228 submarines) remained small relative to leading powers in everything except submarines. The submarine force, though the world's largest, was also concentrated mostly in the Baltic to defend the army's seaward flank, and its effectiveness was to prove low for its size.

While Kuznetsov was commanding in the Pacific, border warfare with Japan had broken out around Lake Khasan, southwest of Vladivostok, and he had become uneasily aware that his fleet's main base was vulnerable to air attack. So after becoming head of the navy he devised and tested a system for bringing the fleets and bases to war-readiness at short notice. Alerted by the growing evidence of German war preparations in early June 1941 he authorized ships and shore installations to fire on unidentified aircraft, and earned a severe rebuke from Stalin for so doing. But when the Germans did attack, his precautions proved justified. The Luftwaffe took the Soviet Air Forces by surprise and destroyed over 800 aircraft on the ground on the first day, but its raids on the naval bases, which Kuznetsov had ordered to 'No. 1 Readiness' during the night, did little damage on shore and sank no ships.

However, the Red Army could not defend the naval bases against attack from the landward side, so that most of them soon had to be abandoned. Operations in the Baltic, especially by surface warships, were severely limited by early loss of the recently acquired bases in Lithuania, Latvia, Estonia and Finland, Germany's laying of a minefield across the entrance to the Gulf of Finland – Kuznetsov was later to admit failure to foresee the need for large numbers of minesweepers – and the impossibility of providing enough fuel oil to the fleet after it had fallen back to Kronshtadt, where it was basically marooned until the siege of Leningrad was lifted in early 1944.

During the siege the improvised naval squadron on Lake Ladoga played an important rôle in organizing and protecting the supply route across the lake to Leningrad, the city's only lifeline from September 1941 until January 1943, when a narrow corridor was opened along the lake's south shore and a railway and road built through it. The navy's rôle here has been overshadowed by the better known 'road of life' across the ice, but for more than half the year the lake was not frozen, and supplies reached the city by water. The Baltic Fleet itself was virtually immobilized for lack of fuel. The guns of the Kronshtadt forts and of its two battleships formed part of the city's artillery defences, but most smaller ships and submarines were deactivated, and their crews formed into infantry and artillery units. Similar units were formed from Black Sea and Pacific Fleet sailors, and many of them gained high reputations in land battles. Some of the credit for this should go to Kuznetsov, who in twenty-six months as head of the pre-war navy tightened discipline, improved training standards, promoted competent officers and insisted on the importance of organization and planning. In a hard-drinking profession and society his refusal to touch alcohol when at sea contributed to his reputation as a martinet, but most officers who served under him described him favourably in their memoirs as fair and courteous, at a time when neither quality was excessively apparent among senior army officers.

Evidence of his skill in choosing subordinates is that, in contrast to the Red Army, where large numbers of generals were replaced (and some shot) for incompetence, all the senior officers he had appointed before the war still held their posts at the end of it, except for those who had died or been promoted, a notable record considering the youth and inexperience of both Kuznetsov and his appointees.

The Northern Fleet had an important task in safeguarding the eastern end of the convoy route through which American and British war materials and food were delivered to Murmansk and Archangel, but lacked resources to do much more than supplement the Royal Navy's rôle. After Finland left the war in September 1944, Northern Fleet ships conducted a number of successful though relatively small short-range amphibious operations in the Pechenga area, and supported the army's advance into northern Norway.

Most active of Soviet naval forces was the Black Sea Fleet. The prolonged defence of Odessa in 1941 and of Sevastopol in 1942 would have been impossible without the supplies and reinforcements it brought in, and, especially at Odessa, it successfully evacuated the survivors. Black Sea Fleet operations often hung by a thread: after its main base at Sevastopol had been lost it had to operate from minor ports on the Caucasus coast, the most important of which, Novorossiisk, was itself closely beset by German forces; they were, however, somewhat facilitated by the relative absence of the German Navy, which operated only minor surface craft and a few submarines brought in sections down the Danube and assembled in Romania. The Romanian Navy offered little opposition, and Bulgaria did not take part in Germany's eastern war. However, the German Air Force proved a major foe at sea, until the Soviet Air Forces gained air superiority in mid-1943, after which Black Sea Fleet ships contributed to several amphibious operations during recapture of the Crimea and western coastal areas.

The nature of the Soviet-German war, fought in terrain intersected by Europe's largest rivers, lent particular importance to naval river forces. Ironically, the then Captain Gorshkov, who was to succeed Kuznetsov as head of the navy in 1956, and to give it a global reach far beyond anything conceived by Kuznetsov or Stalin, distinguished himself on rivers, transporting troops and supplies across the Volga to Stalingrad and later performing similar duties on the Danube.

The surface navy under Kuznetsov's leadership performed competently within its limitations of small size, largely obsolete equipment, and total subordination to army priorities, scoring no major victories, but avoiding major disasters. Kuznetsov claimed on his navy's behalf that no German amphibious landings took place behind Soviet lines, but this is an exaggeration, as a number of such landings occurred, especially on islands in the Baltic in 1941. It is true that Germany attempted no major amphibious operations on the Eastern Front, but that omission resulted more from lack of resources and lack of need than from the activities of the Soviet Navy. In 1941 German and Finnish armies captured the entire Baltic coast apart from Leningrad in less than three months, and in the south all except the Caucasus coast and the besieged base at Sevastopol were in German or Romanian hands within six months of the invasion. In the north the German failure to capture Murmansk owed much to a stubborn Soviet land defence but at least as much to Finnish restraint. Finland had entered the war to regain the territories that Stalin took from it in 1940, and once it had done so it gave no support to German efforts to capture Leningrad, seize Murmansk, or cut the vital rail links along which Allied supplies passed from Murmansk and Archangel to the Russian heartland; so survival of the Northern Fleet's base probably owed as much to Marshal Mannerheim as to Admiral Kuznetsov.

The relative ineffectiveness of the submarine fleet can be explained in part by the interruptions in pre-war training enforced by the annual freezing of the Gulf of Finland, and by inability to operate caused by lack of fuel while bottled up in besieged Kronshtadt. Nevertheless, performance remained poor even after the siege was lifted, and did not improve remarkably after advances on land made it possible for submarines to operate in the southern Baltic, which does not freeze. The Baltic was a difficult sea in which to operate submarines, because its shallowness facilitated detection, hindered evasion, and made it easy to lay minefields. Nevertheless the submarine force does not seem to have justified the faith Kuznetsov placed in it at the time and continued to affirm long after his retirement. A Northern Fleet submarine claimed a torpedo hit on the German battleship *Tirpitz* off Norway, but German records make no mention of any such incident. Baltic Fleet submarine S-13 was responsible for the largest number of deaths in a single sinking, when in 1945 it torpedoed the German liner *Wilhelm Gustlow*, drowning about 6,000 people, mostly civilian refugees.

In January 1945 Stalin entrusted Kuznetsov with responsibility for some of the arrangements of the Yalta Conference with Roosevelt and Churchill. At that time the Western Allies were eager to secure Soviet participation in the war against Japan, and Kuznetsov took the opportunity to present a list of ships which the run-down Pacific Fleet would need. His shopping list included no big ships – the Baltic Fleet's battleships and cruisers had proved unusable in 1944 because of the danger from German mines, and the battleship *Royal Sovereign*, which the British donated to the Northern Fleet in 1944, was never taken to sea because protecting it against air and submarine attack would have consumed too much of the fleet's limited strength. The US Navy had already sunk most of Japan's big ships, and those that remained could not move far for lack of fuel, so the Soviet Pacific Fleet would not have to fight major naval battles. In the circumstances what Kuznetsov wanted was a large number of small ships, capable of taking assault forces right into enemy harbours to overpower the small scattered Japanese garrisons in the Kurile Islands and southern Sakhalin, which Stalin had named as his price for joining the war against Japan.

Kuznetsov got what he wanted. Under Lend-Lease the United States provided the Pacific Fleet with over 250 ships – frigates, minesweepers, submarine-hunters, torpedo boats and landing craft – and these gave the Soviet Navy the capacity to ferry troops of Second Far Eastern Front to all their objectives. Japan was already on the verge of surrender, so the operations, which Kuznetsov supervised personally, involved considerable feats of logistical organization, but no fighting at sea and not very much on land.

So at very small cost Kuznetsov's navy enabled Stalin to more than reverse the defeat of 1905, not only regaining south Sakhalin, which it had then ceded to a victorious Japan, but the Kurile Islands, which it had exchanged for Sakhalin in 1875, and seizing in addition the islands of Kunashiri, Etorofu and Shikotan, and the Habomai islets which had never been part of the Russian Empire.

This was undoubtedly the peak of Kuznetsov's career, but his first downfall lay less than a year ahead. His bluntness in defending naval interests had gained him enemies among both the army and political leaders. Although he generally accepted Stalin's plan for post-war development of the navy, his opposition to Stalin's predilection for heavy cruisers had led the dictator to threaten him with investigation by the NKVD, and he had earned Khrushchev's enmity by telling him in Stalin's presence to stop commenting on naval matters of which he knew nothing. In 1946 Stalin had him and three other Admirals arrested on trumped-up charges of giving secret plans of a parachutable torpedo and maps of Soviet harbours to the British. Expert testimony that the materials were not secret (the maps were simply Russian transcriptions of British Admiralty charts) was withheld from the court. His subordinates received long prison sentences, while Kuznetsov was dismissed and demoted by three ranks to Rear-Admiral. All four were rehabilitated after Stalin's death (though one had died in prison), and Kuznetsov was reinstated in both rank and office. However, he soon fell foul of Khrushchev again, by opposing his plans to make drastic cuts in naval building programmes, so in February 1956 he was dismissed and demoted a second time, this time to Vice-Admiral, and permanently retired at only fifty-one years of age. One of the ironies which punctuated his career was that his re-placement, Gorshkov, though appointed as an 'economizer', extracted funds from Khrushchev's successors over two decades for far more ambitious and costly naval programmes than Kuznetsov had ever contemplated.

The vicissitudes of Kuznetsov's career saw him hold Vice-Admiral's rank three times and all other Admirals' ranks twice. In an active retirement he wrote his memoirs (only now being republished unexpurgated), learned English, and translated several standard naval works from that language into Russian. He died in 1974.

The final irony surrounding him was that following his posthumous rehabilitation in 1988, the navy named its newest and biggest ship, its first full-size aircraft carrier, *Admiral of the Fleet of the Soviet Union Kuznetsov*. Just as it entered service at the end of 1991, the Soviet Union fell apart and his beloved Black Sea Fleet became a bone of contention between Ukraine and Russia, with, as in 1942, its main base at Sevastopol under siege (this time economic blockade), and Novorossiisk its only reliable port.

BIBLIOGRAPHY

Golovko, A. G., *With the Fleet*, Progress, Moscow, 1988.
Kuznetsov, N. G., *Na kanune*, 3rd edn, Voenizdat, Moscow, 1989: see particularly chapter 'About the Author' by the current head of the navy, Fleet Admiral Chernavin.
Kuznetsov, N. G., *Kursom k pobede*, 3rd edn, Voenizdat, Moscow, 1989.
Meretskov, K. A., *Serving the People*, Progress, Moscow, 1971.
Voenno-istoricheskii Zhurnal, no. 11, 1992.
Zhukov, G. K., *Vospominaniya i razmyshleniya*, 10th edn, Novosti, Moscow, 1992; in English, *The Memoirs of Marshal Zhukov*, Jonathan Cape, London, 1971.

Rodion Yakovlevich

MALINOVSKY

JOHN ERICKSON

In the tense days of the Cold War the Soviet Defence Minister accompanying Premier Khrushchev on an official visit to France suggested a drive to the First World War battlefields. There, much to Khrushchev's surprise, he proved to be no stranger. Indeed, the more elderly inhabitants recognized this visitor, one who had arrived in France in 1916 with the Russian Expeditionary Corps along with his regiment parading a bear as its mascot, one who with other Russian soldiers took themselves off to the local wartime *estaminet* to intrigue and beguile the French mesdemoiselles. That Defence Minister, that soldier, was Rodion Yakovlevich Malinovsky, born in Odessa on 23 November 1898 in a poor rural family, never knowing his father, badly disposed towards his mother and brought up by an aunt, working as a farm labourer and errand boy for a haberdashery after leaving the village school. With the outbreak of war in 1914 he ran away to join the army, serving as a private in the trenches, was wounded, and awarded the St George Cross (4th Class) for bravery and devotion to duty. Shipped as a machine-gunner with the Russian Expeditionary Corps to France, he was wounded again and hospitalized. For his service in heavy fighting he was decorated with the Croix de Guerre. But in 1917 war-weariness convulsed the French Army, already in mutinous mood, and Russian troops on the Western Front, infected with the fever of revolution at home, raised their own shouts of 'Down with the war' and proceeded to elect a soldiers' committee as an expression of solidarity with their compatriots at home. The punishment for defiance and mutiny was transportation to North Africa, but Malinovsky, after a variety of adventures, managed to make his way home to Russia via Vladivostok. Together with three of his fellow-soldiers he joined the Red ranks in the autumn of 1919, fighting as a machine-gunner with 240th Tver Regiment attached to the 27th Rifle Division, taking part in the campaign in Siberia to destroy Admiral Kolchak's White forces, and in the capture of Omsk and Novo-Nikolayevsk.

In December 1920 Malinovsky passed out from the training school for junior commanders as a platoon commander, subsequently taking over a machine-gun detachment, and quickly progressing through promotions to command a battalion with the 246th Rifle Regiment. Received into the Party in 1926, the way was clear for his selection to the Frunze Military Academy, which he entered as a student in 1927 and from which he graduated in 1930 to take up a posting as Chief of Staff to the 67th Cavalry Regiment of the 10th Cavalry Division. His career proceeded through a series of staff appointments in North Caucasus and Belorussian Military Districts, culminating in his assignment as Chief of Staff of the 3rd Cavalry Corps commanded by Timoshenko, but 'peacetime soldiering' came to a sudden end in the summer of 1936 with the onset of the Spanish Civil War. Like many Red Army officers Malinovsky volunteered for service with the Republican forces in Spain. With his 'request' approved by the Defence Commissar, he set off on the long winding trail to Spain, taking the train to Helsinki, on to Turku, steamer to Stockholm, another train to Malmö, aeroplane to Rotterdam, thence to Paris and the French frontier with Spain, on to Barcelona and finally Valencia. Learning to ask for '*cafe con leche*' was his first introduction to the Spanish language.

Under his *nom de guerre* of 'Colonel Malino', Malinovsky joined that considerable body of Soviet 'volunteers', notable among them Meretskov, Voronov, Pavlov, Kulik, Smushkevich, Kopets, Berzin and Kuznetsov (from the navy). Fighting with the International Brigades and the Republican forces, Malinovsky played a prominent part in the defence of Madrid but his third summons to return to the Soviet Union carried an ominous message – unless he complied, he would be considered a 'defector', a single, sinister word which sent a shiver down his spine. That recall to Moscow had fatal consequences for senior Soviet advisers other than Malinovsky: Yan Berzin fell victim to the NKVD, as did Stashevsky, Stalin's chief commissar in Spain. Both had reported critically on NKVD high-handedness, interference and espionage fatally compromising Soviet authority. Miraculously Malinovsky escaped the main purge, returning to the Soviet Union in May 1938 to be decorated with the Order of Lenin and the Order of the Red Banner, followed in 1939 by an appointment as a senior lecturer in the faculty of staff duties and staff functions in the Frunze Military Academy.

In the spring of 1941, as German forces continued their build-up on the Soviet frontier, the newly elevated Major-General Malinovsky was assigned to a field command, taking over the freshly raised 48th Rifle Corps in Odessa Military District. It was with 48 Corps that Malinovsky went to war when the German *Blitzkrieg* opened, fighting a defensive battle on the frontier along the line of the river Prut and breaking through German encirclement. In late August German forces closed on Dnepropetrovsk and forced the Dnieper, though their advance was temporarily halted by the Soviet 6th Army (until recently the Southern Front's Reserve Army) fighting under its new commander, Malinovsky, moving up from his corps command. In the middle of December 1941 Timoshenko with the Southwestern Theatre Command prepared a counter-blow at the junction of the Southwestern and Southern Fronts, committing 6th and 12th Armies operating jointly under Malinovsky's command and directly subordinated to Timoshenko himself. This attack pushed the Germans back from the northern Donets as far as the River Bakhmut, recovering much of the territory lost in November. Malinovsky, now a Lieutenant-General, advanced from Army to Front Commander, succeeding Cherevichenko in command of the Southern Front on the latter's transfer to the Bryansk Front.

With the Soviet winter offensive now unrolling, Malinovsky received orders to commit three armies in an attack aimed at Pavlograd and seize crossings over the Dnieper at Dnepropetrovsk and Zaporozhye. The ambitious Soviet offensive finally drew to a halt in the late spring, the Soviet armies exhausted and over-extended. Vastly over-estimating Soviet capabilities, Timoshenko decided on his ill-fated 'Kharkov offensive', launched in May 1942, which brought disaster to his own Front and ruin upon the forces commanded by Malinovsky. The massive German breakthrough to the southeast, spearheaded by Ruoff's XVII Army and Kleist's I Panzer Army, produced near-rout at Rostov for which Malinovsky incurred some of the blame and provoked Stalin's dangerous suspicions. According to Khrushchev, Malinovsky's service in France in 1916–17 fuelled Stalin's doubts, but it was the suicide of Larin, one of Malinovsky's close associates, after Stalingrad that intensified them. As disaster piled on disaster, Khrushchev (according to his own testimony) was charged by Stalin with 'keeping an eye' on this fellow Malinovsky.

In early August 1942 German Army Group 'A' was astride the Don, deep into the Kuban, racing for the northern Caucasus and striking towards the oilfields. Marshal Budenny had already received orders to combine the Southern and North Caucasus Fronts and to split his forces, with Malinovsky taking over the 'Don operational group' covering Stavropol. The defence of the north Caucasus saw Lavrenti Beria, head of the NKVD, move in with the murderous cohorts of his own private army, which was sufficient to bring protests from Malinovsky, at which Beria threatened to arrest him. If Malinovsky escaped Beria's vengeance, the national minorities – the Chechens, Ingushes, Crimean Tartars, Karachai, Balkyrs, Kalmyks and Volga Germans – did not, paying a terrible price in mass murder and deportation. At the end of August Malinovsky was moved to the Stalingrad Front to take command of 66th Army, one of three drawn from Stavka's reserve and committed in the heavy fighting in a desperate bid to halt the German drive on the city. For a brief period from October to November, he was moved again, this time to the Voronezh Front as Deputy Commander, only to return to Stalingrad in December 1942 to command 2nd Guards Army, a powerful striking force, one of the best-equipped and most formidable in the Red Army, with its five rifle corps and a mechanized corps.

The stunning Soviet counter-offensive which opened on 19 November 1942 had trapped the German VI Army inside Stalingrad. But where should 2nd Guards Army strike – against the Germans sealed in the city or against von Manstein bringing relief from outside with his 'de-blockading' force to the besieged German army? Beside himself with rage and desperate to 'finish off VI Army', Stalin grudgingly consented to moving 2nd Guards Army to hold off von Manstein. After forced marches across the steppe in fierce blizzards, Malinovsky's men prepared for action straight off the march behind the river Myshkova, manning the last barrier facing Manstein's relief force. Together with 5th Shock Army and 51st Army, Malinovsky's 2nd Guards held off von Manstein and doomed von Paulus's VI Army.

In February 1943 Malinovsky resumed command of the Southern Front and a month later took over the Southwestern Front (re-designated the 3rd Ukrainian Front in October). Following the defeat of the massive German offensive in the Kursk salient and the onset of the Soviet counter-offensive, Malinovsky's Southwestern Front received orders to liberate the Donbass, followed in turn by an operation with the 3rd Ukrainian Front designed to destroy the German bridgehead at Zaporozhye. Of key importance in the German defensive system, the town fell in a surprise night attack. In the vast operations to destroy the entire German southern wing, Malinovsky's 3rd Ukrainian Front and Tolbukhin's 4th Ukrainian Front prepared concentric attacks to smash German forces in the Nikopol–Krivoi Rog area, clearing the way for a joint advance on Nikolayev and Odessa. The first attempt in October 1943 to storm both Nikopol and Krivoi Rog failed, but in February 1944 Malinovsky finally cracked the tough nut of Krivoi Rog, taking the town on the 22nd, that particular day specified by Stalin in a special signal.

Throughout 1944 the entire Soviet southern wing swept onwards at a furious pace. In the spring Malinovsky's 3rd Ukrainian Front cleared Odessa, his home town, and advanced to the southern river Bug. While preparations were afoot to the north for the giant Soviet offensive to destroy the German Army Group Centre in Belorussia, in the south Malinovsky was given command of the 2nd Ukrainian Front as plans were laid in deepest secrecy for the Jassy-Kishinev operation, designed to unhinge the entire German southeastern flank, burst into Romania, drive into Hungary and isolate Bulgaria. On 20 August 1944 Malinovsky's offensive opened, breaking through the tactical defence on the first day and destroying eleven Romanian and four German divisions within three days. Two days later the entire German Army Group 'Southern Ukraine' was encircled and the remaining Romanian divisions disabled. The political effects were explosive: Romania abandoned Germany, Bulgaria ceded for peace, the route to Hungary, Yugoslavia and eastern Czechoslovakia lay wide open.

Appointed a Marshal of the Soviet Union following this major strategic success, Malinovsky advanced in the early autumn into eastern Hungary, inflicting heavy losses on Army Group South, clearing German forces from Transylvania and together with the 3rd Ukrainian Front closing on Budapest. Stalin demanded an immediate attack on Budapest: 'This has to be done no matter what it costs you.' Malinovsky asked for a five-day delay to bring up a mechanized corps – 'We cannot seize Budapest off the march.' Stalin responded: 'You are arguing to no purpose.' The first attack failed. More than three months of savage fighting followed to reduce the Hungarian capital, the twin cities of Buda and Pest suffering a horrible fate in this dreadful siege. Henceforth Stalin shunned any mention of Budapest. Climbing over these blood-soaked ruins Malinovsky thrust on westwards, operating once more in conjunction with the 3rd Ukrainian Front to drive into eastern Austria and capture Vienna on 13 April 1945.

After the surrender of Germany Malinovsky moved swiftly to the Far East to take part as commander of the Transbaikal Front in the destruction of the Japanese Kwantung Army. In ten days of this Soviet *Blitzkrieg* in the Far East Malinovsky's armies crossed desert, traversed the mountains of the Khingan range and advanced some 400 miles, breaking out to the Yellow Sea and taking that great prize, lost to Russia in 1905, Port Arthur. For the next ten years Malinovsky remained in the Far East, from 1945 to 1947 as commander of Transbaikal–Amur Military District, and as Far Eastern theatre Commander-in-Chief from 1947 to 1953, a key post during the Korean War, prompting Khrushchev to suggest to Stalin at a time of severe North Korean reverses that Malinovsky should be sent – incognito, shades of 'Colonel Malino' – to help Kim Il-sung. Stalin angrily turned this down. Malinovsky soldiered on as commander of Far Eastern Military District until March 1956 when, at Khrushchev's behest, he was recalled to Moscow as Deputy Defence Minister, appointed Commander-in-Chief of the Soviet Ground Forces, and elected a full member of the Central Committee.

Then came the drama of the 'Zhukov affair', the dismissal of Marshal Zhukov as Defence Minister in October 1957, accompanied by charges of 'Bonapartism', 'policy adventurism' and, most damning of all, the pursuit of a 'personality cult'. Many wartime commanders had suffered at first hand from Zhukov's 'personal crudeness', but more serious was the accusation that Zhukov had undermined Party political organs and political work in the Soviet Armed Forces. On 26 October 1957 TASS announced the dismissal of Zhukov and the appointment of Malinovsky as his successor. Malinovsky took office at a time of major changes, even a major upheaval in the Soviet military, Zhukov's removal notwithstanding. The situation became increasingly complex as Khrushchev pursued his own ideas about what direction Soviet strategy should take in the nuclear-missile age, simultaneously proposing a radical programme to refashion Soviet military doctrine and reshape the entire Soviet force structure. In the beginning Malinovsky played a rôle akin to that of referee in what became an increasingly acrimonious debate, attempting to support Khrushchev's policies at large, but also taking into account the reservations, voiced and unvoiced, of the more conservative elements within the Soviet High Command.

The dismissal of Zhukov did not end the debate over the rôle of political organs in the armed forces. In 1958 the commanders began to fight back, attacking the excesses and negative influence of the political organs. Together with Zakharov and Grechko, Malinovsky expressed public concern at the negative effect of excessive political control and indoctrination on discipline and combat-readiness, warning over-zealous political officers not to interfere in operational affairs. The result was a compromise between political control and military professionalism, but stormier days attended Khrushchev's assault on Soviet strategic doctrine and Soviet force structure. In October 1961 Malinovsky's own military report to the XXII Party Congress represented a major step in the military debate, setting out in the framework of a 'new Soviet military doctrine' several of the ideas advanced by Khrushchev himself in his January 1960 speech, pointing to the changed nature of warfare and emphasizing the primacy of strategic missile forces. But, unlike Khrushchev, Malinovsky continued to stress the continuing importance of multi-million mass armies, essential to attain victory in any war. In addition, these forces would be required in a more protracted war which the Soviet Union might have to wage, whatever Khrushchev's notion that the initial phase of any future war with its nuclear exchanges would be decisive (and short), an assumption which clearly destroyed the rationale for large conventional forces.

Malinovsky continued his balancing act between those who espoused the radical Khrushchev line and the more conservative elements supporting a rôle for conventional forces in any future war. To those who hinted at some kind of militia establishment, he vigorously asserted the importance of a regular army and a standing army capable of mastering modern military technology. In May 1962 Malinovsky set out his position (and that of his supporters) in two major articles, the first of which dealt with Party-political problems in the armed forces and the second with strategic questions. While hewing to the 'Party line', he insisted on the need to relate political indoctrination (which should be both curtailed and improved) to practical military requirements. His second article on strategic doctrine, though recognizing change in the nature of warfare, reiterated the need for mass armies and the continued relevance of the combined-arms approach. The appearance in the summer of 1962 of the major work *Voennaya strategiya* ('Military Strategy'), edited by Marshal Sokolovsky, added further fuel to the fire. Its implicit support of Malinovsky's viewpoint signally failed to satisfy either the radicals or the conservatives. As the relationship between the political and military officers took a turn for the worse, a closed conference met to discuss these differences, though the very existence of the meeting was not disclosed until 25 October, at the height of the Cuban Missile Crisis. Malinovsky duly warned NATO about the dangerous game it was playing, at the same time insisting on the highest level of military readiness, as well as criticizing both military 'die-hards' and technologically illiterate political officers for obstructing progress.

In the wake of the Cuban missile crisis a curious pamphlet appeared bearing Malinovsky's name, but it was enough of a hotch-potch of contradictory views to give rise to suspicions about its actual authorship. While it adopts a very accommodating attitude to political control of the military, it also severely criticizes Party intrusion into matters of doctrine at the expense of the professional military and castigates political leaders for their cavalier attitude to military science. The failure of the dangerous gamble over the Cuban missiles did nothing to improve relations between the Party and the military, with the latter, including Malinovsky himself, using the anniversary of the battle of Stalingrad to voice their dissent. The Ground Forces commanders omitted Khrushchev's name entirely, thus denying him any part in the victory at Stalingrad, stressing rather the rôle of military commanders, among them Malinovsky, in the eventual triumph. Malinovsky produced his own surprise by debunking any idea that Khrushchev played a key rôle in planning the Stalingrad counter-offensive and ostentatiously including Zhukov among those who planned and executed the operation.

This rather splenetic article in February 1963 gave way in April 1964 to a more generous appreciation of Khrushchev's contribution on the occasion of the Soviet leader's 70th birthday, though Malinovsky was far from fulsome in his praise. But time was running out for Khrushchev. The Khrushchev era ended suddenly on 16 October 1964 with the public announcements of his resignation. Evidently Malinovsky, who had saluted Khrushchev as 'Supreme Commander-in-Chief' as late as 17 April, did nothing either to assist or prevent the removal of Khrushchev, though he was reportedly invited to take part in the Presidium debates during the political crisis. He may well have given his tacit assent or some assurance of neutrality, either of which would have suited those plotting Khrushchev's downfall. But time was also running out for Marshal Malinovsky, who survived for a while in the new-style 'collective leadership' of the Brezhnev–Kosygin régime. His life ended on 31 March 1967, bringing to a close the remarkable career of this burly fighting soldier, one who rose from humble private in the tsarist army to become a distinguished Marshal of the Soviet Union.

BIBLIOGRAPHY

Bluth, Christoph, *Soviet Strategic Arms Policy before SALT*, Cambridge University Press, Cambridge, 1992.

Erickson, John, *The Road to Stalingrad: Stalin's War with Germany*, vol. I, Weidenfeld & Nicolson, London, 1975.

Garthoff, Raymond L., *Soviet Strategy in the Nuclear Age*, Praeger, New York, 1962.

Khrushchev, N. S., *Khrushchev Remembers*, trans. Strobe Talbot, André Deutsch, London, 1971.

Kolkowicz, Roman, *The Soviet Military and the Communist Party*, Princeton University Press, Princeton, 1967.

Konev, I. S. (ed.), *Za osvobozhdenie Chekhoslovakii*, Voenizdat, Moscow, 1965.

Malinovskii, R. Ya. 'V boyakh za osvobozhdenie Sovetskoi Ukrainy', *V bol'shom nastuplenii*, Moscow, Voenizdat, 1964, pp. 22–38.

Malinovskii, R. Ya. (ed.), *Yassko-Kishinevskie Kanny*, Nauka, Moscow, 1964.

Malinovskii R. Ya., 'Gnevnye vikhri Ispanii', *Pod znamenem ispanskoi respubliki 1936–1938*, Nauka, Moscow, 1965.

Malinovskii, R. Ya. (ed.), *Budapesht Vena Praga*, Nauka, Moscow, 1965.

Malinovskii, R. Ya., *Soldaty Rossii*, Voenizdat, Moscow, 1969.

Seaton, Albert, *The Russo-German War 1941–45*, Arthur Barker, London, 1971.

Tatu, Michel, *Power in the Kremlin*, Collins, London, 1969.

Voenno-istoricheskii Zhurnal, no. 4, 1990, for Malinovsky's autobiography in two parts, the first dated 28 December 1938, the second 4 March 1948.

Kirill Afanasievich
MERETSKOV

GEOFFREY JUKES

Meretskov's war was mostly spent on the northern part of the front. He took no part in the Red Army's great sweep into Eastern and Central Europe and attracted less attention than those who did, but Stalin valued his rôle in defending and relieving Leningrad, and forcing Finland out of the war, highly enough to promote him to Marshal.

Like most of the Red Army's leading generals, Kirill Afanasievich Meretskov, born in 1897 in a village not far from Moscow, claimed to be of poor peasant origin, but his few references to his childhood point to relative rather than absolute poverty. In 1912 he moved to Moscow, where he trained as a fitter, became involved with the revolutionary movement, and avoided conscription by moving frequently. He joined the Communist Party on 1 May 1917, and despite his total lack of military experience was appointed Head of the Military Section of his local Soviet after the October Revolution. Appointment as Chief of Staff of a Red Guards unit followed, the first of ten staff posts he would hold during his career. In the Civil War he was wounded twice, decided to make the army his career, and was a member of the first class of Red Army officers produced by the newly established General Staff (later Frunze Military) Academy. His studies there were twice interrupted by postings to the front, against the Whites in 1919 and the Poles in 1920, including a posting to the First Cavalry Army, where he first met Stalin and the future Marshals Voroshilov, Budenny and Timoshenko. By January 1922 he was already a Brigadier and Chief of Staff of a Cavalry Corps in Belorussian Military District. During the next ten years he held a wide variety of posts in the Chief Personnel Directorate, North Caucasus and Moscow Military Districts, where he was influenced by the future Marshal Shaposhnikov, and in April 1932 returned, this time as Chief of Staff, to

Belorussian Military District. This was then a 'nursery' for outstanding officers, and his colleagues included eight other future Marshals. In 1935 he went to the Far East as Chief of Staff of Special Red Banner Army, but after less than a year was sent abroad, first to Czechoslovakia as chief Soviet observer to army manoeuvres, then to Spain as an adviser to the Republican government, working with more officers destined to rise to the top, including future Marshals Malinovsky and Voronov, and Admiral Kuznetsov, and being decorated for the defence of Madrid and the Battle of Guadalajara. After ten months in Spain he became a Deputy Chief of General Staff under Shaposhnikov, and in 1938 his experience was broadened further by command of a Military District, first on the Volga and very shortly thereafter at Leningrad.

To this point Meretskov's career had run smoothly; he rose high when still very young, met and impressed everyone, from Stalin downward, and acquired a much broader than average range of professional experience in political, staff and command posts in widely separated parts of the country and abroad. But harder trials lay ahead; less than a year after arriving in Leningrad he would plan and lead the attack on Finland, and incur massive losses in repeated futile attacks on the Mannerheim Line. He later claimed in his own defence that intelligence provided by Moscow had underestimated the strength of the Mannerheim Line, but Stalin downgraded him to command of an Army and put Timoshenko in charge over him. His troops eventually breached the Mannerheim Line, and the war ended on 13 March 1940, but the Red Army's poor performance strengthened Hitler's belief that it could be defeated quickly, and the harsh terms imposed on Finland assured Germany of Finnish help in its invasion. Stalin had feared that if the war lasted till the spring thaw, the Finns would flood the Soviet positions, France and Sweden would come to their aid, and the Soviet Union find itself at war with a coalition, so his award to Meretskov of the highest Soviet decoration, Hero of the Soviet Union, was more out of relief that he had averted that possibility than of admiration at his handling of the campaign.

Meretskov was transferred back to staff duties as a Deputy Defence Commissar under Timoshenko, in charge of combat training and military academies. In autumn he replaced Shaposhnikov as Chief of the General Staff, but less than five months later was summarily dismissed from the post, after the summing-up session, attended by Stalin, of a major command and staff exercise in January 1941. Meretskov claimed he was dismissed because Timoshenko and some others took personal offence at criticism in his report; other participants suggested that he angered Stalin by a poor presentation. However, Zakharov, then a junior participant but later himself Chief of General Staff, was probably nearer the mark in linking the dismissal to a professional disagreement over a General Staff study, begun under Shaposhnikov but completed and presented by Meretskov, which argued that the main thrust in the expected German invasion would be through Belorussia and the Baltic states towards Leningrad and Moscow. Stalin, Timoshenko and Zhukov (past and current commanders in Kiev) believed it would be aimed at Kiev and Ukraine's mineral and agricultural wealth, whereas Meretskov's background in Belorussia and Leningrad prompted him to argue for the northern thrust. A few months later Hitler's vacillations post-invasion would show how finely balanced the arguments were, but in January the 'southerners' prevailed. Meretskov was dismissed but not disgraced; he resumed his former post in charge of training, and a plan he had submitted before his dismissal, to re-establish large armour and motorized infantry Mechanized Corps similar to German Panzer Groups, was approved. There was not time to equip them fully or adequately before the invasion, but from 1942 onwards, provided with the new KV heavy and T-34 medium tanks and adequate numbers of trucks (largely US-supplied), they would play crucial rôles in every major battle.

On 21 June 1941 Timoshenko sent Meretskov to Leningrad as High Command representative. War broke out while he was en route, and he was recalled to Moscow on 23 June, first to be appointed a permanent adviser to Stavka (GHQ), but then to be arrested, after his friend General D. G. Pavlov (Commander of Western Special Military District in Belorussia, shot with his two principal subordinates as scapegoats for the early disasters), named him under torture as a member of a fictitious anti-Soviet conspiracy.

He was cleared by September, and Stalin sent him back to Leningrad as a Stavka representative responsible for the Northwestern Direction or Axis, which stretched from the Baltic states to the Arctic coast. His association with that area was to last till the war in Europe ended. On 12 December 1941 a new Army Group, the Volkhov Front, with four Armies (2nd Shock, 4th, 52nd and 59th) was established under his command, to cover the area southeast of Leningrad and if possible lift the siege of the city, which since September had been accessible only across Lake Ladoga. During December he made two attempts to restore control of the Moscow–Leningrad road and railway, but neither succeeded. For this Meretskov blamed broken promises of reinforcements and supplies, but Stavka blamed Meretskov. His neighbour at the Leningrad Front, General Khozin, claimed that he could lift the siege if given command of the Volkhov Front as well, so on 23 April 1942 it was absorbed into the Leningrad Front, and Meretskov downgraded to command 33rd Army, which was being reformed after almost total annihilation in encirclement west of Moscow.

However, Khozin not only failed to lift the siege, but allowed 2nd Shock Army to become encircled, so he was dismissed. On 8 July Stalin sent for Meretskov, admitted error, re-established Volkhov Front with him in command, and asked him to try to rescue 2nd Shock Army. He managed to open a narrow corridor through which its remnants escaped, though its commander, General A. A. Vlasov, was captured (he later headed a German-sponsored Russian Liberation Army, and was executed in 1946).

Attention then turned to lifting the siege. Only the 10 miles of the Shlisselburg–Sinyavino salient separated the Volkhov and Leningrad Fronts, but it comprised mostly swamps and peat-bog workings. Virtually the only dry land was the Sinyavino 'Heights', and these modest hillocks, mostly less than 50 feet high, were to see more deaths to the acre than any comparable area of the Eastern Front. The infantry attacked on 27 August, and by evening on the next day were closing on Sinyavino. But each successive day they gained less ground, and after 4 September none at all, though the operation continued till 6 October.

After this failure it was decided to wait until the swamps froze, and Meretskov went to Leningrad to discuss possibilities with Khozin's successor, General (later Marshal) Govorov. Given the difficulties in supplying the city via Lake Ladoga, Govorov could promise only a short-distance attack, so the Volkhov Front would clearly have to cover most of the distance itself. It could expect few reinforcements or supplies, as Stavka required the lion's share of them for the planned counter-offensive at Stalingrad. However, once the Stalingrad offensive was under way, Zhukov turned his attention to Leningrad, and the relief plan was largely his.

It was decided to attack along the southern shore of Lake Ladoga, where the gap between the two Fronts, from Shlisselburg to Lipki, was only about 7.5 miles and the open flank was relatively safe as Germany had no ships on the lake. The plan was approved on 17 November, but the demands of the Stalingrad offensive, launched two days later, delayed its launching until 12 January 1943. A narrow corridor was opened in six days, and an impressive feat of mid-winter construction saw a railway built through it in two weeks. This, an earth road alongside it, and an oil pipeline and electrical power cable laid on the bed of the lake, made it much easier to sustain Leningrad, though constant repair was necessary, as it proved impossible to drive the Germans back out of artillery range.

Meretskov's hopes that the German surrender at Stalingrad would free resources for him were dashed first by von Manstein's counter-offensive in February 1943, and then by the almost immediate start of preparations for the immense battle of the Kursk salient. This began on 5 July, and Meretskov was ordered to mount an offensive at Mga, synchronized with the major counter-offensive north and south of Kursk. His attack opened on 22 July and ended a month later, and prevented the Germans moving troops to the south, but Meretskov later lamented that he could have achieved more if he had known in August what prisoners told him in September, that Army Group North had committed its last reserves.

The comprehensive though costly Soviet victory at Kursk tilted the strategic balance irrevocably towards the Red Army, which began to plan sweeping advances towards the Baltic, Central Europe and the Balkans. Meretskov now prepared to play his part by finally lifting the siege of Leningrad and advancing to the Gulf of Finland. He began planning this in meticulous detail in September 1943, but maintained very tight security; for example, he told the Commander of 59th Army only on 13 January 1944 that during the next night his troops were to march several dozen kilometres over the ice of Lake Ilmen (in a snowstorm, as it happened) to attack Novgorod. The offensive went well, the siege of Leningrad ended on 19 January 1944, and Novgorod was taken on the next day. By mid-February Soviet forces were on the borders of Belorussia and Meretskov, who knew it well from his pre-war service, asked to be transferred there. But when Stalin summoned him on 15 February it was to send him in the opposite direction. He argued Meretskov's objections down by pointing out that he knew the north well, had more experience than any other Soviet general in attacking through swamps and forests, and in fighting the Finns, so was the obvious man to command the Karelia Front, which extended from the north shore of Lake Ladoga to the Arctic coast west of Murmansk. His task would be to expel the Finns from eastern Karelia during summer and autumn, then remove the Germans from the Pechenga area on the north coast.

But the military tasks were by no means all Meretskov had to consider. The Karelian Front had been quiescent since late 1941 mainly because Finland, unlike Germany, was fighting a war with the limited aim of recovering the territory Stalin had seized from it in 1940. The Finnish Commander-in-Chief, Marshal Mannerheim, a former tsarist general, was well aware of the perils of overprovoking Finland's giant neighbour. In 1939 he had recommended accepting Stalin's initial proposals for frontier readjustment, which would have given Finland twice as much territory north of Lake Ladoga as it ceded in the Karelian isthmus, and had fought a masterly campaign in the Winter War only after his recommendation was rejected. So in 1941 Finnish forces mostly halted at the first easily defensible position beyond their 1939 frontier; they had not collaborated in the siege of Leningrad, made any serious attempts to cut the railway along which Allied supplies passed to the Soviet heartland from Murmansk and Archangel, nor contributed significantly to German efforts to seize the Soviet Northern Fleet's main base at Murmansk. The Red Army, heavily committed in the total war against the Germans further south, had every incentive to keep the sector quiet until 1944, though post-war Soviet-period writings would depict Finland as completely dedicated to the Soviet Union's destruction, and thwarted only by the heroism of the Red Army. Meretskov was no exception, but his memoirs cite a number of factors which showed his and Stalin's awareness of Finland's 'special' position.

Specifically, he knew that the Western Allies classed Finland differently from Germany, that post-war relations with Scandinavia would depend greatly on how the Scandinavians judged Soviet treatment of Finland, and that he must distinguish between government and people.

Realizing that in Germany it had backed a loser, the Finnish government had already asked Soviet terms for an armistice. Stalin's appointment of Meretskov was another move in high politics. Finland would interpret appointment of the general who had broken the Mannerheim Line in 1940 and had just lifted the siege of Leningrad as presaging a large-scale assault, especially as Meretskov's entire headquarters moved with him, and be prompted to accept a dictated armistice as the lesser evil. Meretskov was to pay special attention to the German forces in the north of the country, so that Finland could not argue the damage they might do as a pretext for refusing an armistice or dragging out negotiations.

The new team began work in late February. Its line, longest of any Soviet Front, ran for more than 625 miles, from coastal cliffs and Arctic tundra to the rivers, lakes, forests and swamps of Karelia. It was mostly unpopulated, and four of the Front's five armies (from north to south 14th, 19th, 26th and 32nd) basically defended the very few roads leading to the main centres of Murmansk, Kandalaksha, Ukhta and Medvezhiegorsk, while the fifth (7th Army) defended the line of the River Svir. Meretskov decided to move first against the German XX Lapland Army in the north, and submitted a plan to Stavka on 28 February. It was approved, along with the reinforcements and supplies he requested. Preparations included laying many miles of plank roads, training units to move through roadless swamps and forest, and forming two special light infantry corps of ski troops and marines for off-road movement. Staff war games were held in the three northern armies during April and May, but the operation was never to be mounted. Finland rejected the armistice terms, so Stalin summoned Meretskov to Moscow on 30 May, and told him that to bring the Finns back to the table he must expel their forces from southern Karelia as soon as possible. Meretskov's two armies in Karelia (32nd and 7th) already far outnumbered their opponents, but the occasion required a show not merely of force but of overwhelming force, so Meretskov asked for more reserves, which Stalin at first refused but then conceded. Meretskov left Moscow on 3 June, went straight to 7th Army and, after surveying the terrain from the south bank of the Svir, decided to attack along the northern shore of Lake Ladoga – tactically because the Ladoga Naval Flotilla could protect his flank, strategically because he could thus cut off Finnish forces north of the lake, and politically because that was the shortest route to the frontier. On 9 June Stalin summoned him yet again, to tell him he must attack within ten days, to assist the assault the Leningrad Front was about to mount in the Karelian isthmus. Meretskov pitched his demands for reserves even higher, and got what he wanted, over the opposition of Zhukov and Vasilevsky. But his offensive did not begin until 21 June, by which time the Leningrad Front needed no help – it had attacked ten days earlier, captured Vyborg, and already reached the 1940 frontier.

Meretskov's offensive increased the pressure on the Finnish government. He advanced 10 miles on the first day, and the Finns began to withdraw, slowing the Soviet pursuit by destroying bridges, mining roads, or blocking them with felled trees. But 32nd Army reached the frontier on 21 July. Faced with the prospect of full-scale invasion, President Ryti resigned ten days later, and armistice negotiations resumed. On 25 August Finland accepted Stalin's terms, a cease-fire began on 5 September, and a formal armistice was signed on 19 September. Its terms bound Finland to expel or intern all German forces, and this freed Meretskov to return to his earlier preoccupation with the German forces in the Arctic. These were driven out in a combined operation with the Northern Fleet during October, and pursued into northern Norway. Kirkenes was liberated on 25 October, and on the next day Stalin promoted Meretskov to Marshal. The Karelian Front halted at Neyden on 28 October, leaving the Norwegian Resistance to round up the few remaining scattered groups of Germans, and Stalin ordered Meretskov back to Moscow, where he received his insignia on 31 October.

He had become the first Front Commander to work himself out of a job. However, Stalin had further use for him, so his headquarters were moved to Yaroslavl, but not disbanded. Following the Yalta Conference in January 1945, he was ordered to be ready with his staff for a move to the Far East, where for the second time he would take over forces which had been inactive for years and prepare them for an offensive. Arriving there on 13 April he took command of the armies of the Maritime Group of Forces (1st Red Banner, 25th, 35th and 9th Air), inevitably found them wanting, and set about training them. With the end of the European war other senior commanders began arriving, and with Marshal Vasilevsky in overall charge as Commander-in-Chief three Fronts were established – from west to east Transbaikal (Malinovsky), 2nd Far Eastern (Purkayev) and 1st Far Eastern (Meretskov). The Japanese Kwantung Army was expected to provide serious opposition, so large numbers of experienced troops and their equipment were transferred from Europe. Soviet-period writings were later to magnify the Soviet rôle in defeating Japan by emphasizing that the Kwantung Army was Japan's largest, and ignoring events elsewhere that had brought Japan to the verge of collapse. It had already asked the Soviet government to ascertain Anglo-American armistice terms, but Stalin had not passed the request on; he intended to recover all that Russia had ceded to Japan in 1905 and more, and did not intend the war to end before the Soviet Union entered it.

Soviet forces crossed the Chinese and Korean borders in overwhelming strength at dawn on 9 August 1945. Meretskov peppered his account with mentions of overcoming 'fortified zones' or 'major Japanese formations', and 'breaking through Japanese defences', but his troops' high rates of advance (1st Red Banner and 5th Armies 46 miles in two days, 35th Army 75–94 miles in six days) and his reference to the almost total absence of the Japanese Air Force indicate resistance was neither large-scale nor prolonged. On 14 August Japan requested surrender terms, and on 17 August the Kwantung Army's commander, General Yamada, ordered his troops to stop fighting. The campaign had lasted only nine days, and tested Soviet logistics more than combat skills.

As a field commander Meretskov was solid and reliable rather than outstanding. With his extensive staff experience he inclined to be his own Chief of Staff, at the expense of the actual incumbents, who seldom survived more than a year without requesting a move or being dismissed. But his staff background also ensured that his operations were thoroughly prepared, if sometimes pedestrian in execution, and that his occasional failures were not disasters. He lacked the commanding personality of Zhukov or the intellectual acuteness of Vasilevsky, but was well regarded by his colleagues, and he reciprocated Stalin's obvious regard for him by declining to attack his war leadership after it had become safe and even fashionable to do so. He died on 30 December 1968.

BIBLIOGRAPHY

Anon., 'Delo Generala Pavlova', *Kommunist vooruzhennykh sil/armiya*, nos 8, 11, 13, 1991.

Erickson, John, *The Road to Stalingrad: Stalin's War with Germany*, vol. I, Weidenfeld & Nicolson, London, 1975.

Erickson, John, *The Road to Berlin: Stalin's War with Germany*, vol. II, Weidenfeld & Nicolson, London, 1983.

Meretskov, K. A., *Na sluzhbe narodu: stranitsy vospominanii*, Politizdat, Moscow, 1968; in English, *Serving the People*, Progress, Moscow, 1971.

Semiryaga, M. I., *Tayny stalinskoy diplomatii*, Vysshaya Shkola, Moscow, 1992.

Volkogonov, D. A., *Triumf i tragediya*, 2 vols, Novosti, Moscow, 1990; in English, *Triumph and Tragedy*, ed. and trans. Harold Shukman, Weidenfeld & Nicolson, London, and Grove Weidenfeld, New York, 1991.

Zakharov, M. V., *General'nyi Shtab v predvoennye gody*, Voenizdat, Moscow, 1989.

Zhukov, G. K., *Vospominaniya i razmyshleniya*, 10th edn, Novosti, Moscow, 1992; in English, *The Memoirs of Marshal Zhukov*, Jonathan Cape, London, 1971.

Kirill Semenovich
MOSKALENKO

JOHN ERICKSON

It must have seemed a far cry for a village lad, first risen to the eminence of army commander in a gruelling war, to be involved all too soon in a costly conflict shrouded in the deepest secrecy in far-off northeast Asia, then to discover himself the inquisitor of one of the most terrible inquisitors ever to disfigure Russian or Soviet history, namely Lavrenti Beria, and finally to become entangled in what might well have turned into the ultimate human catastrophe, the realization of 'the unthinkable', global nuclear war.

Kirill Moskalenko was born on 11 May 1902 in the village of Grishino, Ekaterinoslav province, in the Donbas, then a land of grassy steppe intersected by fields and two small rivers, with Grishino running alongside their banks. A pleasant place with its leafy orchards and copses, Grishino had long been a haven for those fleeing serfdom in addition to foreign colonists seeking land together with wealthy Russian landowners. Germans, Poles and Russian incomers might own many an acre while the local peasants subsisted on only an acre or two, forcing them to seek work on the railways or foreign-owned mines, or to hire themselves out on the land as labourers, all for 30 kopeks or so for a day's work. Greedy landowners tried to dispossess the peasants of their small plots and in one such incident the young Moskalenko's father was badly beaten up by a Polish landowner. This misfortune was made worse by his father's fatal fall while repairing a church steeple, leaving a large extended family, since he had married three times: the older children left, leaving two daughters and two sons with Kirill's mother. As the eldest son, aged nine, he became 'head of the family'. Avid for learning, he passed through all the classes of the village school, going on to the 'ministerial school', working during the summer, studying in the winter.

The war stripped men, horses and cattle from the land, conditions steadily worsened and disturbances grew as the hardships increased. After February 1917, Bolshevik agitation grew apace. Amidst growing turbulence, with peasants trying to take empty land, Moskalenko was awarded one of the two scholarships offered by Grishino district for study at the agricultural school, coupled with work on the land. Early in 1918, the 3rd Cavalry Division arrived in Grishino, the war-weary soldiers demanding demobilization. With the officers arrested, the division disbanded, the soldiers throwing away their weapons, some joining the Red Guard and handing out the horses to the peasants, Moskalenko's mother being one of the grateful recipients. But fresh trials awaited as the German Army marched into Ukraine, bringing back the landlords. On holiday from the agricultural school and once again at home, Moskalenko learned that the Germans had swept the place clean. With the family to support, he returned to the land, labouring from dawn to dusk, under German occupation. In the autumn of 1918, with the German Army withdrawing, Moskalenko was back at the agricultural school, but in 1919 teaching ceased and he returned home. With the arrival of Denikin's army, shooting all those associated in any way with the Soviets, Moskalenko went into hiding until the Red Army arrived.

In August 1920 Moskalenko joined the Komsomol and at the same time an armed detachment led by Kulichenko fighting against White Guards and Makhno. At school Moskalenko had received some military training, albeit with wooden rifles and wooden sabres, but the retired NCOs in charge inspired their pupils with great regard for discipline and things military. Such habits stood him in good stead when his detachment, fresh from their encounters with Makhno, joined up with 1st Cavalry Army, victors over Wrangel in the Crimea. In December 1920 Moskalenko, in the company of other young fellows 'with education', was sent to a command training course in Lugansk, though his stay there was brief enough as the entire course was despatched to deal with the Kamenyuk band rampaging through the Don steppes. Still with his three companions, Tsyganenko, Basov and Tkachenko, Moskalenko proceeded in February 1921 to the 5th Kharkov Artillery School, transferring in May to the United Kharkov Military School for Red Commanders. Here the 'fighting four' went their separate ways, Basov to the infantry, Tsyganenko to the cavalry, Moskalenko and Tkachenko to the artillery. The 5th Artillery School, from which Moskalenko graduated with distinction, offered excellent training, the instructors including the well known gun designer V. A. Degtyarev.

Posted in 1922 to 1st Cavalry Army, Moskalenko found himself in command of a platoon of the cavalry-artillery battalion of the 6th Chongar Cavalry Division. The Civil War had ended, but trouble still flared in Central Asia and in parts of the northern Caucasus, the latter involving 1st Cavalry Army – and Moskalenko – in putting down Prince Dzhentemirov's insurgency. Once the fighting died down, the Red Army turned to peacetime training. The older men in the 6th Chongar Division were demobilized, fresh conscripts arrived from Tauride province, considered well-off and whose recruits were mostly literate and largely lacking political affiliation, thus providing fertile ground for political work. By now a candidate member of the Communist Party, Moskalenko found himself in good, even illustrious company. His battery included a number of extremely well educated ex-tsarist officers, one in particular, D. Koropovsky of the Guards, a graduate of the Physics-Mathematical Faculty of Kiev University, while frequent visitors to the Chongar Division – earlier commanded by S. K. Timoshenko, now under O. I. Gorodovikov – were none other than K. E. Voroshilov, commander of North Caucasus Military District, and 1st Cavalry Army commander S. M. Budenny. When in the autumn of 1923 the division was transferred to Belorussia and subordinated directly to the Western Front command, Moskalenko and others came into contact with M. N. Tukhachevsky. Moskalenko was also rising in the ranks, at the age of 22 a battery commander in the 6th Cavalry Division, now attached to the 3rd Cavalry Corps under G. D. Gai in Minsk.

Two years passed in hard training in these crack regular formations, during which time (in 1926) Moskalenko became a full member of the Communist Party and was assigned to the 'command staff educational completion courses' in the former Officers' Higher School in Leningrad, where many of the staff were drawn from specialist ex-tsarist officers, complemented by civilian experts lecturing on a wide variety of subjects – not least the eminent physiologist I. P. Pavlov. On his return to the division in 1928 Moskalenko first took over a training battery, then an artillery battalion, rising to become chief of staff of a regiment. However, after eleven years' service, his time with the 6th Chongar Division was drawing to a close, exchanging European Russia for the Soviet Far East and the 1st Special Cavalry Division of the Special Far Eastern Army under the command of V. K. Blyukhcr. Arriving first in Chita and then moving to Khadabulka, Moskalenko was in for something of a surprise with this new division. Tension in the Far East was growing and the threat from Japan becoming more evident. The Soviet military build-up in the east was gathering pace with the despatch of more rifle and cavalry divisions, independent tank battalions, bomber and fighter squadrons: in April 1932 the Pacific Fleet officially came into existence. Similar efforts went into making the Far East militarily as well as economically self-sufficient. Every inducement was offered to get men (and women) to the area. To combine self-sufficiency with military readiness, M. V. Kalmykov's 'Special Kolkhoz Corps' made up of three rifle divisions and one cavalry division, was formed in March 1932 – 60,000 men in all, its mission to guard the frontiers, exploit rich virgin land and work towards economic self-sufficiency in the Soviet Far East.

In this world Moskalenko came to wondering whether he was a Red cavalryman or a collective farmer, in for what at that time was an impressively mechanized agricultural scene. In between training and building barracks, the cavalrymen turned to repairing tractors, lorries and combine harvesters. In the summer military training and artillery firing practice, went on side by side with harvesting, in winter more training as well as overhauling agricultural machinery for the coming spring. His acquaintance with tractors and other agricultural machines did not come amiss, for, having served as regimental Chief of Staff and latterly as regimental commander, in June 1935 he was posted to the Maritime Provinces as artillery commander to the 23rd Mechanized Brigade presently forming up. There, in Nikolsk-Ussuriisk, amid the tanks, he bade farewell to the cavalry.

To replace the old MS-1 tanks new models, BT-7s and T-26s, were brought into the Far East, tanks which Moskalenko learned to drive and use their armament, his proficiency personally tested by none other than the army commander himself, V. K. Blyukher. His service with this brigade did not last long, however. In September 1936 he was posted back to European Russia, to Kiev Military District and the 133rd Mechanized Brigade (45th Mechanized Corps), mechanized formations representing at that time the pride and joy of the Red Army and the height of Tukhachevsky's influence.

In the autumn of 1938 Moskalenko was sent back to his books, to the Dzerzhinsky Military Academy in Leningrad, joining the course for senior command staff headed by M. N. Chistyakov, a future Marshal of Artillery. Once graduated, Moskalenko continued with his trade as a gunner, acting first as artillery commander in the 51st Perekop Rifle Division in Odessa Military District. It was with this division that Moskalenko fought against the Finns, operating a T-26 tank, emerging as a brigadier-general and rising to artillery major-general in the June 1940 promotions. In his new rank and as artillery commander of the 35th Rifle Corps he took part in the drive into Bessarabia and the northern Bukovina – one of Stalin's 'smash and grab raids' – with the Southern Group commanded by Zhukov.

War began to move closer to the Soviet Union, the alarm bells ringing loudly in the Kremlin with the fall of France in June 1940. Roundly cursing the French, Stalin voiced his fears that 'Hitler will now turn on us and beat our brains in'. The armoured formations disbanded in 1939 were now hastily reformed. In August, confirmed as commander of a tank division, Moskalenko was assigned to the 2nd Mechanized Corps forming up under Major-General Yu. V. Novoselsky in Odessa Military District, ushering in a period of feverish preparation and training. That ended abruptly at the beginning of May 1941 with his appointment as commander of the High Command Reserve 1st Artillery Anti-tank Brigade in Kiev Special Military District, which came as a great surprise: from fighting with tanks he was now to fight against tanks. The District Commander, General M. P. Kirponos, left him in no doubt that time was short, the situation extremely serious: General M. A. Purkayev, Chief of Staff, needed only to point to the growing German troop concentrations on the border.

War came with unrelenting fury on 22 June 1941, engulfing the entire Southwestern Front – where Moskalenko fought throughout the war – in a series of disasters, culminating in the loss of Kiev and a vast encirclement. Fighting with 5th Army against the tanks of von Rundstedt's Army Group South, in early September 1941 Moskalenko handed over his brigade and took command of the 15th Rifle Corps, which was in dire straits. The General Staff's failure to grasp the looming catastrophe and Stalin's refusal to give up Kiev condemned the Southwestern Front to inevitable disaster. Moskalenko managed to break through the German ring and in early December was instructed by Timoshenko to take command of a 'cavalry-mechanized group' attached to 13th Army on the right flank of the Southwestern Front, which was committed to the Soviet counter-offensive about to burst on the German forces ringing Moscow.

Early in 1942 Timoshenko assigned Moskalenko as Deputy Commander in Malinovsky's 6th Army as the Soviet winter offensive rolled on, switching him to the 6th Cavalry Corps and latterly to command of 38th Army. Each new posting presaged offensive action, Moskalenko noted, this time the Red Army's attempt to batter its way to Kharkov. The battle for Kharkov lasted 70 days, with the Red Army reaching a depth of 60 miles, capturing a main German supply base at Lozovya, and carving out the deep Izyum salient, but powerful German counter-attacks and the exhaustion of Red Army divisions brought Soviet operations to a halt. Timoshenko, together with Bagramyan and Khrushchev, resolved to renew the drive on Kharkov. On 12 May 1942, vastly overestimating the Red Army's capabilities, Timoshenko launched an offensive to envelop German forces in the Kharkov area, to drive westwards and on to the Dnieper: Moskalenko's 38th Army formed part of the Northern Attack Group. Five days later Army Group Kleist smashed into the Soviet 9th Army's positions in the south. Rather than reinforcing here, Timoshenko continued his drive on Kharkov, breaking off the action only when 6th and 57th Armies were in danger of being surrounded. Reversing its direction, the Southwestern Front tried to fight its way out of encirclement, suffering terrible losses, 15 divisions destroyed and 200,000 men made prisoner. With 38th Army Moskalenko fought his way back to the northern Donets as the German Army jumped off on a new offensive aimed at Stalingrad and the Caucasus.

In the early summer of 1942 the first defensive phase of what was to become the epic battle for Stalingrad opened. Timoshenko was dismissed. Moskalenko exchanged commands, this time taking over 1st Tank Army and subsequently 1st Guards Army. Lieutenant-General V. N. Gordov, as

Timoshenko's replacement and commander of the Stalingrad Front, kindled little enthusiasm in Moskalenko, who found him not up to his task. If this was his first shock, the second was that 1st Tank Army had yet to form up. Only half-assembled, at breakneck speed 1st Tank Army was thrown into battle on the eastern bank of the Don north of Kalach. At the beginning of August, after almost 400 days at the front, Moskalenko took command of 1st Guards Army at the same time as the new Southwestern Front under Colonel-General A. I. Yeremenko was hived off from the Stalingrad Front.

During September, with Zhukov now on the scene at Stalingrad, Moskalenko's 1st Guards launched its counter-blows in the reaches between the Don and the Volga, fighting to hold off the German thrust on Stalingrad itself. At the end of the month, as these counter-blows drew to a close and 1st Guards Army was disbanded, Moskalenko was summoned unexpectedly to Moscow and to the Stavka. In Stalin's office he was informed that he was to take command of 40th Army on the Voronezh Front under Lieutenant-General N. F. Vatutin (shortly to be replaced by Lieutenant-General F. I. Golikov), some distance from fiery Stalingrad. Having assumed command of his new army Moskalenko sought for some way of obtaining an offensive mission for it and, after much deliberation, decided to telephone Stalin. He proposed an operation with the left flank of the Southwestern Front and the Voronezh Front, using 40th Army, to drive into the great bend of the Don. Stalin agreed, offering reinforcement. But as the Soviet counter-offensive at Stalingrad unrolled in December, trapping von Paulus's VI Army, the Stavka postponed the 40th Army attack, devoting all its resources to holding off German attempts to break through to the besieged German army. Now the whole of the left flank of the Voronezh Front was to attack, 40th Army operating with Major-General P. S. Rybalko's 3rd Tank Army, to destroy the VIII Italian and the II Hungarian Army in the Ostrogozhsk-Rossosh operation. The January offensive conducted by 40th Army and Rybalko's 3rd Tank Army resulted in the encirclement of five enemy divisions, but operations on an even larger scale were planned. At the end of January 1943 Supreme HQ (Stavka) intended to destroy German forces on the Kursk, Kharkov and Donbas axes: the Voronezh Front received orders to attack along the Kharkov and Kursk axes, destroying the remnant of the German Army Group 'B', with 40th, 69th and 3rd Tank Armies committed to regaining the Kharkov industrial region.

The attempt to eliminate the 'Kharkov group' of German forces did not succeed. After the capture of Kharkov itself, no operational pause ensued, as Zhukov suggested there should have been. Soviet armies thrust towards the west and southwest, racing for the Dnieper crossings as von Manstein regrouped for his devastating counter-stroke. German troops recaptured

Kharkov. As the spring mud congealed on the front lines and a momentary lull set in, the entire German southern wing had barely escaped destruction: as a result of these tempestuous battles a huge Soviet salient – the Kursk salient running from Orel in the north to Kharkov in the south – now jutted out to the west. This the German command determined at all costs to eliminate with Operation 'Citadel', designed both to avenge Stalingrad and to break the present stalemate on the Eastern Front.

At long last Stalin stayed his hand, finally persuaded to restrict the Red Army initially to defensive operations at Kursk: more and more armies piled up behind massive defences and dense minefields while the most powerful strategic reserve ever seen in the war assembled under Konev and the Steppe Front, held behind the Central and Voronezh Fronts to block any possible German thrust on either Orel or Belgorod. On the Voronezh Front, now under the command of N. F. Vatutin, Moskalenko's 38th Army joined the first echelon armies holding the right flank on the western face of the Kursk salient and securing the junction with Rokossovsky's Central Front: 40th Army assignment involved holding any German attempt to break through along the northern or northeastern axis. Any breakthrough must be checked with second echelon corps and reserve armies. On 2 July 1943 the Voronezh and Central Fronts received a warning from Stavka about the imminence of the German offensive. Battlefield intelligence fixed the time of German attack as 5 July, at which Soviet guns fired off the greatest 'counter-preparation' barrage so far seen. At dawn Hoth's IV Panzer Army attacked along the southern face, an armoured 'Ride of the Valkyries' which ended in disaster, having covered only 20 miles: in the north Model launched his offensive against the Central Front, running up against bitter resistance. In a final desperate bid to smash in the Soviet defences, Hoth turned towards Prokhorovka in an attempt to drive on Kursk from the south: here, in a great armoured joust, more than 1,000 German and Soviet tanks clashed head-on, with IV Panzer losing 400 tanks. 'Citadel' had failed.

The Red Army now prepared to launch its own counter-offensive. Moskalenko at 40th Army suggested at a command conference with Zhukov a plan for a 'repeat Stalingrad', a huge encirclement of German forces in the Kharkov–Belgorod area. Zhukov told him that Soviet forces were insufficient to undertake such a deep outflanking movement. Stalin wanted the enemy 'knocked on the head, i.e. his main force', Zhukov said. 'And where is this main force? As you know, in the Belgorod area.' On 3 August 1943 the full Soviet counter-offensive opened with the Belgorod–Kharkov operation: Belgorod fell on 6 August, Kharkov on the 23rd. At the end of the month the Red Army stood ready to strike into Ukraine. As 40th Army struck southwestwards, for the third time in the war Moskalenko drew up to the River Psel – the first time in 1941 in fighting to break out of encirclement, the second time in the spring of 1943 fighting west of Kharkov, and now, five months later, resuming the advance towards the Dnieper. On 20 September, Moskalenko's spearheads from the 309th Rifle Division, followed by elements of 10th Tank Corps, reached the broad Dnieper, simultaneously barrier and highway.

Crossing the Dnieper in strength and under fire started during the night of 23 September: 40th Army seized four bridgeheads on the western bank, the largest of them, in the Bukrin bend, taken in conjunction with Rybalko's 3rd Guards Tank Army. For the successful assault crossing of the Dnieper, one of the great epics of the war, decorations and promotions flowed in abundance, with 136 officers and men of the 40th – including Moskalenko – made Heroes of the Soviet Union. Fighting to hold and enlarge the Bukrin bridgehead was fierce in the face of heavy German counter-attacks: ferrying over tanks and artillery took time. At the end of September 40th Army had only seventeen tanks and twenty-seven 76mm guns, 3rd Tank fourteen tanks inside the bridgehead. During the night of 24–25 September Soviet airborne forces dropped into the bridgeheads in an attempt to expand them, but the operation was badly organized and executed: many paratroopers were dispersed or dropped into enemy positions and only half of the original 4,575-strong force remained to continue fighting. Two attempts to charge out of the Bukrin bridgehead south of Kiev and drive on the Ukrainian capital met both difficult terrain and stiff resistance from ten German divisions. Stavka then changed the original plan, concentrating on the possibilities afforded by the Lyutezh bridgehead north of Kiev presently held by Chibisov's 38th Army. Vatutin put the matter succinctly: one infantry army and one tank army would be needed for this attack. The new plan called for a diversionary attack from the Bukrin bridgehead with three armies – 38th, 60th, 3rd Guards Tank Army with 1st Guards Cavalry Corps, supported by Krasovsky's 2nd Air Army – attacking on 1–2 November. The first task was to empty Bukrin of much of its armour and artillery. In pouring rain and amidst clinging mud 3rd Guards Tank and 23rd Rifle Corps withdrew to the eastern bank of the Dnieper and trundled 100 miles to the north; 3rd Tank left only its HQ, radio units and dummy tanks in the bridgehead. If rain hampered Soviet movement, it also helped to conceal it.

On 23 October Stalin informed Vatutin, 1st Ukrainian Front Commander, that it was 'impossible to take Kiev from the south. Now take a look at the Lyutezh bridgehead which is north of Kiev and held by 38th Army.' Four days later, Vatutin instructed Colonel-General Moskalenko to take command of Lieutenant-General Chibisov's 38th Army, earmarked for the main attack from the Lyutezh bridgehead. On 2 November Colonel-General A. A. Grechko arrived as Moskalenko's deputy, immediately supervising the redeployment of 3rd Tank Army, 23rd Rifle Corps, 7th

Breakthrough Artillery Corps and more support units to 38th Army. With four rifle corps, the 1st Czechoslovak Infantry Brigade, 5th Guards Tank Corps and the 7th Artillery Corps Moskalenko's 38th Army received orders to secure the passage of 3rd Guards Tank Army and 1st Guards Cavalry Corps – 1st Ukrainian Front's 'mobile group' – outflank Kiev from the west, liberate the Ukrainian capital and drive south-west. To the north I. D. Chernaykhovsky's 60th Army protected 38th Army's rear. Moskalenko's choice of a narrow breakthrough sector, exposed to enemy fire from the flanks, brought questions from Zhukov at a command conference, but the decision was approved.

The attack directive stipulated that Kiev must fall within forty-eight hours, no later than 5–6 November. Speed the Stavka demanded and speed it got. On the morning of 3 November 1943 Moskalenko's 38th and Chernyakhovsky's 60th burst out of the Lyutezh bridgehead. The following day Vatutin loosed Rybalko's tanks, ordering them to pass through 38th Army, drive southwestwards towards Fastov, Belaya Tserkov and Grebenka. With sirens wailing and headlamps blazing, Rybalko's tanks moved west of Kiev, cutting the Kiev–Zhitomir highway as Moskalenko's lead units entered the outskirts of Kiev. Fighting with 38th Army were men of Svoboda's 1st Independent Czechoslovak Brigade, urged by their commander to fight for Kiev 'as if it were Prague and Bratislava'. Stalin had instructed Vatutin and Moskalenko that, while the Czechoslovak troops should be committed, they should be given every assistance to avoid heavy casualties, because in the Czechoslovak Brigade Stalin saw the core of a future 'Czechoslovak People's Army': Stalin repeated this injunction on the eve of the Dukla operation. At 0600 hours on 4 November 1943, 38th Army reported 'the mother of Russian cities', ancient Kiev, cleared of the enemy. An hour later Vatutin radioed news of the liberation of Kiev to Stalin.

The 'Kiev bridgehead' continued to fill out. As Soviet units west of Fastov splayed themselves out on an ever-widening front, Stavka woke up to the danger of a German counter-stroke: Vatutin was ordered to hold his forces moving westwards at the centre of the 1st Ukrainian Front, reinforce Moskalenko's 38th Army to hold any German thrust on Kiev and only then to resume the advance southwest of Kiev. After beating off German attempts to reduce the Kiev bridgehead, the plan was to chop IV Panzer Army to pieces. Vatutin turned his left and centre over to the defensive, leaving his right flank armies (60th and 13th) free to drive on. In mid-November von Manstein launched his armour in a counter-attack which developed along both sides of the Kiev-Zhitomir highway, aimed at Kiev, but amidst heavy fighting German units came to grief in the mud and Vatutin's 'defensive zones': Grechko's 1st Guards Army took station in the gap between 38th and 60th Armies, holding off one danger. At the end of December Vatutin and Zhukov, in his capacity as Stavka Representative, developed a plan to smash the northern wing of Army Group South and seal the doom of IV Panzer. In late December Vatutin resumed offensive operations, with the aim of finally clearing German armour away from Kiev and to close with Konev's 2nd Ukrainian Front to drive deep into the German rear. Feinting on the right flank, Vatutin aimed to strike along the Zhitomir highway and the Fastov–Kazatin railway line, In the opening phase of the attack, Katukov's 1st Tank Army passed through 38th Army, the T-34s finding reasonable going in the thin snow and shallow mud, both armies clearing Berdichev and Belaya Tserkov by 5 January. The Zhitomir–Berdichev operation proved to be a substantial success but in mid-January, as German reserves piled up, Vatutin reined in both 38th Army and 1st Tank Army, ordering them to block the German attack. Winter obstinately refused to come, the mud persisted. Vatutin's Front was outrunning its supplies, the armies were dangerously spread out, unable to reach the southern Bug, capture Vinnitsa and also encircle German troops at Zhmerinka.

Northwest, southeast and west of Kiev major operations were now in the offing. Between the 1st and 2nd Ukrainian Fronts a huge German salient jutted out as far back as the Dnieper, akin to a cork stopping up the Soviet offensive. The savage battle for the Korsun-Shevchenkovsky salient was about to begin. Heavy German counter-attacks battered 38th and 40th Armies: two encirclements occurred, that of German forces by the Red Army at Korsun-Shevchenkovsky and that by German forces of elements of two rifle corps of the 38th Army. The Soviet divisions broke free: the German forces did not, the two columns making a final break-out in a fierce snow storm, meeting two Soviet armies (27th and 4th Guards) lying in wait across their paths and the Cossacks who showed no mercy. The locking of the flanks of the 1st and 2nd Ukrainian Fronts, together with the elimination of the threat from the Korsun salient, enabled Soviet operations along the southwestern axis to unfold in closer co-ordination of both time and space.

At the end of February 1944 anti-Soviet Ukrainian partisans ambushed and fatally wounded General Vatutin: on 1 March Zhukov assumed command of the 1st Ukrainian Front. Zhukov planned a massive slicing blow to split the entire German southern grouping in two, forcing one part into Galicia and southern Poland, the other into Moldavia and the Danube. But the attempt to trap the whole of I Panzer Army failed when German armour slipped the encircling noose, breaking out not to the south but to the west, finally linking with IV Panzer Army.

By mid-April 1944 Soviet armies had conducted continuous offensive operations for almost four months, in the process smashing in the entire southern wing of the German armies (save for XVII Army trapped in the Crimea). The destruction of German Army Group South brought the liberation of the western Ukraine and carried Soviet armies as far as the western Carpathians. In mid-March 1944 38th Army pushed the enemy back to the southern Bug and established bridgeheads on the western bank before preparing to outflank Vinnitsa from the north. First Zhmerinka then Vinnitsa fell to Moskalenko's 38th. In the race to trap I Panzer Army, Moskalenko was ordered to close with 4th Tank Army and cut off the German escape route to the Dniester at Kamenets-Podolsk. The 1st Ukrainian Front, advancing as far as the foothills of the Carpathians, had effectively chopped the German southern front in two, cutting its communications, save through Romania: to preserve this life-line the German command fought to hold Soviet forces from the approaches to the Carpathians. Moskalenko's preparations to drive on Stanislav together with 1st Tank Army received a rude jolt as the Germans attacked first. The fighting on the Stanislav axis lasted until late April, costing 6,700 Soviet casualties and the loss of 117 tanks. But German attempts to build a new front at the approaches to the Carpathians had failed. In May and June, 38th Army went temporarily on the defensive, a prelude to major new offensive action, first regrouping and then redeploying.

On 1 May 1944 Konev took command of the 1st Ukrainian Front. Zhukov left to co-ordinate the giant offensive against Army Group Centre. Konev now set out to destroy Army Group North Ukraine, waiting until the storm broke over Army Group Centre in Belorussia before concentrating his attack force for the Lvov-Sandomierz operation. Konev drilled his commanders mercilessly in what was required of them. The 1st Ukrainian Front was now one of the most powerful ever assembled, with seven rifle armies, three tank armies and two air armies: Moskalenko's 38th Army, attacking along the Lvov axis, had 90,728 men, 1,841 guns and 85 tanks. Moskalenko's men faced stiff German resistance at the centre, but the first phase of the operation brought the encirclement of the German XIII Corps at Brody while the Soviet armoured advance continued westwards, bypassing Lvov which held out until 27 July. At the end of August Moskalenko ordered 1st Ukrainian Army to go over to the defensive, but on 2 September Konev informed him of a change of plans: 38th Army would take part in the offensive to move through the Carpathians in order to help the Slovak rising. The attack on the Dukla Pass, connecting Slovakia with southern Poland, was carried out by 38th Army, the 1st Czechoslovak Corps and Grechko's 1st Guards Army operating with the 4th Ukrainian Front. After 38 days of continuous fighting 38th Army was in sore need of reinforcement and replenishment, but moving up steep cliffs – heights of 2,000 feet and more – on 6 October the Dukla Pass was secured. One month later, on 29 November, despite Konev's appeal, Stalin ordered the transfer of 38th Army to the 4th Ukrainian Front. For Moskalenko it was farewell to any hopes of fighting along the Berlin axis, and a final farewell to Konev's powerful 1st Ukrainian Front.

At the beginning of 1945 the Red Army stood at the frontier of the Reich, smashed its way into Poland, shattered the German forces in Romania, marched peacefully into Bulgaria, pushed into Hungary and through the Carpathians deep into Slovakia. By the beginning of March almost all of eastern Czechoslovakia had been cleared: 38th Army and 1st Guards had meanwhile advanced through southern Poland, outflanking the Carpathians from the north and closed once more on the Czechoslovak frontier and the Morava-Ostravska industrial region. Stavka now committed the 4th Ukrainian Front to an offensive spanning forty to forty-five days and reaching to a depth of 350 kilometres, clearing German forces from Morava-Ostravska, then striking out for Olomouc and finally Prague. In April, General Yeremenko assumed the Front command, displacing General I. E. Petrov – who was dismissed at the instigation of Lev Mekhlis, the 'Inquisitor of the Red Army'.

The Morava-Ostravska operation lasted fifty-two days, followed by a final drive on Olomouc and Prague. With Berlin in Soviet hands, Konev's 1st Ukrainian Front swung down from the north: 4th and 2nd Ukrainian Fronts advanced from the east and southeast. In the Czech capital the citizens took up arms against the German troops, radioing for assistance, at which Yeremenko ordered Moskalenko to form a 'mobile group' to advance on Prague. This assignment Moskalenko entrusted to Lieutenant-General Bondarev and 101st Rifle Corps. On 7 May 1945 Germany capitulated unconditionally. On the morning of 8 May three Soviet Fronts were converging on Prague, on the following day lead elements of 38th Army's 'mobile group' entered Prague, to be met by three or four tanks, hatches closed, ready for action. They proved to be from Lelyushenko's 4th Guards Tank Army with Konev's 1st Ukrainian Front. The remnants of Schörner's Army Group Centre were completely trapped.

With this gruelling, barbaric war ended, Colonel-General Moskalenko assumed command of a peacetime army in the immediate post-war period, which was one of both demobilization and reorganization. In April 1946 the Northwestern Air Defence District was established out of what had been the Central Front Air Defence command under Lieutenant-General of Artillery P. E. Gudymenko. Two years later, in September 1946, in a further reorganization the Moscow Air Defence Region (to become subsequently the Moscow Air Defence District) replaced it and was put under the command of Moskalenko, with Major-General P. F. Batitsky as his Chief of Staff.

This was a period of rapidly deteriorating relations between former wartime allies, marked by the Berlin blockade in 1948, but much intensified with the outbreak of the Korean War in June 1950. Almost immediately, in August of that year Moskalenko ordered General Lobov, commander of the 303rd Fighter Aviation Division of the Moscow Air Defence District, to proceed to Vladivostok, though he was expressly forbidden to take his advanced MiG-15 fighters with him. Early in October 1950 two American jets shot up a Soviet base near Vladivostok and American bombers were attacking targets close to the Soviet border: General MacArthur's UN troops had entered North Korea and were moving close to the Soviet and Chinese borders. The Communist régime in North Korea was near to collapse, prompting desperate appeals for help to Stalin and Mao Tse-tung, the former promising aircraft, the latter ground troops. Stalin went back on his promise; Mao Tse-tung did not, pouring his armies across the Yalu.

As UN troops closed on the Soviet frontier General Lobov received fresh orders to move to northeast China at a time when, through 'connections' and the 'co-operation' of Soviet pilots, he had managed to lay his hands on some MiG-15s, the first of which went into action on 1 November 1950. Orders came directly from Moscow, though the Soviet pilots wore Chinese uniform (their documents and personal identification removed to maintain secrecy), their aircraft bearing Chinese markings. An attempt to have the pilots communicate in Chinese, basic Chinese, failed – they could not avoid reverting to Russian in air-to-air dogfights. As the 'secret' air war intensified, with life for the pilots made unnecessarily difficult by the lack of real co-operation between the Air Defence command and the Soviet Air Force, in October 1951 Lobov was promoted to command the 64th Air Defence Fighter Aviation Corps, 'home' to all Soviet personnel involved in the war – 120–130 air crew, Soviet Navy pilots and many thousands of personnel. More than 200 Soviet pilots died in the Korean skies, losing 345 of their aircraft. Chinese losses were much heavier.

The Korean War did not erupt into an overt Soviet–American clash. It was the death of Stalin in March 1953 which introduced internal upheaval and turbulence in the Soviet Union. At 9 a.m. on the morning of 25 July 1953 Khrushchev telephoned Moskalenko and asked: 'In your immediate circle, do you have people as devoted to the Party as you are?' Moskalenko replied affirmatively, whereupon Khrushchev instructed him to bring them to the Kremlin to what used to be Stalin's office and to the Chairman of the Council of Ministers, Georgy Malenkov. Khrushchev also suggested that Moskalenko bring Air Defence operational plans and maps with him – and also some cigars. Moskalenko replied that he would bring the papers but he had stopped smoking in 1944: Khrushchev responded by saying that others, not Moskalenko, might need the cigars. Following a broad hint from Khrushchev, it dawned on Moskalenko that he might need to be armed.

Moskalenko summoned Major V. I. Yuferev, special assignments officer, Major-General A. I. Baksov and Colonel I. G. Zub, advising them that it was necessary to proceed to the Kremlin – armed. He instructed the staff commandant, Major M. G. Khizhnyak, to issue weapons and ammunition. Since this was such a small group, Moskalenko telephoned Major-General

Batitsky, his former chief of staff but now Air Force Chief of Staff, suggesting that he accompany the group and that he come armed. Shortly afterwards, Defence Minister Bulganin telephoned to say that Khrushchev had suggested that Moskalenko should first call on Bulganin at the Defence Ministry. Bulganin met Moskalenko's squad alone. Beria was to be arrested, along with his numerous, loyal and well armed guards. Moskalenko said he had five reliable, battle-tested men. 'Fine,' replied Bulganin, 'but that's not many. Who can we get here without further delay?' Moskalenko suggested Bulganin's deputy, Vasilevsky, but Bulganin, for reasons best known to himself, turned this down. 'Who else is to hand?' asked Moskalenko. Bulganin mentioned Zhukov and when Moskalenko suggested that he, Zhukov, accompany the group, Bulganin agreed but insisted that the Marshal not come armed. Moskalenko was unclear why Khrushchev had selected him for this task, but in a subsequent talk Khrushchev explained that he had approached one Marshal – unnamed – but he had refused. Moskalenko had known Khrushchev during the war in the Southwestern and Ukrainian Fronts and had met him from time to time after the war, all in friendly fashion. What Khrushchev and Bulganin suggested Moskalenko took to be 'a commission at the behest of the Party'.

At 11 a.m. on 26 July, Bulganin and Moskalenko took the Minister's car to the Kremlin. At the Council of Ministers building both took the lift, leaving Moskalenko's group of officers on the staircase. Zhukov, Brezhnev, Shatilov, Nedelin, Getman and Pronin followed in another car. All were assembled in the waiting-room to Malenkov's office, at which Bulganin left them and went in to Malenkov. A little later Khrushchev, Bulganin, Malenkov and Molotov came out to the officers, starting to explain that of late Beria had conducted himself with much effrontery towards members of the Central Committee Presidium, spying on them, tapping telephones, noting their contacts. Shortly the Presidium would meet, after which Malenkov's assistant Sukhanov would give a special signal and then the Soviet officers were to move in and arrest Beria. Beria had not yet arrived. Shortly everyone assembled and the session of the Presidium began. It did not last long – but it seemed interminable to Moskalenko and his fellows. Some 15–17 persons gathered, some in uniform, others not, most of them Beria's men. None of them had any inkling of what was about to take place as they stood chatting. One hour later, at 1 p.m., at a given signal five armed officers, plus the unarmed Zhukov, burst into the room. Malenkov announced: 'In the name of Soviet law arrest Beria.' The officers drew their weapons, Moskalenko aimed his directly at Beria and ordered him to put up his hands. Zhukov searched Beria, finding nothing. Moskalenko and his officers ushered Beria into Malenkov's retiring room, Presidium members stayed on to continue their session in the room. Zhukov stayed with them.

His arrest took Beria completely by surprise, leaving him wholly disoriented. In his briefcase was a sheaf of papers with 'Alert' marked on each in red pencil – he had evidently meant to hand these over to the Kremlin guard if the Presidium tried to censure him. But no one, save for Bulganin, Malenkov, Molotov and Khrushchev, either knew of or expected Beria's arrest. After twenty minutes the Presidium session ended and all left including Zhukov. Moskalenko and his five officers were left face to face with Beria. Outside Brezhnev, Getman, Nedelin, Pronin and Shatilov kept guard. Beria acted nervously, peering out of the window, frequently asking for the lavatory, to which he was escorted there and back by all five officers, weapons at the ready. He seemed to want to signal to the guards milling about, some uniformed, some in civilian clothes but armed. The time dragged on, everyone was hungry, Sukhanov went and organized some tea.

It was still not dark enough to get Beria out of the Kremlin unnoticed. At midnight Moskalenko ordered five ZIS-110 vehicles with government pennants and sent them to the Moscow Air Defence staff headquarters in Kirov Street, where, on his orders, thirty officer-Communists under the command of Colonel Yerastov, Chief of the Operations Staff, were waiting, all armed. They arrived unchecked at the Kremlin and immediately on their arrival changed the guard inside the building where Beria was held. Beria was hustled out and seated in the middle passenger seat of a ZIS-110 together with Batitsky, Baksov, Zub and Yuferev. Moskalenko sat in the front with the driver: the other vehicle carried six of the officers from the Air Defence staff. Both cars drove off without stopping through the Spassky Gate to the main military detention centre in Moscow. The next day, Saturday, Beria's deputies, Colonel-Generals Kruglov and Serov, came to the guardhouse with a commission from Malenkov and Khrushchev that they, together with Moskalenko, should investigate the 'Beria case'. Moskalenko objected, insisting that Batitsky and Getman should be present. Kruglov and Serov disagreed. Moskalenko tried to telephone Malenkov, finally tracing him at a performance at the Bolshoi. Malenkov ordered all three to come to the theatre where the whole Presidium was meeting in a special room. Serov and Kruglov argued that Beria's arrest and detention were illegal. Moskalenko responded by saying that he was neither a Chekist (secret policeman) nor a lawyer – just a soldier and a Communist. He had comported himself properly to a declared 'enemy of the people and the Party'. Malenkov and Khrushchev supported Moskalenko, the Presidium in turn supported them. The investigation of Beria would be conducted by the Procurator-General R. A. Rudenko in the presence of Moskalenko. The confrontation with the two KGB officers left Moskalenko somewhat uneasy. (For some months after Beria's arrest he receive death-threats in the post. Some of the letters he forwarded to Serov who took no action.)

On leaving the Bolshoi, Beria was taken to the Moscow Military District staff and lodged in an underground bunker which served as a temporary command post. On 29 July 1954 Rudenko met Moskalenko and both, for six long months, day and night, investigated the 'Beria case'. Rudenko put most of the questions, Moskalenko added some of his own, the entire proceedings transcribed by legal-investigator Tsaregradsky. No physical force was used against Beria, who wrote many letters first to the Presidium, then to Malenkov, insisting that his arrest was a mistake. Finally Malenkov, Bulganin and Khrushchev ordered that Beria be given neither paper, pencils nor pens. The six-month investigation produced forty volumes of evidence. At 10 a.m. on 18 December 1953 in Moscow, a special judicial session of the Soviet Supreme Court met *in camera*. Konev presided over the proceedings with Moskalenko among the members of the tribunal. The proceedings lasted five days: on 23 December 1953 Beria was found guilty and shot on the spot. The Soviet Colonel deputed to carry out the execution could not face it. Batitsky personally finished Beria off. The body was cremated.

Moskalenko's wartime association with Khrushchev and his show of personal loyalty and Party steadfastness during the Beria affair served him well. Like others of the so-called 'Stalingrad group' – wartime associates of Khrushchev – he was assigned a key command position in 1953, that of Moscow Military District. Khrushchev also emplaced his close associate, L. I. Brezhnev, as deputy head of the Main Political Administration. One month after Malenkov was removed from power in 1955, six officers of the 'Stalingrad group' including Moskalenko were promoted to the highest rank, Marshal of the Soviet Union. The 'southwestern theatre' was winning the war all over again. With Zhukov dismissed in 1957 Khrushchev gained a tighter hold on the military, but with Khrushchev's growing 'missile mania' and the future of conventional forces in doubt, dissent was growing. The 'Stalingrad group' split, though Moskalenko together with Marshals Biryuzov, Chuikov and Yeremenko still actively supported Khrushchev. However, in 1960 Moskalenko's career took another unexpected turn. On 24 October Chief Marshal of Artillery M. I. Nedelin, commander of the newly created Strategic Missile Forces – Khrushchev's pride and joy – was killed along with hundreds of others in a giant explosion at an ICBM site. Moskalenko now took up his old associate's command, for both had been commanders of the new anti-tank brigades in Kiev Military District in 1941.

In April 1962 Moskalenko's command career came to a strange, secretive, bizarre end when he was removed from the Strategic Missile Forces and transferred to the Defence Ministry Inspectorate, home for retired Marshals. In June 1962 Khrushchev stated publicly that 'we are helping Cuba with weapons and other things'. What Khrushchev did not disclose was the highly secret, vastly ramified operation involving a major logistics effort, Operation 'Anadyr', to ship forty-two ballistic missiles and many thousands of men into Cuba, the operation which in October precipitated the Cuban Missile Crisis. The decision to place ballistic missiles in Cuba obviously affected Moskalenko directly and it was a decision he evidently disapproved of, either for operational reasons or from concern over the risk, for the Cuban missile venture was inherently a gamble – and a nuclear gamble entailing the highest possible risk. Moskalenko was not alone in falling from favour and suffering dismissal. Golikov, head of the Main Political Administration, clearly faced with the duty of explaining away the Cuban adventure and evidently baulking at it, was removed and replaced by A. A. Yepishev (who had served from 1943 to 1945 with Moskalenko as the third political member of the military soviet of 38th Army).

In July Moskalenko's fortunes slipped further, having been deprived of his post as Deputy Defence Minister, but towards the end of the year his standing recovered somewhat, for his ranking of Deputy Minister was restored. But he never again assumed an active command. In 1978 he was awarded a second Hero of the Soviet Union gold star, seven years before his death in 1985 closed a career committed to the Red Army and devoted to the Communist Party, marked by strange twists of circumstance and a final brush with what could have been unparalleled calamity.

BIBLIOGRAPHY

Glantz, David M., *From the Don to the Dnepr: Soviet Offensive Operations, December 1942–August 1943*, Cass, London, 1991.

Kolkowicz, Roman, *The Soviet Military and the Communist Party*, Princeton University Press, Princeton, 1967.

Konev, I. S. (ed.), *Za osvobozhdenie Chekhoslovakii*, Voenizdat, Moscow, 1965.

Konev, I. S., *Zapiski komanduyushchego frontom, 1943–1944*, Nauka, Moscow, 1972.

Lobov, G., 'V nebe Severnoi Korei', *Aviatsiya i kosmonavtika*, no. 10, 1990.

Moskalenko, K. S., 'Kievskaya operatsiya', *Voenno-istoricheskii Zhurnal*, no. 12, 1973.

Moskalenko, K. S., *Na Yugo-zapadnom napravlenii: Vospominiya komandarma*, 2 vols, Nauka, Moscow, 1973.

Moskalenko, K. S., 'Intervyu polkovodtsev', *ViZh*, no. 2, 1978.

Nekrasov, V. F. (ed.), *Beria: konets karyery*, Politizdat, Moscow, 1991.

Sadarananda, Dana V., *Beyond Stalingrad: Manstein and the Operations of Army Group Don*, Praeger, New York, 1990.

Sovetskie vosdushno-desantnye: voenno-istoricheskii ocherk, 2nd edn, Voenizdat, Moscow, 1986.

Tatu, Michel, *Power in the Kremlin*, Collins, London, 1967.

Vladimirskii, A. V., *Na kievskom napravlenii*, Voenizdat, Moscow, 1989.

Alexander Alexandrovich
NOVIKOV

JOHN ERICKSON

One fine day in 1922 a junior 'Red Commander', Alexander Novikov, currently attending the Vystrel (Higher Rifle School for Commanders) infantry training course, won a fifteen-minute flight as a passenger from an airfield near Moscow, the prize in a lottery draw. Completely smitten with the 'aviation bug', the young Novikov henceforth dreamed only of aeroplanes and pilots, but not even in his wildest dreams could he have thought that exactly twenty years later he would take command of the entire Soviet Air Force, fighting the Luftwaffe, one of the most formidable and battle-tested aerial armadas the world had ever seen.

Novikov was born in November 1900 into a poor peasant family in the village of Kryukovo in Kostroma province, learning to work on the land from an early age but attending to his books with both diligence and eagerness. After attending primary and elementary school he was successful in the examinations for the Kineshemsk-Khrenovsk teaching training college, subsequently taking up a teaching post in a primary school in nearby Peshevo. Being a teacher suited him and he was more than satisfied with his choice of profession. The thought of the army never entered his head, though even the unenthusiastic accounts his father gave of his military service as an NCO in the Russo-Japanese War and in the Great War kindled a certain curiosity.

Like millions of others Novikov's life changed dramatically as a result of the events of 1917. As a former NCO, his father was mobilized for the new Red Army, leaving the young Novikov the 'man of the house' responsible for looking after his younger sisters and brother. His monthly wage consisted of one *pud* (36 lbs) of flour which he had to collect from the granary. His mother knew he was keen to get a higher education and, though it meant leaving her alone with three small children, she let him leave to improve his education.

Not quite eighteen, Novikov decided to risk it and travelled to Ivanovo, where he applied to the agronomy faculty of the Polytechnical Institute evacuated from Riga in 1916. In these lean and hungry times Novikov decided to return home to resume teaching children, thinking that the Civil War would not last long. But a year later, in the autumn of 1919 Novikov found himself called up to the Red Army, a country lad from the far north posted a long way from home, finding himself 'in the thick of it' with the 27th PriVolga Regiment stationed at Nizhni Novgorod. Novikov was evidently marked out by the commanders and military commissars as a young man receptive to their views, and in February 1920 he was posted to the Nizhni Novgorod infantry course for junior 'Red Commanders'. Three months later, on 24 May, by unanimous vote he was made a member of the Communist Party.

On his infantry course he became acquainted with Boris Kuznetsov, a former tsarist officer, and a 'military specialist', who not only taught tactics but tried to inform his students about the personalities and achievements of both White and Red commanders – firing Novikov with a resolve to try to serve under Uborevich, the Red Army *Wunderkind*, in his early twenties, 9th Army commander and victor in the north Caucasus. But his new posting took him to the opposite end of Russia, first as assistant company commander then chief of reconnaissance in the 348th Rifle Regiment of the 43rd Rifle Division attached to 7th Army, operating on the relatively quiet Northern Front in the area of Petrozavodsk. Novikov asked for a transfer to the Western Front but was refused, only to be posted on 10 March 1921 to the 128th Rifle Brigade in Petrograd, arriving there just two days after the outbreak of the Kronshtadt mutiny.

Reconnaissance troops were badly needed; the first assault on the Kronshtadt forts had failed. Tukhachevsky was recalled from the Western Front to take command of 7th Army and the operations to crush the mutineers. Novikov was attached to Tukhachevsky's staff and put in charge of field reconnaissance for the left flank of the Northern Group, one of the two battle groups set up by Tukhachevsky. It was from Tukhachevsky that the young Novikov learned of the value of aerial reconnaissance on the Western Front, even with a few aircraft. Taking part in the assault on No. 6 Fort, Novikov saw his first demonstration of aircraft in a ground-attack rôle when, as the fog lifted, Semen Korf's small Red squadron bombed and machine-gunned the defenders holding out in the forts and on the warships. The massacres on the icebound Gulf of Finland, the whole bloody suppression of Kronshtadt, ended on 18 March 1921, whereupon Novikov returned to the 128th Rifle Brigade.

As the 128th disbanded, out of the blue came a request from Kuznetsov, now Chief of Staff of the Independent Caucasus Army, for Novikov to be posted to the south. Kuznetsov urged him to apply for admission to the Vystrel course, and in November 1921 Novikov was admitted to the 'field academy' of the Red Army, a focus for intensive and impressive political activity with speakers drawn from the luminaries of the international Communist movement – Bela Kun, Palmiro Togliatti, Ernst Thälmann, Georgy Dmitrov, Wilhelm Pieck. But these military and political excitements paled into insignificance compared with that one breath-taking flight. As soon as his feet touched the ground Novikov determined to apply for admission to the Red Air Fleet Zhukovsky Engineering Institute. His superiors, however, decided otherwise.

As the huge Civil War Red Army gradually demobilized, 'quality' rather than 'quantity' became the watchword, necessitating special attention to the training of commanders. As a result Novikov, now a Vystrel graduate, found himself assigned as assistant to the head of the 14th Command Course in Batum, but in February 1923 he was sent to Tbilisi to take over successively a company and a battalion in the Caucasian Army's military-political school. Novikov was also assigned in 1924 to those special units fighting Cholokayev's insurrection and crushing the Menshevik rising in Georgia. Now married and with a son, Lev, in 1925 he took advantage of the visit of Ordzhonikidze and Kuznetsov to the training school to ask abut the possibility of entry to the Military Academy: he hankered after the Air Force Academy though as yet he lacked the necessary specialist education and skills.

In 1927 Novikov finally entered the Frunze Academy at a time when Tukhachevsky held the chair for strategy, Triandafillov lectured on operational art, Kalinovsky on armoured troops, Karbyshev on military engineering, Novitsky on the history of the Great War. Novikov became acquainted with the early work on the theory of 'deep operation' (see article 'Tukhachevsky') and combined-arms offensive operations employing massed armour, aviation, artillery and airborne troops. He graduated among those at the top of the examination list and was duly posted to Belorussia Military District at Smolensk, as chief of reconnaissance with the 11th Rifle Corps commanded by the Civil War hero E. I. Kovtyukh. The district was at this time a hive of activity under Yegorov, but when Uborevich took over in August 1931 the emphasis began to shift towards intensive training and experimentation.

I. P. Uborevich (an expert on military developments in Germany which he had visited as part of the secret Red Army–Reichswehr collaboration) took a keen interest in aerial reconnaissance. In September 1932 he detached both Novikov and Argunov, chief of operations with the 8th Rifle Corps, to the staff of the District Air Force to study air operations. Due to illness Argunov could not fly, leaving Novikov alone on this special posting – a half-way house, as Uborevich fully intended it should be, to inch Novikov into the Air Force. The Central Committee in 1931 had already decided on the reorganization of the air force, as well as on an expansion of political and technical training. The new aviation units needed more officers, which the

Central Committeee proposed to find by transferring the best trained and most forward-looking army men to that service.

Uborevich suggested such a transfer to Novikov, but there remained the matter of his defective eyesight: already one medical board had turned him down and even during his time at the Frunze Academy Novikov had been graded 'unsuitable' for Air Force service. Uborevich suggested that Novikov could 'compensate' with his knowledge of ground operations – and also advised Novikov to read Giulio Douhet, the Italian air warfare strategist. Uborevich clearly disagreed profoundly with Douhet. Aviation, according to Uborevich, should be used primarily in a ground-support/ground-attack rôle rather than for independent strategic air operations, hence the importance of assigning Red Army officers to Air Force units. Two days after this exchange A. Ya. Lapin, the District Air Force commander, instructed Novikov to report to him. Here Novikov learned that by order of Uborevich he had been appointed chief of staff to the 450th Aviation Brigade in Smolensk. Not that this type of transfer was at all unique. Over an entire decade, from 1928 to 1938, 5,670 Red Army officers were assigned to the Air Force, among them Vershinin (from a rifle battalion), Vorozheikin (divisional commander), Naumenko (cavalryman), Falaleyev (regimental commander), each one destined to become a leading wartime air commander.

Life in an Air Force unit proved to be far from easy for Novikov, since pilots did not take kindly to being instructed by and associated with a mere infantry 'foot-slogger'. However, things improved when brigade commander Yungmeister was transferred to the Far East and his place was taken by Ye. S. Ptukhin, commander of a fighter squadron from the Bryansk aviation brigade. Ptukhin believed in what Yakov Alsknis, a qualified military pilot and the head of the Air Force since 1931, preached, namely, good order and strict discipline both on the ground and in the air. Soon finding himself on familiar terms with Ptukhin, Novikov gingerly broached the question of taking flying lessons, whereupon Ptukhin arranged a special programme for Novikov who quickly mastered basic flying on a U-2 trainer, soloed and then moved on to the R-5 fighter.

The year 1935 brought success coupled with personal tragedy. In April his wife, Militsa Konstantinovna, died of tuberculosis, leaving Novikov with three small children to bring up. However, the 1935 manoeuvres conducted by Uborevich were, in public at least, a spectacular success, with massed parachute drops, the capture of an 'enemy' aerodrome and transport planes landing light tanks, artillery and ammunition. In yet another interview with Uborevich, at that time in high good humour, Novikov formally requested a transfer to flying duties and was told that he must begin by taking command of a squadron, which could mean a drop in rank. More than content with this, while on leave in Sochi he accepted a posting as commander of the 42nd Light Bomber Squadron with four flights of R-5s, ten aircraft to a flight.

His promotion to Colonel came on 28 March 1936. In the 1936 manoeuvres watched by Voroshilov, Tukhachevsky and Yegorov at the General Staff and a bevy of foreign observers, Colonel Novikov's bomber squadron excelled itself. But the triumphs of 1936 all too quickly faded beside the grimmer portents of 1937. Novikov had earlier met Ordzhonikidze in the Caucasus and news of his death – rather the rumours of his suicide – shook Novikov badly. The military purge began to bite. Arrests of 'enemies of the people' flowed in quick succession: more than seventy-five men of the 450th Aviation Brigade were arrested in a matter of weeks. Uborevich himself was arrested. Though not a single accusation from the 42nd Regiment was levelled at Novikov, Moscow peremptorily demanded his expulsion from the Party. Novikov was relieved of his duties. The Party commission of the 116th Aviation Brigade was forced on 2 June 1937 to administer and record a severe reprimand, whereupon Novikov appealed to Commissar 2nd Rank A. I. Mezis, a member of the Military Soviet of Belorussia Military District. He at once ordered Novikov to be restored to his rank and command – but Mezis himself was arrested in January 1938. Novikov languished only briefly on the reserve. Miraculously, in March 1938 the Party commission of the 116th Aviation Brigade, recognizing that Novikov was 'neither a tippler nor an associate of women of doubtful virtue', withdrew the 'severe reprimand'.

One month later during a visit to Moscow, Novikov quite by chance came upon Ptukhin. His old friend was fresh from acting as an 'adviser' to the Republican forces in Spain and full of information about the latest German fighter aircraft. In the course of these exchanges Ptukhin intimated that he had been appointed air commander of Leningrad Military District. He immediately proposed that Novikov take the post of his Chief of Staff, if higher authorities approved. With that duly sanctioned, Novikov moved to his new post with the Leningrad Military District Air Force which included over seven aviation brigades and mustered over 1,000 aircraft. But for all its impressive numbers, the Soviet Air Force as a whole was in poor shape, suffering not only from creeping technical obsolescence but also from the severe damage inflicted by Stalin's massive military purge. Most of the senior air commanders disappeared between 1937 and 1938. Alksnis was shot in 1938, Loktionov, a one-time rifle brigade commander and with little experience of the Air Force, took over for a brief period until Ya. V. Smushkevich, fresh from a triumph over the Japanese in fierce fighting at Khalkin-Gol in Outer Mongolia, assumed the post of Head of the Air Force Administration in September 1939. Not only the purges wreaked havoc. Stalin regarded the Air Force as his own special fiefdom, priding himself on his technical knowledge, subjecting designers, engineers and commanders alike to arbitrary decisions and excessive demands. Failure meant the firing squad or the Gulag, where a number of distinguished designers, Tupolev among them, languished in Beria's prison 'design bureaux'.

The disastrous 'Winter War' with Finland in 1939–40 revealed the lamentable state of the Soviet Air Force. Indifferent air gunnery, poor training, neglect of night and bad-weather flying, the lack of personal initiative and faulty navigation, shortage of radio communication, all brought calamity to the Red Air Force in operations over Finland. On the ground an early attempt by 7th Army to storm the Mannerheim Line off the march failed. Meretskov, the army commander, protested at the lack of air support for the assault troops, for which Novikov had inevitably to accept the blame. As the war dragged through the winter the Northwestern Front was established in January 1940 under Timoshenko, with Novikov acting as chief of staff to Ptukhin's Front Air Force. Whenever it was authorized he seized the opportunity to fly as a pilot-observer during the preparations for the massive, pounding assault on the Mannerheim Line.

Massed fire-power and overwhelming numbers finally broke Finnish resistance and pierced the Mannerheim Line. The cost of the war to the Soviet Air Force through enemy action and accidents amounted to some 640–650 aircraft. The Red Army suffered horrendously and, in a grim portent of things to come, the 6,000 Soviet prisoners-of-war repatriated by the Finns were handed over to the NKVD once on Soviet soil. Smushkevich paid for this poor performance by the Air Force with dismissal (and ultimate execution). Stalin, as usual, re-shuffled the command, selecting a 29-year-old lieutenant-general, P. V. Rychagov, who had served as a fighter pilot in China, to head the Air Force administration. Stalin also decided in August 1940 to transfer Ptukhin to Kiev Special Military District. Over the question of who should replace Ptukhin he promptly answered himself – Novikov, 'good worker, proved himself in the Finnish war'. The new Defence Commissar Timoshenko, himself a replacement for the incompetent, boastful Voroshilov whose blunders cost the Red Army dear in Finland, duly assented.

The Soviet Air Force did not lack for sheer numbers – between 1938 and June, 1941 Soviet industry turned out 9,690 bombers and 12,995 fighters, but more modern aircraft materialized only late in the day and only in limited numbers, 86 in 1940, rising to 2,653 by 1941, with 322 LAGG-3 and 460 Pe-2 bombers delivered up to June 1941. Pilot conversion proceeded even more slowly. The MiG fighter programme was more successful in terms of numbers delivered, but pilots feared the new fighter and many tried to steer clear of the MiG-3 if at all possible. By June 1941 only nineteen air regiments had acquired new combat aircraft. Radio communication suffered from shortages and poor equipment. Airfields suitably fitted out with hangars and prepared runways were also relatively few in number, while aviation 'rear services' (logistics, supply, maintenance and repair) suffered from an acute shortage of transport, repair shops, spares and trained mechanics. Most damning of all, however, was the lack within the Soviet command of any realistic concept of an operational application of air power and the failure to recognize the need for effective centralized control of air assets. During the Finnish war Novikov had seen for himself the damage inflicted by the dispersion of effort and the dissipation of assets due to the separate existence of 'Front' aviation and 'Army' aviation.

Throughout 1941 the accident rate in the Air Force increased alarmingly. When taxed about this by Stalin, Rychagov rounded on him intemperately and bitterly: 'There are accidents and there will be more of them because you are driving pilots to their graves.' Without raising his voice Stalin replied: 'You shouldn't have said that.' Rychagov's fate was sealed, and he was executed later in the year. In April 1941 Stalin appointed 40-year-old Lieutenant-General Pavel Zhigarev, former cavalryman, graduate of the command faculty of the Zhukovsky Air Academy, to head the main administration of the Soviet Air Force. In the course of three and a half years five heads of the Air Force had come and gone, some to their deaths. This lack of continuity at the top was made worse when more than 91 per cent of the commanders of major air formations had been in their posts for less than six months. In 1940 a report from the Air Force command had commented adversely on both the absence of theoretical knowledge among the bulk of a youthful command group and the lack of 'organizational habits' among 'yesterday's fliers in command of their comrades from earlier days'. To repair this and other gross deficiencies in organization, equipment and training, little enough time remained in 1941 before the German onslaught.

Shortly after 1 a.m. on Sunday 22 June 1941 Major-General Novikov returned home in Leningrad, about to travel to Kiev to take up the post of commander of Kiev Special Military District Air Force from Ptukhin. General D. N. Nikishev summoned Novikov urgently to headquarters. A directive from Moscow signalled that a surprise attack by German forces might ensue in the course of 22–23 June. At 3 a.m. Hitler's forces went to war on the Soviet Union, launching a devastating surprise attack across a 1,000-mile front. Luftwaffe bombers, their targets carefully marked by earlier aerial reconnaissance, carried out the greatest aerial massacre in history, wiping out uncamouflaged Soviet aircraft on the ground neatly parked in parade order, destroying more than 1,000 aircraft by noon. (Losses for the 'initial period' amount to 2,062 aircraft, 72 per cent destroyed on the ground, 12 per cent shot down by German fighters.) Four days into the war Novikov mustered all available aircraft to cover a front running from the Gulf of Finland to the Barents Sea, massing them as best he might, launching them on a series of nineteen consecutive raids on German airfields in Finland and northern Norway, as well as Finnish bases and communications. But as the Soviet Northwestern Front crumpled and the German drive to the south on

Leningrad gathered frightening speed, Novikov realized he would now have to fight on two fronts.

As German forces and Finnish troops closed on Leningrad from the northwest and southeast, Novikov decided to concentrate his force in the critical battle to the south, forming aviation 'fists'. Early in July 1941 Stalin set up three high commands, Northwestern, Western and Southwestern: Voroshilov took over the Northwestern with Novikov as air commander, though in less than a month this command was wound up and split up into the Leningrad and Karelian Fronts. With 326 aircraft (a third of them battle-damaged) Novikov prepared to defend the immediate approaches to Leningrad and the city itself, now in mortal danger. Stalin peremptorily re-called Voroshilov in virtual disgrace, and ordered General Zhukov to Lenin-grad on 10 September to organize a last-ditch defence. The hard-hitting, overbearing Zhukov evidently found in Novikov an air commander after his own heart. By way of reinforcement Zhukov managed to wring one regiment of Pe-2 bombers and a regiment of Il-2 ground-attack aircraft from Stalin.

On 7 October Zhukov flew back to Moscow. German armour swung southwards to join the offensive aimed at Moscow. The German bid to capture Leningrad had been beaten off, but the city was completely besieged. Leningrad began to starve. An 'aerial bridge' of transport planes brought in supplies but never enough for a whole city and its defenders. Novikov sought no privileges for himself, living on sparse, dwindling rations. His own son grew weaker. In spite of the youngster's pleas to stay, Novikov had him flown out with other young evacuees. With the coming of winter the ice across Lake Ladoga provided another supply route, a hazardous life-line into and out of the city to which Novikov assigned air cover to fend off German bombers harrying the columns of lorries and smashing the ice-road.

The grim winter of 1941–2 closed with the Red Army fighting doggedly to lift the Leningrad blockade and with the Moscow counter-offensive slowly grinding to a halt. Suddenly, disconcertingly, Novikov was ordered to Moscow. Stalin met him on the evening of 3 February 1942, informing him brusquely that he was to become Zhigarev's first deputy. Novikov's new responsibilities involved building up air reserves, but his immediate task was to report to Zhukov at the Western Front – evidently it was to Zhukov's influence with Stalin that he owed his transfer to Moscow. Novikov planned and co-ordinated air operations, including a major airborne assault, in the closing stages of Zhukov's winter offensive. Reporting on these operations to Stalin, Novikov criticized the division into 'Army' and 'Front' aviation which ruined any attempt at the mass employment of air assets: 'Army aviation' held on grimly to 'its' aircraft, Front aviation was equally posses-sive. To remedy this Novikov proposed the creation of an 'aviation corps' with up to six or eight air regiments in each corps. Stalin was incredulous: 'Six to eight regiments in each?!'

Early in March Stalin and Stavka (GHQ) despatched Novikov to the Volkhov Front to co-ordinate air operations in a joint offensive with the Leningrad Front to lift the blockade. With air commanders I. P. Zhuravlev, A. Ye. Golovanov and S. I. Rudenko, Novikov seized on the absence of aviation divisions to create a 'temporary air group' consisting of eight regiments under Rudenko's command. For the first time in the war one senior Soviet air officer – Novikov himself – commanded and co-ordinated the air assets of two Fronts, Leningrad and Volkhov. Further south the Red Army had trapped a powerful German force in the 'Demyansk pocket'. Here Novikov was assigned to impose a full aerial blockade which proved to be beyond the resources available to him. If that was impossible, he could at least attack the Ju-52 transports flying in reinforcements, food and ammunition. In an unorthodox tactic, Novikov threw in the heavily armoured ground-attack Il-2s, the *shturmoviki*, 'flying tanks', to take on the lumbering Junkers. The Red Air Force learned to expect the unexpected from him – 'Novikov's here, watch out for novelties!' – playing on his name.

His promotion to Lieutenant-General in April 1942 coincided with his appointment by Stalin to full command of the Red Army Air Force and as Deputy Commissar for Aviation. Several air commanders who failed Stalin had gone before a firing squad. Novikov shook up the entire organization of the Air Force, first picking his own staff. G. A. Vorozheikin was appointed his First Deputy with S. A. Khudyakov taking over from Vorozheikin as Chief of Staff. New deputies took over rear services, engineering-technical support the inspectorate and navigation. New combat aircraft began arriving in great numbers. Soviet industry produced 21,681 aircraft in 1942, with Pe-2 bombers, Yak-7b, Yak-9 fighters, Tu-2 bombers and Il-2 *shturmoviki* now forming more than half the current front-line strength. Novikov embarked energetically on plans to replace Frontal and army aviation with an entirely new organization, the 'air army'. 'Air strike groups' deploying between three and eight regiments had been formed earlier in March 1942, a further 'strike group' followed by May, but these alone did not solve the critical problem of air reserves.

In April 1942 the Military Council of the Red Army Air Force formally abolished Front and Army air components, establishing in their place unified Frontal aviation with designated 'air armies'; reserve formations were in turn designated 'aviation armies'. The first 'air army' was established on 5 May 1942 with two fighter divisions (four air regiments in each), two composite air divisions (two fighter regiments, two ground-attack regiments and one bomber regiment in each division), a training regiment, a long-range reconnaissance squadron, a liaison squadron, and a night bomber regiment flying the ubiquitous U-2 biplanes, the noisy 'sewing machines', many of them flown by women pilots. By November 1942, thirteen air armies had been formed, no longer subordinate to the field armies, whose only air assets were one air regiment for reconnaissance and liaison. In March 1942, Major-General A. Ye. Golovanov had taken command of the newly established Long Range Aviation, directly subordinated to Stavka for independent operations against the deep rear. A final move in this centralization was to subordinate the Civil Air Fleet to Novikov for transportation and evacuation duties, as well as maintaining communications with Soviet partisans operating behind the German lines.

Stalin demanded increasingly powerful Supreme High Command air reserves. In addition to numbers, Novikov required flexibility and mobility of these 'aviation armies', the first three of which were formed on 1 July 1942 (two fighter and one bomber army). But deploying an 'air army' together with an 'aviation army' on one front without a single air commander worked badly and impeded the co-ordination of air operations. The 'air corps' rather than the 'air army' was found to be a better way of organizing air reserves, thirteen such corps being assembled by the end of 1942 (four fighter, three ground-attack, three bomber and three composite groups). At the cost of plundering the 'air armies', as yet under strength, an immediate air reserve was built up, representing one-third of the entire Soviet tactical air strength. (By 1945 that figure had risen to no less than 43 per cent of all front-line combat aircraft.)

In the summer of 1942 the Soviet Union faced fresh calamities. Timoshenko's ill-fated spring offensive to retake Kharkov had ended in disaster, the whole Southern Front crumbled, German armies drove into the Caucasus threatening the oil fields, and advanced towards the Volga, pressing on to Stalingrad. On 12 August 1942 Novikov arrived in Stalingrad as Stavka Representative for Front and Long-Range Aviation operations. At the end of the month Zhukov, Deputy Supreme Commander, flew into Stalingrad with instructions from Stalin to assign control of all fighter aviation on the Stalingrad and Southwestern Fronts to Novikov. In addition to ordering the intensification of night bombing raids, Novikov also introduced an experimental system using ground-based radio stations to control fighter aircraft and air engagements, sending twenty-five air commanders to the front to act as fighter controllers and instructing them to compile an operational manual for future use.

Stalin suddenly recalled Novikov to Moscow from these gruelling air battles to adjudicate in a dispute over whether or not to continue production of the I-16 and I-153 aircraft (the latter the 'manoeuvrable fighter biplane'), old war-horses whose time had passed. Khudyakov, 1st Air Army commander on the Western Front, supported by Bulganin, wrote to Stalin suggesting discontinuation. Stalin refused. Novikov, however, playing on Stalin's preference for the offensive mode, argued that, while the I-16 and the I-153 were well suited to defensive actions, they were not adequate for offensive operations or for winning air superiority. Stalin duly stopped production of these aircraft.

The battle for Stalingrad raged day and night. The Soviet defenders were driven back to the very edge of the Volga, but Stalin, closeted with Zhukov and Vasilevsky, worked on plans for a massive counter-offensive designed to encircle the German forces. Novikov had meanwhile been assigned to report on the situation on the Kalinin Front, but in early November he was summoned again by Stalin and ordered to fly at once to Stalingrad, where the huge counter-offensive was in the offing. Novikov pointed out that Major-General Vorozheikin was already the acting Stavka Representative on the spot. 'I haven't forgotten, comrade Novikov,' Stalin remarked. But Zhukov had asked specifically for Novikov, saying, 'We work well together.' Displacing Vorozheikin was no reflection on him, but agreeing to Zhukov's request would help 'to get the job done'. Zhukov met Novikov at the Serafimovich bridgehead, bringing him into the 'mighty magic circle' of senior commanders – Vasilevsky (General Staff), Voronov (artillery), Fedorenko (armour), Golovanov (bomber aviation). Air reinforcement poured in, three aviation corps and seven independent divisions to supplement 17th, 16th and 8th Air Armies, five bomber divisions plus the 102nd Fighter Regiment from Air Defence, in all 1,414 aircraft.

Working on the preparations for the attack, Operation 'Uranus', Novikov discovered to his consternation that the air effort would not be ready by 12 November, the date originally planned. Zhukov duly informed Stalin by telegram. Stalin's reply underlined the vital rôle of air operations in ensuring success and set out specific air missions. If Novikov needed more time and more aircraft, then this would be allowed. Before Soviet guns opened fire in fog and blizzards at 0730 hours on 19 November, Novikov organized some special air support for the ground forces. In the sub-zero temperatures tank engines seized up as anti-freeze supplies ran out. Novikov's solution was to mobilize his spare heavy transport gliders to get anti-freeze to the tank troops.

Driving panic-stricken Romanians before them and breaking through the German lines, attacking from north and south of Stalingrad, the Red Army snapped the encirclement shut at Kalach, trapping two German armies. In a repeat of the Demyansk operation German transport planes began to fly in supplies to 330,000 beleaguered men, soon close to starvation, as Novikov ordered his aircraft to hold off von Manstein's relief attempt and to mount their own 'aerial blockade'. In December 1942 Novikov moved to Rokossovsky's Don Front to provide air support for Operation 'Ring' to reduce the trapped Stalingrad garrison, the German VI Army, which on 3 February 1943 surrendered with Field-Marshal von Paulus at its head. From 19 November 1942 to 2 February 1943 Soviet aircraft flew 35,929 sorties, dropped 141,000 bombs, fired 30,000 rockets and claimed 3,000 enemy aircraft destroyed.

Fresh from the triumph at Stalingrad, Novikov flew north on Stalin's orders to the 'Demyansk pocket', the stubborn, half-encircled German force still holding out after eighteen months. Novikov's orders prescribed that the 'Ramushevo corridor' be cut, the encirclement sealed and the garrisons reduced. The Northwestern Front attack opened on 15 February 1943 with Novikov using Polynin's 6th Air Army to enforce an 'aerial blockade', exploiting the experience gained at Stalingrad. For this and for Stalingrad Colonel-General Novikov was awarded the Order of Suvorov 1st Class and in less than a month, on 17 March, named Air Marshal, the first appointment of its kind in the Soviet Union. Ahead gigantic battles loomed as the Red Army fought to seize the strategic initiative. Novikov now mustered thirteen air armies supported by nineteen aviation corps of the Supreme Commander's Reserve, with special fighter regiments of the air defence forces assigned to cover front-line aerodromes and eight bomber corps for independent operations commanded by Golovanov. Front-line strength stood at 5,892 aircraft, tangible proof of the extraordinary exertions of Soviet workers.

The sweeping Soviet offensive to unhinge the entire German southern wing slowed on meeting increasing resistance. In March von Manstein's slicing counter-stroke recovered Kharkov, the front line stabilized, leaving the Red Army holding the giant Kursk salient. But defeat at Stalingrad placed German forces in the Caucasus in great danger as they carried out a perilous withdrawal. In the lower Kuban and on the Taman peninsula, however, German XVII Army dug itself in and drew on ample supplies. Overhead, over a narrow section of the front in the Kuban, the Soviet Air Force fought a two-month battle for air superiority, opening with massive attacks on German airfields. In the three phases of the air battle the Soviet Air Force flew 35,000 sorties and claimed the destruction of 1,100 German aircraft, 800 of them in air-to-air battles. These Kuban air battles marked a new phase for the Soviet Air Force, introducing the 'air offensive'. In the subsequent command conference analysing the results of the fighting, Novikov stressed the vital importance of operational air supremacy, the rôle of the 'air offensive' and the effectiveness of control by radio from air commanders at forward posts at the front.

In July 1943 a mighty armoured encounter opened in the Kursk salient, the decisive battle of the war. Commanding 2,900 aircraft (including Long-Range Aviation) to counter the Luftwaffe strength of 2,050 bombers, fighters, ground-attack and reconnaissance aircraft, Novikov issued strict orders that aviation corps attached to air armies must only be used on main sectors and under *no* circumstances be dispersed. At long last Stalin was persuaded that the Red Army should first remain on the defensive, ordering the air force to interdict German rail and road movements by day and by night. Air Marshal Novikov, working with Zhukov, was responsible for co-ordinating air operations, assisted by his deputy Vorozheikin and Khudyakov (recently appointed Chief of Air Staff). One important tactical change involved the Il-2s, the 'tank-busters', instructed to fly in staggered line abreast to make specific diving attacks from under 1,000 metres, releasing their ordnance when 2–300 metres from the target and then making strafing runs with their cannon and machine-guns. In the air battles the Luftwaffe's Bf-109Gs and FW-190s continued to have an edge, but the newest Soviet La-5FN and Yak-9 fighters proved to be formidable opponents, the Soviet air force claiming the destruction of 3,700 German aircraft in fifty days of air combat.

With the German tank thrusts on Kursk deflected and Hoth's IV Panzer Army battered at Prokhorovka, the Red Army turned to a sweeping offensive designed to reach the eastern Ukraine and the Dnieper river line. Though satisfied with the outcome at Kursk, Stalin was furious at the failure of General Sokolovsky's offensive operations further north aimed at Smolensk. On a unique visit to 'the front' (but not *too* near the front-line!) Stalin learned in detail of the slow Soviet progress. In late August 1943 he ordered Marshal Voronov and Air Marshal Novikov to the Kalinin Front to co-ordinate the offensive. Major-General Gromov and Novikov worked out an operational air plan with Sokolovsky and liaised with General Yeremenko on the Kalinin Front to mount an extensive deception manoeuvre. Novikov's ruse of committing Golovanov's bombers to pound the apparent line of advance succeeded in diverting German reinforcement from Sokolovsky's main thrust directed at Smolensk. Once recaptured, the city where Novikov had spent almost eight years, had buried his wife and young son Igor, had learned to fly, lay in ruins.

In December 1943, as he had done after Stalingrad, Novikov held a command conference with officers from the air armies, military district air commanders and reserve air brigades to examine the results of Soviet air operations at Kursk and elsewhere on the Soviet-German front, con-centrating on means to improve pilot training in reserve regiments and developing new training courses for fighter, ground-attack and bomber pilots. Soviet air strength continued to rise, growing from 8,500 aircraft in January 1944 to 13,500 in June, though a much weakened Luftwaffe continued to inflict heavy losses, claiming the destruction of 6,900 Soviet bombers and 5,100 fighters in 1943.

In December 1943 the Red Army liberated Kiev and the offensive by four Soviet Ukrainian Fronts continued to unroll against the entire German southern wing, with Air Marshal Novikov co-ordinating the air operations. Late in January Konev's 1st Ukrainian Front and Vatutin's 2nd Ukrainian Front, supported by 5th and 2nd Air Armies, encircled a large German force at Korsun-Shevchenkovsky, a 'touch of the Stalingrad whip', as Konev put it. Novikov had also been involved in making preparations to receive the American Army Air Force bombers flying 'shuttle missions' in raids on Germany and landing in Ukraine at Poltava, Mirgorod and Priyatin. General

A. R. Perminov was put in charge of the 169th Special Air Base and the administration entrusted to General S. T. Levandovich, directly subordinated to General A. V. Nikitin, one of Novikov's deputy commanders. To protect the airfields to be used by the American bomber groups with their fighter escort, Novikov ordered extra air defences and increased vigilance. Prophetic instructions indeed, to no avail. During the night of 22 June the Luftwaffe, with Hungarian bombers making their last foray, raided Poltava, destroying forty-three B-17 'Flying Fortresses' on the ground.

Suddenly Stalin summoned Novikov to Stavka. The head of Red Army Armoured and Mechanized Troops, Marshal Fedorenko, was already present. Looking at Novikov Stalin spoke: 'Tell me, Comrade Novikov, can aircraft stop tanks?' 'It's possible,' Novikov replied. (He recalled Il-2s using hollow-charge ordnance to knock out German tanks at Ponyri in the Kursk salient.) 'Then tomorrow fly down to Vatutin and take the necessary measures to stop the tanks. Everyone trumpets that they have encircled the enemy at Korsun-Shevchenkovsky but so far they can't finish him off.' In an ill humour Stalin stopped Novikov short when he mentioned Khudyakov, Stavka Representative for air operations with Vatutin's 1st Ukrainian Front: 'I don't need Khudyakov there. Get rid of him.' Novikov emphasized the good work being done by the Air Force Chief of Staff but Stalin rounded on him: 'I don't need him there. Fly to Vatutin yourself and stop the tanks.' Novikov might be able to halt German tank attacks but he could not erase Stalin's malice towards Khudyakov, who paid dearly for it later. (Khudyakov's real name was Armenak Artemevich Khanferyanz, born in Nagorny Karabakh and Armenian by nationality. He changed his name to Khudyakov – that of a commander killed in action – to throw Beria off his scent, for his father had discovered Beria's rôle in the shooting of the twenty-six Baku commissars in 1918: Beria had been a guard taking them to be shot. On 14 December 1945 Khudyakov, commander of 12th Air Army, en route from the Far East to Moscow, was arrested in Chita and never seen again. Charged in 1947, his family was promised his release but he was shot on 23 April 1950.)

German attempts to relieve the encircled force at Korsun-Shevchenkovsky were beaten off by ground-attack aircraft and artillery, with the Il-2 *shturmoviki* of 2nd Air Army attacking German tanks. To interdict German air supply Novikov organized four 'destruction zones' covered by fighters and assigned bombers to strike airfields beyond the outer encirclement ring. When the relief attempt failed, German troops formed into columns to fight their way out to the southwest: in a horrendous maelstrom of blood and the mud of an early spring thaw the German columns were decimated and the Korsun 'pocket' reduced on 18 February 1944. On 21 February Novikov was at Vatutin's command post. Also present was Marshal Zhukov recently arrived from Moscow to co-ordinate the forthcoming operations of the 1st and 2nd Ukrainian Fronts. In the evening the telephone rang with a call from Moscow. Zhukov took the receiver. 'Alexander Alexandrovich,' he said, 'you have just become the first ever Air Chief Marshal.' Stalin's own congratulatory telegram arrived shortly afterwards.

In the late winter and early spring of 1944, the year of the 'ten decisive blows', four Soviet southern fronts (1st, 2nd, 3rd and 4th Ukrainian) advanced deep into the Ukraine and closed on the Romanian frontier. Novikov again co-ordinated the massive air operations involving 66,000 sorties in heavy attacks on the German front-line and the rear. One German strong point at Ternopol, straddling the Red Army's supply route, caused Zhukov (1st Ukrainian Front commander after Vatutin had been fatally wounded) great disquiet. He consulted Novikov about eliminating this 'thorn in the flesh'. Novikov used two divisions of U-2 biplanes flying by day with fighter cover to hold off the Me-109s. Raining down light bombs the biplanes finally brought about a German surrender.

In mid-May 1944 Novikov returned to Moscow to receive not only his second Order of Suvorov but also orders to fly north to prepare air operations to drive Finland, already suing for peace, out of the war. Just before leaving Moscow Novikov met the United States Ambassador Averell Harriman, whom he understood to have promised the Soviet Air Force a squadron of B-29 bombers, aircraft which Novikov very much admired and hoped to use against the Finnish defences. But Harriman told Novikov that the 'promised' B-29s would not be forthcoming. Stalin took the news calmly enough.

Novikov flew to Leningrad on 6 June in the dual-seat version of a Yak-7 fighter. He intended to find out for himself why Soviet pilots complained about the poor workmanship of their headsets, making radio communication difficult. They did work badly and once in Leningrad Novikov ordered General N. P. Seleznev, head of Air Force procurement, to pass this to the factories for modification.

Soviet air activity in the north had long been on a relatively limited scale, though in the January 1944 offensive to deblockade Leningrad two air armies (13th and 14th, supported by Baltic Fleet naval aviation and aircraft from 15th Air Army of the adjoining 2nd Baltic Front) deployed some 1,200 aircraft. The forthcoming offensive against the Karelian isthmus reminded Novikov of assaulting the Mannerheim Line in those far-off days in 1940, but in 1944 'air armies' now led the attack. At 0800 hours on 9 June General S. D. Rybalchenko, 13th Air Army commander, and General M. I. Samokhin, commander of Baltic Fleet aviation, launched 360 aircraft to attack the first line of defensive positions. Even General Govorov, Leningrad Front commander and famous for his extreme taciturnity, expressed his satisfaction with the result. Further north Novikov worked with General I. M. Sokolov's diminutive 7th Air Army to provide air support for the forthcoming Svirsk-Petrozavodsk operation and finalize the co-ordination of two bomber divisions (334th and 113th) with Red Army operations on the Karelian Front.

Before flying to Leningrad Novikov compiled a directive, summarizing the results of air operations during the winter and spring of 1944, as well as setting out summer missions. Underlining the tactical nature of Soviet air operations, Novikov instructed air crews to study their targets closely and air staffs to pay closer attention to the interaction of aviation with tank and mechanized corps not only in the breakthrough phase but also throughout the depth of the enemy defences. All fighter commanders and the staffs of air armies were ordered to master radio air-control procedures. The control of small groups of aircraft by air army commanders was expressly forbidden: they were to issue general directives to corps and divisional commanders who would then assign sorties according to the tactical situation, a move designed to counter increasing inflexibility in the centralized control of air operations. In fighting for air supremacy each air army had to establish a specialist fighter corps or a division operating specifically under radio air-control.

From Leningrad Novikov flew straight to Belorussia, where Stalin and Stavka planned the giant operation 'Bagration' to destroy the remaining German Army Group, Centre, still a formidable opponent. Five air armies, 1st, 3rd, 4th, 16th (plus 6th assigned to the second phase of the operation) deployed 6,000 aircraft in the greatest concentration of tactical air power yet seen in the war. Air Chief Marshal Novikov worked with Marshal Zhukov on the 1st and 2nd Belorussian Fronts; Aviation General F. Ya. Falaleyev was Stavka's air Representative with Marshal Vasilevsky on the 1st Baltic and 3rd Belorussian Fronts. At Novikov's suggestion and with Zhukov's approval Golovanov's bombers blasted targets in the rear ten days before the offensive opened while tactical units raided enemy airfields. Women pilots from squadrons staffed entirely by women (ground staff, armourers, mechanics) flew flimsy biplanes only recently equipped with a machine-gun to defend themselves, raiding airfields at night, contributing to the 24,000 sorties flown by women pilots throughout the war. In three devastating days from 22 to 24 June massive Soviet attacks unfolded, engulfing first the flanks and then the centre, hurling German units back in confusion or simply smashing them to pieces. Harrying the chaotic German retreat the air force flew 3,000 sorties in five days and sealed the escape route to Minsk, where the Soviet encirclement snapped shut on 3 July, grim retribution for the catastrophe which befell the Red Army in the Bialystok-Minsk encirclement early in July 1941. On 4 July 1944 Army Group Centre ceased to exist as an organized force. Enjoying absolute air supremacy in 'Bagration', the Soviet Air Force flew 55,000 sorties from 22 June to 4 July with Golovanov's bombers proving especially effective in attacking breakthrough zones. (In December, 1944 Golovanov's bomber force was redesignated as 18th Air Army and subordinated directly to Novikov.)

New Year 1945 found the Red Army hammering at the gates of the Reich, its main attack aimed along the Warsaw–Berlin axis. The Soviet Air Force deployed ten air armies and mustered 15,815 aircraft with substantial reserves, with Soviet pilots flying the latest aircraft, the Yak-3, La-7 fighters and Il-10 *shturmoviki*. For the forthcoming Vistula-Oder operation, another mighty offensive, Novikov emphasized two factors – deception and reconnaissance. Aircraft flew to forward positions in stages with great secrecy shrouding their movement; fifty-five dummy airfields were built with 818 dummy aircraft on them, the realism increased by operational aircraft actually using these 'airfields'. New pilots were introduced to their squadrons, others practised dive-bombing small targets, reconnaissance aircraft flew missions deep into the German rear.

Originally planned for 20 January, Stalin advanced the date of the offensive to 12 January in response to an Allied request for Soviet action to relieve German pressure in the Ardennes. Konev in the south attacked first, supported by 400 aircraft of 2nd Air Army operating in bad weather to cover the armoured spearheads. On Zhukov's 1st Belorussian Front, attacking on 14 January, 16th Air Army, heavily reinforced by Novikov, also found itself hampered by bad weather but two days later the weather cleared, bringing the Luftwaffe to battle. The Red Army sped ahead: Novikov thought ahead to the coming thaw. To keep his forward airfields operational during the spring mud, he ordered special metal sheeting for them. At the request of the Front commanders Novikov re-assigned aircraft to harass the German retreat, committing fighter aircraft to this mission, but logistical difficulties mounted as the Red Army, across the German border on 29 January, outran the air force and its airfields. Units of 2nd and 16th Air armies were ordered to use the autobahns as landing strips, with Colonel A. I. Pokryshin making the first landing, followed by the entire fighter division.

Further north Soviet troops of the 3rd and 2nd Belorussian Fronts fought their way into East Prussia supported by 3,000 aircraft of the 1st and 4th Armies. General I. D. Chernyakhovsky, 3rd Belorussian Front commander, was fatally wounded on 18 February and to fill his place Stalin despatched Vasilevsky, who then requested Novikov as his air commander. It fell to Novikov to plan the air assault on Königsberg (Kaliningrad), the great urban barrier blocking the way to the final reduction of East Prussia. For this operation three air armies (1st, 4th and 18th) plus two bomber corps (from 4th and 15th Air Armies) and Samokhin's planes from the Baltic Fleet, 2,144 aircraft in all (1,124 bombers and twenty torpedo bombers) supported one entire Front committed on this occasion on a very narrow sector. Two days of preparatory air strikes began on 1 April. More than 500 Soviet aircraft flew 4,000 sorties, the bombers followed by the *shturmoviki* supporting armour and infantry, with top cover provided by three fighter divisions. Fighters were assigned ground-attack missions, their large number requiring prescribed altitudes along fixed corridors. On 7–8 April the weather cleared, allowing 18th Air Army to launch a massed daylight raid with fighter cover on a city now pulverized by bombs and shells and obscured by smoke. Two days later Königsberg fell.

Further south early in April 1945, three Red Army Fronts (Rokossovsky's 2nd, Zhukov's 1st Belorussian and Konev's 1st Ukrainian) lined up for the final assault on Berlin, with only 37 miles separating Berlin from Zhukov's bridgehead on the Oder. On 9 April Novikov, still with Vasilevsky, was ordered to join Zhukov to prepare and co-ordinate the giant air assault involving 7,500 aircraft (including 297 from the 1st Polish Aviation Corps and the 4th Polish Aviation Division). An air armada of such size had never before been assembled. Three air armies (4th, 16th and 2nd) deployed sixty-five formations: 16th Air Army, the largest in the Soviet air force, fielded over half of them (twenty-eight divisions and twenty-seven independent regiments) with 3,033 front-line combat aircraft. Directly subordinated to Novikov, Golovanov's 18th Air Army with 800 heavy night bombers also operated with the 1st Belorussian Front. To keep this mass of aircraft flying the Red Army helped to build or repair 290 airfields and build up stocks of fuel, ammunition and spares sufficient for ten to twelve days. Novikov was well informed about the enemy's air situation. Luftwaffe air strength was put at 3,300 aircraft including 123 of the latest Me-262 jet fighters. German troops were protected by 200 anti-aircraft batteries, Berlin itself defended by 600 anti-aircraft guns assisted by an excellent radar network, and the dwindling fighter force also had the advantage of short flying times from a network of local aerodromes. To facilitate a rapid advance by the tank armies Novikov assigned 75 per cent of the aircraft from 2nd and 16th Air Armies to tactical air support of the breakthrough and deep into the defences. For support of two tank armies and two combined armies on the axis of Zhukov's main assault Novikov assigned the bulk of 16th Air Army's strength – 2,453 aircraft. He also warned his commanders and aircrews against complacency. Such an attitude could only lead to unjustifiable losses.

To the south Konev's armour moved forward with great speed, forcing the Neisse supported by General Krasovsky's 2nd Air Army flying 2,380 sorties in support of the main attack. During the night of 18 April Stavka adjusted Konev's line of advance, swinging his tank armies to force the Spree and strike directly on Berlin. Novikov ordered Krasovsky to see that the assault river crossing went without a hitch or a bottleneck and to guarantee a 'sterile sky' for Soviet aircraft. Zhukov's massive drive encountered stiff German resistance on the Seelow Heights. He demanded of Novikov that Golovanov just pour bombs on the German defenders rather than, as Novikov proposed, attacking German reserves. But with a breakout achieved and Konev closing on Berlin, the assault on the capital began with massed bomber strikes by 16th, 2nd and 18th Air Armies, while fighter aviation maintained an aerial blockade and supported the intense ground fighting, and it ended with the German surrender on 2 May. In the Berlin operation Soviet air armies flew 91,000 sorties. Almost 60 per cent of the sorties flown by 16th Air Army, whose commander Rudenko acted as Novikov's tactical deputy, were in support of the ground troops. Soviet fighter aircraft fought 1,317 air engagements reportedly losing 527 planes to German fighters and anti-aircraft guns.

On 12 May Novikov flew back to Moscow to take part in planning Soviet operations in the Far East against the Japanese Kwantung Army. Plans to transfer air assets to the Far East had already been prepared in April and the operational directive was ready on 24 June. As far back as 1944 obsolete I-66s and I-153s had been withdrawn and replaced by modern aircraft in Transbaikal and Far East Military Districts. On 30 July the Far Eastern High Command was established under Vasilevsky with Novikov as air commander who followed his wartime principle – 'collective work, individual responsibility' – in organizing his 'air group'. That group consisted of Khudyakov's 12th Air Army from the Transbaikal, Sokolov's 9th Air Army, 10th Air Army, 19th Bomber Corps from 18th Air Army and naval aircraft of the Pacific Fleet. Novikov concentrated 12th Air Army in the Transbaikal, assigning the 10th to support the 2nd Far Eastern Front in forcing the River Amur and the 9th to support the 1st Far Eastern Front in breakthrough operations against Japanese fortifications in the Maritime Provinces.

To support 6th Guards Tank Army in its advance through the Khingan mountains and into the central Manchurian plain Novikov decided to commit bombers instead of ground-attack planes once the tanks moved beyond their range. Recalling the losses incurred in the airborne operations on the Western Front in 1942, Novikov ordered strict control of fighter cover for the drops at Port Arthur, Mukden, Changchun, Dairen and Harbin.

With Japan defeated, Novikov returned to Moscow, to post-war life and the advent of the 'jet age'. Aircraft designers such as A. S. Yakovlev were well aware during the war of the potential of the jet engine, but the demand was for more and ever more proven front-line combat aircraft. After examining captured German jet engines Novikov was persuaded of the importance of this development, supporting Yakovlev's proposal in December 1945 to produce the Yak-15 and the MiG-9. 'If you don't let us down,' Stalin commented, 'and if the machines are built on time, put them in the next Tsushino air show.' A. N. Grinchik flight-tested the MiG-9 in April 1946, but Novikov was not there to see it. During the night of 23 February he had been arrested on Beria's orders together with A. I. Shakhurin, the wartime head of aircraft production. Not only was this the purge of the Air Force but also part of Stalin's malevolent 'purge of the victors' which swept through all branches of the Soviet armed forces, with Beria intent on snaring Marshal Zhukov himself. Stripped of rank and decorations, Novikov was interrogated for days and nights by Beria's henchman, Abakumov, using threats, tricks and physical beating, before being sentenced to five years' deprivation of liberty.

Novikov spent almost six years in strict isolation in prison, taking, as he said of himself, 'the complete course of the Stalinist Academy'. In May 1953, after Stalin's death, the 'Novikov case' was reviewed, the sentence quashed and on 29 June, in the age of the jet bomber and nuclear weapons, Air Chief Marshal Novikov was appointed commander of Long-Range Aviation and Deputy Air Force C-in-C. Amidst new aircraft and new weapons he also found a new wife, Tamara Potapovna Fomina, a military aeronautical engineer, graduate of the Military Academy. But the successful test of a Soviet ICBM and the rise of Khrushchev, speedily mesmerized by missiles, boded ill for the future of the manned bomber and evidently that of Novikov himself. In March, 1955 Khrushchev made his dubious choice and placed Novikov 'at the disposal of the Ministry of Defence'.

Formally retired on the grounds of ill-health, for the eleven years between 1956 and 1967 as head of the Higher Civil Aviation School, Novikov exchanged jet bombers for jet airliners, the TU-104, the AN-24 and the TU-124, adding professor to military pilot in January 1959. Seventeen years later, on 3 February 1976, the life of Air Chief Marshal A. A. Novikov, twice Hero of the Soviet Union, pilot and professor, among the greatest air commanders of the Second World War, drew to its close.

BIBLIOGRAPHY

Aptekar, P. A., 'Opravdany li zhertvy', *Voenno-istoricheskii Zhurnal*, no. 3, 1992.

Bekker, C., *The Luftwaffe War Diaries*, trans. F. Ziegler, Macdonald, London, 1966; original *Angrisshohe 4000*, Hamburg, 1964.

Bezborodov, V. G., 'The 90th Jubilee', *Voennaya mysl'*, no. 1, 1992 (in English).

Boyd, A., *The Soviet Air Force since 1918*, Macdonald Jane, London, 1977.

Chechneva, M. P., *Nebo ostaetsya nashim*, 2nd edn, Voenizdat, Moscow, 1976.

Glantz, D. M., *August Storm: The Soviet Strategic Offensive in Manchuria, 1945*, US Command and Staff College, Fort Leavenworth, Kansas, n.d.

Hardesty, V., *Red Phoenix: The Rise of Soviet Air Power 1941–1945*, Smithsonian Institution Press, Washington DC, 1982.

Khorobrykh, A. M., *Glavnyi marshal aviatsii A. A. Novikov*, Voenizdat, Moscow, 1989 (contains Novikov's unpublished memoirs).

Martel, Lt-General Sir Giffard, *The Russian Outlook*, Michael Joseph, London, 1947.

Noskov, A. M., 'Severnyi uzel', *ViZh*, no. 7, 1990.

Novikov, A. A., *V nebe Leningrada: Zapiski komanduyushego aviatsiei*, Nauka, Moscow, 1970.

Simonov, K. M., *Glazami cheloveka moego pokoleniya: Razmyshleniya o Staline*, Novosti, Moscow, 1980.

Konstantin Konstantinovich
ROKOSSOVSKY

RICHARD WOFF

One of the remarkable factors in the Soviet victory over Nazi Germany was the crucial rôle played by a group of officers who had suffered and survived imprisonment during Stalin's purge. Contemplating the Allied victory over Nazi Germany in 1945, Stalin fêted 'our good Generals', at the same time regretting that many lacked 'breeding and culture'. One could have added that the repressive system he conjured up had sacrificed many of his best generals who had embodied the traditional professional ethos of the Russian officer. One survivor was Konstantin Konstantinovich Rokossovsky. Of the leading Red Army wartime commanders, Rokossovsky combined outstanding professional ability with self-effacing modesty, and a sense of traditional military values. There were times during the war when, amid the destructive urge for bestial vengence on both sides, Rokossovsky displayed humanity and compassion for the suffering of the once powerful adversary, and the hapless German population.

Considered by many senior wartime German commanders as 'the Red Army's best general', to a great extent the Allied view of Rokossovsky was shaped by the image created by the wartime and early post-war Soviet and British news media. Reports put out by the English-language Soviet wartime propaganda machine cynically lauded Rokossovsky's 'aristocratic Polish roots'. BBC and British press reports from 1941 onwards created a contrasting image which evoked comparison with such historical Russian figures as Suvorov and Kutuzov. At the height of the 'Cold War' in 1949 *The Times*, on the other hand, greeted Rokossovsky's appointment by Stalin as Polish Minister of Defence with a scathing article entitled 'Russian and Pole', quoting from the official Polish biography where Rokossovsky was described as 'the boy who . . . once worked on the building of the Poniatowski

Bridge – named after the Polish patriot who became one of NAPOLEON's Marshals – and now himself returns a Marshal of Poland . . . ROKOS-SOVSKY becomes ROKOSOWSKI!' Russian or Pole? 'Aristocrat' or 'soldier-worker' in the cause of the Revolution? The biographer will always have to contend with the enigma of Rokossovsky's early background.

Rokossovsky himself was reticent regarding his family background, and Soviet and Polish sources are inconsistent. He was born on 21 December 1896, either to a railway official in Velikie Luki, Pskov province, or to a minor Polish landowner near Warsaw. The most reliable account, published in Moscow in 1982, stated that he was born in Velikie Luki, the son of a Polish railway worker married to a Russian. Later in life he was bilingual, his Russian having a marked Polish accent. Some years after his birth the family moved to Warsaw, at the time a province of the Russian Empire. His father died in 1904 in a railway accident, and his mother in 1910. Consequently, according to a Polish account, Rokossovsky abandoned the Warsaw technical school at fourteen to earn a living as a stone-cutter. He was 'inevitably drawn into the struggle for the liberation of the working classes and the Polish nation'. In 1912, following a demonstration of Warsaw workers, he was arrested by the tsarist police. While in the Pawiak Prison, according to the same account, he developed 'a clearer idea of class warfare for a better future for the people and the Motherland'. This account was a device by Stalin's Polish lackeys to create a credible image of the Polish patriot dedicated to the struggle against tsarism, 'one of many thousands of Poles who fought for the cause of socialism and fraternity of nations under the great Stalin's leadership in the name of the Soviet Republic', a record that conflicts with the next significant phase in his life.

On the outbreak of the First World War Rokossovsky volunteered for service in the Russian Army, serving until 1917 as a private, NCO, officer cadet, and junior commander in the 5th Kargopolsky Dragoon Regiment (5th Cavalry Division), one of the oldest and most distinguished in the Imperial Army. By any standard Rokossovsky's wartime record was credit-able; he was wounded twice, and awarded the St George Medal, Classes 4, 3, and 2. This Soviet account once again contradicts the Polish 'official life' published in 1949, which talks of his joining the army in 1914 and immediately contacting 'revolutionary currents by which means he could reach the voice of socialism . . . of Lenin and Stalin'.

The collapse of tsarism in February 1917 put a temporary end to Rokossovsky's military career. The October Revolution, however, opened up new opportunities for thousands of ambitious, able junior commanders willing to bury their scruples and throw in their lot with the Bolsheviks. In late 1917 Rokossovsky was elected assistant to Adolf Yushkevich, commander of what was now the Kargopolsky Red Guards Cavalry Detachment. Through-out the Civil War Rokossovsky served as commander of a cavalry squadron, distinguishing himself in engagements against Kolchak at Yekaterinburg and in Central Siberia, and was wounded twice. By 1921 he was commanding the 35th Independent Cavalry Regiment, fighting against the forces of Baron von Ungern-Sternberg in Mongolia, the start of a relationship with the Soviet Far East which was to shape his early career in the Red Army. In recognition of his bravery he was decorated twice with the Order of the Red Banner.

By the end of the Civil War Rokossovsky had established a reputation as a dashing cavalry commander of outstanding ability. Ahead lay a promising career, shaped by the friendships he forged with many future commanders, above all Timoshenko, Zhukov and Konev. For a brief period Rokossovsky continued to serve in the Far East, eventually commanding a cavalry brigade. In 1924 he was assigned a place in the Leningrad Higher Cavalry School, joining other rising stars, such as Yeremenko, Zhukov, Romanenko and Bagramyan. Almost fifty years later Bagramyan recorded his memories of the young Rokossovsky: extremely likeable, elegant, generous and correct in his personal relationships; he possessed an impressive and well-proportioned physique, every inch a cavalryman, with a keen analytical mind. 'Among us inveterate cavalry officers he was deservedly regarded as the most experienced cavalryman, and most knowledgeable regarding cavalry tactics.'

On completing the course in 1925 Rokossovsky returned to the Far East to command a cavalry regiment. Shortly after his return, however, he was seconded to the Soviet Military Mission in Ulan Bator as an instructor to the infant Mongolian People's Army. Here he met Pavel Rybalko, a Soviet advisor, destined to achieve fame as an outstanding wartime tank troops commander. It was also at about this time that Rokossovsky married Yulia Petrovna, daughter of an official in Kyakhta, a small town on the Soviet/Mongolian border. Despite parental opposition to marrying 'an officer', it proved an ideal marriage. The wartime correspondence between the two provides an invaluable insight into Rokossovsky's thoughts during some of the most epic moments of his service. They had one daughter, Adia.

In 1928 Rokossovsky returned to Moscow to attend the Senior Officers' Course at the Frunze Military Academy. This was followed by a further tour of duty commanding the 5th Independent Cavalry Brigade in the Transbaikal region, where a brief military confrontation was soon to take place between the Soviet Union and militant Chinese nationalism, the legacy of Russia's nineteenth-century expansion into the Far East.

With mounting nationalism in China, and the struggle for control between the Kuomintang and the Chinese Communists, Moscow followed a dual and at times conflicting policy, seeking to retain Imperial Russia's acquisitions, while supporting the Moscow-trained Nationalist, Chiang Kai-shek, against the Communists. Moscow had helped the Kuomintang to establish the Wampoa Military Academy, and maintained a strong military mission in China, headed at one time by the future Marshal Vasily Blyukher. Fear of provoking Japan and the British none the less precluded open Soviet intervention in the internal feuding. Matters came to a head in the summer of 1929, when the Kuomintang seized the Chinese Eastern Railway – the principal strategic link between the Soviet Union and Vladivostok on the Pacific – and arrested over 200 Soviet officials. Consequently, the Kuomintang's campaign to subvert Soviet rights – supported by anti-Soviet elements in the Communist Party – was a clear provocation. After months of hesitation in Moscow, on 7 August 1929 the Special Far Eastern Army was set up under Blyukher's command. Arriving some weeks previously, Rokossovsky played a distinguished rôle in the first major successful military operation since the Civil War. After initial successes in September and October, Blyukher launched a major operation in November to drive the Chinese out of the Transbaikal region and regain control of the railway. The 5th Independent Cavalry Brigade mounted an outflanking movement to encircle and in effect emasculate the Chinese garrison of Manchouli. Soviet success not only deterred further Chinese action: the Japanese were also prompted to reassess the rôle and effectiveness of emerging Soviet military power in the Far East.

Apart from invaluable combat experience and recognition for his handling of a large cavalry formation in support of a vital operation, the period spent amid the rigours and freer atmosphere of the Far East was to influence Rokossovsky's later career. Of the officers in the 5th Independent Cavalry Brigade many served later under Rokossovsky in the Second World War. Links with Blyukher, however, later threatened Rokossovsky's career with total eclipse, as Voroshilov moved to settle old scores during the purges of the 1930s.

In 1930 Rokossovsky was promoted commander of the 7th Cavalry Division of 3rd Cavalry Corps commanded by Timoshenko and located in Belorussia Military District. It was the beginning of a long professional relationship which continued down to Rokossovsky's death in 1968. Another officer who subsequently played an influential rôle in Rokossovsky's career was Zhukov, then commander of a cavalry regiment in Rokossovsky's division. Later their careers underwent a remarkable reversal in fortune, in Rokossovsky's case a tragedy which, despite mutual respect, was to colour their professional and personal relationship. Indeed, one senses a note of bitterness, if not resentment, with Rokossovsky chafing at Zhukov's authoritarian style and recalling that Zhukov served under his command in the early 1930s. Zhukov himself was also aware of the dilemma, and in his turn supported Rokossovsky. To refer to Rokossovsky, however, as 'Zhukov's protégé', is to distort the nature of the relationship between the two outstanding wartime commanders, both of whom suffered humiliation under Stalin.

In 1935 Rokossovsky returned to the Far East to command the 15th

Cavalry Division, renewing the fateful association with Blyukher. The link, however, was brief. In February 1936 he was promoted commander of 5th Cavalry Corps, located in Leningrad Military District. The Corps had been reorganized earlier that year and Rokossovsky was given the task of commanding the new formation. He performed well, and his ability to bring the Corps up to a high standard of training within six months was praised by Shaposhnikov, the District Commander, in his report on the summer exercises.

Departure from the Far East, and praise from Shaposhnikov, could not obliterate the links with Blyukher in the eyes of the vindictive circle around Stalin. By early 1937 the protracted campaign to cleanse Blyukher's Far Eastern Command was underway. On 17 August 1937 Rokossovsky was arrested, initially on the suspicion of 'sabotage', and impairing 'combat-effectiveness'. In the Kresty NKVD special internment centre accusations of being both a Polish spy and in the pay of the Japanese were added to the list of his 'crimes against the people'. The evidence rested on a 'confession' by 'fellow conspirator' Adolf Yushkevich. The 'trial' was a farce. Declaring that 'the dead cannot give evidence', Rokossovsky reminded a perplexed prosecutor that Yushkevich had died in the cause of the Revolution seventeen years previously. Despite weeks of torture, Rokossovsky retained his composure. Reprieved, he spent the next three years in gaol near Leningrad. The final act, symbolized by Blyukher's execution in November 1938, was probably delayed following a renewal of Japanese military activity in the Far East. On 22 March 1940, 'the case against him having been dropped', he was released a month after the end of the Soviet–Finnish War. The world had changed, and the Soviet Union was facing the threat from Nazi Germany. Rokossovsky, still a Colonel, set about mending a shattered career.

'The spring of 1940 was spent together with my family in Sochi. After this I was invited to visit Defence Commissar Marshal S. K. Timoshenko. He greeted me warmly and sincerely.' Thus Rokossovsky opened his memoirs, marking in effect the beginning of his wartime career. Having been commander of the corps in which he had served in the early 1930s, Timoshenko's confidence in Rokossovsky's ability remained unshaken, and within weeks of his emergence from incarceration he had no hesitation in recommending he take command once more of 5th Cavalry Corps. The Corps had meanwhile deployed to Kiev Special Military District as part of a restructuring of the western strategic defences. Promoted Major-General in June, one of Rokossovsky's first missions was to assist District Commander Zhukov in assessing 'the strengths and weaknesses' of Soviet defences on the crucial Southwestern Axis. The next task was the 'liberation' of Bessarabia in the summer of 1940. Ostensibly a move to claim the Soviet share in Hitler's new European order, its purpose was to create a defensive glacis on the exposed southern strategic approaches, as Germany's military power assumed threatening proportions following the defeat of France.

On returning from Bessarabia in October 1940 Rokossovsky was appointed commander of the recently formed 9th Mechanized Corps. The challenge now was to prepare the new formation, virtually from nothing, to fulfil its mission in wartime. In keeping with new concepts, the new formation consisted of three divisions: 131st Motorized Division and 35th and 20th Tank Divisions. Designed to combine mobility with 'punch', in late 1940 Rokossovsky's formation had to contend with serious material shortcomings, above all in tanks. The Corps was part of 5th Army, commanded by the ill-fated Major-General M. I. Potapov, and was assigned a key rôle in confronting a German assault on the southwestern approaches.

As Rokossovsky's memoirs make clear, overshadowing any shortcoming below was the general mood of malignant complacency in both the High Command in Moscow and in Kiev. In June 1940 Zhukov was appointed Chief of the General Staff and was replaced as Commander of Kiev Military District by Lieutenant-General Mikhail Kirponos. There could be no greater contrast between the leadership displayed by Zhukov and the lethargic inactivity of Kirponos. While Kirponos was an able commander, it was indicative of the post-purge situation that an officer of his modest accomplishment could be appointed to command one of the two Military Districts that would be crucial in the initial phase of any major military confrontation with Germany. In his memoirs, published posthumously in 1968, Rokossovsky painted a depressing picture, not merely of Kirponos, but of the general mood of disarray in the local civil administration and Party organization in drawing up contingency plans. The problems, however, revolved around poor leadership from the District Commander down to sub-unit level. The full extent of the malaise was not revealed until the late 1980s when the Soviet military press published sections of Rokossovsky's memoirs deleted by the censor as late as 1984 (3rd edition). Rokossovsky's account was supported by the publication in 1989 of a number of interviews by former officers of Kiev Special Military District, originally given in the 1950s and 1960s, and the documents reproduced in Dmitri Volkogonov's *Stalin*.

The first signs of an impending invasion came in early June 1941. While the local senior commanders sought to discount the omens, a number of officers like Rokossovsky acted, stepping up reconnaissance activity and preparing a response. When the invasion came the main German axis of advance aimed to split 5th and 6th Armies of what was now the Southwestern Front under Kirponos. By late June, with the Red Air Force eliminated at the start, and overwhelmed by German superiority in the air and on the ground, the Soviet line of strategic defence had been breached. In his memoirs Rokossovsky, while emphasizing German superiority, singles out the divisional commanders and men of 9th Mechanized Corps for their professional skill, bravery and devotion to duty 'in these first testing battles', achieving local successes, and blocking the German advance on Kiev.

A more sinister threat, however, faced Moscow as Field Marshal von Bock's Army Group Centre ground down the first strategic echelon of the Red Army. By mid-July the German advance had reached Smolensk and the Soviet Army High Command began to panic. In an effort to stem the German advance a number of new formations were hastily assembled and dispatched to the front. The first weeks of the German offensive had also taken a devastating toll of the senior commanders and shattered the reputations of others.

On 12 July, as Rokossovsky was preparing to defend Novograd-Volynsk in a hopeless effort to halt the German advance into central Ukraine, Stavka ordered him to take command of 4th Army on the Western Front, now under the command of Timoshenko. The move was prompted by the disaster which had overwhelmed that army and its unfortunate commander, Major-General A. A. Korobkov, who was court-martialled and shot. On 14 July Rokossovsky took leave of a dejected Kirponos and headed for Moscow. By the time he arrived, 4th Army had been disbanded, and instead he was given command of an 'operational group', consisting of two or three tank divisions, and one rifle division, deployed in the defence of Smolensk. The Battle for Smolensk, in effect the last of the 'frontier battles of 1941', dragged on from 10 July to 10 September. The rôle of 'General Rokossovsky's Group' was to support 16th Army, holding Smolensk, and 20th Army. In the event his first task was 'to collect what I could' before the Group could be deployed. While the Red Army was forced on to the defensive, as in the case of Napoleon's advance on Moscow following the Battle of Smolensk of 1812, the German offensive of 1941 had temporarily lost momentum.

The delay eventually forced the Germans to fight a winter campaign for which they were not prepared, thus denying Hitler the prize of taking Moscow 'before Christmas'. It was Rokossovsky's first taste of command of a major mobile operational group, albeit under-manned and under-equipped. These deficiencies, however, were outweighed by the quality of some of the officers Rokossovsky 'recruited' to serve under him: Colonel M. S. Malinin, Chief of Staff; Major-Generals V. I. Kazakov, V. I. Vinogradov and L. M. Dovator, commanders respectively of artillery, 7th Mechanized Corps and 3rd Cavalry Corps. Malinin and Kazakov remained on Rokossovsky's staff until the last months of the war.

Two weeks after the fall of Smolensk, the battle for Moscow commenced. Appointed commander of 16th Army in late September 1941, Rokossovsky was to play a vital rôle astride the main Volokolamsk highway leading to Moscow. By late 1941, 16th Army consisted of remnants of battle-scarred formations, Moscow militia and volunteer units, and the first of the 'reserve' formations raised in Siberia (like 16th Army itself) and Central Asia. It was once again Rokossovsky's task to mould them into a cohesive and effective force, commanded by officers for whom 'no retreat' became the order of the day.

Meanwhile, Zhukov had replaced Timoshenko as commander of the Western Front, a reversal of fortune, as Rokossovsky recalled. The feeling of repressed resentment may have led him on occasion to question Zhukov's decisions affecting 16th Army. On one famous occasion Rokossovsky wished to withdraw to a more defensible position to avoid further losses. Overruled by Zhukov, he appealed to and was supported by Shaposhnikov. The matter was finally settled by Zhukov's stern reminder that he was commander of the Western Front, and all officers under his command obeyed his orders – no matter what the General Staff might say. Indeed, by late November 1941 Zhukov's iron will not to give an inch, as the German offensive continued to batter its way towards Moscow, was the vital element underpinning the morale of the Red Army at the time. The affair did not, however, affect the close relationship and mutual respect which developed between Zhukov and Rokossovsky thereafter.

The main German elements facing Rokossovsky's 16th Army were V Army, XL Motorized Corps, XXXV Infantry Division, four Tank Divisions, and the SS 'Das Reich' Division. By late November 1941, 16th Army had been pressed back to a line Krasnaya Polyana–Kryukovo–Istra, and already the Moscow skyline was visible. By early December, however, the initiative was passing to the Red Army. Having expended their reserves, and hit by the early onset of the Russian winter, the German offensive ground to a halt. Meanwhile, the Red Army went over to the offensive, and by early January 1942 von Bock's forces had been thrown back 100–250 kilometres west of Moscow, losing thirty-eight divisions. A notable feature of the Soviet counter-offensive was the growing rôle of the Air Force, sadly lacking in 1941. As for 16th Army, it had fought with depleted formations and scarce resources on one of the key sectors barring the approaches to Moscow, and, while Rokossovsky paid tribute to his staff and men, it was his tactical skill that had imbued them with a will to fight. The battle for Moscow demonstrated that the nucleus of a regenerated Soviet High Command had finally emerged.

The Red Army continued to push the Germans back, consolidating the gains of December 1941–January 1942. For the moment, however, with the Wehrmacht still enjoying superiority and in a position to mount large-scale operations, despite Stalin's prodding the Red Army lacked the ability to mount a strategic counter-offensive. Consequently, from mid-1942 to late 1943 the western Soviet Union resembled a vast chessboard over which the contestants marshalled powerful forces on the main axes, each hoping to wrest the strategic initiative. With the German High Command moving its forces now on a central axis, now a southern axis, for the 'final knock-out blow', the Red Army High Command had the advantage of a flexible strategic command and control structure, creating *ad hoc* Army Groups, or Fronts, to make optimum use of scarce resources. From early 1942 to the end of the war Rokossovsky was destined to be one of the most important 'knights' on the 'chessboard', commanding in turn a number of key Fronts astride the strategic axis directed at the heart of the Third Reich. In the end, however, it was Zhukov who was to get to Berlin first in May 1945.

By mid-1942 the Germans, having been baulked before Moscow, were massing to cross the Caucasus and seize the Baku oilfields. In July 1942 Rokossovsky, still recovering from a serious back injury sustained that March, was designated Commander of the Bryansk Front in place of Golikov. 16th Army was taken over by Bagramyan. Rokossovsky asked for, and was given, the senior group of officers who had assisted him during the Battle for Moscow: Malinin (Chief of Staff), Kazakov (Front artillery), and Orlov (armoured tank forces). He also made the acquaintance of able officers who were to serve him until the end of the war, among them his deputy on the Bryansk Front, General Batov.

In the event, Rokossovsky's command of the Bryansk Front was to be relatively brief, and compared with the epic events ahead uneventful. None the less, intensified operations against German forces on the Tula and Voronezh Axes were subsequently to influence events further south. In September, as VI Army and IV Tank Army closed in on Stalingrad in their advance into the North Caucasus, Stavka was forced to reorganize the strategic defence structure. Recalled to Moscow in early September, Rokossovsky was given command of an 'operational group' comprising three combined-arms armies and two or three tank corps, designated as a mobile force to harry the northern German flank and support the forces defending Stalingrad. Even as he was being briefed by Zhukov, however, events on the Volga were quickly moving towards a crisis, forcing Stavka to revise its plans. Consequently, Rokossovsky was ordered instead to accompany Zhukov to the Stalingrad Front to assess the situation, with the German forces closing in on 62nd Army, pinning it down in a narrow corridor on the Volga 10 kilometres wide.

For the next five months Rokossovsky played a crucial rôle in the battle of Stalingrad. The campaign had been in progress since 17 July 1942, and the day after Rokossovsky's arrival in September yet another Soviet counter-attack had been repulsed, convincing Zhukov that drastic changes were required. Rokossovsky was appointed Commander of the Stalingrad Front virtually 'on the spot', replacing Yeremenko. This arrangement lasted merely a week. On 28 September the Stalingrad Front was redesignated the Don Front, under Rokossovsky's command, while the Southeastern Front became the Stalingrad Front under Yeremenko, an arrangement which gave Rokossovsky virtual control of operations. Initially the Don Front comprised seven armies; by 1 January 1943, Rokossovsky was commanding eleven armies of all arms. The increase in Rokossovsky's authority resulted partly from his own pleas to Stavka to combine all forces at Stalingrad under one command.

The initial task entrusted to the Don and Stalingrad Fronts in September –October 1942 was to relieve the hard-pressed 62nd Army by exerting pressure on the northern flank of the German VI Army and IV Tank Army under the overall command of General von Paulus. The Red Army counter-attack of 19–23 November, entrapping the bulk of the 250,000 strong German 'Stalingrad Army' in a 'cauldron', could not, however, disguise the gravity of the threat still facing Rokossovsky. Attempts to liquidate von Paulus's forces throughout late November and the first half of December proved unsuccessful for the time being, with the Red Army still lacking the strength to maintain pressure on all the crucial sectors, confronted by a clotted mass of fanatical and desperate German resistance. Moreover, in mid-December two Armies – 51st and 2nd Guards Tank – were detached to deal with a German attempt to relieve von Paulus from the south. The task of delivering the *coup de grâce* to the beleaguered German forces was entrusted to Rokossovsky's Don Front. Initially, Operation 'Ring' envisaged a general assault on the encircled Germans; Rokossovsky, however, proposed splitting up the 'cauldron' into a 'north' and 'south' group, liquidating each in detail. This plan was finally accepted by Stalin.

Before mounting the operation, Rokossovsky, mindful of the extreme privations being endured by the German soldiers, not to mention the strain on his own men, drew up a draft 'surrender' document in early January 1943. After discussing the matter with General Antonov, Vasilevsky's new senior Deputy on the General Staff, Rokossovsky was eventually given permission by Stalin to press ahead. In the event it was rejected by von Paulus, and the final operation to liquidate the remnants of VI Army was launched on 10 January, with Batov's 65th Army spearheading the assault. German resistance was snuffed out, and on 31 January 1943 the newly promoted Field Marshal von Paulus surrendered to Rokossovsky and Colonel-General Nikolai Voronov, the Chief of the Red Army Artillery. The battle of Stalingrad was over.

Like the battle for Moscow, Stalingrad was a 'turning point'. It was a milestone in the evolution of the Red Army in other important respects also, with the growing effectiveness and power of Soviet artillery, the re-emergence from total eclipse of the Air Force, and the first demonstration of the latent destructive power of Soviet armour. Some time was to pass, however, before the Red Army gained the strategic initiative. None the less, for Rokossovsky, promoted Colonel-General in January, Stalingrad marked a point of no return. One crucial element in his success was a pragmatic approach to the critical problem of senior command and control. The fifty or more generals in key posts and commands throughout the battle of

Stalingrad represented a disparate pack of unusual personalities, many possessing unique ability and experience. While it was vital to establish and impose authority from above in the wider interests of 'the commander's battle', it was equally important not to smother ability, but to exploit the talents of each commander. The relationship Rokossovsky forged with his senior officers is best illustrated by three examples: Batov, Malinovsky and Chuikov. Reference has already been made to Batov, commander of 65th Army, on whom Rokossovsky could rely to carry out the most challenging mission.

By contrast, Malinovsky, commander of 2nd Guards Army during the battle of Stalingrad, while unusually able, courageous and keenly intelligent, was also headstrong, ambitious, prone to vanity, and at times ruthless when the occasion warranted. Once his mind was made up nothing could shake his determination to do things his way. Consequently, his ideas on command and control frequently differed from those of Rokossovsky. None the less, their professional and personal relations were based on mutual respect. The third element in the trio, Lieutenant-General Chuikov, was commander of 62nd Army defending Stalingrad, the epicentre of the titanic struggle. Before Rokossovsky visited Chuikov's headquarters on the banks of the Volga at the height of the battle in mid-December 1942 the two had never met. Rokossovsky's first impressions of Chuikov were favourable. An officer of stubborn nature, somewhat limited in intellect, but of solid professional ability, Chuikov – as Stalin had long recognized – could be relied on to stand with his back to the wall faced with the most daunting challenge, considered tantamount to suicide by any other officer. At their first meeting, impressed by the general air of confidence pervading 62nd Army amid the surrounding desolation, Rokossovsky recorded his 'feeling of deep respect' for Chuikov, whose subsequent briefing on the situation was 'a model of clarity, and brevity', adding that 'this man made a strong impression on me, and . . . we became the best of friends'.

On 15 February 1943 the Don Front was redesignated the Central Front under Rokossovsky's command. He retained 21st and 65th Armies, together with 16th Air Army. In addition he was given 70th Army, comprised of former Border Troops units. It was some time before Rokossovsky could knock it into shape, removing many senior officers, mostly ex-NKVD. The timing of the next major operation – mid-February 1943 – with a week in which to redeploy several hundred kilometres north, re-assemble and prepare the Front for a resumption of operations, presented Rokossovsky with a daunting task. Poor or non-existent communications, and lack of transport, forced many formations to rely on tractors and farm carts to move equipment. To speed up progress Stavka sent in the NKVD to 'administer' the shattered rail network, a move resented by Rokossovsky. Following the shooting of some senior railway officials for 'sabotage', and with a complete breakdown of rail communications, the measure was rescinded. Grappling with a multitude of problems, however, did bring its rewards. On 27 April 1943 Rokossovsky was promoted Army General.

From late March 1943 intelligence reports indicated that the Germans were assembling a huge force to attempt a strategic breakthrough in the Kursk region. The battle of Kursk, or Operation 'Citadel', arose out of Hitler's determination to deny the Red Army the fruits of the Stalingrad victory, and thus retain the strategic initiative. Two German Army Groups were to be involved in a huge battle of encirclement: Army Group Centre under Field Marshal von Kluge was to assault the northern flank from the Orel area; Army Group South under Field Marshal von Manstein was to strike at the southern flank from the general area of Kharkov. The two Groups were then to link up in the general area of Kursk. In all, six Soviet Fronts were to be involved throughout the Battle of Kursk which lasted from 5 July to 23 August, and consisted of a 'defensive' phase, followed by a massive counter-attack.

To meet the German assault against the Central Front Rokossovsky, advised by Zhukov and Vasilevsky, planned to construct six lines of defence with an overall depth of 150–190 kilometres, consisting of an elaborate system of trenches, barbed wire, anti-tank obstacles, firing points, and minefields. Some 400,000 mines were laid, of which no less than 170,000 were on an 11-kilometre sector where Rokossovsky expected the main attack. The whole operation was under the direct control of Major-General A. M. Proshlyakov, Chief of Engineers on the Central Front, for whom, along with Zhukov, Rokossovsky reserved his warmest praise. It was hoped that the Germans would, like the French at Verdun in 1916, 'bleed themselves to death' on the 'defensive wall'. On the Central Front the Battle began on 5 July with a massive artillery exchange, followed by a German assault on General N. P. Pukhov's 13th Army, succeeded in turn by a counter-attack by 2nd Tank Army to stem the German advance. The operation was not an entire success, and the commander was replaced by Lieutenant-General S. I. Bogdanov. None the less, the new Soviet armoured formations, now up against the new German 'Tiger' tanks, were to make a decisive contribution to Rokossovsky's battle, although on its debut 3rd Tank Army under General Pavel Rybalko had to be withdrawn without fulfilling its mission.

Rokossovsky's reliance on defence in depth, however, paid off. By 9 July the main German assault was flagging, and with some 50,000 dead, 400 tanks and self-propelled guns, and 500 aircraft destroyed, von Kluge went over to the defensive without having achieved a breakthrough on Rokossovsky's Central Front. This was followed on 15 July by the Soviet counter-offensive, with Central Front operating in conjunction with the Bryansk and Western Fronts to wipe out the German Orel grouping. On 5 August the last German was driven out of Orel, one of the most formidable German strongpoints since 1941. The threat of a renewed German assault on Moscow was finally extinguished. This was the signal for a general Red Army counter-offensive across a broad front from Orel to the Sea of Azov. The last German strategic offensive had failed and the strategic initiative had now passed to the Soviet side.

Despite the triumph at Kursk, Rokossovsky noted that things had not gone as well as expected. German determination, skill and experience had told in the early stages of the battle, forcing him to commit crucial reserves earlier than planned. Co-ordination between his northern and southern Fronts had left much to be desired. Moreover, the supply chain channelling reinforcements from the rear was 'organized chaos'. Between 26 August and 30 September, following the break-out from the Kursk salient, Central Front was to advance some 300 kilometres to the Dnieper, liberating the northern Ukraine, and positioning itself for the liberation of western Ukraine and ultimately Belorussia. For Rokossovsky, however, there were frustrations, as when Stavka realigned the main Front axis north, robbing him of the satisfaction of liberating Kiev. Perhaps to relieve his frustration, he vented his spleen on Vatutin, Commander of the 1st Ukrainian Front, upbraiding him on a visit to his HQ in November for the way he was handling his staff. Meanwhile, on 20 October the Central Front was redesignated the Belorussian Front, depriving Rokossovsky of the two armies which had distinguished themselves at Kursk – Pukhov's 13th, and 60th Army commanded by the brilliant, ill-fated Jewish General Ivan Chernyakhovsky, both transferred to Vatutin's command. The change also entailed a major redeployment north during the muddy season through a region with poor communications and intersected by large stretches of marsh. Adding to Rokossovsky's administrative headaches was the enforced diversion of some 30,000 troops, 300 officers, and over 6,000 vehicles to assist in the harvest, collect fodder and requisition cattle.

The establishment of the Belorussian Front in October, redesignated the 1st Belorussian Front on 17 February 1944, was part of a major restructuring of the strategic command on the Eastern Front, as Stalin moved to exploit the victories of 1943. From late 1943 Rokossovsky was in effect responsible for major operations on the 'Western strategic axis' along which the Red Army would battle its way into central Europe. With the successful conclusion of the Gomel-Rechitsa operation (December 1943) and the Rogachev-Zhlobin operation (February 1944), the 1st Belorussian Front paused to reorganize before the next operation: the destruction of German Army Group Centre, now commanded by Field Marshal Model. Based on Minsk, this powerful force stood astride the main strategic axis into central Europe, namely Minsk–Warsaw–Berlin.

In all, five Soviet Fronts participated in the Belorussian operation 'Bagration'. Rokossovsky's 1st Belorussian Front was deployed on a line extending west from Rogachev on the Dnieper to Kovel, and comprised nine Armies plus one Air Army. The first mission of 'Bagration', which opened 23 June, was to destroy the German defensive strong points. Rokossovsky's forces advanced over marshy ground, negotiating rivers and lakes, pinning down IX Tank Corps, which was then pounded by Rudenko's aviation. On 3 July Minsk was liberated and by 24 July Rokossovsky had crossed the River Bug, liberating Lublin. The next day a Polish National Committee was set up, the first step in installing a Communist government in post-war Poland. Two days later Brest-Litovsk fell, completing the liberation of Belorussia. With the crumbling of German resistance the road to Warsaw lay open. Rokossovsky was promoted to Marshal and made a Hero of the Soviet Union.

Rokossovsky's advance on Warsaw was marked by one of the most tragic events of the Second World War – the Warsaw Uprising of the Polish underground army led by General Tadeusz Bor-Komarowski. Planned for several months, it cannot have been a surprise to London or Moscow. It began on 1 August, and what ensued was one of the ghastliest episodes of the war, with an assorted German force under Himmler's emissary SS Obergruppenführer von dem Bach-Zelewski waging a battle of butchery against under-armed and out-gunned Poles. The battle lasted until 2nd October, leaving over 15,000 Polish fighters dead.

Throughout, Stalin, then negotiating the future of Poland with a delegation from the London-based Provisional Government, adopted a cynical stance, now promising relief by Rokossovsky's forces, now deriding the 'handful of power-seeking criminals who launched the Warsaw adventure'. Although the Red Air Force dropped arms, medicine and food supplies to the insurgents on 13 September – the day units of 1st Polish Army moved into the southern outskirts of the city – in the end no effective relief was to come from Rokossovsky. In his memoirs Rokossovsky adopted a laconic, at times derisive attitude towards the uprising. When Front intelligence reported the rising on 2 August, it was assumed to be a German ruse, although 'the news put us in a great state of alarm'. If it was a Polish decision the timing 'was most unfortunate'. With regard to the failure of the 1st Belorussian Front to provide timely relief, Rokossovsky explains that 48th and 65th Armies 'were engaged in operations 100 kilometres or more to the east and northeast of Warsaw'. With his right wing denuded of two further armies, other formations were either pinned down by strong German resistance, or still engaged in mopping-up operations. On the left wing the remaining three armies, having forced the Vistula south of Warsaw, were preoccupied in establishing a bridgehead on the west bank.

Rokossovsky is on less solid ground in claiming that the uprising came as a complete surprise to Moscow, and that Bor-Komarowski, despite being given 'the required codes', refused to establish direct contact with the 1st Belorussian Front, insisting instead on going through London. Finally, refuting 'the spiteful slurs in the Western press accusing the 1st Belorussian Front – and of course me personally – of as it were deliberately refusing to support the Warsaw insurgents and condemning them to death', Rokossovsky points out that the Belorussian operation was a gigantic undertaking, 'an immense cost in men and resources'. To have attempted to seize Warsaw, 'with its strong defences and substantial enemy garrison', would have required time and preparation and 'overstretched our logistics'. Despite the odds, he concludes, 'at the time we would have gone to any lengths in order to help the insurgents'.

While the Red Army lost 130,000 men in the Belorussian operation, the scale of German losses heightened the chances that Warsaw would be taken by early August 1944. The Warsaw Rising a week after the Soviet-backed 'Lublin Government' was formed, however, placed Stalin in a dilemma, faced with the unpalatable prospect of a hostile faction liberating the capital from the Germans. If it was felt at the time that the Russians had deliberately stood back while the Germans pounded the insurgents into submission, it is equally probable that the precarious situation of Rokossovsky's armies, following the exertions of the Belorussian campaign, was exploited by Stalin to advance his post-war policy in Eastern Europe. In the event, what was left of Warsaw was not liberated until 17 January 1945.

One evening in early November 1944, as Rokossovsky was about to sit down for supper, a telephone call came from Stalin, ordering him to hand over command of the 1st Belorussian Front to Zhukov and take command of the 2nd Belorussian Front from Army General G. F. Zakharov. Unable to control his emotions Rokossovsky asked, 'Why the disgrace – why am I being transferred ... to a sector of secondary importance?' Stalin said he was wrong to see it in this light: 'Your sector is part of the main Western strategic axis' comprising the 2nd and 1st Belorussian and 1st Ukrainian Fronts, and final victory would only be achieved by acting in close support of one another. 'We therefore need the best men for the job.' Sensing that Rokossovsky had already set his sights on Berlin, Stalin added: 'If you and Konev do not advance, then Zhukov will have to mark time, too.'

Stalin was in fact correct; the Stavka directive of November 1944 was based on the need to reorganize the three Fronts on the Berlin strategic axis in preparation for the final assault. Giving Rokossovsky command of the vital northern flank was a decisive move to secure the Berlin operation. None the less, considering the way Stalin had manhandled his senior commanders in the past – and would again – it says something for the respect Rokossovsky now enjoyed with the 'Supreme One' that he could discuss such issues so frankly. Turning aside Stalin's suggestion that he retain Malinin as his Chief of Staff, Rokossovsky departed for the 2nd Belorussian Front HQ the next day without awaiting Zhukov's arrival.

Rokossovsky opened the East Prussian operation of 14–26 January 1945 by striking north over the Narew with five armies, deploying another two to the east to link up with Chernyakhovsky's 3rd Belorussian Front in East Prussia. On the way the advancing units passed through the Masurian Lakes, bypassing Tannenberg, scene of Russian defeat in 1914 by Hindenburg. Buried on the site of his victory in 1934, Hindenburg's remains and those of his wife were spirited away to safety by the retreating Germans hours before the arrival of the Red Army. The Narew posed a formidable barrier. Heavy mist and swirling snow grounded the air force and limited tank operations. Progress was slow. On 16 January, however, the weather improved and with strong support from Vershinin's 4th Air Army, 48th Army was able to break through the German defences, enabling Rokossovsky to launch General V. T. Volsky's 5th Guards Tank Army into the breach the following day. By 19 January Rokossovsky was in East Prussia. On 20 January, however, he received 'the unexpected order' to switch four armies north to complete the isolation of German forces in the province. He had misgivings, for the move would disrupt close co-ordination of the 1st and 2nd Belorussian Fronts, with only two armies on his left flank in support of Zhukov's thrust towards the Oder. Consequently, having broken through to the Baltic at Elbing by 26 January, and 48th Army having survived a counter-attack by IV Army in an attempt to break through south to the Vistula the following day, for the moment the 2nd Belorussian Front ground to a halt.

In his memoirs Rokossovsky described East Prussia as Germany's 'age-old springboard for attacking her neighbours', and as the 2nd Belorussian Front lunged towards Königsberg he sensed the war was rapidly moving towards its end. The smell of victory also affected his troops, some of whom had recently liberated the inmates of Nazi death camps in Poland. The scale of destruction, pillage, rape and indiscriminate slaughter endured by the civil population, as the Red Army swept over East Prussia in early 1945, can only be compared to the mutilation endured by the province three hundred years before during the Thirty Years War. While much of the destruction could be attributed to fanatical resistance by German commanders and local 'Gauleiters', despite the offer of 'surrender terms', Rokossovsky understood the emotions which took hold of his troops. But he was also appalled at the sight of Soviet soldiers murdering and raping defenceless civilians. Moreover, the excesses were beginning to erode discipline. Given the record of German atrocities in the occupied territories, the problem was to be expected, 'but hatred for the enemy did not permit acts of blind vengeance on the German people', he noted, adding that 'we are fighting Hitler's army, not the peace-loving population of Germany'. A hurriedly assembled Front Military Council ordered all commanders to take measures to 'uphold the honour of the Soviet Army', and punish anyone – irrespective of rank – guilty of any crime against unarmed civilians. None the less, uncontrolled rape and looting remained the order of the day as the Red Army swept through Germany.

Meanwhile, the German High Command had not hesitated to exploit the ever-widening gap between Zhukhov and Rokossovsky, and the threat to the 1st Belorussian Front's exposed northern flank some 150 kilometres in length. By early February remnants of II, III, IX and XI Tank Armies had joined to form Army Group Vistula in Eastern Pomerania, under Himmler's control. To meet the threat Stavka detached the 2nd Belorussian Front from the East Prussian operation, ordering Rokossovsky instead to advance into Pomerania in an attempt to close the gap. The operation opened on 10 February, and within a few days Rokossovsky's leading formations were fighting III Tank Army, which halted and eventually forced 47th Army to retreat. But on 1 March Rokossovsky counter-attacked, and by 5 March had broken through to the Baltic at Kolberg and Köslin. Strengthened by 1st Guards Tank Army, 'on loan' from Zhuykov, Rokossovsky concentrated his forces for the final assault on Danzig, which surrendered on 30 March.

On 1 April Zhukov and Konev visited Moscow to complete plans for the final stage of the Berlin operation. Antonov presented the main plan: a general offensive by Zhukov, Rokossovsky and Konev commencing on 16 April on a broad front from Stettin in the north to Görlitz in the south. With the seizure of Berlin, the Red Army would link up with the British and US forces on the Elbe twelve to fifteen days from the commencement of the operation. Rokossovsky was not present at this conference, but was summoned to Moscow some days later to be briefed by Antonov. The 2nd Belorussian Front was to regroup and be ready for operations by 16 April, protecting Zhukov's northern flank and taking over a sector bounded by the Baltic in the north, and south by a line Schneidemühl–Arnswalde–Pyritz –Schwedt–Angermünde–Wittenberg. Faced with the problem of having to wheel five armies westwards, across some 300 kilometres of virtually impassable devastated terrain, Rokossovsky again asked for a delay in mounting the operation, and the crossing of the Oder commenced on 20 April on a 80–90 kilometre front between Stettin and Schwedt, spearheaded by Batov's 65th Army, followed by 70th, 2nd Shock, and 49th Armies.

The fall of Stettin on 26 April opened the way for the 2nd Belorussian Front to advance across northern Germany, supported by Admiral Tributs's Baltic Fleet, in the process grinding down the remnants of the 'Vistula' Group, and finally demolishing General von Manteuffel's III Tank Army. By early May 1945 the 2nd Belorussian Front fanned out for the final surge to the Elbe and the Baltic. At Wismar on 3 May forward units of General A. T. Panfilov's 3rd Guards Tank Corps made contact with advanced elements of the British 2nd Army. The occupation of the Baltic islands of Wollin, Usedom and Rügen by 2nd Shock Army concluded the 2nd Belorussian Front's wartime operations. For Rokossovsky meeting Field Marshal

Montgomery in Wismar on 4 May provided a fitting end to his wartime career.

In July, on his first visit to Berlin, Montgomery invested Zhukov, Konev, Rokossovsky and other Red Army commanders as Knights Commander of the Bath. For Rokossovsky it was but the latest honour testifying to a brilliant military career: St George Cross (three grades); Hero of the Soviet Union twice; seven Orders of Lenin; Order of October Revolution; six Orders of the Red Banner; Order of Suvorov 1st Class; Order of Kutuzov 1st Class; Order of Victory; six Orders of Red Star; Order of Virtute (Poland); and other foreign orders. The final honour, however, was to command the triumphant Victory Parade on Red Square on 24 June to the acclaim of the Soviet people, with Zhukov taking the salute, as Stalin peered down from Lenin's Mausoleum.

As the Red Army was completing the extinction of the Third Reich, a Soviet–Polish Agreement signed in Moscow on 21 April resurrected Russian rule in Poland. On 29 May the 2nd Belorussian Front was wound up and redesignated the Northern Group of Forces 'temporarily stationed in Poland', and Rokossovsky was appointed Commander-in-Chief. This was part of a pattern whereby certain Soviet wartime Fronts were redesignated 'Groups of Soviet (Occupation) Forces' – in Germany, Austria, Hungary, Romania and Bulgaria – ostensibly to provide efficient administration and a framework for restoring economic and political order out of chaos. Ultimately, they served as instruments of Soviet control, underpinning Stalin's post-war order in Eastern Europe well into the 1950s.

In Poland, as Commander-in-Chief of Soviet troops, Rokossovsky's authority was wide-ranging, far beyond that of military commander. He was in effect Stalin's Viceroy in Warsaw. Meanwhile, in April 1946 he was summoned to Moscow for a meeting of the Collegium of the Defence Ministry convened to arraign Zhukov. While Rokossovsky himself did not play the leading role – reserved for Konev – it was indicative of the fissures within the High Command, exploited by Stalin, and later Khrushchev.

In Poland Rokossovsky remained Commander-in-Chief of Soviet troops until November 1949, when he was replaced by Colonel-General K. P. Trubnikov. Some days later the Soviet and Polish media announced his appointment 'at the request of the Polish Government' as Polish Defence Minister, and a member of the Politburo of the Polish Communist Party. At the same time, Rokossovsky was officially declared a Polish national and invested with the rank of Marshal of Poland. Recent events in Yugoslavia, where Tito had broken away from Moscow, lay behind this move, by which Stalin intended to forestall the Poles from emulating the Yugoslav heresy. From the point of view of the Soviet High Command, it was regarded as a necessary step to reorganize and improve the Polish Armed Forces. There followed an influx of Soviet 'advisors' into the Polish Defence Ministry, intelligence and security services. Rokossovsky at times attempted to appease injured Polish pride, deferring to Polish custom and national sentiment when the opportunity afforded, and indeed added a touch of dignity to the ruling clique, many of them old-guard Jewish émigrés. None the less, while he resided in Warsaw he was regarded as the symbol of Stalin's repressive rule, and on one occasion narrowly survived an assassination attempt by a reckless Polish general.

The death of Stalin, and Khrushchev's eventual accession to the Soviet leadership, subsequently raised hopes throughout Eastern Europe of a relaxation in Moscow's grip. Indeed, there were moves towards realigning Soviet policy, with the Austrian Peace Treaty of 1955, followed by the creation of the Warsaw Pact. None the less, the new mood in Moscow did not satisfy aspirations even within the ruling Communist Parties. In Poland tension mounted throughout the first half of 1956, highlighted by the Poznan riots of June, and calls for national consolidation to deal with the precarious economic situation. The Soviet leadership at first attempted to negotiate, redefining Communist orthodoxy, and dispatching a high-level delegation to Warsaw, including Marshals Bulganin and Zhukov. Khrushchev's reaction reflected Poland's strategic importance astride the lines of communication with East Germany. Matters, however, came to a head in October with the risk of armed insurrection. In the attempts to find a solution Rokossovsky became the principal sacrifice. On 19 October he was not re-elected to the Polish Politburo, and the first alarm sounded in Moscow that Poland might attempt to leave the bloc. With reports of Soviet troop movements, on 23 October Khrushchev backed down, assuring Gomulka, the new Polish leader, that Soviet troops would return to barracks by 25 October. Rokossovsky appears to have played no part in negotiations between Moscow and Warsaw, and on 13 November, despite opposition within the Soviet High Command, Khrushchev replaced him with Marshal Spychalsky as Defence Minister. His departure was followed by the replacement of the Soviet commanders of the Polish Air Force and Warsaw Military District by Poles, and the return to Moscow of over thirty senior 'advisors'.

Throughout the next decade Rokossovsky was to hold a number of important posts; in November 1956 he became a Deputy Defence Minister, and in July 1957 Chief Inspector of the Ministry of Defence. Inevitably, he could not avoid being drawn into the fractious debate over military doctrine, policy and the wider relationship with the leadership. In October 1957 he was appointed Commander of Transcaucasus Military District, removing him from Moscow at a critical time as Khrushchev manoeuvred to strike the final blow at Zhukov. The arrogant, obstructive and naïve Zhukov, turned military reformer, the upholder of armed forces authority and military efficiency when threatened by political quacks posing as military strategists, was dispatched to irredeemable disgrace in October 1957. While Rokossovsky's removal to Tbilisi was generally regarded as evidence of his support for Zhukov, the text of the October 1957 Central Committee plenum summoned to arraign the unrepentant Marshal sought to align Rokossovsky with Zhukov's accusers.

With the Zhukov affair out of the system, in early 1958 Malinovsky, now Defence Minister, recalled Rokossovsky, appointing him Chief Inspector once more, where he had the responsibility, among others, of monitoring the modernizing reforms and reorganization instituted by Zhukov in the mid-1950s. In 1962 Rokossovsky joined the senior Group of General Inspectors of the Ministry of Defence on virtual retirement. Already he had developed symptoms of the illness from which he was to die. In the final months in the Central Military Clinic his visitors included many of his old wartime comrades-in-arms. None gave him greater comfort than Batov, to whom he entrusted the task of revising and later publishing his memoirs. He died on 3 August 1968.

A statue of Rokossovsky erected in 1952 in the Polish town of Legnica, was torn down in October 1992 by order of the town council, which, after forty years, found it an incongruity in the Street of Popes.

The centenary of Marshal Rokossovsky's birth fell on 21 December 1996, within three weeks of the Zhukov centenary. Inevitably, celebrations in Russia and throughout the CIS in honour of Zhukov's wartime sparring partner were delayed. Judging by comment in the Russian and CIS press, the year 1997 will be devoted to Rokossovsky, described as 'the Marshal of two countries' (the Soviet Union and Poland) and 'commander, Marshal and citizen'. While praising Rokossovsky's outstanding wartime role, in general he is portrayed as a commander of humanity, charisma and a brilliant team leader. As in the case of Zhukov, to immortalize Rokossovsky's memory and inspire future generations of Russian officers, the 'Order of Rokossovsky' has been instituted.

BIBLIOGRAPHY

The Infantry Review (in Polish), Warsaw, 12 December 1949, for the Polish account of Rokossovsky's life.
Bagramyan, I. Kh., *Tak nachalas' voina*, Kiev, 1974.
Izvestiya, 8 May 1992.
Krasnaya zvezda, Moscow, 13 December 1964.
Rokossovsky, K. K., *Soldatskii dolg*, 3rd edn, Moscow, 1984.
Voenno-istoricheskii Zhurnal, nos. 4–6, 1989; no. 2, 1990; no. 7, 1991; no. 12, 1991; no. 3, 1992, for previously censored sections of Rokossovsky's autobiography.
Voenno-istoricheskii Zhurnal, no. 7, 1990, for interviews of Kiev staff officers.

Sergei Ignatievich

RUDENKO

RICHARD WOFF

Fifty years after the traumatic defeat suffered by the Red Army in June 1941, the need to make adequate provision for national defence still colours debate in Moscow. The memory of 1941 has a warning today, as Russian military leaders contemplate the decline of Soviet power in Eastern Europe, and – to quote Russian Defence Minister General Pavel Grachev – the loss of the first strategic line of national defence. He was referring in part to Moscow's concern at the CIS's failure to make adequate provision for an effective joint strategic air defence command structure. To support their case senior Russian officers point to the disaster inflicted on the Red Air Force by the Luftwaffe. While the Red Air Force was able to recover and turn on the Luftwaffe, thanks to the devotion and ability of a small group of senior officers who survived Stalin's purges, based on the record of the first decades of the century the defeat could have been avoided. None knew more about the trauma, played a greater rôle in the revival of Soviet air power, and took a keener pride in its traditions than the Ukrainian-born Marshal of Aviation Sergei Rudenko.

The origins of the Russian Air Force were laid well before the First World War, throughout which the Imperial High Command continued to support successful investment in the air. Belief in the future of Russian air power survived the October Revolution, thanks to a few pioneers, and Lenin. Consequently, the 1920s and early 1930s were a period of progress for the Red Air Force. The expansion of Soviet air power, buttressed by state economic planning, modernization, and help from the Reichswehr, was a legacy of Lenin's belief in technical progress for its own sake, and the future of Communism in Russia. Moreover, the evolution of the Red Air Force, and its expanding rôle in Soviet military doctrine, had influential friends elsewhere in the Red Army, notably Tukhachevsky. In a speech in 1936 he stressed the importance of 'the mobility of aviation'. As early as 1930–1 Red Army exercises displayed the first attempts to develop a theory of combined operations in which tactical aviation, 'air artillery', was used to gain command of the air, attack unprotected flanks and communications, adding a new and significant dimension to the Soviet view of the battlefield.

The 1935 and 1936 manoeuvres, attended by many foreign visitors, demonstrated the growing effectiveness of the Red Air Force. Of the 1936 manoeuvres General Sir Giffard Martel, while not impressed with the 'tactical handling' of tank units, with regard to the Red Air Force noted the effectiveness of 'the low-flying attacks of troops on the march', the aircraft's rôle in forcing rivers, and in 'air-landing' operations deep in the enemy rear. Giffard Martel also recorded his high opinion of the senior air force command, including the Commander-in-Chief Yakov Alksnis, a Latvian and veteran of the Imperial Air Force, and Vasily Khripin, like Tukhachevsky a protagonist of the long-range bomber. None the less, compared to the Red Army and Navy, the Air Force was a 'young', indeed 'radical' service, with no military tradition to match that of the other arms. Any early move to stifle its growing esprit de corps and achievements would stunt its growth, if not threaten its future. Consequently, Stalin's purge threatened to eliminate the Red Air Force and the gains of the 1920s and 1930s.

The Red Air Force command was decimated, creating a crippling command vacuum. Among Stalin's victims were Alksnis, his deputy Khripin, and over a hundred senior commanders. Nor did the pioneer aviation research and development institutes escape. Many victims were ferried to Moscow from distant regions in the 'prison plane', commanded by Alexander Golovanov, unscrupulous and destined for wartime command of Long-Range Aviation. Despite the bloodletting at the top, the late 1930s saw Soviet pilots in action in Spain, Mongolia and Finland. Consequently, in terms of size and combat experience, on the eve of the Second World War Soviet air power was regarded as second only to that of the Luftwaffe. None the less, within a week of the German invasion, Stalin's Air Force was to be virtually obliterated, many units immobilized before carrying out a single mission. It was a disaster for which many senior officers paid with their lives in the first weeks of the war. Over a year was to elapse before the Red Air Force was to challenge German air superiority. By early 1944 the balance had been adjusted, with Soviet air power supporting and covering the Red Army strategic counter-offensive.

Hopes for a revival rested with a younger generation, a mixture of former infantry officers like Alexander Novikov, careerist adventurers like Golovanov, and the cream of the academies in the 1930s. Sergei Rudenko was typical of the latter group: ambitious and of outstanding professional ability moulded by experience. As commander of 16th Air Army from late

September 1942, he was in the vanguard of the Red Army's reversal of fortune, from Stalingrad to Berlin. His maxims regarding essential features of the air battle, and air power, remain valid today. A leading exponent of effective night and day air support to ground formations, his advice on air operations was sought, and appreciated, by Zhukov and Rokossovsky. After 1945, overshadowed by many wartime comrades-in-arms, Rudenko's career went into reverse, only to recover in the early 1950s. Eventually, he played a significant part in the 1950s and 1960s evolution of Soviet air power, jousting at times with Khrushchev when the future of the Air Force was threatened, and going on to influence the reassessment of the doctrine of Soviet air power throughout the 1970s. One ambition Rudenko was never to achieve – command of the Soviet Air Forces.

Born the son of a small craftsman on 7 October 1904 in Chernigov Province, Rudenko was one of hundreds of young communists who 'volunteered' for service in the Red Army in the mid-1920s. After a brief apprenticeship with an aviation unit, in 1924 he entered the First (Ukrainian) Military School for Pilots, graduating in 1927. His first three years were spent perfecting his flying skill, before selection in 1930 for a junior command course at the Zhukovsky Air Academy. He graduated in 1932 and spent the next three years commanding an air squadron. In 1935 Rudenko returned to the Air Academy to study in the Operations Faculty, graduating with distinction in 1936. Subsequently he commanded an air regiment and brigade, in turn. Appointed Deputy Commander of 31st Air Division located in Western Special Military District, in January 1941 he took over command of the division. Following the German invasion, Rudenko participated in some of the first aerial combat missions against the Luftwaffe. One of the few senior Soviet commanders to distinguish himself during the disaster of the first weeks, in October Rudenko was promoted Major-General of Aviation. Some weeks later he was appointed Commander of Aviation of 61st Army, and soon after Commander of Aviation on the Kalinin Front at the height of the battle for Moscow. After a brief period on the Main Air Staff, he was transferred to the Volkhov Front in the spring of 1942 as Deputy Commander of Aviation, Commander 1st Air Strike Force, and Commander 7th Strike Air Group of the Supreme High Command, in turn.

In retrospect, Rudenko's service on the Volkhov Front was a turning point in the fortunes of the wartime Red Air Force. He arrived in March 1942, together with Stavka Representative Novikov and Major-General Golovanov, commander of Stalin's pre-war 'Special Aviation Unit'. Their mission was to co-ordinate planning and execution of one of the first wartime Soviet 'air offensives' on 10–20 March 1942, a series of 'mass air strikes' against German formations, airfields and defences, followed by a counter-offensive by 2nd Shock, 4th and 59th Army Volkhov Front, and 54th Army Leningrad Front. For the remainder of the war the trio virtually formed a senior field operations staff, co-ordinating the Soviet strategic air offensive throughout the Stalingrad, Kursk, Belorussian, Vistula-Oder and Berlin operations.

In early June 1942 Rudenko was transferred to the Southwestern Front, initially as Deputy Air Commander, and subsequently Deputy Commander 8th Air Army, created out of Southwestern Front air assets, taking part in the defence of Poltava and the subsequent air battles, as the Germans advanced on Stalingrad in late summer 1942. To increase air support to the retreating Red Army, and having decided to defend Stalingrad 'at all costs', Stavka carried out a major reorganization of air assets on the Southwestern and Southeastern Fronts in mid-summer 1942, most significantly creating a number of air armies, one of which was 16th Air Army, formed 8 August 1942, and consisting of elements from 8th Air Army and the Supreme High Command Reserve, and placed under command of Major-General P. S. Stepanov. Soon after, Rudenko was appointed Deputy Commander for Training, and on 28 September Commander 16th Air Army, a post he was to hold for the remainder of the war.

Overall control of air operations at Stalingrad was exercised by Novikov, as Stavka Representative, and since April 1942 Commander of the Red Air Force. He was assisted by his Deputy Major-General Grigory Vorozheikin, and Golovanov, now Commander Long-Range Bomber Aviation and Stalin's favourite 'high-flyer' within the Air Force command. Their task was twofold: to co-ordinate air operations of the four air armies at Stalingrad, and to provide close support to the ground formations. Building on the experience of early 1942, the tactics evolved at Stalingrad, the seminal experience of co-ordinated air/ground command and control, and the costly mistakes, influenced and shaped Soviet air operations for the remainder of the war.

Throughout the defensive phase of the battle of Stalingrad, the German IV Air Fleet had overwhelming air superiority with 1,640 aircraft of which 1,200 alone were assigned to support VI Army in an attempt to pound Chuikov's 62nd and Shumilov's 64th Armies into submission throughout September and October. Against this armada in early July 8th Air Army mustered 454 aircraft. In an unsuccessful attempt to stall the German advance on the Stalingrad Axis, and hold the Don crossings, this force was reinforced in mid-August by a mixed assortment of 450 aircraft, some drawn from other fronts. Later in August there followed 150–200 long-range bombers under Golovanov's command, and 60–100 fighters to increase close ground support and air defence capability. From September to late November successive reinforcements held the total of Soviet aircraft at around 1,000. None the less, down to late 1942 the Luftwaffe retained a margin of air superiority.

Assigned initially to support the Stalingrad Front, on 30 September 1942, Rudenko, with a relatively small force of some 300 aircraft, was resubordinated to the Don Front under Rokossovsky. This was the beginning of a close association between Rokossovsky and Rudenko's 16th Air Army which was to last until November 1944, and in his memoirs Rokossovsky constantly refers to the invaluable support and advice he received from Rudenko in the planning and execution of some of the crucial offensive operations.

Perhaps Rudenko's greatest contribution to the defence of Stalingrad was the inventiveness and flexibility he brought in deploying his resources, using fighters in close support of the hard-pressed defenders, and the defence of the Volga crossings, co-ordinating operations with the artillery and the commander on the ground, and stepping up operations 'round the clock', with pilots in some cases carrying out three to four missions in one day. By early November, thanks to the joint efforts of 8th and 16th Air Armies, and having seized the vital bridgeheads on the western and southern Don, the Red Army was poised to mount the counter-offensive of 19 November, ending in the encirclement of VI Army. By the end of the 125-day battle for the city, 16th Air Army had carried out some 10,000 combat missions, 5,718 in October alone, dropping around 5,000 tonnes of bombs, and destroying some 100 enemy aircraft in the air and over 50 on the ground.

In the weeks before the counter-attack, Stalin stressed the crucial rôle of the Air Force, informing Zhukov on 12 November that 'experience to date demonstrates the absolute importance of achieving air superiority in operations against the Germans.' With this objective in view, Stavka concentrated on reinforcing the air armies involved in the offensive phase of the battle. In order to improve offensive capability, in early November 16th Air Army was reinforced by 2nd Bomber Corps, commanded by a senior officer of Polish birth, Major-General I. L. Turkel, bringing the total force at Rudenko's disposal to some 460 aircraft, many 'rehabilitated' by an increasingly effective technical maintenance organization. For the first time since June 1941, despite periodic shortages of fuel, the Red Air Force enjoyed local superiority over their German contestants: 1,350 versus 1,200 aircraft.

Working to a co-ordinated plan under Novikov's control, despite severe weather conditions, the three air armies maintained a constant air barrage, with the objective of suppressing enemy air activity in support of the beleaguered VI Army, while providing close air support to ground formations. By early December the Red Air Force was winning the air battle; with von Paulus's surrender on 2 February 1943, the battle of Stalingrad was over. Subsequently, the main thrust of the counter-offensive switched from the southwestern to the central strategic axis, and with it the battle for air superiority.

Promoted Lieutenant-General in late March, the experience and lessons of Stalingrad were to loom large in the planning of Rudenko's next major operation, providing air support to Rokossovsky's Central Front during the battle of Kursk, 5 July–23 August 1943. Like Stalingrad, Kursk had a defensive phase and an interlocking offensive phase. It was, however, in scale and execution a totally different battle, designed to call Hitler's bluff, 'bleed' the German offensive, and finally roll back Army Groups Centre and South. From late March to late May 16th Air Army was engaged in the hazardous regrouping phase, as Rokossovsky's Central Front moved north ready to face von Kluge's Army Group Centre. Rudenko's mission in the weeks before and during the battle of Kursk, was to suppress the German air offensive, blunt the combat-effectiveness of German ground formations, harry enemy lines of communication and supply, and provide strategic air cover to Soviet ground operations. Throughout April–June, 14,309 sorties were carried out, in the course of which 308 German aircraft were destroyed in the air and 104 on the ground. Soviet air-photo reconnaissance played a crucial part in defining German intentions, tempting Rudenko to propose a massive air strike to destroy leading German formations, an idea vetoed by Rokossovsky who considered it of greater importance 'to convince the enemy that we know nothing of his intentions'. Compared with Stalingrad, 16th Air Army's offensive power had more than doubled, with over 1,000 aircraft at Rudenko's disposal, carrying out over 22,000 sorties between 13 July and 15 August.

The defeat of the German summer 1943 offensive was followed by the liberation of much of Ukraine, the industrial heartland of the Donbas, and eastern Belorussia by late 1943. Red Army success went hand-in-hand with growing air superiority. Kursk had important lessons for the evolution of tactics and strategic command and control, and the improvement in organization at regimental and divisional level. These changes were to have an impact on 16th Air Army operations during the Belorussian operation.

A total of five air armies, with a strength of over 6,000 aircraft, were now ranged against IV Air Fleet with under 1,400 aircraft. 6th Air Army was assigned to Rokossovsky's 1st Belorussian Front, and a further indication of the importance of Rudenko's sector of operations was the arrival in mid-June of a high-level group of staff officers headed by Turkel, co-ordinating 16th Air Army with Novikov and Golovanov. As senior Stavka Representative, Zhukov, accompanied by Novikov, visited Rokossovsky's headquarters shortly before the operation opened, emphasizing the crucial rôle assigned to Rudenko's 16th Air Army, which now comprised five air corps and eight independent air divisions. Throughout the operation out of a total of 153,545 sorties, 16th Air Army carried out over 27,500, blasting German communications and formations on the ground, and completing the destruction of encircled groups. Zhukov later recalled his impressions, and admiration, of the havoc wrought by 16th Air Army on the German Bobruisk Group in support of General Romanenko's 48th Army, with 'hundreds of bombers . . . striking blow after blow'.

The following November Rokossovsky moved sideways to take command of the 2nd Belorussian Front, Zhukov taking over the 1st Belorussian Front astride the main axis to Berlin. Ahead lay the Oder-Vistula operation, designed to complete the destruction of Army Groups Centre and 'A'. By early February the combined forces of the 1st Belorussian and Konev's 1st Ukrainian Fronts had carved out a huge salient, establishing bridgeheads on the Oder merely 60 miles from Berlin. Rudenko's 16th Air Army provided air cover, pinned down enemy artillery and disrupted the German retreat. While the Luftwaffe no longer enjoyed air superiority, with 1,050 aircraft facing a combined Soviet force of some 5,000, VI Air Fleet could still threaten to stall Zhukov's advance. Consequently Rudenko received significant reinforcements from the Supreme High Command's Reserve. It was now the turn of 16th Air Army to reverse rôles, immobilizing hundreds of German aircraft, grounded for lack of fuel and pilots, in the final weeks of the Berlin operation.

The Berlin operation marked the close of Rudenko's wartime career. He retained command of 16th Air Army for a further three years, surviving Stalin's vindictive assault on the senior command of the former 1st Belorussian Front. Finally, in December 1948, Rudenko was appointed Commander Soviet Airborne Troops. The two years spent in this post marked perhaps the nadir of his post-war career. The Airborne Troops had a number of singular wartime successes as a strategic element of the Supreme High Command. Assigned to administrative control of the Air Force, in April 1946 they were reorganized as an independent command, and resubordinated to the Defence Ministry 'in keeping with their strategic rôle'. None the less, the first two post-war decades was a period of 'doctrinal vacuum', marked initially by frequent changes of command. Rudenko was the third commander since 1946, two highly decorated wartime all-arms commanders having 'died' or been 'removed' little over a year after appointment. In March 1950 Rudenko himself was succeeded by another outstanding all-arms commander, Colonel-General Alexander Gorbatov.

Throughout the last three years of Stalin's rule Rudenko was to occupy two senior posts: Chief of the Main Air Force Staff, March–August 1950, and Commander Long-Range Aviation, August 1950–June 1953, demonstrating Stalin's renewed confidence in Rudenko, who now controlled the expanding strategic strike force in the early years of US–Soviet nuclear confrontation.

The death of Stalin in March 1953 inevitably ushered in a prolonged period of upheaval in the Soviet High Command. In June 1953 Rudenko returned as Chief of the Main Air Force Staff, and in 1955 was promoted Marshal of Aviation in a round of Khrushchev promotions honouring his military friends, in the main members of the wartime 'Stalingrad group'. In February 1958 Rudenko moved up on appointment as First Deputy Commander-in-Chief Air Forces and senior aide to Marshal Vershinin. It was a crucial period in the post-war history of Soviet air power, with Khrushchev's ambitions to build up strategic nuclear power, downgrading the rôle of the manned bomber, which was later upgraded by Khrushchev's successors.

While Rudenko was to play a major part in developments throughout the 1960s, in 1968 he was transferred to head the Air Force Academy. The move was possibly part of a power struggle between the wartime and post-war generation of commanders prior to Vershinin's retirement in 1969. None the less, the next five years afforded Rudenko an opportunity to study Soviet wartime experience, and US experience in southeast Asia in the late 1960s, and apply the lessons to the reassessment of the rôle and structure of Soviet air power for the last decades of the century. In August 1973 Rudenko retired as head of the Academy and was awarded the title of 'Professor' and 'Doctor of Military Science', marking his contribution to the evolution of the doctrine of Soviet air power. Throughout the 1970s and 1980s he continued to publish writings, including his wartime memoirs, in which he evaluated the wartime experience and set out his vision for the future. He died in July 1990.

BIBLIOGRAPHY

Kozhevnikov, M. N., *Komandovanie i shtab VVS Sovetskoi Armii v Velikoi Otchechestvennoi voine 1941–1945*, Institute of Military History, Moscow, 1977 and 1985.

Rudenko, S. I., 'Osobennosti boevykh deistvii aviatsii v Belorusskoi operatsii', *Voenno-istoricheskii Zhurnal ViZh*, no. 2, 1971.

Rudenko, S. I., 'Aviatsiya v bitve za Stalingrad', *ViZh*, no. 7, 1972.

Rudenko, S. I., 'Aviatsiya v kontrnastuplenii', *ViZh*, no. 11, 1972.

Rudenko, S. I., *Kryl'ya pobedy*, Moscow, 1976 and 1985.

Tsupko, Colonel N., 'Aviatsiya i kosmonavtika', *ViZh*, no. 12, 1992 reassesses the faulty deployment of Red Army air power in the western military districts 1939–41, and draws lessons for the Russian Air Force in the 1990s.

Pavel Semenovich
RYBALKO

RICHARD WOFF

The German invasion found many future outstanding commanders serving in relatively minor posts in military academies or schools, where they passed on valuable ideas on Red Army doctrine to a younger generation. Not content to languish in the classroom while the fate of their country hung in the balance, among those who hoped for active service in the first months of the war was Pavel Semenovich Rybalko. A former political officer, military advisor and diplomat, Rybalko's intellect and ideas blossomed late. Out of the dedicated political commissar evolved the theorist, innovator of a unique concept of tank operations, and one of the most genial of wartime commanders. Many of his 'disciples' served in key posts within the High Command of the 1970s and 1980s. The secret of Rybalko's success was confidence in his own abilities, a passion for hard work, determination to challenge entrenched prejudice higher up, pragmatism, a willingness to take matters into his own hands, and candour.

Born 23 October 1894 in Kharkov province, Ukraine, Rybalko was the fourth of seven children of a poor craftsman. After a basic education in a local school, he worked in a local sugar factory. Within weeks of the outbreak of the Great War, he found himself at the front as a private in an infantry regiment. He spent most of the war on the Galician Front, and was wounded once.

Soon after the October Revolution Rybalko enrolled in the Red Guards. In the first months of the Civil War he was a political officer with the partisans fighting against the German Army in his native Ukraine. Before long he had been elected commander of the detachment, his first experience of independent command. Combat activity was combined with chairmanship of a local soviet. Soon, however, he was promoted, and spent most of 1919 as a political officer on the Turkestan Front. In late 1919 he was sent to the

Bashkir region to help set up a Bolshevik government. One of his first tasks was to organize measures to fight a typhus epidemic, and it was here that he met and soon married a young nurse, Nadezhda Denisova. Another indication that Rybalko's abilities were being recognized was his transfer in April 1920 to 1st Cavalry Army. There were others serving in 1st Cavalry Army with whom Rybalko's own career became closely associated later, notably Timoshenko. As Budenny said at their first meeting, Rybalko's arrival was 'timely', and throughout 1920 and early 1921 he helped establish Bolshevik power in Ukraine, and later the North Caucasus. In the last months of the Civil War Rybalko commanded the 61st Cavalry Regiment of the Special Cavalry Brigade, a valuable experience in mobile operations.

As with many junior commanders, the Civil War broadened Rybalko's grasp of the basic principles of combat. None the less, he had never had the benefit of a military education, and he sensed the need to apply himself to disciplining his mind and broadening his outlook in the interest of his future military career. He therefore embarked on a course of 'self-study' in his spare time, poring over books into the small hours. Luckily he had been transferred to Moscow in 1924, where he soon became adept at 'knocking on the right door'. When he felt he had made sufficient progress he applied for a senior course. Initially rebuffed, in 1926 he was selected to attend a Senior Officers' Course at the Red Army (later Frunze Military) Academy. Despite initial difficulty in adapting to academic routine, he graduated with distinction, and was initially posted to a cavalry regiment stationed on the Mongolian/Chinese border, spending the next two years as an advisor to the Mongolian Army. This was followed in 1928 by three years as commander-commissar of 7th Cavalry Regiment of the Chervon Cossack Division, one of the few surviving Cossack formations in the Red Army, located near Starokonstantinov on the old Soviet–Polish border. With the changes now affecting the Red Army in the late 1920s, however, Rybalko still felt the need 'to catch up on my education', and in 1931 he was among a promising group of junior commanders selected to attend a three-year course at the All-Arms Faculty of the Frunze Military Academy, graduating in 1934.

In his confidential report on Rybalko, the Head of the Academy, Shaposhnikov, noted his 'thirst for knowledge, widening military erudition, and breadth of view', which placed him among the best of the students. The emphasis on 'academic' achievements explains why, none the less, in contrast to most of his fellow students, Rybalko spent the next eight years in a number of posts far removed from the promotion ladder. Thus, on leaving the Academy he returned to the Far East as military advisor attached to a mountain cavalry division in China. Recalled to Moscow in 1935, he served the next two years as a senior aide in the Auto-Armoured Tank Directorate at a time when ideas on the organization and deployment of armoured troops were undergoing fundamental reassessment. He himself had now become converted to the concept of armoured warfare, influenced among others by the studies of Western theorists, including Fuller and von Kleist. Unfortunately, with any progressive ideas on the use of large armoured formations extinguished for the time being by Stalin, in the late 1930s the Soviet concept regarding the rôle of armour went into reverse. This may explain Rybalko's next move in late 1937 as Military Attaché in Warsaw, a posting which, however, removed him from the internal turmoil of the next two years.

Rybalko's correspondence shows that he was not sympathetic towards the Poles. He noted that he preferred 'crossing swords with the Polish gentry in 1920' to dealing with officials in Warsaw, tending to regard the régime as pro-Nazi. The reason for his recall to Moscow on the eve of the German–Soviet Agreement of August 1939 is, none the less, glossed over, merely recording that the Second World War began with the German attack on Poland. Meanwhile, in early October Rybalko returned to China, this time as Military Attaché. His second tour of duty was relatively short. Replaced in late December 1940 by Lieutenant-General V. I. Chuikov, Rybalko returned home as lecturer in tactics at the Kazan Tank School.

While the post of lecturer was congenial, affording an opportunity to study the German *Blitzkrieg* of 1940, Rybalko was soon frustrated, 'shut away in a classroom' while the Germans threatened Moscow and the existence of the Soviet Union throughout late 1941 and early 1942. Repeated appeals to serve at the front fell on deaf ears, until one day in May 1942 he decided to write to a former comrade-in-arms, Colonel-General Andrei Yeremenko, Commander Bryansk Front. Within a week he received a summons from Moscow, and in late May he was appointed Deputy Commander of 3rd Tank Army on the Central Front, part of the Reserve of the Supreme High Command, now in the process of forming under General P. L. Romanenko.

Within a few weeks Rybalko had noted the crucial flaws besetting the new tank armies now being formed: lack of all-arms co-ordination; a tendency to undervalue the rôle of the artillery; a misconception regarding the rôle of the tank army itself; a chaotic supply and distribution system which was to paralyse effective operations throughout 1942–3. After a brief interval commanding 5th Tank Army, he was back in command of 3rd Tank Army, a personal decision by Stalin, Romanenko in turn taking over 5th Tank Army. The fortunes and reputation of Rybalko and 3rd Tank Army were to be inseparable for the remainder of the war.

The German invasion had come at a time when the Red Army was already attempting to reassess its doctrine of armoured warfare, and repackage an impressive inventory in tanks into larger combat-effective formations. It was to be some time, however, before the mistakes and U-turns of the late 1930s, regarding the structure and rôle of tank formations, could be compensated for. Indeed, it was not until March 1942 that Field Regulations governing armoured brigade-corps operations had been drawn up. Between May and

July 1942 five tank armies were raised, in four cases out of former all-arms armies. A sixth tank army was created in January 1944. They were the Red Army's answer to the powerful German armoured groupings, injecting lethal 'punch', mobility and manoeuvrability to the strategic counter-offensive. Though they were to adopt Guderian's concept of 'the hammer' as opposed to being deployed in 'packets' to support other arms, Stalin's tank armies evolved an organization, rôle and esprit de corps distinctly Russian. By March 1945 all six tank armies had been awarded 'Guards' honorifics.

3rd Tank Army was originally raised in May 1942 in the Moscow region out of the former 58th Army. In April 1943 it was redesignated 57th (all-arms) Army. In turn a new formation was raised in May 1943 under Rybalko's command – 3rd Guards Tank Army – the first tank army to be honoured by the 'Guards' title. On taking over 3rd Tank Army in September 1942 Rybalko's first task was to reorganize training and supervise re-equipment to make up for the serious losses of the previous operation. From September to late December the army was part of supreme High Command's Reserve, and early January 1943 was transferred to the Voronezh Front, taking part in the Ostrogozh-Rossoshan Operation and the liberation of Kharkov on 25 February. The triumph was short-lived. As three Soviet armies were tightly concentrated in and around Kharkov, the Germans saw a chance to accomplish a 'German Stalingrad', to surround and annihilate the powerful Red Army grouping. At the mercy of a massive air offensive, and confronted by local superiority, the Kharkov defensive operation (4–25 March 1943) failed to halt the German offensive, and on 15 March forces of the 1st Ukrainian Front were forced to withdraw, as Rybalko ruefully noted, abandoning the local population to its fate, but denying Hitler his 'Stalin-grad'. The operation had its lessons, with Rybalko having to adapt tactics, deploying mobile groups to stem the German counter-attack. For his contribution to the liberation of Kharkov, Rybalko was promoted Lieutenant-General in late February 1943, and awarded the Order of Suvorov 1st Class. The successes of the early 1943 operations, however, were gained at some cost, under extreme conditions with 30 degrees of frost, and with insufficient resources. It was Rybalko's first experience of commanding a major armoured formation in combat, and the lessons were to bear fruit, in particular redeploying over large distances, difficult terrain, often at night.

The reformation of 3rd Guards Tank Army in May 1943 was part of the major preparations for the strategic counter-offensive, as the initiative slipped from German control throughout 1943. For the first of the counter-offensives, the battle of Kursk, 3rd Guards Tank Army was deployed initially on the Bryansk Front, and from 27 July on the Central Front under Rokossovsky's command. For their rôle in the Orel operation on the northern wing of the Kursk salient 12th and 15th Tank Corps were redesignated respectively 6th and 7th Guards Tank Corps. In his memoirs Rokossovsky, none the less, expressed reservations on the rôle of 3rd Guards Tank Army, handicapped as Rybalko was by a chaotic supply system.

In mid-August 3rd Guards Tank Army was withdrawn to Supreme High Command's Reserve in preparation for the great push into the heart of Ukraine in late 1943. The aim of the offensive was the liberation of Kiev, in the course of which Rybalko had to carry out a major regrouping operation in late October. The redeployment on 26–29 October from Bukrin, south of Kiev, some 60 miles north to the Lyutezh bridgehead, followed by the forcing of the Dnieper, was regarded by Soviet military historians as a classic operation of its kind. Recalling the task of clearing the German minefields a month later, Mikhail Sakson, a former senior NCO attached to 9th Mechanized Corps, claimed that the sappers were the real heroes of the operation. Having cleared the advance route, 3rd Guards Tank Army moved north on two main axes some 30–40 miles apart, across difficult terrain at night, achieving comparatively high rates of advance, using tactical deception, radio silence, and finally assembling after forcing the Dnieper for the assault on Kiev, which was liberated on 6 November by forces of the 1st Ukrainian Front. There followed the Kiev defensive operation 11 November–22 December, with IV Tank Army mounting a determined assault to re-take the Ukrainian capital. The German offensive was repulsed, with the Soviet grip on the main central axis into central Europe firmly established.

The Zhitomir-Berdichev operation of December 1943–January 1944, followed by the Proskurov-Chernovits operation of 4 March–17 April, was directed at the destruction of German Army Group South by combined forces of 1st and 2nd Ukrainian Fronts. After advancing some 400 miles by May 1944 the 1st Ukrainian Front was about to complete the liberation of Ukraine. The Lvov-Sandomir operation of 13 July–29 August was launched to eliminate Army Group North Ukraine and establish a foothold in southern Poland, with 3rd Guards Tank Army operating as the 1st Ukrainian Front mobile operational group, a rôle in which Rybalko could display outstanding talent as a commander and tactician of innovative enterprise, a master of manoeuvre, under Konev's scrutiny. The liberation of Lvov involved a major encircling movement to cut off the entrapped German garrison, which surrendered on 27 July 1944.

The next major operation in which 3rd Tank Army played a major part was the Sandomir-Silesian operation of 12 January–1 February 1945. After breaking through the German defences on the first day of the operation, by 23 January elements of Rybalko's forces had established a bridgehead on the Oder, and then went on to take part in the final liquidation of Army Group Centre and the advance into Saxony. The Berlin operation of 16 April–8 May formed the final assault on Nazi Germany. Four tank armies took part in the operation. 3rd and 4th Guards Tank Armies formed the mobile punch of Konev's 1st Ukrainian Front, engaging the city from the south and becoming enmeshed in the remorseless street fighting which marked the final stages of the operation.

There remained only the Prague operation of the 1st Ukrainian Front, requiring 3rd Guards Tank Army to disengage from the carnage of Berlin, regroup and wheel south over difficult mountainous terrain into Czechoslovakia. The whole operation took three days, and Prague was liberated on 9 May. Rybalko deployed a hastily organized mobile group acting as an advanced guard, under Major-General Ivan Ziberov, 6th Guards Tank Corps under Major-General Vasily Mitrofanov, and 7th Guards Tank Corps under Major-General Vasily Novikov – three of Rybalko's most talented and experienced lieutenants. The operation, depicted as a model of planning and execution by Soviet military historians, brought to a brilliant conclusion Rybalko's wartime career. A Colonel-General since December 1943, in late 1945 Rybalko was promoted Marshal of Armoured Tank Troops. He was twice awarded Hero of Soviet Union, in November 1943 for his part in the liberation of Kiev, and in April 1945 for his contribution in the closing stages of the war. In July 1945 3rd Guards Tank Army redeployed to what was now the Soviet Group of Occupation Forces Germany, establishing its headquarters near Wittenberg. Reorganized in early 1946 as 3rd Guards Mechanized Army, it remained in East Germany until the late 1950s, when it was disbanded.

Of the six tank armies, 3rd Guards is acknowledged to have been the most distinguished, due above all to the charismatic qualities of command displayed by Rybalko. He was to survive the war by only three years. He retained command of 3rd Guards Tank Army until March 1946. In April Rybalko returned to Moscow on appointment as First Deputy Commander of Armoured Tank Troops. Shortly after he was summoned to join other senior commanders, including Konev and Rokossovsky, at a meeting of the Higher Military Council in the Kremlin to arraign Zhukov. At the conference Zhukov was condemned by Stalin, Molotov, Beria and Bulganin. Of the military present Konev was lukewarm. Although Stalin wanted to arrest Zhukov on the spot, he was prevented from doing so by opposition from other senior officers present: Rokossovsky, Vasilevsky, Sokolovsky and Rybalko. Indeed, Rybalko was the only senior officer to speak up in defence of Zhukov.

In January 1947 Rybalko, deputizing for the ailing Marshal Yakov Fedorenko, Chief Main Armoured Tank Troops Directorate, was among the senior Soviet officers met by Field Marshal Montgomery while on a visit to Moscow. A photograph published during the visit clearly demonstrates the rapport established between the most outstanding Red Army wartime tank troops commander and Montgomery. Two months later Rybalko was to succeed his old friend Fedorenko on his death in late March 1947. It was a time of reassessment of the wartime experience, in particular the rôle and structure of the armoured tank troops, and Rybalko was looking forward to playing a leading part in a programme of modernization. The war, however, had taken a toll of his health, and on 28 August 1948 he died suddenly, leaving his successors, and Zhukov as Defence Minister in the mid-1950s, to carry out the modernization of tank troops.

BIBLIOGRAPHY

Alferov, S., 'Peregruppirovka 3-ei gvardeiskoi tankovoi armii v bitve za Dnepr (oktyabr 1943)', *Voenno-istoricheskii Zhurnal*, no. 3, 1980.
Belikov, General V. A., 'Kommanduyushchie', *Voennyi vestnik*, no. 3, 1987.
Melnikov, S. I., *P. V. Rybalko*, Kiev, 1980.
Narodnaya armiya, 5 September 1992, Kiev.

Boris Mikhailovich
SHAPOSHNIKOV

OLEG RZHESHEVSKY

On 7 August 1941, at the height of the Wehrmacht's offensive in Russia, German radio broadcast the following address in Russian to Marshal Boris Shaposhnikov, head of the General Staff of the Red Army:

Marshal Shaposhnikov has been vested with supreme military powers. He is the only tsarist officer in the General Staff to have survived after 23 years of service to the Bolsheviks, thanks to his astuteness and cunning at a time when other tsarist officers such as Tukhachevsky and Yegorov were shot down. So now we are addressing Comrade Shaposhnikov or, to be more precise, Colonel Shaposhnikov.

Mr Colonel, you've been in the Bolshevik service for 23 years now – for lack of courage rather than prompted by your Communist views: you did not wish to take any heroic decisions, hoping to bide your time by lying low and adapting to the situation. You explained to other officers, who had gone over to the Reds' side, that you had acted like this because the enemy was threatening your country and that it would be better to serve with the army in order to save it. That was just subterfuge. In spite of everything, you've carved out an excellent career for yourself in the Red Army, were awarded the highest decorations and promoted to the rank of marshal, having braved all dangers and overcome all obstacles, thus making your way to a quiet harbour. In all these years, however, you've been assailed by doubts and troubled by pricks of conscience. You've been tortured by the thought that you have not acted the way a Russian officer should, being well aware that you were assisting a régime that was totally hostile to the Russian people. Perhaps there are not so many years ahead of you, but won't it be better to tell the truth at long last, after 23 years of treachery to the Russian people or its butchers? By doing so you will atone for the injustice done by your conscience and history. You know how best to do it, how to revenge yourself on the Kremlin ringleaders.

Mr Colonel, you are above all a Russian man and your rank of marshal comes only next. You should not leave this world with an ignominious Soviet brand. The time to act is now.

Boris Shaposhnikov was born on 20 September 1882 into the family of a distillery manager (later manager of a storehouse) in the town of Zlatoust, in the south Urals. His mother was a teacher. 'Mysterious and magnificent in its quiet dignity,' Shaposhnikov wrote in his memoirs, 'the south Urals, which was the bulwark of traditional Russian customs and mores, is my native land. Its people . . . were self-confident and capable of enduring any hardships, industrious and ready to face any danger . . . . Many of those traits have been preserved and do credit to the Urals inhabitants, who form part of the core of the Russian population of vast Russia.'

As a youngster in 1900 Boris finished the Perm Modern School with distinction. He was keen on history and literature, and his favourite writers were Pushkin, Tolstoy, Saltykov-Shchedrin and Victor Hugo. His family was too poor, however, for him to continue his studies at university. In his desire for an education, he entered the Alexeyev Military School at Lefortovo, a suburb of Moscow, where studies were free of charge. Cadet Shaposhnikov stood out among his comrades by his exceptional ability, phenomenal memory and rare modesty. Apart from military subjects, he acquired fluent German and French (and later Polish and some other languages), and his name was added to the Academy's Board of Honour, giving him the privilege of choosing for himself the place of his future service. He chose Tashkent, where he was appointed commander of a half-company for novices with the rank of second lieutenant, in the 1st Turkestan Rifle Battalion.

Hard climatic conditions and meagre monthly pay (10 roubles or £1 for pocket money) did not discourage the young officer. He performed his duties to the letter, became a good horseman (the only means of transportation for officers) and swordsman. He knew how to drill recruits, showed good ability for staff work, and was put in charge of the officers' library. In 1905 he was appointed chief of the battalion drilling command and started preparing for entry exams to the General Staff Academy. He kept abreast of all military and political developments and was deeply hurt by the Russian army's defeat in the Russo-Japanese war (1904–5) and shocked by 'Bloody Sunday', 9 January, when troops in St Petersburg opened fire on peaceful demonstrators, and earlier by the shooting of workers in his native Zlatoust. But on the whole he was proud of Russia and its army, although he could not understand why it was necessary 'to have one general for every 500 soldiers'.

In 1907 Shaposhnikov entered the General Staff Academy, having passed two rounds of exams and collected 9.82 points out of 12. The academy was founded in 1832 on the initiative of Antoine Jomini. Subjects were taught exhaustively and there were talented lecturers among its teaching staff (generals and professors N. A. Danilov, A. A. Neznamov, S. F. Platonov), who stood out. Their lectures provided a wealth of material (especially in strategy and tactics) for most of the students, who thus got an insight into the life of the state and army and of human existence in its complexity.

The Russian, Shaposhnikov thought, was a man of many talents. 'He can draw up plans of fortresses as well as compose opera and write novels, but usually he is a dabbler in both spheres.' Shaposhnikov showed special interest in history, which he described as a beacon lighting his path. On 3 June 1910, he was appointed to serve with the General Staff in the same Tashkent Military District. After a period of service in the district headquarters, which, according to Shaposhnikov, 'was bogged down in bureaucracy', he was appointed commander of a company (180 men) of the rifle battalion where for a period of two years he served prior to his studies at the Academy. He was promoted to the rank of staff-captain.

Turkestan's Governor-General, General A. V. Samsonov, who was also commander of Turkestan Military District, took the matter of drilling recruits seriously and employed the most capable young officers for the purpose. Shaposhnikov was among them. He read a paper at a meeting of the district's generals and officers, entitled 'Approaches to the Battlefield and Reinforced Reconnaissance on the Basis of the Experience of Borodino and Wafanggou'. The lecture was highly praised by the audience, including by Samsonov, whom Shaposhnikov deeply respected. During the discussion Shaposhnikov raised a cautious objection, but Samsonov took no offence. While describing this episode in his unfinished memoirs, Shaposhnikov wrote: 'Of course, only young people permit themselves to object to their superiors and even criticize them in a small way. Later, in my mature years, I happened to find myself in the same situation – but with different results.'

The tempestuous revolutionary situation and the gloomy prospects of the war put Shaposhnikov's views to a severe test. He neither sympathized with nor condemned a mutiny by the sappers of the Tashkent garrison, but continued to carry out his duties diligently. And he continued with his studies. He was invited to lecture in remote garrisons and at officers' meetings, and his erudition and potential were far beyond his rank of company commander. However, he showed no sign of ambition or arrogance and went on with his duties of drilling recruits. 'I asked,' he wrote in his memoirs, 'why riflemen took their aim with an open mouth. And the platoon commander said: "that was sergeant-major's order". The latter in turn explained that when he was a recruit, his commander taught them to open their mouths when taking an aim, as this slightly raised the right eye, which made you see the fore-sight better. I had to explain to him that the effect was quite the opposite,' Shaposhnikov concluded.

In November 1912, after the Balkan War had broken out, Shaposhnikov was appointed to the staff of Turkestan Military District, probably on the advice of Samsonov, who must have picked him out as a talented officer.

However, according to the list of vacancies offered by the General Staff to the Academy graduates, Shaposhnikov had the right again to choose his posting. He decided to continue his service in another district, as he put it, where he 'would have an opportunity to gain some experience in manoeuvres and war games on a large scale', and, now a full captain, was appointed adjutant of the 14th Cavalry Division, located in Czestochowa (a four-hour journey from Warsaw in those days). Shaposhnikov's desire to change location was partly motivated by his state of health, which had been undermined by malaria and Turkestan's arid climate.

As adjutant, Shaposhnikov served mainly as head of the divisional HQ. During this eve-of-war period, he became an experienced and capable officer, with an obvious talent for handling operational training, an essential for staff officers at all levels. He worked to a packed timetable which shows that, after an hour of riding at 8 a.m., he would work at headquarters until 8 p.m., then prepare his ciphers and go through the Russian, German and Polish press, retiring at 1 a.m. and rising again at 7 a.m. His service in Poland both added to his experience and enabled him to study the future theatre of military operations, although, he recalled, no one expected the war to break out.

On 18 July 1914 general mobilization was proclaimed in Russia and on 19 July Germany declared war on Russia. On 2 August forward units of the 14th Cavalry Division were engaged in initial fighting against the 7th Austrian Cavalry Division, supported by artillery, in the Kielce district. The Austrians retreated for no good reason. In the Battle of Galicia, a major strategic operation on the Russian Front (18 August–21 September 1914), the Russian cavalry division was located on the left bank of the Vistula with the task of carrying out reconnaissance and preventing the enemy from capturing Ivangorod. Although the Russian division lost one of its regiments, it proved quite battle-worthy and neither side won. Meanwhile Shaposhnikov was making rapid progress in his military career. In October 1917 he was promoted to the rank of colonel and was appointed commander of the 16th Mingrelian Grenadier Regiment of the Caucasian Grenadier Division, and he had received six decorations.

The Russian Revolution brought radical changes in his life. First he had to decide which side to take. His memoirs do not reveal the motives behind his decision. No doubt Russia's major war losses, a result of the tsarist government's and High Command's blatant political and military mistakes, played a major part, as well as the situation in the country, the fact that many of his colleagues were joining the revolution and, not least, his appointment as commander of the Caucasian Grenadier Division at the congress of delegates of revolutionary-military committees in November 1917. In any event, the die was cast.

From May 1918 until the end of the Civil War Shaposhnikov held various posts in the country's supreme military bodies, including that of head of operational command of the field staff of the Revolutionary-Military Committee of the Republic. Together with former tsarist generals and old colleagues of his academy days, such as M. Bonch-Bruevich, N. Suleiman and S. Lukirsky, he planned and prepared virtually all the main operations carried out by the Red Army. In June 1918, while holding him prisoner for a short period, the Whites tried to persuade Shaposhnikov and his colleagues to change sides, but nothing came of it. In recognition of his services in the years of the Civil War Shaposhnikov was awarded the Order of Red Banner in 1921. After the Civil War he took an active part in reorganizing the Red Army, whose strength was cut from 5.3 million to 600,000.

In 1921–8 Shaposhnikov successively held the posts of first assistant to the Chief of Staff and Commander of Leningrad and later Moscow Military Districts. In 1928–31 he was head of the Red Army Staff. During this time, he summed up Russia's experience in the First World War in articles and books which revealed a deep knowledge of military affairs, in both the sphere of operational staff work and in theory. His book *The Cavalry* (Moscow, 1923) was the first such work and aroused great interest. In it he analysed the use of cavalry units during the war and their value in the future. His views were shared by Budenny and Voroshilov, but not by Tukhachevsky. While Shaposhnikov was no doubt expounding his own views, when the clash for leading positions in the army later arose between the 'cavalrymen' (led by Voroshilov) and advocates of the war of the future as 'the war of motors' (led by Tukhachevsky), Shaposhnikov's views won the support of the Defence Commissar when Voroshilov was appointed to that post.

Another fundamental study by Shaposhnikov was entitled *The Vistula: The History of the 1920 Campaign*. In it the author took issue with Tukhachevsky, whose book, *The Vistula Campaign*, came out in Smolensk in 1923. Shaposhnikov showed that the initial correlation of forces put the Red Army's success in question. He remained neutral, as it were, with respect to mutual accusations by the commanders of the Western (Tukhachevsky) and the Southwestern (Yegorov) Fronts. Views of this kind might have impressed Stalin, who was a member of the Military Council of the Southwestern Front and, together with Lenin and Trotsky, bore his share of responsibility for the Soviet defeat in the Warsaw campaign, which had exceedingly unfavourable consequences for the Red Army and the country as a whole. Bearing in mind the repressions of the 1930s, Shaposhnikov's assessment of the prospects for the development of cavalry, and of the Soviet–Polish war, was perhaps significant for his own destiny, although it is also likely that his personal qualities were of crucial importance: as a top-notch military commander he was unequalled for erudition, professional skill and intellectual development – the only exception being A. I. Antonov, a very gifted individual who was Head of the General Staff later.

In 1927–9 Shaposhnikov published his fundamental work, *The Brain of the Army*, in three volumes (it was partially reprinted in 1974), in which he discussed a wide range of problems of army management and proved the need to set up the General Staff as a single agency for directing the Red Army. The fact was that prior to 1935 the managerial functions of the relatively small territorial Red Army were divided between the Headquarters Staff and the Main Administration. The former was not in a position to draw up realistic plans for the strategic deployment of the armed forces in case of war, since it was not empowered to handle mobilization work, nor to supervise training, while the latter, separated as it was from the planning body, was not competent to conduct combat training, either. In *The Army's Brains*, Shaposhnikov analysed the nature of a future war, the guidelines for preparing the country's defence and the tasks confronting the General Staff. Shaposhnikov shared the view of A. Svechin (1878–1938), another prominent military theorist of the period, that in a future war it would be advisable to set up new military-industrial complexes in the trans-Volga region and the Urals, rather than in the south.

On the other hand, Shaposhnikov contested Svechin's idea that the main forces should be concentrated in the south, arguing that they should be deployed in the western sector and poised against the main enemy force. Shaposhnikov was also sceptical with respect to Svechin's illusions about the imminent world revolution, which, Svechin believed, would undermine the imperialist coalition from within, in case of war. At the same time Shaposhnikov supported V. Triandafillov (1894–1931), a military leader and theorist (who died very young), one of the authors of the theory of deep operation (a theory proved during the Second World War), described in his book *The Character of Operations of Modern Armies* (Moscow, 1926). 'Although Comrade Triandafillov's book has a number of shortcomings,' Shaposhnikov pointed out, 'we should promote the development of our young people's creative thinking and not criticize it too severely.'

Shaposhnikov believed that the theoretical discussion then being launched served the important practical task of setting up (or to be precise, restoring) the General Staff as a centralized body of the armed forces command. Despite strong resistance from a number of prominent military leaders, e.g. Dybenko and Budenny, Shaposhnikov won the issue and the General Staff was set up in 1935. In 1936 the General Staff Academy was opened and its first students entered that year.

The stress of Shaposhnikov's duties proved a heavy burden on his health, with the result that the Defence Commissar wrote to the Central Committee Secretariat in 1929 (a rare document for that period), stating that:

> B. M. Shaposhnikov, Chief of Red Army Staff, has for a long time suffered from a serious case of tropical malaria. His condition was especially grave last winter in view of his overwork. Shaposhnikov's ten-year-old son also suffers from the same disease.

A group of doctors insists that Comrade Shaposhnikov should be sent abroad (to Germany) for ten weeks of treatment, first to Hamburg to the Tropical Institute and later to Nauheim.

Since Comrade Shaposhnikov is one of the most valued Red Army specialists, and a successful course of treatment for his disease can be secured only abroad, I request your permission for Shaposhnikov and his son to stay in Germany for ten weeks and for allocation of the necessary amount of hard currency for this purpose. Signed: K. Voroshilov. (Shaposhnikov Archive, 1. 37).

In 1939 Shaposhnikov joined the Communist Party: he was admitted by a special decision without a probationary period. In his application for membership he wrote that he was doing so in order 'to uphold the proletarian cause in its iron ranks to the end of his life'.

In the period from April 1931 to May 1937 Shaposhnikov held successively the posts of commander of Volga Area Military District, chief and military commissar of the Frunze Military Academy and commander of Leningrad Military District. He survived a Party purge in 1933. A special commission of 10 December 1933 was generally in his favour, noting that he was 'versatile and knowledgeable, his only weak point being lack of character'.

In 1935 Shaposhnikov was promoted to the rank of Commander of the Army, First Class, corresponding to the present-day General of the Army. As Chief of the Academy, he introduced changes in the curriculum: operational and tactical training became the leading subjects, while war games on maps and theoretical discussion, etc., using domestic and foreign experience, were part of the course. One of the academy's former students wrote of Shaposhnikov in those years: 'he wears a tired but attentive look and has manly and regular features. He is well made and looks trim and smart and his blue eyes are quite penetrating. He is one of the most talented leaders of the Workers' and Peasants' Red Army, one of the few academy graduates of the pre-revolutionary Staff who joined the army in the first days of the October Revolution.'

In the spring of 1937, Shaposhnikov replaced Yegorov as Chief of Staff, in August 1940 he was appointed Deputy Defence Commissar, and from late July 1941 to the second half of 1942 he was again Chief of Staff. Thus, he held that post in the critical years of the Stalinist repressions against the military leaders, and during the Soviet–Finnish War, as well as in the initial and most difficult and tragic period of the struggle against the Nazi invaders. Shaposhnikov escaped unscathed by the repressions, and his attitude to those events is unclear, although we know that he was appointed a reserve member of the Supreme Court.

In the period of the Czechoslovak crisis in 1938 and of the British–French–Soviet talks in August 1939, Shaposhnikov performed the novel duties of a military diplomat. Soviet foreign policy at that period underwent considerable changes in view of the realignment of forces, resulting primarily from France's refusal to perform its obligation to assist Czechoslovakia. A statement in late April 1938 by Soviet President Mikhail Kalinin, about possible Soviet assistance to Czechoslovakia even without France, was impracticable. The atmosphere at the talks held in Moscow with representatives of the Czechoslovak General Staff in August–September 1938, with Shaposhnikov's participation, was therefore tense. This was mentioned by V. Potemkin, Deputy Commissar for Foreign Affairs, in his report to Stalin and other Politburo members on his talks with Z. Firlinger, the Czech envoy, held on 9 September 1938:

> Fajfr, the Czech Air Force Chief, who arrived in the USSR on an urgent mission to discuss some practical issues, went back home obviously disappointed. According to Firlinger, Fajfr's talks with Shaposhnikov were of a formal nature and did not yield specific results, Firlinger asserts that the facts described by him were interpreted in Prague as proof of our reluctance to render any kind of assistance to Czechoslovakia in its period of crisis.

The stand adopted by the General Staff and personally by Shaposhnikov was most likely due to the unresolved question of the passage of Soviet troops through Poland and Romania, which made it practically impossible for the USSR to render effective military assistance to Czechoslovakia.

In the course of the British–French–Soviet military talks Shaposhnikov described what could be done by the Red Army and Navy and offered possible versions of joint action with the British and French armed forces in responding to Nazi aggression. That Shaposhnikov regarded trilateral military alliance as both possible and necessary is shown in his 'Theses on Talks with Britain and France' of 4 August 1939, written a week before the talks opened in Moscow and used by him as the basis for his contribution to the talks. However, according to another hitherto unknown document, namely, notes made by Voroshilov probably when he was received by Stalin on 7 August and which may be regarded as instructions for the talks, the Soviet leadership viewed the occasion pessimistically (AVP, op. 06, n. 27, d. 2, I. 19).

The 'instructions' said, in particular: 'If it transpires that our troops will not be permitted to pass through the territory of Poland and Romania, we should declare that in the absence of such permission the signing of an agreement is impossible.' And that was exactly what happened.

By that time the General Staff and Shaposhnikov were preoccupied with a military solution of the 'Finnish problem', should it not be resolved peacefully. The records of the British–French–Soviet military talks show that Moscow even at that time regarded the threat of an attack through Finland, Estonia and Latvia as quite real.

Plans on preparing for the war were discussed. One could be called the

Shaposhnikov plan, and the other the Meretskov plan. (General Meretskov was Commander of Leningrad Military District.) The former, which was supported by Voroshilov, argued the need to offer a rebuff to a strong enemy and to break the resistance of the Mannerheim Line, whereas the latter advocated a ramming strike with the active support of the local Finnish population. Eventually Meretskov's plan was adopted and sanctioned by Stalin. However, the war was not over in three months, which not only proved that Meretskov's plan held no water but also revealed major shortcomings in the Red Army's combat training and material support. Moreover, all this undermined the Red Army's prestige in the world.

Voroshilov was removed from the post of Defence Commissar. Shaposhnikov lost his post, too, but was given the rank of Marshal and put in charge of the construction of defence fortifications on the western border. Stalin explained to him that, although he had been right on many points in his calculations and forecasts with respect to the Finnish campaign, especially in his assessment of the Finnish army's combat-worthiness, his reappointment was meant to bring it home to the public that 'the lessons of the Soviet–Finnish conflict have been learned'. This 'explanation' was somewhat contradicted by the appointment of Meretskov as Chief of Staff in place of Shaposhnikov.

Meanwhile, events in Europe, especially the rapid defeat of France and the British–French coalition, showed that the Soviet leadership's stake on a protracted war in the west had proved futile. The debate on defence was conducted essentially between Shaposhnikov and Stalin. The former believed that the main Soviet forces should be concentrated in the central and northern sectors of the front – from the Baltic coast to Polesye, in Belorussia – but Stalin insisted that they be concentrated in the southwestern sector, as indeed they were. Stalin believed that the Germans would make for the country's richest natural resources, and that their attack would therefore come in the southwest. Shaposhnikov's plan was put to Stalin in his absence by Timoshenko, the new Defence Commissar, in September 1940 and did not receive Stalin's support. Events proved Shaposhnikov and Timoshenko right. Stalin's strategic miscalculation had the most tragic and costly consequences for the army and the country as a whole.

On 22 June 1941 Shaposhnikov was in Minsk to organize the city's defence when it came under a massive bombing raid. For some time he acted as Chief of Staff of the Western Sector. (On 10 July 1941, commands were formed for the main three axes: the Northwestern Axis Command under Voroshilov; the Western Axis under Timoshenko; and the Southwestern Axis under Budenny.) The same State Defence Committee decree appointed Shaposhnikov a member of the Supreme Command headed by Stalin.

On 29 July 1941 Shaposhnikov was again appointed Chief of Staff. The

Red Army was retreating rapidly. In a short time the Germans made a great forward thrust of 300–800 km in all directions and advanced to the approaches of Leningrad, Smolensk and Kiev. 10 July marked the beginning of the battle of Leningrad. In September/October, after heavy fighting, the Red Army abandoned Kiev, Odessa and part of the Crimea, and Sevastopol was besieged by German troops. Soon the enemy was occupying some 1.5 million sq.km. of Soviet territory with a population of 74.5 million (according to the pre-war census) and several million people had either fallen in battle or were taken prisoner and thrown into concentration camps.

Some two weeks after Shaposhnikov became Chief of Staff, Stalin, Shaposhnikov, Molotov, Budenny, Voroshilov and Timoshenko signed Order No. 270 sanctioning the arrest of servicemen's families: 'Commanders and political officers,' the order ran, 'who tear off their insignia in the course of battle and desert to the rear or surrender to the enemy should be considered malicious deserters whose families should be arrested as being related to people who have broken their oath of allegiance and are guilty of state treason.'

Shaposhnikov's first difficult strategic decision was over whether to permit the troops defending Kiev to retreat, as they were threatened with complete encirclement. He could not bring himself to adopt any decision for some time. On the night of 11 September, in response to the request of the Southwestern Front Command for permission to withdraw the Front's main forces eastward, Shaposhnikov, naturally expressing Stalin's opinion, gave the following reply by telephone to General Mikhail Kirponos, the Front commander: 'A retreat along the entire Front is not so simple, it is a very complicated and delicate matter. Apart from the fact that any retreat reduces the units' fighting capacity, in this particular war the enemy moves its motorized groups in between the retreating units, involving them in fighting when they are least prepared for it, that is, when artillery is on the move and not in combat position . . . . The Supreme Command believes it necessary to go on fighting in the same positions the troops of the Southwestern Front now occupy.' The hopes of Stalin and Shaposhnikov that they would be able to render assistance to the Front were not realized, and on 17 September they gave permission for the troops to retreat. But it was too late: the defenders of Kiev were completely encircled. As a result Soviet casualties in dead, wounded and POWs totalled 700,000. General Kirponos also fell in battle.

The main events, however, were taking place along the Moscow Axis. The Battle of Smolensk, which broke out on 10 July 1941, took place on a vast area 650 km long and up to 250 km wide. The Soviet capital's fate largely depended on its outcome: in those months the Germans regarded the capture of Moscow as their prime goal. The rapid formation, equipping and transportation of ever new troop reserves from the rear became a matter of life or death, and success depended on the Red Army's ability to rebuff the enemy and halt his offensive. Shaposhnikov was well aware of the need to solve those two closely interconnected problems and he concentrated the General Staff's efforts on tackling them. For the time being Smolensk was saved from capture. However, after heavy fighting the Wehrmacht was obviously gaining the upper hand, although its offensive on Moscow was held up for almost two months, which made it possible for the Soviet side to muster new reserves. Nevertheless, the enemy succeeded in breaking the Front by new strong attacks on the Moscow Axis, with the result that five Soviet armies were encircled near Vyazma. However, in mid-September the enemy met with formidable defence in the most important operative sectors which it was unable to overcome: 16th Army under the command of General Konstantin Rokossovsky on the Volokolamsk Axis, 5th Army under the command of General Leonid Govorov on the Mozhaisk Axis, 43rd Army under the command of General K. Golubev on the Maloyaroslavets Axis, and 49th Army under the command of General Ivan Zakharin on the Kaluga Axis.

Under Shaposhnikov's command the General Staff seemed to be performing the impossible: it adopted operative decisions, presenting them for consideration to Stalin as Supreme Commander-in-Chief, sent instructions to front headquarters on demand, and in strict secrecy prepared for a counter-offensive by concentrating reserves from the deep rear and less threatened sections of the Front. No stone was left unturned to supply the army with hardware and ammunition. On 16 October, the General Staff with Shaposhnikov at its head was evacuated from Moscow by special train, but they returned a month later and actively contributed to the preparation of the counter-offensive.

The task of encircling and eliminating German Army Group Centre was not fulfilled, but the results of the successful Soviet counter-offensive were of crucial importance for the subsequent course of events. The Wehrmacht's defeat in the Battle of Moscow meant more than the failure of the 'Barbarossa' plan, which had envisaged elimination of the Red Army's main forces, and the establishment of Nazi control in the European part of the USSR as far as the Urals in the course of a single campaign, in five months at most. In fact, Nazi Germany's hopes of winning victory in the war and enslaving the world's nations were dashed then. The staunch position of Great Britain and the entry into the war of the United States at the time of the Soviet counter-offensive at Moscow brought to nil the prospects of the aggressive bloc's final victory.

Concentration of army reserves in total secrecy and the surprise counter-offensive were among the major achievements of Soviet military skill and personally of Boris Shaposhnikov who as Chief of Staff was for a long time responsible for the army's operational actions in the battle that proved to be of historic importance.

In planning the spring and summer campaigns of 1942 Shaposhnikov was guided by long-term considerations. He suggested at a session of the Supreme Command that during the next spring only defensive operations should be carried out along the Soviet-German front, since the Soviet troops were utterly exhausted by the winter campaign, and the configuration of the front line was unfavourable for an offensive. Temporary defence operations, he believed, would make it possible to build up forces and undertake thorough preparation to ensure the success of a major offensive.

Shaposhnikov's plan was not approved, however. It was decided instead to carry out mostly defensive operations and to attack on several sectors simultaneously. The first attempt at offensive, near Kharkov, ended in a crushing defeat of the Soviet forces with the result that the Wehrmacht divisions broke through to Stalingrad, thus putting in jeopardy the entire southern section of the front.

The terrific strain of the job led to a sharp decline in Shaposhnikov's health, and in May 1942 he applied to the State Defence Committee for a transfer to less arduous work. In the period May 1942 to June 1943 he held the post of Deputy Defence Commissar and concentrated his efforts on the needs of the training sector. Already during the battle of Moscow he had been responsible for publishing 'Instructions on the Field Service of Red Army Staffs' which became operative on 17 March 1942. He was well aware of the need to update the old manuals and instructions in the light of experience. The new Military Manual was adopted on 9 May 1942. The importance of these documents for the army in the field could hardly be overestimated. The new Field Manual (FM-43) was published and distributed in 1943. At the same time a number of collections which summed up the wartime experience were brought out under Shaposhnikov's editorship. In the same period he headed a group of authors of a three-volume collection devoted to the battle of Moscow which was, in fact, the first fundamental study of wartime experience.

In June 1943 Shaposhnikov was appointed Chief of the General Staff Academy (Voroshilov Higher Military Academy, as it was then called). Attending it were officers who were to pass through as rapidly as possible for appointment as commanders of large army units and staffs. He introduced changes in the Academy's curriculum by replacing the less necessary subjects with war games; he sent instructors for training periods at the front, introduced regular analyses of successful and unsuccessful operations, and started preparing peacetime curricula. He was well aware that his service at the Academy was to be his last term of military service.

Marshal Zakharov, who was among Shaposhnikov's close associates, wrote of him: 'He accepted with the quiet courage of an old soldier the idea that his end was near and made haste to convey as much of his experience as possible to the students.'

Stalin quite often enquired after Shaposhnikov's health. Their relations are still a mystery in many respects. Stalin had more than enough reasons to remove Shaposhnikov, whose most important proposals he often declined with tragic consequences. This happened in 1940, when Shaposhnikov insisted on preserving fortifications of the old western frontier and providing only the necessary protection for the new one; it was the same with planning the Finnish War and the spring/summer campaign of 1942. Shaposhnikov, however, retained his position in all cases. Moreover, the phrase 'the Shaposhnikov school', coined by Stalin, gained wide currency. Stalin addressed Shaposhnikov formally, using his name and patronymic, whereas all other military leaders were addressed by him by their surname, except Voroshilov, with whom he used the familiar form. This can best be explained by Shaposhnikov's outstanding abilities: he was indispensable as a theoretical and practical military expert. Stalin valued him so much that virtually not a single operational decision was adopted without preliminary studies of the General Staff's proposals which were reported by Shaposhnikov in person. Of no small importance was also the fact that, on the one hand, if his arguments were not accepted, he never objected, and on the other hand, he never renounced them, and he implemented the adopted decision with exemplary discipline, firmly confident that experience would prove him right. He once said: 'I was born in the Urals, so I've always been independent in my views and openly said what I thought.' This was perhaps not always the case.

He held to the officers' code of an earlier generation, something not commonly encountered among his peers. On one occasion, for instance, Stalin asked him about the fate of a general who had exaggerated the results of his troops' activities. Shaposhnikov said that the general had been reprimanded.

'Is that all?' Stalin asked.

'That's a severe punishment,' Shaposhnikov replied with conviction. 'If he's been reprimanded by the Chief of General Staff, he is in duty bound to resign.'

Shaposhnikov never wrote anything about his family in his memoirs, as if he had none. Many years ago the author of these lines had occasion to meet his wife, Maria, and his son, Igor. His wife was employed at the Bolshoi Theatre and Lieutenant-General Igor Shaposhnikov was an engineer by profession. Both are no longer alive. They were cultivated people, a close-knit family, and deeply attached to one another. On the morning of 26 March 1945, Maria Shaposhnikova read the latest report about the situation at the fronts to Shaposhnikov who was on his deathbed. He died in the evening of the same day – forty-two days before victory – and was buried in the Kremlin wall. During the burial ceremony a salute of twenty-four salvoes was fired from 124 guns. That was the closing chapter of the glorious and complicated life of Boris Shaposhnikov, and a proper study of him has yet to be written.

BIBLIOGRAPHY

Foreign Ministry Archives, Moscow.
Gorelik, Ya., *Boris Mikhailovich Shaposhnikov*, Voenizdat, Moscow, 1961.
Shaposhnikov, B., *Vospominaniya*, Voenizdat, Moscow, 1974.
Shaposhnikov Archive.
Vasilevsky, A., *Delo vsey zhizni*, 2 vols, Politizdat, Moscow, 1973.
Zakharov, M., *Uchenyi i soldat*, Politizdat, Moscow, 1978.

Sergei Matveyevich

SHTEMENKO

GEOFFREY JUKES

Most young officers joined with visions of command and outdoor physical activity, did not relish desk duties, and regarded staff officers with suspicion. However, the complexity of modern warfare inevitably made staff work an obligatory part of a military career. Shtemenko, born in 1907 in Uryupinsk and proud of his Cossack lineage, is a classic example of a reluctant entrant who became a staff officer *par excellence*.

In August 1938 Sergei Matveyevich Shtemenko was happily commanding an Independent Heavy Tank Training Battalion at Zhitomir in Kiev Military District, and reacted with distinct lack of enthusiasm to an order posting him to a course at the General Staff Academy. Established for only two years, it had as yet few graduates, and they were generally believed doomed to perpetual chairborne careers. So he tried hard to have the posting cancelled; but the army was expanding, trained officers were acutely needed, so the order was repeated and he left reluctantly for Moscow.

Although he enjoyed his time there, especially assignments to the invasion force in western Ukraine in September 1939 and to the General Staff during the war with Finland, he opted on graduation in autumn 1940 to return to command work. But all the graduates who had worked in the General Staff during the Finnish War were posted to its Operations Directorate; yet another request for a command posting was turned down, his new superior, Major-General M. N. Sharokhin, told him sternly to stop his nonsense and get down to work, and Shtemenko embarked on what was to prove a lifetime career.

The early weeks of the war were almost as chaotic in the General Staff as in the front line. Communications with the border Military Districts (now transformed into Fronts) constantly broke down, and officers sent to them to get information frequently returned empty-handed because the Front HQs had lost contact with their Armies and Divisions. In this information vacuum it was hard to know where to deploy the newly mobilized divisions coming from elsewhere in the vast country. One trainload after another of newly mobilized divisions rolled westward and the staff officers sent to unloading stations to give the commanders their instructions (often outdated even before delivery) were often compelled to clear the tracks by moving trains on before unloading had finished, so that troops ended up in one place, headquarters in another.

Changes at the top of the General Staff made matters worse. The Chief, Zhukov, resigned at the end of July to command a Front, and the Head of the Operations Department, Malandin, went as Chief of Staff to the Western Front, replacing Klimovskikh, shot with his commander, Pavlov, officially as a traitor but actually as a scapegoat. These moves did nothing for morale; nor did the atmosphere of mutual suspicion engendered between officers by the early disasters and shootings, in an organization still struggling to recover from Stalin's purges. Out of patriotism mingled with fear and disgust one officer after another applied for posting to the front; few were released, but some, Shtemenko among them, were given short assignments to the headquarters of Fronts, i.e. Army Groups; the insights they derived into problems field commanders faced in implementing high-level decisions improved the quality of their subsequent staff work.

German air raids on Moscow began on 22 July; the General Staff responded at first only by ruling that officers not on duty should go to its basement air raid shelter, but it also began to evacuate officers' families from the city. After the first raid Shtemenko put his wife and children on a train to Novosibirsk, with a letter asking a former colleague to find somewhere for them to live. But night raids became more frequent, the basement shelter had to be used as a workplace as well, and proved quite unsuitable. So half of the Metro station at the Belorussia railway terminus was taken over; every evening at dusk the General Staff night shift packed up its documents and tramped over there, to work till dawn in a central command post on the platform, separated only by thin plywood partitions from the civilian shelterers who thronged the other half of the station.

However, the inconvenience of constant packing and unpacking prompted a search for a better solution, which was found by taking over a building on Kirov Street, closing the Kirovskaya Metro station beneath it, and walling the platform off from the tracks by high plywood panels. A communications centre was installed at one end, offices for Stalin and the Chief of General Staff at the other, and rows of desks and tables filled the space between them. As September wore on much of the government moved to Kuibyshev (now Samara) but Stalin and the two war-directing bodies he headed – Stavka, the headquarters of Supreme High Command (set up on 23 June 1941 as the

High Command, renamed on 8 August) and State Defence Committee (established on 30 June) – remained in Moscow.

Stavka had no staff of its own, and the General Staff, as its executive tool, also remained in Moscow, but as the Germans drew closer Stalin decided to evacuate most of it along with its Chief, Marshal Shaposhnikov, so that the Fronts could still be directed if the capital fell. In mid-October they left Moscow in two trainloads for a destination Shtemenko, commandant of the one in which Shaposhnikov travelled, did not identify even when writing thirty-four years later. He returned immediately to Moscow by car, to join the small operations group under Vasilevsky which remained with Stalin. Moscow's situation in late October was perilous, following the encirclement and destruction of seven armies and parts of several others in the first half of the month. Vasilevsky's small staff worked round the clock, snatching sleep whenever they could on the seats of a railway carriage shunted into the Metro station (it was later replaced by a sleeping car). Stalin and his staff worked in the building above, descending to the underground offices only during air raids, until a bomb fell in the courtyard on 28 October. After that they worked permanently in the Metro station.

The victory outside Moscow eased the pressure. The main body of the General Staff returned in December, and life assumed a more regular rhythm. Some of the section heads moved on to become Chiefs of Staff of Fronts or armies, and younger men, Shtemenko among them, moved up. He became Head of the Near East section, where he dealt mainly with matters affecting the Soviet forces which had occupied northern Iran at the end of August 1941. This broadened his experience in two ways; first, in dealing with the Foreign Ministry on matters requiring liaison with the British forces occupying southern Iran, and second, reporting regularly to Shaposhnikov, whom Stalin, mistrustful of Churchill, had ordered to keep a close eye on affairs there.

During the lull imposed by the spring thaw of 1942, the General Staff was reorganized. Heads of 'Directions', all of them former Front or Army Commanders or Chiefs of Staff, were interposed between the sections and the Chief, in the hope that these experienced senior officers would have more influence and better relations with the field commands.

But the arrangement was found to slow the upward movement of information without adding any new insights, and after about a month the previous system was reinstated. At the end of April Shaposhnikov's continuing ill-health forced his withdrawal to a quieter life as Head of the Higher Military Academy, and Vasilevsky took his place. No sooner had he done so than the attack on Kharkov began to go wrong, and Shtemenko was among the officers from other sections called in to try to find a way out. There was only one – a change of plan, urged vainly by Bagramyan on Timoshenko and by Vasilevsky on Stalin on 18 May, but Timoshenko's optimistic reports persuaded Stalin against intervention, and when Timoshenko himself cancelled the advance on the next day it was already too late.

Shtemenko's first encounter with Stalin came in August 1942, when he was summoned to report to Stavka on the military situation in his 'Near East' area, which included the Caucasus, then threatened by the southward push of German Army Group 'A'. Apart from purely military problems of providing additional troops from Central Asia and the armies in Iran, there was uncertainty whether Turkey might use the opportunity of a German success to join the war and invade Transcaucasus. Shtemenko's mastery of his brief was to lead in due course to rapid advancement to one of the most demanding posts in the General Staff, the headship of the Operations Directorate.

Stalin shared with Hitler and Churchill the habit of rising late and working well into the night. For those around him, who had to stay up late to receive his decisions and then rise early to implement them, this régime was extremely taxing, and in addition the frequent absences of Vasilevsky who, on Stalin's orders, spent more time with the Front Commands than in the General Staff, threw additional responsibilities onto his subordinates, not all of whom could stand the strain for long. The post of Head of the Operations Section proved extremely hard to fill, changing hands no less than seven times in six months during 1942. Stalin eventually realized that he was overstraining the officers, and as the staff had to operate throughout the twenty-four hours he personally prescribed the duty and rest hours for all the senior officers. His timetable, though an improvement on the previous situation, was a punishing one. Shtemenko, Head of Operations Section from May 1943, came on duty between 6 and 7 in the evening and went off duty at 2 the next afternoon. Antonov, Deputy Chief, and effectively Chief during Vasilevsky's long absences, came to work at noon and went off duty between 5 and 6 the next morning. Stalin required three daily reports, the first by Shtemenko, usually by telephone, between 10 and 11 a.m., the second by Antonov between 4 and 5 p.m. The third report was the most important and both attended to present it, always after midnight, in Stalin's Kremlin office or at the 'nearby dacha', his villa in Kuntsevo, usually with Stavka or Politburo members present. They would first report events on each Front in order of importance, then submit draft orders. The most important ('Directives') would be signed by Stalin and Zhukov or Vasilevsky, or if both were out of Moscow, by Antonov, who would sign less important orders ('Instructions') himself 'By Order of Stavka'. If an order had to be composed on the spot, Stalin would dictate it, Shtemenko would write it down, read it aloud, amend it as Stalin wanted, and take it to the adjacent signals office for immediate transmission.

It would then be time to open the 'blue file' of requests from the Fronts, usually for reinforcements, equipment or fuel. These had previously been reviewed in the General Staff, and its recommendations were attached for Stalin to approve, reject or modify. It was usually between 3 and 4 a.m. by the time they returned to their offices, and this régime of seventeen- or eighteen-hour working days, seven days a week, was a severe test of stamina. Shtemenko wrote, not surprisingly, that a number of his colleagues later suffered nervous or cardiac disorders, and that many resigned prematurely as soon as the war ended. Shtemenko, however, had the necessary stamina, and Stalin's search for a Head of Operations was over. He showed his gratitude by promoting Shtemenko to Colonel-General in 1943, and to Army General and Chief of General Staff after the war, but right up to his death he maintained draconian pressure on staff officers, whose working day continued to start between 10 and 11 a.m. and finish at 3 or 4 o'clock the next morning. Shtemenko would probably have become a Marshal had he not fallen foul of Khrushchev, who demoted him by two ranks. Under Brezhnev he worked his way back to Army General and became Chief of Staff of the Warsaw Pact. He died in 1976, aged sixty-nine.

BIBLIOGRAPHY

Erickson, John, *The Road to Stalingrad: Stalin's War with Germany, vol. 1*, Weidenfeld & Nicolson, London, 1975.
Erickson, John, *The Road to Berlin: Stalin's War with Germany, vol. 2*, weidenfeld & Nicolson, London, 1983.
Shtemenko, S. M., *General'nyi shtab v gody voyny*, 2nd edn, 2 vols, Voenizdat, Moscow, 1981.
Vasilevskii, A. M., *Delo vsey zhizni*, 6th edn, 2 vols, Politizdat, Moscow, 1988.
Zakharov, M. V., *General'nyi stab v predvoennye gody*, Voenizdat, Moscow, 1989.
Zhukov, G. K., *Vospominaniya i razmyshleniya*, 10th edn, Novosti, Moscow, 1992; in English, *The Memoirs of Marshal Zhukov*, Jonathan Cape, London, 1971.

Semen Konstantinovich
TIMOSHENKO

VIKTOR ANFILOV

Among the cohort of Soviet military leaders Timoshenko occupies a prominent place. In the long course of his military service he experienced the elation of victory and the bitterness of defeat, and the corresponding swing of Stalin's attitude towards him between kindness and anger.

Born in 1895 in the village of Furmanka, Odessa province, the son of a poor peasant, from an early age Semen Timoshenko went out to work. When the First World War began he was conscripted, served as a machine-gunner in the infantry and won two St George Crosses. He joined the Red Army in April 1918, commanding in turn a unit, then a squadron and finally the 1st Crimean Cavalry Regiment which took part in the defence of Tsaritsyn. In October he was appointed commander of a cavalry brigade, in February 1919 commander of the 6th Cavalry Division, which in November became part of 1st Cavalry Army, and then in August 1920 commander of the 4th Division. As a capable leader, as demanding of his subordinates as he was concerned for their welfare, and as a man of personal courage and loyalty, Timoshenko enjoyed the affection and the support of his officers and men.

It is plain now to see that the Russian Civil War was fratricidal. Both the Red and White forces were essentially composed of Russian peasants in uniform who were commanded by men on opposite sides of the barricades. Each group of leaders thought they were fighting for a good cause and for the interests of the working people. The working people for their own part were heartily sick of war and cordially detested both sides. An order issued by Timoshenko on 29 November 1919 makes this plain: 'Arms alone cannot win the war as quickly as a conscientious attitude towards the rear which gives us new fighters and friends, and sometimes also powerful enemies. Be attentive to the civilian population which is suffering the hardships of war as you do, do not carry out arbitrary requisitioning and looting which officers sometimes permit through ignorance, and understand once and for all that you are bringing liberation to the poor, not oppression and violence.'

Like the overwhelming majority of Red Army commanders, Timoshenko accepted Bolshevik propaganda and believed in the world revolution. Addressing his cavalrymen in November 1919, he declared: 'We summon you to go bravely forward to victory. We shall soon cut off the hydra head of the counter-revolution and plant the Red Banner of Socialism throughout the world.'

For his leadership as a cavalry divisional commander in the Soviet–Polish war, and for a decisive attack on Wrangel's forces at Novo-Alekseyevskaya, in which, despite being seriously wounded by a hail of machine-gun fire, he threw himself onto an armoured trainload of White officers and continued to command his division for several hours, on 12 November 1920 he received his second Order of the Red Banner.

Unlike the military opposition in which Voroshilov played a leading rôle, while the Civil War was still in progress, Timoshenko was a strong advocate of military discipline: 'Remember, Comrades,' he stressed in an order of 1 November 1920, 'the guarantee of success and the strength of any army are founded on order and discipline.' He maintained this approach throughout his military service. For a prolonged period after the Civil War, Timoshenko commanded the 3rd Cavalry Corps which included the 7th Division commanded by K. K. Rokossovsky, and one of the cavalary regimental commanders in this division was Zhukov. Timoshenko went out of his way to broaden Zhukov's horizons, in both theory and practice. In 1922 Timoshenko completed the higher academic courses for officers and in 1930 the course for commander-commissars in the Military-Political Academy.

In August 1933 Timoshenko was appointed Deputy Commander of Belorussia Military District, transferring to a similar post in Kiev District in September 1935. On his arrival in Kiev, he took part in large-scale manoeuvres under the leadership of the District Commander, I. E. Yakir. These were the first manoeuvres to take place anywhere in the world using large tank, aircraft and airborne formations. Witnessing the exercise was General (later Field Marshal) Wavell from England who reported to his government: 'If I had not witnessed this myself I would never have believed such an operation possible.'

Timoshenko was Yakir's deputy until the latter's arrest in May 1937. The onset of the mass arrests meant that he was constantly being sent from one post to the next. In June 1937 he was posted as Commander of North Caucasus Military District with his HQ at Rostov-on-Don, in September of the same year he became Commander of Kiev District and in February the following year he returned to Kiev as District Commander. He explained these peregrinations at a meeting of the staff council of the Soviet

Institute of History on 19 February 1968: 'You know about the very dangerous, difficult years, the years which in fact encouraged the German Fascists to think they could successfully carry out a lightning war against the Soviet Union. During those years many party, state and military cadres were wiped out. Of the old guard only Voroshilov, Budenny and [I] Timoshenko remained. No one else was left alive. I commanded practically every military district as a trusted agent of Stalin and Voroshilov. I would just manage to install a little order and then they'd telephone and ask, "Everything all right? We've sent a plane for you, fly straightaway to Rostov because there's no one in charge there and the local Cossacks are dangerous; from there go straight on to Kharkov, which has been stripped bare." I'd be making these trips from place to place the whole time.'

Timoshenko did not tell us, and we were too timid to ask, how he had felt about the fact that his predecessors, Yakir and Fedko, had been arrested during the previous six months. He did not oppose the outburst of mass arrests of officers, nor did he condemn them. This is documented by a report on the state of cadres in Kiev Military District, signed by himself and another member of the defence council, Khrushchev, on 26 March 1938:

> The Military Council set as its central task the rooting out of enemies of the people and the selection for senior posts of loyal, up and coming officers. In carrying out the orders of Comrades Stalin and Voroshilov the Military Council has done great work in purging the highest ranks of senior officer cadres, and also the middle and upper ranks, of all hostile and politically unstable elements and it will continue with this work in the future.

It is only fair to point out that Timoshenko himself did not write any denunciations and took no part personally in the repressions. But it was in the context of the most difficult domestic and foreign relations that as District Commander he had to prepare his troops for the approaching conflict.

With the outbreak of the Second World War on 3 September 1939, Germany seized almost the whole of Poland, creating a threat to the independence of the peoples of western Ukraine and western Belorussia, which had been detached from Russia in 1920. The Soviet government responded by ordering the Red Army to launch a 'liberation campaign'. A Ukrainian Front was created using troops of Kiev Military District under Timoshenko's command. On 17 September Soviet troops entered western Ukraine. Most of the population greeted them with joy, but some Polish units offered armed resistance. Despite the notorious secret protocol appended to the Soviet-German Pact of 23 August 1939, the German leadership received the news of the Soviet advance with disapproval, but was nevertheless compelled to order its units to call a halt. On Timoshenko's demand, the German troops who had been about to enter Lvov were obliged to retreat.

His authority rose in Stalin's eyes, and when results seemed slow in coming in the war which the USSR had launched against Finland on 30 November 1939, Stalin appointed Timoshenko commander of the North-western Front on 7 January 1940. The task facing the troops was to break through the strongly defended Mannerheim Line, destroy the enemy's main forces on the Karelian peninsula and emerge in the region of Vyborg. This action was meant to determine the outcome of the war, since the main Finnish forces were concentrated there.

After long preparation, on 11 February Timoshenko launched his offensive, but despite considerable superiority in strength and weapons, it was slow to gnaw through the enemy's defences. The Soviet government achieved its aim at a high cost, and while Timoshenko was made a Hero of the Soviet Union, he was not consoled by his victor's laurels. He had seen with his own eyes the damage caused by the mass purge of senior officers and the prolonged leadership of the army by the talentless Voroshilov, who was now removed as Defence Commissar. The Finnish War exposed many flaws in the Red Army's preparedness, in its equipment, organization and leadership. On 8 May 1940, Timoshenko was appointed Defence Commissar, having just been created a Marshal of the Soviet Union, the highest military rank. His name is associated with the restructuring of the army, its reorganization and rearming. He undertook to uproot in the shortest possible time the old defective training methods, with their political conditioning and abstract planning. In his Order No. 120 on training, issued in the summer of 1940, he demanded that the troops be 'taught only what they need for war, and only in the way things are done in war'. Quoting Suvorov's famous maxim, 'the harder you study, the easier the battle', he pointed out that 'the main thing is to develop high battle qualities in every soldier and officer, firm discipline, initiative, energy, audacity, doggedness, persistence, camaraderie and self-sacrifice.' At his suggestion the institution of military commissars was abolished. It had been created by Stalin in 1937 with the aim of sniffing out 'enemies of the people'. At a December 1940 meeting, Timoshenko said the move to the system of combined command had been absolutely necesary, for 'to train the Red Army in the spirit of the new demands, to prepare it for the successful conduct of modern warfare, and to teach it to beat not merely weak but also strong enemies, would be impossible without the fully empowered combined commander' – that is, holding military and political responsibility.

At the time the German Army was carrying out one lightning operation after another in Western Europe. A key role was played by tank formations, airborne troops and aircraft, that is, the kinds of forces which the Soviet Union had been developing since the early 1930s. The Germans invented nothing new. As the *New York Times* defence correspondent, G. Rossinsky, noted on 19 May 1940, the combination of paratroop attacks to seize aerodromes and siege troops to use them had been demonstrated by the Red Army in its large-scale manoeuvres of 1936. Large tank and aircraft formations had, however, been disbanded in the USSR in 1939 because they had been created by such 'enemies of the people' as Tukhachevsky, Yakir and Uborevich. To try to correct the appalling mistake committed by Voroshilov and his supporters, Timoshenko urged on the government the need to form ten tank and five airborne corps, and in June 1940 the task of doing this was begun.

In September–October 1940 Timoshenko inspected the tactical and staff courses in the western frontier districts and at the 99th Rifle Division course. He reported that the previous system of training was seriously deficient: 'At all levels we have been operating too simplistically . . . . Having an army of vast resources, but training it in the conventional way, was a criminal act. We taught the army how to die, but not how to win. We taught our forces indiscriminate tactics, based on the idea that we can always oppose force with considerably greater force, send a division to beat a battalion, as we did in the Finnish war.' On 31 August at the 42nd Rifle Division course, he re-emphasized the point: 'In the current year, taking recent military experience into account, we have drastically altered the methods and nature of our battle training. We have started firing live rounds over the heads of our troops when attacking "enemy" defences, because it is impossible to get the desired co-operation between artillery and infantry without such training. In the Finnish war, even though I'm supposed to have a heart of stone, it made me suffer to watch a mass of officers and men spill their blood in vain, only because they hadn't been trained for the conditions of war.'

At the 1st Rifle and 6th Mechanized Corps, he turned his attention to the officer cadres, pointing out that 'the Finnish war showed that our junior officers at unit and formation level had only a vague notion of how to lead their troops in warfare'. Officers had been incapable of co-ordinating different kinds of forces, i.e. combined operations, 'but mainly they did not know how to command'. The war in Western Europe, he concluded, should serve now as an object lesson.

At a meeting of senior officers, convened by the chief war council at the end of December 1940, Timoshenko, as Defence Commissar, stressed that, given the large-scale nature of modern warfare, it was no longer possible to think in terms of the outcome being decided by one decisive operation. The war would be conducted as a series of intermittent goals, any one of which might turn out to be of major strategic significance. He also underlined the importance of mixed forces, noting that the war in Western Europe had demonstrated the rôle of aircraft and motorized forces as a weapon of surprise, making it necessary for the anti-aircraft and anti-tank weapons to remain on constant alert. 'Wherever they were neglectful, they paid in blood.'

He criticized Soviet inadequacies in the use of aircraft, pointing out that Air Force Command had no agreed policy either for planning operations or conducting aerial warfare. He did nothing, however, to correct the mistake of his predecessor who had divided the Air Force into three levels, Front, Army and Unit. The battle for air supremacy, in that view, should be conducted within the framework of Front and Army operations. This miscalculation on Timoshenko's part would make it impossible to use massed aircraft to gain air supremacy at the outbreak of the war. He did, however, stress the need to overtake the West in the use of airborne troops.

Summing up, he made it clear that the restructuring still had some way to go and would need more time and effort: 'Each one of us has to expunge in himself harmful arrogance and self-satisfied complacency. Let us recognize that some comrades have yet to justify the rank of general and their high posts by working on themselves tirelessly, studying minutely the theory of military art and the practice of war, and acquiring practice in leading their troops in battle.'

The December meeting resulted in a directive from Timoshenko dated 25 January 1941 on operational training, an order on the tasks of battle training and political instruction for 1941, and a series of further regulations. Zhukov later declared that Timoshenko had advised district commanders to exercise their troops near the state frontiers, thus making them available for deployment according to the cover plans.

The army's cover plans for the first echelon of the western frontier Military Districts were contained in the 'Plan for the Defence of the State Frontier in 1941', sealed in 'red packets' and kept in safes for use on the signal 'Threat'. The defence plan was worked out by the General Staff on Timoshenko's instructions. Assuming the USSR's adversaries to be Germany and Japan, with the likely addition of Finland, Romania, Hungary and Italy, in September 1940 he had submitted his ideas on the principles of the strategic deployment of the armed forces. He proposed concentrating about 170 divisions on the western frontiers and suggested two variants for a possible response to German aggression. Stalin demanded that a main grouping of forces be maintained in Kiev Military District for use in a counter-attack.

In accordance with the plan, Timoshenko ordered District Commanders 'not to allow the incursion of enemy troops into Soviet territory; to cover the mobilization, concentration and deployment of the Red Army's main forces with firm defence in the reinforced military districts; to achieve air supremacy by using aircraft and to hamper the enemy's concentration and deployment of forces by bombing bridges and railway junctions, and thus create favourable conditions to go over to counter-attack.' The plan essentially expressed outmoded ideas on the opening phase, namely, that the war would not be started by entirely mobilized and deployed forces, but only by covering forces. It was to last fifteen days during which time the Red Army would be fully mobilized, concentrated and deployed, but it was silent on the question of how to beat off the massed attacks of an enemy who was fully mobilized and deployed. The movement of troops from their permanent locations to their appointed defence districts was to be carried out by a special order of GHQ, an order which did not reach the troops before 22 June.

Given the international situation and the state of the forces' unreadiness, Stalin made it his aim to avoid war in 1941 at any cost, and he insisted firmly and persistently that Timoshenko give Germany no excuse for armed conflict. The cost of this 'no provocation' policy was the forces' battle-readiness and many other measures which ought to have been taken to prepare the country for war.

While it was important to exercise caution over possible provocations, it was also essential to maintain the highest possible degree of alertness against enemy incursions, and to ensure the capacity to put troops into battle-readiness well in time. But this was not done. Strategy was the servant of politics, and Timoshenko was obliged to observe the orders of a dictator. Unlike the boastful tone of propaganda coming from the Political Section of the army, which talked of an easy victory, Timoshenko foresaw the hardships. Reviewing a collection of articles by A. I. Zaporozhets, head of the army's Political Section, entitled 'The glory of these days will not fade', Timoshenko wrote: 'There is much unnecessary posturing and eulogizing here. Victory is depicted invariably as being easy, simple, a matter of hurrahs, as in days of yore. But we cannot train our youth in this way. The authors evidently have learnt nothing from the restructuring that is going on in the Red Army.'

In May, by which time the enemy was on the frontier, Timoshenko succeeded in persuading Stalin to order some strategic deployments in the western Military Districts: four armies began to move to the defence ridge of the western Dvina and the Dnieper, but it was not until 12 June that Stalin would agree to let him move troops from internal districts to the state frontier itself. Divisions of the first echelons, however, had to stay put, and only a special order could effect their movement, an order that was not given until after the enemy had already begun to invade by land and air.

Stalin ordered the troops into full battle-alert only during the evening of 21 June. Timoshenko's order read: 'Our forces' task is on no account to respond to provocative actions which might lead to major complications. Simultane-ously, the forces of the Leningrad, Baltic, Western, Kiev and Odessa Military Districts are to be in full battle-readiness to meet any sudden attack by the Germans or their allies.' Timoshenko ordered Zhukov to despatch the order to District Headquarters at once. After leaving the Kremlin, he summoned the Naval Commissar, Admiral N. G. Kuznetsov, and told him to prepare the navy to repel any attack by sea or air.

Timoshenko spent the last night of peace in his study. He knew that many defence measures were still incomplete, the Red Army was neither fully restructured nor rearmed with the new weaponry. Because of Stalin's recalcitrance, the frontier units were not ready. The outlook for the Soviet Union was bleak.

Nevertheless, the fact is that after the XX Congress Timoshenko was angered by the claim made by many historians and writers that the country had been totally unprepared for war. 'The problem is not so simple,' he said at the above-mentioned meeting at the Institute of History. 'From Moscow to the farthest corners of the country, we were trying to put industry on a war footing. And what was done before the war was also significant. In the first half of 1941 alone, when I was Defence Commissar, we built 2,650 aircraft of new design, 636 heavy and 1,225 medium tanks. But we couldn't do everything in so short a time.'

No doubt that was what he was thinking that sleepless night. He maintained constant contact with Zhukov and other District Commanders. From 5 a.m. reports starting coming in of one German land and air incursion after another. Timoshenko and Zhukov reported this to Stalin who replied that, until they had conferred with the German ambassador, they must order no response, and he told them to come to the Kremlin. At that moment the Deputy Commander of Western Military District, General I. V. Boldin, came on the line and reported that German aircraft were continuing low-level strafing of Soviet troops and the civilian population. German forces had crossed the frontier at many points and were advancing. According to Boldin, Timoshenko listened carefully and said: 'Comrade Boldin, take note that you are not to begin any action against the Germans without our knowledge.' Boldin yelled, 'What do you mean? Our troops are retreating, towns are in flames, people are dying. . . . ' Timoshenko replied: 'Iosif Vissarionovich [Stalin] believes this could be a provocation by some German generals. . . . ' This account was published by Boldin while Timoshenko was still alive and it was not challenged.

It was only after Foreign Commissar Molotov reported to Stalin that the German ambassador, von der Schulenberg, had declared that Germany was in a state of war with the USSR that Stalin gave the order to start fighting. At 8 a.m. Timoshenko signed a directive calling on the forces 'to use all their strength and means to fall upon the enemy forces and destroy them in the districts where they had violated the Soviet frontier. Do not cross the frontier until further orders.' This wording suggests that Stalin still thought it possible to curtail the conflict. By the time the order was received at front headquarters, first-echelon troops were already being drawn into defensive fighting and, finding themselves outnumbered, having to retreat. As communications were cut, commanders lost control of their forces. Not knowing precisely what was happening, they could not properly inform the Defence Commissar. Nor could he assess the position in the air, for, although the battle for air supremacy was continuing, its outcome was predetermined on the first day. Only inadequate knowledge of the full position can explain Timoshenko's third directive, despatched late on 22 June and ordering the forces to go over to counter-attack with the aim of seizing the strategic initiative and destroying the enemy.

On 23 June Supreme Headquarters was created, headed by Timoshenko, with the purpose of co-ordinating the armed struggle, but he still needed Stalin's permission before he could make any decision, a fact which could not but have a negative effect, since orders were subject to delay and therefore frequently no longer relevant to the rapidly changing scene. This situation could not continue and Timoshenko asked Stalin to take full power into his own hands. On 30 June Stalin was duly named Chairman of the State Defence Council, then next day Chairman of the General Staff and soon also Defence Commissar. As for Timoshenko, he became Commander-in-Chief of the Western Front. His adjutant's diary records that on 1 July at 2100 hours he drove to the headquarters of the Western Front, on 2 July at 0700 hours he arrived in Smolensk, then drove off to the command post at Gnezdovo. By this time a large part of Soviet Western Front forces had been encircled and destroyed. The former Front Commander, D. G. Pavlov, had been arrested and quickly shot, and this was the post Timoshenko took over. He had to create a new front on the Dnieper using reserves from the interior.

He had hardly got his bearings, when one after another messages started coming from Stalin. On 2 July he asked whether the Orsha–Minsk highway had been mined. Timoshenko replied that the explosives had arrived but that they hadn't started laying them yet because the highway was full of the retreating troops. Ignoring the explanation, Stalin, in the name of all the Politburo members who happened to be in his study, demanded the immediate mining of the highway, adding that it should be done at intervals, so that the road could be blown up as the need arose.

The chief task set by Timoshenko was to halt the enemy's tank groups at the river Dnieper, to bleed the enemy and create the conditions for a counter-attack. This aim, however, was not to be achieved. On 10 July the German Tank Groups under Hoth and Guderian renewed their advance on Smolensk, and the battle began for this main strategic sector which would last two months. On the same day, Timoshenko was appointed Commander-in-Chief of the Western Axis, which included both the Western Front, which he continued to command, and the Central Front. When the German mobile units broke through, Timoshenko ordered the army commanders 'to withdraw the troops systematically, quietly but fighting, to rear defence positions. In order to destroy the enemy's tanks,' he went on, 'create in each division mobile detachments, combine them up to army strength, then surround and destroy the enemy.' He ordered the building of tank traps to restrict the enemy's mobility and brought aircraft into play to destroy the German tanks.

The fierce Soviet resistance caused heavy enemy losses and slowed the German advance. On 14 July Timoshenko was able to cable Stalin that he had ordered the forces 'to close the gap caused by the German breakthrough, to cut off the enemy's mechanized units and to throw everything we have into destroying the groups that had broken through.' The same day, Soviet troops for the first time used rocket-propelled mines, or *katyushas*, at Orsha, and Timoshenko reported on their success to Stalin, requesting that several more batteries be sent together with more ammunition.

In mid-July, Hoth and Guderian broke through to Smolensk. Stavka resolved on 19 July that they should be destroyed. The same day Timoshenko was summoned to Moscow where he remained until 21 July, discussing the organization of an offensive with Stalin and Zhukov. Five newly created strike groups began mounting counter-attacks under Timoshenko's direct command. Slowly but surely the Red Army began to overcome enemy resistance and to advance. In the second half of July Western Axis forces deprived the Germans of their freedom of manoeuvre, harrassed and bled their attack groups and forced them onto the defensive, a fact accepted by Hitler on 30 July when he ordered Army Group Centre to adopt a temporary defensive position.

By coincidence, that day the Reserve Front under Zhukov assisted in the destruction of Field Marshal Bock's Group. As Timoshenko's adjutant recorded, 'on 5 August the Marshal drove to Zhukov's HQ at Gzhatsk, whence at Stalin's request they both drove on to Moscow. On 6 August by 1600 hours the Marshal returned to the Western Front HQ in the district of Kasnya on the former estate of Prince Volkonsky.' In Moscow they were ordered to develop the offensive. In August and early September the forces of the Western Axis carried out offensive operations at Dukhovshchina and Yelnya, causing serious damage to Army Group Centre. The break in the German advance on Moscow was of strategic and great political significance. The first cracks had appeared in the German *Blitzkrieg*.

Like Zhukov's, Timoshenko's authority now rose in Stalin's eyes. In early October, Stalin replaced Voroshilov with Zhukov, while Timoshenko was put in place of Budenny and given the task of holding Leningrad and then Kiev 'at all costs'. Timoshenko's adjutant wrote: '11 September at 0145 hours Stalin called. At 0845 we drove to Moscow. Arrived 1230 hours. Summoned to Kremlin 1700 hours. Returned to apartment 2200 hours. Brought with us two pipes . . . from Comrade Stalin. One pipe had a deer engraved on it, symbolizing our transfer from north to south. At 2400 hours we were on board the Moscow–Poltava train.'

Timoshenko arrived at Poltava on 12 September in the evening and as Commander-in-Chief at once plunged into the whirlpool of events taking place along the Southwestern Axis, where Soviet forces were being encircled by Kleist's and Guderian's tank groups in a pincer movement. Budenny, Timoshenko's predecessor, had seen this coming and had sought

Stalin's permission to abandon Kiev and move his forces to a rear defence position, but Stalin had refused. Stalin told Timoshenko of this, and demanded that he take steps to annihilate the tank wedges. Having been briefed by the commanders of the Southwestern and Southern Fronts, Timoshenko ordered the concentration of forces for an attack on the German tank formations.

Despite the seriousness of the situation, Timoshenko still shared with Stavka the hope that a counter-attack against Guderian's group might succeed. The catastrophe, however, drew remorselessly closer. Contact was lost with a number of Front Commanders. But there was no slowing down. Therefore on the morning of 16 September Timoshenko orally transmitted the following order to the chief of operations Southwestern Front, General I. Kh. Bagramyan, to be passed on to his commanding officer, General M. P. Kirponos: 'The main forces of the Front are to withdraw without delay to a defensive ridge on the river Psel.' Bagramyan finally found Kirponos later in the day and reported Timoshenko's order, but since this important order, which contradicted the earlier one issued by Stalin, had been given only orally, Kirponos decided he must seek confirmation. But the Front HQ was unable to establish contact either with GHQ, or with the C-in-C's HQ, which was mobile, having moved to Akhtyrka to evade the Germans who had broken through at Poltava. Having made contact with the Chief of General Staff, Shaposhnikov, Timoshenko requested that his order be confirmed. A report was made to Stalin and permission was finally given, but by this time the enemy had closed the circle. Among those killed in the encirclement was General Kirponos. He was succeeded as Front Commander by Timoshenko himself. The outcome of the fighting on the east bank of the Dnieper in September 1941 was extremely unfortunate for the Red Army. The Southwestern Front had to endure the same bitter lesson the Western Front had suffered in June.

From the end of September the forces of the Southwestern Axis carried out defensive operations along the Kharkov and Rostov Axes. Thanks to the concentration of main force at Moscow, the German command was unable to organize a major advance to the south. The last task of Rundstedt's Army Group in 1941 was to attempt a siege of Rostov, a vitally important stage on the way to the Caucasus. Realizing Rundstedt's intentions, Timoshenko decided to forestall him by launching a counter-offensive. On 31 October, he discussed this with Shaposhnikov who warned that 'in war nothing can be gained without risk', and cabled the request to Stalin. On 4 October Timoshenko visited the Southern Front HQ to raise the morale of the Front commander, General N. T. Cherevichenko, prior to the offensive. 'We have to think only of a real, major offensive,' he told the members of his military council, 'and particularly here at Rostov. Only by this means can we disrupt Hitler's plan to reach the Caucasus.' It was agreed to begin preparing the offensive, and although the next day the German Army Group South resumed its advance, Timoshenko stuck to his idea of a major counter-offensive. According to Bagramyan, nothing would deflect Timoshenko from this idea.

Timoshenko did not expect Kleist's tank army to cease its advance towards Rostov completely, and so he asked Cherevichenko to start planning and preparing for the intended counter-offensive. On 9 November Stalin spoke with Timoshenko by telephone. He said he was satisfied that Timoshenko had a correct understanding of the position, as far as the counter-offensive at Rostov was concerned, but he warned him not to lose sight of the position of the spearhead on the Western Front.

On 20 November Kleist's tank force captured Rostov, an event proclaimed by German propaganda with great pomp, and when the Stalin counter-offensive opened on 23 November it met stubborn resistance. Stalin called Timoshenko on the evening of 28 November and said, 'Rostov must be retaken tonight.' The Red Army launched a night attack, destroying the enemy grouping. Next day Timoshenko informed Stalin that Rostov had been liberated. His adjutant recorded the conversation: 'Good-day, Comrade Stalin. Thank you. I report that the mission has been accomplished. Four divisions have been smashed to smithereens. We're now pursuing the enemy towards Taganrog, beating him mercilessly. Yes, yes, that's right. Good-bye. It is my honour.' Stalin replied: 'We're going to drink your health today.'

Following this conversation, during which Khrushchev and Cherevichenko were present, Timoshenko conveyed Stalin's greetings to everyone. The same day, for the first time in the war, Stalin sent congratulations to the troops on the liberation of a major city. It was published on 30 November in the main newspapers. On 5 December Churchill wrote to Stalin of the admiration the British people felt at the brave defence of Leningrad and Moscow and the brilliant victory at Rostov.

The victory at Rostov enhanced Timoshenko's authority still further. He now felt added confidence in his own ability to predict the enemy's intentions and to make accurate assessments of the two sides' capacities. But he was now prone to miscalculation, as a telephone conversation with Zhukov, recorded by his adjutant, shows: 'In a couple of days I'll take Taganrog. I'll liberate the south. Then I'll move closer to you. Bear in mind that the enemy is weakened and we must now beat him.' This could not but reflect badly on his subsequent actions.

A meeting of Stavka took place on 27–29 March 1942 at which the situation at the front was assessed and measures were outlined for the spring and summer. 'We don't have to wait for the enemy to strike the first blow,' Stalin said. 'We must start by striking a number of blows on a wide front, we must exhaust and bleed the enemy and disrupt his plans for an offensive.'

Timoshenko declared: 'I and the war council of the Southwestern Axis believe we are now in a position to deliver a warning blow to the enemy in the south and to disrupt his plans for an offensive, that is to say, to seize the initiative. If we do not deliver a warning blow then we can be sure our sad experience of the beginning of the war will be repeated.' With the exception of Zhukov, the majority of those present supported the proposal.

With Timoshenko in Moscow were his Chief of Staff and Chief of Operations. By 7 April, working with the General Staff, they had carried out his instructions and evolved the 'Plan of action by Southwestern Axis forces for April–May 1942'. Timoshenko ratified the plan on 10 April. It envisaged reconquering the district of Kharkov, regrouping the forces and by attacking along the axis of Dnepropetrovsk–Sinelnikovo depriving the enemy of the most important crossing-points on the Dnieper.

Officers at all levels and the troops themselves were carefully prepared for the forthcoming offensive. Timoshenko visited all the armies and took all possible measures to secure the operation, putting the last details on the plan which he personally submitted for Stalin's approval on 29 April. On 11 May his adjutant noted that Timoshenko was very confident of the outcome, as he told Boldin in a radio conversation, adding: 'Better not convey the appointed hour when you report to the boss.' At 1700 hours Stalin called to give his agreement and blessing.

The offensive was launched on 12 May. The Southern Front, which came under the command of the Southwestern Front, had the task of securing the strike group from the southwest, which was where the enemy had concentrated a large force to resist the offensive. The offensive opened well. In the first day the troops advanced some 15 kilometres. At 2 a.m. Timoshenko reported to Stalin and the Supremo expressed his satisfaction. Things looked as if they were going to turn out as expected. Three days later, however, the Germans attacked the lightly defended left flank of the strike group. Zhukov recalled: 'On the evening of 17 May I was personally present during a radio conversation between Stalin and Timoshenko, and I well remember Stalin's concern. Timoshenko said that the war council considered the news of danger from Kramatorsk as exaggerated and that there were no grounds for stopping the offensive.' It was not until 19 May, when the forces of the Southwestern Front were half-encircled, that Timoshenko began to take steps to get them out. But it was too late.

As in the summer of 1941, the Red Army was forced again to swallow the bitter pill of defeat and retreat. Timoshenko was summoned to Moscow on 20 May where from 5 p.m. to 11 p.m. he had to account for the catastrophe along the Southwestern Axis. Next day he was relieved of his post. When Zhukov was asked why Timoshenko got off so lightly, he replied: 'I think Stalin limited himself to just taking his job away because the idea of the warning strike had been his own originally.'

By 25 July Timoshenko was on his way to command the Northwestern Front. His adjutant recorded: 'So it's the front again. From the south to the north, from the heat to the rain, the mud and the mosquitoes. From the expanse of the Don steppes to the forests and marshes of the Ilmen lowlands and the Valdai highlands.'

With his southern command apparatus dismantled, Timoshenko transferred his special services general, L. F. Minyuk, to Zhukov, who had just become Deputy Supreme Commander-in-Chief, together with a letter of congratulations on his new post. Zhukov said to Minyuk, 'Semen Konstantinovich must be offended by the way things have turned out. This post is his by rights, but he was badly hurt by the Barvenkovo-Kharkov operation. He was too sure of himself over it and it turned out to be a huge miscalculation. Still, he's not the only one who's to blame.'

In the north Timoshenko had time for reflection and taking stock. He also read the newspapers, and in four issues of *Pravda*, for 24–27 August 1942, he read Korneichuk's play *The Front*, which depicted a number of generals of the older generation in a sarcastic way. Timoshenko had cause to recognize himself among them. Angry, he wrote to Stalin on 28 August that the play 'deserves special attention. It is harmful to us, it should be taken off and the author be called to account.' Stalin replied by telegram the same day: 'I've received your telegram about Korneichuk's play. Your judgement of it is not correct. The play will have great educational significance for the Red Army and its officers. The play correctly exposes the shortcomings in the Red Army. One should have the courage to admit these shortcomings and take steps to liquidate them. That is the only way to improve and perfect the Red Army.'

Timoshenko commanded the Demyansk offensive on the Northwestern Front. Before he arrived the German XVI Army had been partially encircled in an area of 2,500 square kilometres. It was connected with its rear by a narrow corridor 10 kilometres long. To avoid unnecessary bloodshed, Timoshenko suggested to the German commander, General Busch, that he capitulate, but his ultimatum was rejected. On 15 February 1943 the Red Army launched its offensive. At first the Germans were able to withdraw their troops. In pursuit of the retreating enemy, the Red Army emerged at the River Lovat on 28 February and there destroyed the Demyansk bridgehead which the enemy had held for seventeen months. Nevertheless, Timoshenko's troops were unable to execute their task fully, as the enemy managed to bring out his main forces and avoid their total annihilation.

The operation failed to help Timoshenko re-establish his prestige. He was soon relieved of this post, too, and for the duration of the war Stalin would give him no other Front to command. Instead he served as Stalin's representative on various Fronts, and also took part in planning a number of operations, including one of the biggest, that of Jassy-Kishinev, in August 1944.

Timoshenko has been treated in Soviet historiography in contradictory ways. 'In some works he is depicted quite wrongly,' Zhukov declared. 'Almost like a man with no willpower who wormed his way into Stalin's favour. That's not the case.' In Zhukov's opinion, Timoshenko was an old and experienced war leader, stubborn, strong-willed and well versed in tactical and operational terms. 'In any case,' said Zhukov, 'he was far better than Voroshilov as Defence Commissar, and in the short time that he held that post the army started to improve . . . . But Stalin was angry with him over Kharkov, and it affected his career for the rest of the war.' According to Zhukov, Timoshenko never fawned on Stalin, 'in fact, had he done so, he might well have been given a Front to command.' And despite Stalin's attitude, he still awarded Timoshenko the Order of Victory.

After the war Timoshenko commanded various Military Districts. From 1960 he was an Inspector General of the Defence Ministry and from that time until his death in 1970 he chaired the Soviet Veterans' Committee. His ashes were buried in the Kremlin wall.

BIBLIOGRAPHY

Anfilov, V. A., *Proval 'Blitskriga'*, Moscow, 1974.
Central State Archives of the Soviet Army.
'Glasnost', 11 July 1991.
Marshal Zhukov. Kakim my ego pomnim, Moscow, 1988.
Marshal Zhukov: polkovodets i chelovek, Moscow, 1988.
Simonov, K. M., *Glazami cheloveka moego pokoleniya*, Moscow, 1989.
Zhukov, G. K., *Vospominaniya i razmyshleniya*, 10th edn, Moscow, 1992.

Mikhail Nikolayevich
TUKHACHEVSKY

SHIMON NAVEH

On 15 February 1963 a formal but modest ceremony was held in the Frunze Military Academy in memory of Marshal of the Soviet Union Mikhail Nikolayevich Tukhachevsky, who was executed by firing squad on 12 June 1937, in one of the NKVD's yards in Moscow. The memorial ceremony, which was accompanied by music provided by the Marshal's close friend, Dmitri Shostakovich, and attended by his daughter, Svetlana, signalled the rehabilitation of a man who had been a 'non-person' for twenty-five years. It seemed that the rehabilitation of one who symbolized more than any other in modern historiography the Great Purge of the Red Army High Command, and about whom so little had been written, would spark a significant wave of historical research and writing. That, however, has not occurred, either in the Soviet Union or the West.

A nostalgic article appeared in the April 1963 issue of the Journal of Military History (*Voenno-istoricheskii Zhurnal*) by G. Isserson, a former Red Army officer and close friend of Tukhachevsky. Later the same year a shallow biography, containing elements of rehabilitation, was published in the Soviet Union by A. I. Todorsky. In 1964 Tukhachevsky's 'Selected Works' was published by the Soviet military establishment, and also a biography by L. Nikulin. In 1964, with the publication of a volume of memoirs by surviving friends and comrades-in-arms and edited by N. I. Koritsky, the feeble flow stopped. The latest mention of Tukhachevsky was in a personal note by his sister, Elizaveta, in *Ogonek* of 23 April 1988. And Western output on Tukhachevsky has not exceeded that of the Soviet Union. One is tempted to ask why this is so. The question becomes even more obvious in view of events that followed the Marshal's rehabilitation, and that were related directly to his theoretical achievements.

Around the beginning of 1965 an essay illustrating the extraordinary evolutionary process of the Soviet theory of operational art during the 1930s was published by G. Isserson in the January and March issues of *Voenno-istoricheskii Zhurnal*. Both Isserson and his theme had been absolutely taboo since 1937 because of their close association with Tukhachevsky. Moreover, Isserson's essay, which could not have appeared without the 1963 rehabilitation of Tukhachevsky, represented a new military trend which formed the later stage in what has been called in Soviet military literature a 'revolution in military affairs'. Since one of the features of this 'revolution' concerned the reapplication of the deep operation theory, in its original form, it may be assumed that Isserson's essay served as an indicator of future trends. The changes that followed the re-adoption of Tukhachevsky's original idea of deep operation were revealed by a continuous current of theoretical, organizational and technological activities lasting twenty years.

Two questions arise: first, what lay behind the rebirth of Tukhachevsky's theoretical brainchild, and, second, what caused the apparent indifference towards the other aspects of his past and personality? The answer to the first question will emerge when we examine the evolution of the operational theory and discuss its merits. The second question requircs the setting of Tukhachevsky's personality in the historical context. First, the theory.

The theoretical form into which the deep operation idea crystallized in the summer of 1937, when Stalin's hand fell upon Tukhachevsky and other members of his group, was best demonstrated in Tukhachevsky's article 'New Questions of War' (1931), and in Isserson's book, *The Evolution of Operational Art* (1937). The final version of the deep operation theory specified the offensive and defensive as the basic forms of manoeuvre, at the operational level, and the 'operational shock' as its end. Furthermore, the pattern of the 'turning-manoeuvre' was defined as the most advanced state of operational shock that can be attained by an operational strike. Finally, the operational synergy between the 'holding force', the main 'manoeuvring force' and an 'element of reserve', was identified as an essential condition for the completion of a successful operational manoeuvre.

The main manoeuvring element, or the chief means for creating the shock effect, was the column form, representing three 'efforts' or components: the 'breaking' or 'assaulting effort', which was composed of mechanized-rifle formations reinforced by armour, self-propelled artillery, tactical aviation and engineers, aimed at breaking through the tactical zone and bisecting the defensive front. The second component, or the 'echelon for developing the breakthrough', consisted of armoured-mechanized formations reinforced by aviation, and was designed to accelerate the break-up of the defender's lay-out and to build up a manoeuvring mass beyond the defender's centre of gravity. The 'deep' or airborne effort (*desant*), which relied on mechanized-airborne formations, was designed, after landing in the defender's depth, to neutralize his calculated use of his own depth and to serve as a bolstering manoeuvring vector, operating from the depth towards the front and thus promoting the advance of the main manoeuvring effort. We shall return to some aspects of the theory below. Now, however, let us attempt to set Tukhachevsky's personal biography in context.

Any attempt to reconstruct Tukhachevsky's image and personal life immediately stumbles over several technical and historiographical obstacles that distort the main picture and blur our view of the facts. First, there is a surprising lack of documents and other reliable evidence, thanks to Stalin's obsessive efforts to eradicate proof of Tukhachevsky's achievements, as well as the physical extermination of those who were related to the Marshal and his activities, and also reluctance on the part of Russian historians to let the genie out of the bottle, even fifty years after its incarceration. In the province of historiography the problem is even more complex, owing to the wide differences of approach to the subject.

Second, Tukhachevsky's achievements have become blurred by the three apocalyptic upheavals that embraced the two decades of his adulthood, namely, the Bolshevik Revolution, which overshadowed his performance in the Civil War and his meteoric rise; the Great Terror, which obscured his technical-military innovations; and finally the Second World War, which dwarfed his intellectual contribution to the Red Army, in the form of the deep operation theory. On this last point, Richard Simpkin has written, in his *Deep Battle*, a book dedicated to Tukhachevsky's deep operation theory: 'One tends to think of him as the great captain that never was, because he was dead when his thinking at last, from 1942 onwards, provided a springboard for the Red Army's victory over Germany.'

Third, in attempting to assemble the biographical material, both before and after Tukhachevsky's execution, one confronts an unbridgeable gap between approaches. On the one hand, there are the bizarre writings of Geneviève Tabouis (1942) and J. F. C. Fuller (1956), bordering on the absurd, and portraying the Marshal as a prince of darkness, Bonapartist, the Anti-Christ, anti-Semite, admirer of the Nazis, butcher, militant Communist inclined towards paganism, and romantic Mongol, a veritable Genghis Khan. On the other hand, there are the accounts of his colleagues and comrades, the reports of German officers such as Blomberg and von Manstein who met him in person, the accounts of British officers such as Sir Giffard Martel and Sir John Dill, the memoirs of the French Chief of the General Staff, Gamelin, and of Maisky, the Soviet ambassador in London, all portraying him as a charming intellectual, a sensitive and artistic human being who possessed a penetrating and creative mind, and an admirer of Western civilization. Todorsky recounts in his biography that during a Politburo session in 1938,

Stalin personally mentioned Tukhachevsky's exceptional military faculties, noting that his was the dominant contribution to the Red Army's development in theory, technology and organization.

There is no doubt that the enigma surrounding the story of Tukhachevsky derives, among other things, from the disjointed nature of his personality. Richard Simpkin illustrates this complexity thus: 'Perhaps he was both – Jekyll and Hyde in conscious co-operation. And perhaps that was the secret of both his achievements and his downfall.' Tukhachevsky combined in his personality the qualities of a visionary creator with a remarkable talent for organization, an aptitude for deep and abstract philosophical thinking with unique faculties for operational command, a realistic political outlook with an ardent belief in Communism, artistic proclivities with an acute awareness of technology – a living combination of intellectual and military charisma.

Thus, we face a heterogeneous personality functioning inside an opaque milieu within one of the most tempestuous epochs of modern history. Furthermore, the fact that his short life was terminated abruptly, without any of those who were closely related to him being able to amend the grievance, only adds to the distortion which historiography had already committed against his image.

Mikhail Nikolayevich Tukhachevsky was born on 16 February 1893 on the Alexandrovsky estate near Vyshegor Station on the Smolensk–Vyazma railway, 150 miles southwest of Moscow. Mikhail (Misha) was the fourth child of the nine born in the Tukhachevsky family. His father, Nikolai Nikolayevich, descended from an aristocratic family of impoverished gentry. Since the name Tukhachevsky suggests Polish connections, the purely Russian origin of the family was doubtful – a fact which might have added weight to his final fall in 1937. His mother, Mavra Petrovna Milokhava, came from a peasant family near Knyazhino, and was employed as a servant girl by Mikhail's grandmother prior to her marriage to Mikhail's father.

Mikhail's father was a progressive liberal, a highly cultivated humanist, possessing intellectual curiosity and a genuine interest in music. In his manner and demeanour he communicated simplicity and composure. Thus, the origins of Mikhail's future zeal for learning, his penchant for music – the composer Shostakovich was to describe him as 'my patron' and his hobby was to be making violins – and the arts, his leaning towards science and technology, and even his political outlook, should all be sought in his father's personality and in the mentality which he bequeathed to his children.

The spiritual harmony of Tukhachevsky's family life was generally expressed in music. His grandmother, father and younger brother, Igor, all played the piano, while Mikhail and his elder brother, Nikolai, played the violin, and his other elder brother, Alexander, played the cello.

When Mikhail was eleven, the family was in financial difficulty, the estate was sold and they moved 450 miles eastward to the town of Benza. In 1909, following Mikhail's graduation with distinction from Benza gymnasium, the family moved again, this time to Moscow. There, Mikhail joined the 10th Moscow High School and concluded his secondary education after two years, again with distinction. At this point, he took one of the crucial decisions that would influence his future life: he embarked on a course of military higher education. It is not altogether clear, however, whether the decision was made voluntarily, or was due to the family's inability to support him at university, which might have been more in tune with his current interests.

On 16 August 1911 he entered the élite Catherine II Moscow Cadet Corps, an institution which guaranteed its successful graduates admission to one of the more prestigious higher military academies, and from there an assured transition to one of the Guards regiments. On 1 June 1912 Tukhachevsky joined the Alexandrovsky Military College in Moscow, where, under the guidance of the leading military historian V. A. Verezovsky, he discovered an interest in military thought, and with his mastery of German, French, English and Russian, he gratified his intellectual appetite among the rich holdings of the library. On 12 June 1914 Tukhachevsky passed out from the Alexandrovsky College as one of the best students in its history, and was commissioned instantly as a subaltern in the renowned Semenovsky Guards Regiment.

In the autumn of 1914 Tukhachevsky was sent with the 7th Company 2nd Battalion of the Semenovsky Regiment to the Prussian Front. On the night of 19–20 February 1915 his regiment was tasked with blocking the Lomza–Kolno axis, northeast towards Warsaw. After undergoing a German attack, his company was cut off from the rest of the regiment, and while leading an attempt to break through the encirclement, Tukhachevsky was injured and taken prisoner. The only feature worth noting of his stay in the prisoner-of-war camp at Ingolstadt were his frequent attempts to escape, and the presence of Charles de Gaulle among the French prisoners, a fact that was to become a future source of gossip and speculation.

Late in October 1917 Tukhachevsky returned from captivity, and on rejoining his family in Vrazhskoe he learned the bitter fact that during his years of absence, his father, his brother Igor and his sister Nadia had perished in the harsh conditions prevailing in wartime Russia. The other event that he witnessed on his return home was the apocalyptic occurrence of the Russian Revolution.

Under the influence of his mother, who had been left to sustain her four small daughters, Tukhachevsky returned to Petrograd and reported to the Semenovsky Regimental Depot. After staying for some time with his old regiment and observing the chaotic events of early 1918, he moved to Moscow and reported to Trotsky, who was heading the Military Department of the All-Russian Executive Committee, offering him his services as one of the 'military experts' whom Trotsky was exhorting to join the ranks of the revolutionary army. It was this decision which gave rise in later years to claims portraying him as a Bonapartist and ruthless opportunist. On 5 April 1918 Tukhachevsky formally joined the Communist Party, and soon became a prominent military commander of the Civil War and a leading figure in the endeavour to repel the Intervention.

Tukhachevsky's life, brief as it was, was characterized by a series of personal tragedies: first, the fateful decision to enter higher military studies, reflecting the financial straits of many of Russia's gentry before 1917. Instead of turning toward a musical or academic career, he embarked upon that of a soldier; second, at the age of twenty-four, he confronted both the physical ruin of his family and the collapse of the old world in which he had been brought up; the suicide of Marusia Ignatieva, his first wife, marks the third tragic highlight of his life. In the autumn of 1918, after several months of marriage, when paying Mikhail a visit on the Eastern Front, the young wife was caught carrying food which she had stolen from the army for her family. To save her husband's face and to protect his career, the desperate Marusia shot herself. Later, his second marriage to Nina Yevgenieva collapsed because of his total dedication to his professional career and his absorption by the vast military demands of the 1920s.

From the middle of the 1920s onwards, Tukhachevsky was pushed through a gradual process, initiated by Stalin, into a state of physical, mental and political isolation. In 1925 he was dealt a heavy blow when his mentor, friend and political supporter, People's Commissar for the Army and Navy Mikhail Frunze, died mysteriously. In 1928, after serving as Chief of the General Staff for three years, Tukhachevsky was removed from office and transferred from the centre of affairs to Leningrad Military District. In 1931 his closest friend, and his partner in the formulation of operational theory and development of mechanized forces, V. K. Triandafillov, was killed in an air crash. Many of his friends, for example the corps commander, Gaia Dmitrievich Gai, were arrested in the second half of the 1930s and simply disappeared. In the winter of 1937, when the final torrent of terror started rolling, Tukhachevsky's last political ally, the Head of Heavy Industry and a key figure in the Communist Party, S. Ordzhonikidze, committed suicide, thus leaving him an easy prey to Stalin's machinations. Being aware of both his delicate political position and the number of victims the vicious terror was taking from among his colleagues, Tukhachevsky lived with the constant oppressive fear that his own liquidation was only a matter of time.

The last tragic aspect of Tukhachevsky's life concerns his struggle to implement his advanced theories and to mechanize the Red Army against the acrimonious ignorance of Stalin's military cronies, Voroshilov and Budenny.

Tukhachevsky's experience during the Civil War revealed the remarkable speed and effectiveness with which he was able to respond to the challenge of conducting vast operations and handling huge formations. This, despite being only in his mid-twenties and having had no command experience beyond the level of a rifle company. In June 1918, when operating in the Moscow area, he attracted Lenin's attention and was sent to take part in the formation of the First Revolutionary Army on the precarious Eastern Front. In a short time he stabilized the front and scored some achievements for the Reds.

He clearly had a talent for solving operational problems and crises. At the end of 1918 Tukhachevsky was called to eliminate a threat that had developed along the Southern Front – a mission he accomplished by using 8th Army in a vigorous counter-strike. At the end of January 1919 he conducted a general counter-offensive, with two armies along the entire Southern Front, which stabilized the operational situation in that theatre for some time. In March 1919, he returned to the Eastern Front to deal with a new crisis that had developed in his absence. After a summer of dynamic manoeuvres with 5th Army, he had eliminated the problem and stabilized the front. In November the same year, aged twenty-six, he was appointed Commander-in-Chief of the Southern Front. Three months later, to deal with a new crisis, he was assigned overall command of the Caucasus Front. Finally, in May, Tukhachevsky was called urgently to deal with the gravest threat that occurred in the course of the war against the Intervention – a general catastrophe had developed all along the Western Front due to the invasion of Russia and Ukraine by Polish armies under Piłsudski. When Tukhachevsky was recalled to take command of the Western Front, four Polish armies, reinforced by two Ukrainian divisions under Hetman Simon Petliura, had reached the river Berezina, some 300 miles deep into Russian territory, and taken Kiev.

The Polish Campaign has been described by J. F. C. Fuller as one of the decisive operations of the twentieth century, and referred to as the 'Battle of Warsaw'. The operation involved four Soviet armies (3rd, 4th, 16th, 12th), Gai's Cavalry Corps and Budenny's 1st Cavalry Army, and developed in four succeeding stages from the middle of May 1920 to the beginning of October.

In the first stage, lasting two weeks, Tukhachevsky checked Piłsudski's advance along the line Vitebsk–River Desna, and counter-attacked towards the town of Molodechno. During July, he conducted a vigorous advance and pursuit operation over a distance of 400 miles, attempting, unsuccessfully, to encircle the Polish forces in the area between the rivers Dvina and Pripet. The third stage, at the beginning of August, involving the deployment of both armies in front of Warsaw, ended with a Polish counter-offensive that broke through the Soviet lines, and caused a general collapse of the Red Army on Polish territory. In the last stage, which persisted through September, the

Red forces under Tukhachevsky retreated to what under the Treaty of Riga of March 1921 became the eastern Polish border.

The first lesson Tukhachevsky learned from the Polish campaign was the importance of thorough logistical planning and proper organizational groundwork to secure the effective conduct of large-scale operations. Second, he learned that it was essential to define intelligible strategic aims and operational objectives. Third, he recognized the fundamental contribution made by the strategic co-ordination and synchronization of operational groups. Finally, he saw the futility of the linear form of operation and that of the frontal approach in modern manoeuvre. The experience gained in the Polish Campaign, and indeed the entire Civil War, crystallized later into a tendency to stress the element of depth and the operational use of highly mobile manoeuvre by columns. None the less, the Polish campaign, which represented a blatant check to this early attempt to spread world Communism by military means, contained the seeds of future conflict and animosity between the school of the Western Front, represented by Tukhachevsky and Gai, and that of the Southwestern Front, represented by Stalin, Voroshilov and Budenny.

In the spring of 1921 Tukhachevsky was sent to crush the anti-Communist insurrections in Kronshtadt and Tambov, earning himself the title of ruthless butcher, according to some Western historians (e.g. Fuller). Later in the year he was tasked with refounding the military academy, an appointment reflecting both general recognition of his professional abilities and a determination to settle the military on an institutionalized professional future path. In the course of the war Tukhachevsky was decorated twice with the Order of the Red Banner.

In May 1924 Tukhachevsky was appointed deputy to Frunze, Chief of the General Staff. Together, and against the hostility of the Party establishment, represented mainly by Stalin and Voroshilov, they embarked on the immense task of reforming the Red Army, which was in poor shape in most respects. Tukhachevsky displayed energy and resourcefulness, both in his official post and in the additional responsibility he undertook of directing military theory studies at the Academy. With the unexpected death of Frunze, with whom he had developed a deep friendship and excellent working relations, Tukhachevsky was appointed Chief of the General Staff.

Following an argument with Voroshilov, who was Chief of the Military Revolutionary Council and Commissar for Military and Naval Affairs, and now lacking Frunze's protection, in May 1928 Tukhachevsky was forced by Stalin to leave his office and was sent to command Leningrad Military District. Despite the fact that for three years he was kept far from the centre, and his access to major decision-making was barred, Tukhachevsky kept pushing forward the development of operational theory, the application of mechanization and armour, and the development of airborne troops. His professional insight, organizational skills and dedication to modernization were all demonstrated in war games, resourceful discussions and manoeuvres that he conducted within his territorial command.

Thanks to the influence of Ordzhonikidze, Chairman of the Supreme Council of the National Economy (VSNKh, later to become the Commissariat for Heavy Industry), a close associate of Stalin and a leading personality in the Communist establishment, on 19 July 1931 Tukhachevsky was brought back to Moscow to replace Uborevich as Head of the Army's Technology and Armament Department. Tukhachevsky's achievements in this post were recognized and highly praised by the German, British and French missions that visited the Soviet Union in the course of 1931–6. At the beginning of 1934 the Red Army's mechanized formations were armed with the most advanced weaponry and armoured fighting vehicles in the world, both in quality and quantity. Soviet Airborne Forces were unique in their scale, operational concepts and rich assortment of arms, such as light tanks, highly mobile armoured vehicles, recoilless guns and light artillery. Under Tukhachevsky's supervision Soviet industry started manufacturing a whole variety of advanced fighter, reconnaissance and bomber aircraft, and was the first to develop self-propelled artillery and assault guns. His creative touch was to be felt in the realms of technological development, production and operational concepts.

On 21 November 1935 Tukhachevsky's achievements received official recognition, perhaps for the last time, when he was awarded the rank of Marshal of the Soviet Union, concurrently with Voroshilov, Budenny and Yegorov, who were Stalin's favourites, and Blyukher, who, like Tukhachevsky, deserved it for his military accomplishments.

On 26 January 1936 Tukhachevsky was chosen with Foreign Commissar Maxim Litvinov to represent the Soviet Union at the funeral in England of King George V. During various meetings in Britain and France, he impressed the foreign military and political leadership with his magnetism, his wit, his wide range of languages, his political insight and the originality of his military thinking.

In his original research on the Soviet High Command during the 1930s, Boris Orlov maintains that Stalin's terror campaign against the military leadership was uninterrupted since its initiation early in the decade. Thus, the tendency to focus exclusively on the events of 1937, while compelling, is artificial, and derives mainly from the clamour that followed the events of June that year. Dr Orlov rightly claims that, on Tukhachevsky's departure for his mission to Britain and France, the plot against him was already in place, and Stalin was merely waiting for a suitable opportunity.

With Tukhachevsky's return from Western Europe, the process of his political and military exclusion began, leading to the *coup de grâce*. In April 1936 Tukhachevsky was forced to hand over his post as Chief of the

Technology and Armament Department to Khalepsky. Thus, although he kept his nominal position as a Deputy Defence Commissar, it was clear that he had lost his authority in matters of strategic force-building, as well as the planning and development of mechanized troops. It was therefore with the innocuous title of Deputy Defence Commissar and Inspector of Military Training that he devoted the last year of his life to the task of composing the 1936 Field Manual.

At the beginning of May 1937 the tempo of events increased and the final stage of the Great Terror materialized. On 6 May Tukhachevsky's last article, concerning the new Field Manual, was published in *Krasnaya Zvezda*. On the same day he received indirect notification that his arranged trip to the coronation of King George VI had been cancelled. On 11 May he read in the press that, due to a sequence of new military appointments, he was being transferred to the marginal post of commanding Volga Military District. On 26 May he was arrested, probably at the headquarters of his new command in Kuibyshev.

The complex nature of Tukhachevsky's relations with Stalin derived first and foremost from profound differences of personality which precluded any sort of normal rapport. Moreover, Tukhachevsky's advanced military concepts, his political perceptions after Hitler's rise to power, his good relations with Frunze and Ordzhonikidze, and his bad relations with Stalin's cronies, only deepened Stalin's hostility. The web of relations that existed between the two was that of constant conflict, with its ups and downs, but generally tending towards the inevitable end.

Stalin's initial attitude towards Tukhachevsky was biased by the prejudice he held against the group of ex-tsarist officers, recruited by Trotsky as a nucleus of military specialists, around whom he intended to form the future Red Army. The debate that followed the Civil War, and centred on the conduct of the Polish campaign, not only intensified Stalin's basic distrust of the military specialists, but in fact turned the argument between him and Tukhachevsky into a purely personal conflict. Tukhachevsky attributed the failure in Poland to the fact that the Southwestern Front's command, of which Stalin was the political commissar, had withheld co-operation and support from its sister Front in the west. Since it was well known that Stalin had opposed the idea of spreading revolution by military means, he was the obvious target for Tukhachevsky's accusations. Stalin, on the other hand, blamed Tukhachevsky for the lack of military proficiency he had demonstrated throughout the campaign. The admiration and honours Tukhachevsky had earned in the eyes of Lenin, Frunze and Trotsky, and in those of the Russian public in general, only exacerbated Stalin's sense of resentment and envy. Indirectly, Stalin attacked Tukhachevsky through a book, *Lvov–Warsaw* (1929), by his, Stalin's, wartime comrade, Yegorov, and also had his agents, particularly Budenny, hurl unrestrained verbal attacks at Tukhachevsky during political and military gatherings.

After Frunze's death in 1925 Tukhachevsky's isolation was exploited by the veterans of the Southwestern Front and 1st Cavalry Army in order to foil his efforts at reforming and modernizing the Red Army. On 16 April 1928, Inspector of Cavalry Budenny, Head of the Army Supply Department F. A. Dybenko, and Commander of Belorussia Military District Yegorov, wrote to Voroshilov to protest against the 'dangerous centralization of the whole problem of organization, force-development and operational thinking in the hands of a single authority – namely, M. N. Tukhachevsky'. Hence, Tukhachevsky had been forced to leave his influential position and sit on the sidelines as commander of a military district. The appointment of Shaposhnikov in Tukhachevsky's place reflected not only Stalin's personal preference, but also his perception of the position of the Chief of the General Staff.

The issue of the mechanization of the Red Army, which was Tukhachevsky's brainchild, constituted another focus for tension between him and Stalin. For Tukhachevsky, who introduced the concept of mechanization when he was Chief of the General Staff, pushed it forward while in Leningrad and finally brought it to a peak in his last operational assignment, the entire question of the Red Army's future centred on the use of armour and the adoption of mechanization. Stalin's antagonism derived from three sources. First, he detested anything initiated by the group of progressive officers headed by Tukhachevsky. Second, because he was fixated on his experience in the Civil War, his military perceptions were archaic. And finally, he believed that the application of mechanization could lead the army to excellence, which for him constituted the greatest threat, since he associated military excellence with militarism. Thus, by abstaining from excellence, Stalin hoped to avert the eventuality of Red military élitism. Stalin expressed his hostility directly when he brusquely rejected Tukhachevsky's memorandum of 1930. In his memorandum, Tukhachevsky stressed that the Red Army's survival in a modern war would depend on its mechanization. On reading the document Stalin remarked: 'This memorandum is nonsense! Moreover, it comprises arguments that do not suit a Marxist.' Stalin also used indirect means to express his hostility through a series of speeches by Budenny and Voroshilov at military conferences and party meetings. Budenny and Voroshilov emphasized the pre-eminence of the horse and cavalryman over mechanization and the tank. In 1931, by a campaign of persuasion conducted by Ordzhonikidze and a group of officers, Stalin appeared to have been convinced of the operational potential offered by mechanization and the use of armour. Nevertheless, at the 17th Party Congress of 1934, Budenny openly blamed Tukhachevsky for pushing forward his programme of modernization through mechanization.

As late as May 1936 an official article in *Pravda* attacked the theory of mechanization for preferring machines over horses. The explicit object of this attack was of course Tukhachevsky.

The obsession against Tukhachevsky was so deeply embedded in Stalin's mind that, after his execution, the main elements of his conceptual, technological and organizational achievements were almost entirely eradicated, so that in the last four years preceding the Second World War, the Red Army regressed more than a generation in its operational capabilities.

Despite his being fully aware of Tukhachevsky's prominence as a military theorist, Stalin made every effort to restrain his activities in that field and moderate the degree of his intellectual impact. Stalin was first and foremost motivated in this by his fear that the creative thinking, which Tukhachevsky wanted to introduce among the senior ranks of the Red Army, might create independent-minded officers and thus generate political dangers for himself. In 1935, through Tukhachevsky's initiative, the Faculty of Military History and Strategic Studies was established adjacent to the Frunze Academy, with the aim of promoting creative thinking at the operational level of command. After it opened, the course of strategic theory was dropped from the syllabus by Shchadenko, who was deputy commandant for political affairs and had served in 1st Cavalry Army during the Civil War. His main argument was that strategic thinking was an occupation reserved exclusively to Stalin. One of Tukhachevsky's close assistants in this venture, G. Isserson, has testified that the order to cancel the course was given personally by Stalin, and that Yegorov, Commandant of the Frunze Academy, was instructed to ensure that the order was obeyed. There was, however, a personal side to Stalin's scheming against Tukhachevsky on the theoretical level. Stalin could not bear the idea of sharing his renown as the initiator of new ideas with anybody, and in Tukhachevsky he recognized a menacing contender.

In January 1934 Yakir had requested that the Revolutionary Military Council appoint Tukhachevsky to conduct advanced courses on operational theory for high-ranking officers of the General Staff and commanders of the military districts. His request was rejected on the grounds that Tukhachevsky was preoccupied with armament matters. Yakir paid dearly for this miscalculation when later he was barred from the Advisory Council of the Defence Commissariat. Isserson, who in 1937 was Deputy Head of the Operations Department, revealed that he came across a draft of one of Tukhachevsky's last articles, entitled 'The Art of War', which had been passed to Voroshilov for endorsement, prior to publication. It bore the remark, in Voroshilov's hand, 'not to be published'.

Another possible reason why Stalin imposed restrictions on Tukhachevsky's lecturing on operational theory may have been that Tukhachevsky's approach to the subject of the operational defensive was different from his own. Stalin, with the support of Voroshilov and Yegorov, dictated a unilateral adherence to the offensive at the operational level. This trend was reflected in instruction programmes, field exercises and programmes of force-building. Tukhachevsky, on the other hand, argued that a thorough understanding of the defensive was a prerequisite for comprehending the operational level of war, as a whole. Moreover, the principle of depth, the cornerstone of the deep operation theory, could be properly understood only by meticulous analysis of the operational defensive. Because of these differences of approach, Tukhachevsky's theoretical activity had now been confined to dealing with tactical defence. The achievement of this last venture of his was expressed in the composition of the Field Manual for 1936, which laid great emphasis on defence at the tactical level.

Despite the fact that Tukhachevsky, unlike his colleagues Blyukher and Yakir, refrained deliberately from any involvement in internal politics, his pragmatic observations on external politics provoked a complex and deadly conflict with Stalin. With Hitler's rise to power, Tukhachevsky and Gamarnik demanded an end to the co-operation between the Red Army and the Reichswehr that had lasted for over a decade. Stalin rejected the demand, and when finally relations were terminated by German initiative, Tukhachevsky was the only senior officer in the Soviet High Command to refer with scepticism to the future reinstatement of collaboration between the two armed forces. He kept on criticizing Nazi Germany, despite the frequent pro-German sentiments expressed by Voroshilov, Yegorov and other high-ranking officers. At the beginning of 1935 Tukhachevsky published an article entitled 'The War Plans of Germany in Our Time', in which he argued that Hitler was moving towards invading the Soviet Union and striking at the West. The publication of the article provoked a wave of sharp protests from the Nazi political and military establishment.

On 15 January 1936 Tukhachevsky addressed a plenary session of the Soviet High Command on the 'defensive trends of the Soviet Union'. Focussing on the German threat to the Soviet western border, and highlighting the likelihood of German–Japanese military co-operation, he demanded that appropriate defensive preparations be made to deal effectively with these threats. Maxim Litvinov, with whom Tukhachevsky co-operated in pushing forward the idea of collective security during their visit to Britain in 1936, recounted that both Tukhachevsky's article of 1935 and his address of 1936 were intended to inform the Western powers of the growing military might of Germany and to warn them of Hitler's aggressive designs. General M. Gamelin, who met Tukhachevsky in February 1936, reported that during one of their meetings his Soviet colleague spoke about Germany's war plans and warned him of an impending German attempt to remilitarize the Rhine region.

As far as Stalin was concerned, Tukhachevsky had committed a dual sin by expressing his attitude towards Germany in public. On the one hand, he was the only senior officer to claim an understanding of the entire depth of Hitler's strategic aims, and being too original was a mortal sin. On the other hand, his perceptions contradicted the course which Stalin had adopted towards Germany, and dissent was the gravest of all sins.

The Great Terror, which hit the higher ranks of the Red Army in the summer of 1937, was not unforeseen, despite the impression created by the abrupt blow that fell in the month of June. Boris Orlov has shown that the terror against the Red Army persisted right through the 1930s. The widespread arrests and mass liquidation of the officer cadres were commonly accompanied by provocations fabricated by Stalin's secret services. Stalin was primarily motivated by an irrational fear of the Red Army as a permanent threat to his régime.

The first phase of the terror was launched in the summer of 1936 with the trials of Zinoviev and Kamenev. In this phase Divisional Commanders Chapayev, M. O. Zyuka and Yu. Savelin, Corps Commander S. O. Turovsky, Deputy Commander of Leningrad Military District V. M. Primakov and V. Putna, Military Attaché in London, were arrested. The second intensified phase corresponds to the trials of January–February 1937 and an attempt to formalize the judicial process. The third stage began in May 1937 with the formal announcement of the reinstitution of the Military Councils and Military Commissars. Soon afterwards, the news of Tukhachevsky's alleged plot was announced. It is clear from the various testimonies that Tukhachevsky was not only aware of what awaited him, but understood precisely the entire course of events, and knew who had initiated the whole affair. General I. P. Deznit has testified that he was being interviewed by Tukhachevsky in his office in mid-May when the latter was interrupted by a telephone call, informing him of the arrest of his friend B. M. Feldman. Tukhachevsky reacted by exclaiming: 'What a grand provocation!'

The news of Tukhachevsky's trial was published by the Procuracy on 11 June 1937. A special tribunal was composed of Alksnis, Belov, Blyukher, Budenny, Dybenko, Goryachev, Kashirin, Shaposhnikov and Ulrikh. The group of conspirators consisted of: Eideman, Feldman, Kork, Primakov, Putna, Tukhachevsky, Uborevich and Yakir. The news of their execution was announced on 13 June in *Pravda*, and on 14 June in *Krasnaya Zvezda* and *Izvestiya*. Various reports confirmed that Tukhachevsky died honourably, and that the firing squad had been commanded by his close friend, Blyukher, a point that reveals the full extent of Stalin's sadism, since Blyukher had tried desperately to abstain from even participating in the tribunal. Furthermore, while he was commanding Tukhachevsky's firing squad, Blyukher's own death warrant had already been signed by Stalin.

The case against Tukhachevsky was initially based on documents allegedly showing that he had had secret contacts with German officers. This obvious provocation had various origins. According to the version propagated in the West by Nazi secret service officers Wilhelm Hoettl and Walter Schellenberg, the provocation was planned initially by SD chief Heydrich, after he had received information from the Russian monarchist General Skoblin, in Paris, that Tukhachevsky intended to attempt a coup d'état against Stalin. By removing Tukhachevsky, Heydrich hoped to damage Soviet military capability and sabotage Soviet–French co-operation, which Tukhachevsky had initiated. Hitler and Himmler had approved the plan in December 1936. At the beginning of 1937, documents referring to the Reichswehr's co-operation with the Red Army were stolen from the archives of the General Staff. In April 1937, in four days of concentrated work at Gestapo headquarters, materials were forged under the supervision of SD General Behrens with the assistance of four GPU agents (as the Germans referred to the NKVD) who were being held prisoner by the Gestapo. The documents included faked correspondence between Tukhachevsky and German officers concerning his willingness to deliver to the Wehrmacht strategic secrets in exchange for support of his coup against Stalin. They also showed faked evidence of telephone calls and faked signatures of Soviet officers on receipts showing the transfer of German money into their hands. In May 1937, after Hitler's final approval, and through a Czech intermediary, the Germans passed to the Soviets the information about the existence of a conspiracy against Stalin. Finally, the forged documents were delivered by the SD to Stalin's agents, who paid a legendary sum in what was later found to be counterfeit money.

According to Boris Orlov, the idea of incriminating Red Army officers by fabricating a story about a military plot supported by external elements against the Communist régime, was born in the Soviet Union in the late 1920s. Given this, Stalin did not need the assistance of the Germans to raise the idea, and the only reason for postponing its implementation was his inclination first to liquidate the opposition within the party. The accounts of a German intelligence agent named Jahnke and a Soviet diplomat named Barmin, who had served in London prior to his defection to the West, show that some furtive contacts regarding the Tukhachevsky provocation did indeed exist between the Soviet and Nazi secret services, and also that General Skoblin, i.e. the source behind Heydrich's initiative, was in fact an agent of Yezhov, head of the NKVD. Moreover, General Behrens, who was involved in both the decision-making and the implementation of the Tukhachevsky provocation, argued that the whole affair was a Soviet contrivance, in which Heydrich and the Gestapo were manipulated by Stalin to facilitate his intrigue. The fact that Soviet agents assisted the Germans in forging the documents, and the fact that Simon Dragatch, the Czech link, was another Soviet agent, both help to strengthen the assumption that the entire Tukhachevsky affair, from start to finish, was indeed a Soviet provocation.

The question now arises, not whether Stalin was motivated by a psychological need to liquidate Tukhachevsky, but rather why he needed a provocation that would link the Marshal through forged documents to a secret German connection? The answer to the question centres on Stalin's endeavour to allay the opposition of the moderate faction in the party, led by Ordzhonikidze, who rejected the terror against both the army and the Party. With Ordzhonikidze's removal in February 1937, the moderate opposition was broken, a fact that contributed to Stalin's abrupt loss of interest in the forged documents. This last fact is confirmed by Schellenberg's version of how the documents were passed to Stalin's agents. Thus, it is safe to assume that the documents played no part in Tukhachevsky's fall, and that Stalin consented to carry on the game to its natural conclusion to assuage Hitler.

Finally, when one considers Tukhachevsky's posture as a Russian nationalist, his rational approach to the German threat, as well as the fact that three persons in the Tukhachevsky Group were Jews (Yakir, Feldman and Gamarnik), the notion of an anti-Soviet conspiracy with Nazi elements becomes absurd.

Until the emergence of the American air land battle theory in the 1980s, the Soviet theory of deep operation represented the most advanced ideas ever attained in the history of military theory. The deep operation theory was developed through a deliberate process, led essentially by Tukhachevsky and lasting thirteen years, in the course of which the outdated notion of the linear battle of destruction was replaced by this advanced operational concept.

Unlike the Germans, who almost at the same time were developing their own conceptual version of operational manoeuvre but did not go further and formulate it into a theory, the Soviets turned their collection of embryonic ideas into an institutionalized theory and uniform nomenclature. This achievement, which derived from Tukhachevsky's grasp of the need for a universal theory for the proper functioning of a massive and dynamic system, was a major factor in crushing the Wehrmacht, despite the superior training and background of the German officers.

In the mid-1960s, when they restructured their operational perceptions, the Soviets applied the deep operation theory, almost literally. Moreover, when the Americans embarked on developing their own operational theory, it was to Tukhachevsky's brainchild that they turned for intellectual backing, and the United Nations campaign in Kuwait and Iraq in 1991 represented the latest and most complete application of the theory.

The background to the deep operation theory lay in the lessons of the Civil War, Frunze's legacy and the environment that prevailed in the USSR of the 1920s. The war experience provided the operational knowledge, the environment rendered the revolutionary approach and critical attitude towards any traditional concept and Frunze bequeathed to the young military radicals the framework of a massive conscript army, a preference for dynamic manoeuvre, and the ideas of tactical initiative and unified command (*edinonachalie*), i.e. single command of combined arms, but also sometimes used to signify political and military command in one person.

The first stage in the evolutionary process called for a thorough analysis of the causes of failure in the First World War, as well as a critical assessment of the experience of the Civil War. The main theoretical conclusions of this stage, which were published in two of Tukhachevsky's early works ('The Battle of the Bugs' and 'Questions of Higher Command', 1924) rejected both the Clausewitzian paradigm of the grand battle of destruction and the outdated patterns of linear manoeuvre, and presented instead a basic understanding of the operational dimension. Further, in his early works Tukhachevsky characterized the operation as a series of engagements that develop towards a predetermined operational goal. He stressed the physical relation between manoeuvre and attrition at the higher level of operations, and he also suggested the concept of operational shock (*udar*), as a substitute for that of annihilation, in the operational context of war.

In the course of the next stage, Tukhachevsky and his colleagues sought to define the universal characteristics of modern war. The essence of this analysis was best demonstrated by Tukhachevsky's closest friend, Triandafillov, in his book, *The Character of Operations of Modern Armies* (1929):

> Modern wars will consist of massive armies, possessing abundant combat means and immense fire power . . . The outcome in modern war will be attained not through the physical destruction of the opponent, but rather through a succession of developing manoeuvres that will aim at inducing him to see his inability to comply further with his operational goals. The effect of this mental state leads to operational shock or system paralysis, and ultimately to the disintegration of his operational system. The success of the operational manoeuvre is attained through all-arms combat at the tactical level, and by combining a frontal holding force with a mobile column to penetrate the opponent's depth at the operational level. The element of depth is a dominant factor in the conduct of modern operations both in the defensive and the offensive. And finally, in the modern context of war, technological development will be governed by operational concepts which are anchored deep in an institutionalized theory.

By the end of the 1920s Tukhachevsky's 'think-tank' was able to define the specific qualities of the operational level of war. The group's activity resulted in a wave of writing that defined the operation as a series of manoeuvres and tactical battles, developing in the direction of an operational objective or towards an operational situation, which, when attained, represented a secondary stage in the complex of the entire campaign.

The group evolved three specific definitions of the phenomena that occur at the operational level, according to their quality and magnitude: the term 'campaign' which referred to the entire operational event within a theatre of operations, centred upon a strategic aim; the term 'operation' which was oriented towards an operational objective and constituted a complete act within the campaigns; the term 'engagement' which indicated an operational engagement characterized by randomness. After delineating the element of randomness as a key factor in any modern operational manoeuvre, the group developed patterns of the 'encounter battle' and the 'meeting engagement' to face this challenge at the tactical and operational levels, respectively. Finally, the group defined the field of operational conduct as an art and an expertise distinct from that of tactics. Thus, in order to meet the need for promoting creative thinking in officers at the operational level, the group advocated the establishment of a special academy of operational art.

Meanwhile, Tukhachevsky headed another working group, called the Fourth Directorate, in an attempt to elaborate a structural framework for the universal comprehension of an operation. The formula they devised implied that the evolution of a universal operational pattern would occur through the synergy of force, time and space in three stages: the first stage concerned the penetration by an infantry-oriented combined force of the tactical outer layer of the defender's lay-out. The second operational stage referred to the breakthrough or break-out of the defender's operational depth by an armoured-cavalry combined force. The third stage concerned the rout of the defender beyond his operational depth. This formulation of a universal operational pattern emphasized the acute link between the concepts of depth, simultaneity and operational shock. Thus, the simultaneous paralysis of the defender throughout his entire depth was defined as a prerequisite of the shock effect, and also as the preferred pattern of manoeuvre. Finally, the Fourth Directorate recommended a universal scheme for modern force-building, which comprised three operational components: a complex of combined-arms mechanized-infantry formations, a complex of combined-arms armoured-cavalry formations and a complex of combined-arms mechanized-airborne formations.

In the course of 1928–33 the Tukhachevsky group paused in its operational activities and concentrated on the final development of the theory of the deep battle. This tactical enterprise, which served as a model for experimenting with the more serious problems of the operational level, stressed the idea of combined-arms combat as the basis of the tactical manoeuvre. The final version of their efforts was composed personally by Tukhachevsky in the form of the Field Manual of 1936.

The theory, or perhaps visionary concept, of the deep operation was first applied, in part at least, by the Red Army in the terrible summer of 1942. Precisely on whose initiative is unknown, but at that time Stalin brought

Isserson back into service, the sole survivor of the extraordinary group that had been responsible for developing the theory, and it was with his assistance that it was applied in the battle of Stalingrad. Thus, Stalin's effort to eradicate Tukhachevsky's fame was mocked by his own hand. Tukhachevsky's intellectual victory over his executioner was complete.

BIBLIOGRAPHY

Alexandrov, V., *The Tukhachevskii Affair*, London, 1963.

Butson, Thos. G., *The Tsar's Lieutenant, The Soviet Marshal*, New York, 1984.

Erickson, J., *The Soviet High Command: A Military Political History*, London, 1962.

Fuller, J. F. C., *A Military History of the Western World*, 3 vols, New York, 1956.

Isserson, G., 'Zapiski sovremennika o M. N. Tukhachevskom', *Voenno-istoricheskii Zhurnal*, no. 4, 1963.

Isserson, G., 'Razvitie teorii sovetskogo operativnogo iskusstva v 30-e gody', *ViZh*, no. 1, 1965 and no. 3, 1965.

Koritsky, N. I. (ed.), *Marshal Tukhachevskii, Vospominaniya druzei i soratnikov*, Moscow, 1964.

Lomov, N., 'Izbrannye proizvedeniya M. N. Tukhachevskogo', *ViZh*, no. 7, 1965.

Nikulin, L., *Tukhachevskii*, Moscow, 1964.

Orlov, B., 'The High Command of the Red Army and the Terror of the 1930s in the USSR', unpubl. Ph. D thesis, Tel Aviv University, 1986.

Simpkin, R. and Erickson, J., *Deep Battle: The Brainchild of Marshal Tukhachevskii*, London, 1987.

Tabouis, G., *They Call Me Cassandra*, New York, 1942.

Todorsky, A. I., *Marshal Tukhachevskii*, Moscow, 1963.

Triandafillov, V. K., *Kharakter operatsii sovremennykh armii*, Moscow, 1937.

Tukhachevskii, M. N., *Izbrannye Proizvedeniya*, Moscow, 1964.

Alexander Mikhailovich

VASILEVSKY

GEOFFREY JUKES

The strong Orthodox Church backgrounds of both Vasilevsky's parents, and his record as an officer in the Tsar's army, did not presage advancement in the armed forces of the new Soviet state. Nor, as an infantryman, did he enjoy the advantages of the First Cavalry Army 'old boy network' which had already brought officers of promise such as Timoshenko, Zhukov, Meretskov and Yeremenko to the attention of Stalin and Voroshilov as early as 1919–20. Against Communist Party suspicion he advanced entirely on his qualities as a soldier, and ultimately became one of the two generals most trusted by Stalin. Though Red Army officer cadets were again being taught formerly despised social skills (including ballroom dancing) by the end of the 1930s, many of their seniors despised polite behaviour as dangerously bourgeois, and cultivated a pseudo-proletarian uncouthness which was not Vasilevsky's style. Though reluctant to become a staff officer, he found himself in complete rapport with its soft-spoken chief, Marshal Shaposhnikov, who carefully guided and groomed Vasilevsky to succeed him, and whom Vasilevsky would afterwards cite as the most important single influence on his thinking. After becoming Chief of General Staff, he worked for most of the war in tandem with the prodigiously gifted but imperious Zhukov, and some of his talent had to go into smoothing feathers ruffled by his domineering colleague; but he also contributed intellectual solidity and organizational skills which made the pair Supreme Headquarters' most formidable trouble-shooters. Together they supervised a series of major victories hard to match in the history of warfare.

Alexander Mikhailovich Vasilevsky, born fourth of eight children in 1895 in a village on the middle Volga, was unusual among Soviet generals in not claiming peasant or proletarian origin. He did in his memoirs make the obligatory Soviet claim to pre-revolutionary poverty, but said that the peasants were even worse off. Both his parents were connected with the Orthodox Church; his mother's father was a cantor, and so was his father, who later became a village priest. He was educated in a church school, was intended to become a priest (as, so Stalin would remind him later, were he and Mikoyan) or teacher, and entered the seminary at Kostroma in 1909, though his real ambition was to be an agronomist. The outbreak of war brought on an upsurge of patriotism, and he volunteered for the army in January 1915. He was selected for officer training at the prestigious Alexeyev military school in Moscow, emerging after four months as an Ensign, and with the basis for his future as a military commander and thinker already being laid in voracious reading of the works of Suvorov, Kutuzov and other famous Russian generals. In September 1915 he was posted to 409th Infantry Regiment of 9th Army on the southern sector of the front, and in 1916, promoted to Staff-Captain, commanded a company in Brusilov's offensive.

Disillusioned by his war experiences, he greeted the fall of the monarchy with enthusiasm, left the army in November 1917 and went home. In December his regiment, then in Ukraine, elected him to command it and invited him to return, but in view of the uncertain political situation there the military section of his local soviet advised him not to go, and offered him employment as a military instructor. His family and tsarist officer background made the local authorities reluctant to offer him active service in the Civil War, so in September 1918 he became a teacher. But in May 1919 a different local authority enrolled him in the Red Army, and his active service in the next three years ranged from confiscating grain to fighting in Poland. By 1924 he was head of a divisional NCO training school, was nominated for the Red Army (later Frunze) Military Academy, but refused, as he considered himself inadequately prepared. He then commanded 143rd Regiment of Moscow Military District, and in 1926 first came under the influence of the former tsarist Colonel Shaposhnikov, then commanding the District and writing his seminal work on the General Staff *The Brain of the Army*, the first two volumes of which appeared in 1927 and the third in 1929. In 1928 I. P. Uborevich succeeded to command of the District, and transferred Vasilevsky from 143rd Regiment, considered the best, to 144th, one of the worst, a move Vasilevsky resisted but which benefitted his career when by 1930 it was rated best in its Division. But because of his pre-1917 background the Communist Party took ten years to accept him, even though he had prepared the ground for an application by breaking off all contact with his parents in 1926. He first applied in 1928, but was not approved as a 'candidate for membership' until August 1931, and it was March 1938 before he was accepted as a full member.

The military leadership clearly did not share the Party's doubts. In the spring of 1931 he was posted, again over his objections, to what he saw as an 'office job', to the newly established Combat Training Directorate, where he spent three years. He was delighted to find his objections unfounded. The work in fact involved frequent visits to units to inspect and advise on training, demonstration exercises for commanders, developing new ways to train and to fight, testing the regulation manuals by field exercises, and developing new ones for formations up to and including corps. His duties included editing a new 'Combat Training Bulletin', and assisting the editors of the existing 'Military Herald'. At the time Tukhachevsky, then Deputy Commissar for the Army and Navy, was pushing the Red Army to develop a theory of combined-arms deep-penetration battle, and many of its propositions were tested in field exercises, staff war games, or the sand table in Tukhachevsky's office. The post considerably broadened Vasilevsky's experience, which hitherto had all been with infantry, and marked the start of his career in the operations branch of staff work. It was followed by two years as Deputy Chief of Staff of Volga Military District; although his duties there were mainly to do with training, he played the part of an Army Chief of Staff in a major strategic field exercise in Belorussia in 1935, in which the Volga District headquarters staff took part.

In the autumn of 1936 Colonel Vasilevsky was selected as one of the first class to attend the new General Staff Academy. Members of this class would hold important posts in the coming war. Two (Vasilevsky and Antonov) would become Chiefs of General Staff, four would command fronts, eleven would be Front Chiefs of Staff, and at least eight others would command armies or head important sections of the central defence apparatus. But only a quarter of the 137-man class would ever complete the eighteen-month course, because Stalin's purge of the military began while it was in progress. Tukhachevsky, Yegorov, Alksnis, Uborevich, Yakir: all had lectured or conducted war games at the Academy and all vanished into oblivion. More than thirty of the class were withdrawn early to fill vacancies caused by the purge, and about twice that number vanished because they themselves were purged.

With Vasilevsky's bourgeois background he might well have been among them. But in August 1937 he was instead offered the Academy's Chair of Rear Services (Logistics), an appointment he claimed to find incomprehensible as he had never worked in the area, but which can be explained by Stalin's slaughtering of more qualified candidates. However, he would be Professor of Logistics for less than two months, because Shaposhnikov had him appointed to head the section of the general staff responsible for operational training of senior officers.

He held that post until June 1939, but spent most of his time working on tasks set by Shaposhnikov, who in hindsight can be seen to have been grooming him. His basic tasks were to update the annual orders and directives governing the training of senior officers, but Shaposhnikov used suitable occasions to broaden his understanding of the international situation and the rôle each branch of the armed forces would be expected to play in a future war. After the fighting with the Japanese around Lake Khasan in July–August 1938 had exposed some weaknesses in troop training, in particular unnecessary losses arising from the troops' reluctance to dig in (one of the reasons why Stalin had had the Soviet commander, Marshal Blyukher, killed), Vasilevsky helped draft a directive, for which he received official thanks and promotion to Brigade Commander. Shaposhnikov broadened his responsibilities in 1939; he remained head of operational training, but also became deputy head of the operations section.

Like Meretskov and all Soviet-period writers, Vasilevsky obligatorily maintained the fiction that Finland attacked the Soviet Union in 1939. He helped draft the plan for the 'counter-offensive' under the guidance of Shaposhnikov, but the Main Military Council (essentially Stalin and Voroshilov) rejected it (Vasilevsky did not say why) in favour of one drawn up by Leningrad Military District. Vasilevsky was involved in the re-evaluation that took place in early January 1940 following the early failures and it was then that he had his first meetings with Stalin and the Politburo, accompanying and being guided by Shaposhnikov at meetings in the Kremlin.

Following Finland's request for an armistice, Vasilevsky was included in the Soviet negotiating team, and drew up the proposals for the new frontier line under the guidance of Molotov and Shaposhnikov.

He was now in the 'inner circle' and further advancement soon followed. Evaluation of the tragi-comedy of the Winter War resulted in Voroshilov's replacement as Defence Commissar by Timoshenko, and a sweeping reorganization of the armed forces. In April 1940 Vasilevsky was promoted to Division Commander and to First Deputy Head of the Operations Directorate, and was one of a three-man team (the others being Generals Vatutin, Head, and Malandin, Deputy Head, of that Directorate) which Shaposhnikov set to produce a new plan for defence against the expected German attack.

Before the plan was completed Shaposhnikov was replaced by Meretskov, officially for health reasons. However, he told Vasilevsky that Stalin, while acknowledging that Shaposhnikov had been right and the Main Defence Committee wrong about Finland, had said 'but only we know that', and told him that dismissing only Voroshilov was not enough to persuade the outside world that the lessons of the Finnish campaign had been learned.

The plan as presented expressed the view of both Shaposhnikov and Meretskov that the main German thrust would come north of the river San and Pripet marshes, aiming at Leningrad and Moscow. Stalin, however, believed it would be in the south, aimed at Ukraine. The arguments were finely balanced, and Hitler himself would vacillate between the two objectives, but the main initial German thrust did indeed come where

Shaposhnikov and Meretskov expected it. However, with Stalin and Timoshenko (whose previous post had been in Kiev) both believing in a southern push, and Shaposhnikov not there to exert his great influence over Stalin, the plan had to be amended, and all consequential revisions (for example in the Railways Commissariat plans for moving troops) taken into account, so that the border Military Districts' tasks could be amended and they could begin to make their own plans immediately after 1 January 1941.

In November 1940 Vasilevsky was a member of the team which accompanied Molotov to Berlin. The talks were fruitless and left Vasilevsky convinced that war was inevitable. But illness kept him away from work from late November 1940 until February 1941, so he missed the important meetings in December and January which preceded Meretskov's replacement by Zhukov.

The outbreak of war caught the Red Army in the middle of a vast reorganization, with large numbers of inexperienced officers in leading positions, with forces brought to the alert only at the last moment, and, to the extent that they were deployed at all, deployed in accordance with a plan which was wrong about the direction of the main German effort. The first weeks were as chaotic for Vasilevsky as for anyone else. But on 29 July Shaposhnikov was reinstated, and on 1 August obtained Stavka's agreement to appointing Vasilevsky as Head of the Operations Section and Deputy Chief of the General Staff. In this capacity Vasilevsky renewed his acquaintance with Stalin, accompanying Shaposhnikov to meetings with him at least once a day.

In mid-August 1941 the most acute problem was the danger of encirclement threatening Kirponos's armies in Ukraine, and both Shaposhnikov and Vasilevsky joined in attempts to convince Stalin of the need to abandon the attempts to hold Kiev. Stalin's faith in Yeremenko's assertions that he could stop Guderian's southward push enabled him to put off decisions about Kirponos, and on 7 September, when it was already clear that Yeremenko had failed, and Shaposhnikov and Vasilevsky tried to persuade Stalin of the need to pull Kirponos's armies back across the Dnieper, he abused them both for joining Budenny (commander of the Southwestern Axis, who made the same recommendation and was dismissed for it) in taking the line of least resistance and trying to run away from the enemy instead of hitting him.

Army Group Centre's attempt to take Moscow began on 3 October, and Vasilevsky acknowledged the General Staff's total failure to identify its most likely lines of attack. After the loss of the Vyazma-Bryansk battle the situation was so desperate that Vasilevsky found himself, as Stavka Representative, tasked with rounding up retreating troops and transporting them to the Mozhaisk defence line. With the evacuation of Shaposhnikov and most of the General Staff on 16–17 October, Vasilevsky became Stalin's closest military confidant. At the end of the month Stalin asked him to sign an order promoting a General; Vasilevsky agreed, but demurred when he found the General was himself, thanked Stalin and asked him for promotions for three other members of the group. Stalin agreed, and Vasilevsky became a Lieutenant-General on 28 October. As he was to do later with Antonov and Shtemenko, Stalin in October 1941 ordered Vasilevsky to have a daily rest period (in his case from 4 to 10 a.m.), checked that he was taking it, and abused him roundly when he found he was not. As night-time Stavka meetings often went on until 4, and the consequent Staff work could take several hours, Vasilevsky took to stationing an adjutant at the telephone, ordered to reply if Stalin rang, 'He's resting till ten o'clock.'

The successful counter-offensive at Moscow in December made it possible for the main body of the General Staff to return to Moscow. From mid-April to 8 May 1942 Vasilevsky was with the Northwestern Front as Stavka Representative overseeing the attempt to liquidate the German force cut off at Demyansk. On 24 April Stalin telephoned to say Stavka had decided to relieve Shaposhnikov of his post for health reasons, and that he, Vasilevsky, had been appointed temporary acting Chief of General Staff. Two days later Stalin promoted him to Colonel-General, but not till 9 May did he summon him back to Moscow.

There were new failures to analyse. First was the unsuccessful Kerch operation in Crimea, resulting in a hasty evacuation across the Kerch Straits, heavy losses of men and equipment, and an increased threat to already besieged Sevastopol. A Stavka directive blasted all the leaders involved, from the Stavka Representative to the Front and Army Commanders and Chiefs of Staff, and demoted most of them.

Even more serious was the situation developing in Ukraine, where Timoshenko's assault on Kharkov was going badly wrong. After talking to Timoshenko's Chief of Staff on the evening of 17 May, Vasilevsky asked Stalin to order the offensive halted, but Stalin decided to talk to Timoshenko first, and accepted his assurance that he had taken adequate measures to deal with the threat. Next day the situation was worse, and at six or seven that evening Khrushchev (whom Bagramyan had asked to intervene when he himself failed to persuade Timoshenko earlier that day) telephoned to say Stalin had rejected a request to stop the offensive, and asked Vasilevsky to try again. Vasilevsky replied that he had already tried more than once, and suggested that Khrushchev, as a member of the Politburo, should ring Stalin himself. Shortly afterwards Khrushchev rang back to say he had tried to, but Malenkov had answered, Stalin had refused to come to the telephone, and had confirmed his refusal to intervene. Although Timoshenko and Stalin changed their minds the next day, the Germans were already by then ripping into their forces from behind, and three Armies were destroyed. The consequent enfeeblement of the Southwestern Front meant that when the

Germans launched their main summer offensive on 28 June they would not be stopped until they reached the Volga and the Caucasus foothills.

In May 1942 Shaposhnikov on medical advice formally asked the State Defence Committee to transfer him to less taxing work, and was put in charge of the military academies. Vasilevsky continued as acting Chief, but several times rejected Stalin's offer of the post, claiming that after watching Shaposhnikov for years he knew he could not fill his shoes. Stalin ultimately abandoned the charade of asking him, and on 26 June simply issued an order appointing him.

He was to hold the post almost until the end of the war, but to spend more time away than present. This was more because of Stalin's reliance on him as a Stavka Representative than because of his own wish, though his past scorn of an 'office job' suggests that Stalin's wishes and his own preferences were not far apart. In his long absences the burden of highest-level staff work fell on his Deputy and the Head of the Operations Section. The Deputy's post (first Vatutin and then Antonov) presented no problem, but it proved extremely difficult to find a successor to Vasilevsky himself as Head of Operations, and the problem was not solved until Shtemenko was appointed in May 1943.

The first big crisis after the Barvenkovo débâcle was the German offensive in the south. On 19 June a German light aircraft was shot down by Soviet anti-aircraft fire and found to contain various documents relating to the planned offensive, including a map with the assignments of XL Panzer Corps and IV Panzer Army marked on it. Timoshenko, rightly as it turned out, considered them genuine, but Stalin dismissed them as a 'plant'. The Red Army was ill-placed to meet the threat because, apart from the losses at Barvenkovo already mentioned, Stalin and the General Staff believed that Moscow would inevitably be the main target in 1942, and were reluctant to accept evidence that this was not the case (hence Stalin's rejection of the captured documents). They were even more reluctant to move their strategic reserves away from Moscow, and Timoshenko's appeals for replacement divisions fell on deaf ears; worse, on 20 June Stalin told him scathingly, 'If they sold divisions in the market I'd buy you five or six, but unfortunately they don't.' As Army Group South's advance took it further and further from Moscow, these reserves began to be released, and by August, when representatives of Stavka (Vasilevsky and Air Force chief Novikov) and the State Defence Committee (Malenkov) were installed in a bunker at Stalingrad, divisions were arriving at the rate of five a week.

This period saw the beginning of Vasilevsky's partnership with Zhukov, who on 26 August 1942 was appointed Deputy Supreme Commander. Both were in the Stalingrad area in early September, supervising attacks intended to eliminate the German corridor from the Don to the Volga and re-establish connection west of the Volga between 62nd Army in the city and the main forces further north. The idea of a counter-offensive to take the Germans in the rear originated in a discussion between Stalin, Zhukov and Vasilevsky in September. Once it had been provisionally decided to conduct it before the end of the year, Stalin sent Zhukov to the Stalingrad Front and Vasilevsky to the adjacent Southeastern Front to study the terrain, determine where and in what directions to strike, and establish details as precisely as possible. Stavka and State Defence Committee approved the outline plan (code-named 'Uranus') at the end of September, and it was then passed to the General Staff to work out in detail. The Fronts were reorganized, and the pair shuttled between Moscow and the south, where they supervised counter-offensive preparations, Zhukov controlling the Southwestern and Don Fronts, Vasilevsky the Stalingrad Front. Both conducted the briefing conferences for commanders down to Division level, on 3 November for the Southwestern Front, 4 November for the Don Front and 10 November for the Stalingrad Front. They then returned to Moscow and reported on the final plan to Stavka on 13 November. Zhukov then went to arrange a diversionary attack by the Kalinin and Western Fronts, while Vasilevsky returned to Stalingrad to co-ordinate all three Fronts in the counter-offensive which began on 19 November. He remained there until 1 January 1943, then Stalin sent him to the Voronezh Front before he returned to Moscow.

In mid-February Manstein launched a counter-offensive which took the Soviet Southwestern Front completely by surprise and forced it to retreat eastwards. This bared the left flank of the adjacent Voronezh Front, so Stalin sent Vasilevsky back there at the beginning of March. As the situation continued to worsen, he sent Zhukov there as well on 18 March, and on the next day they reported to him the steps they had taken, which included moving three armies, two tank corps and several artillery regiments. The situation was stabilized, and the scene set for the next major battle, which would be in the Kursk salient. Vasilevsky received permission to return to Moscow on 22 March.

Soviet intelligence on German intentions improved vastly between mid-February and late March; on 8 April Zhukov, who was still at the Voronezh Front, sent a message to Stalin forecasting very accurately what the Germans would do, and opting for an initial defence rather than a pre-emptive attack. Vasilevsky happened to be with Stalin when the message arrived, and had already told him that the General Staff shared Zhukov's view. Stalin decided to seek the views of the two Front Commanders in the salient, Vatutin (Voronezh) and Rokossovsky (Central), and telephoned them to submit their assessments by 12 April. Both agreed with Zhukov's assessment, but Vatutin confined himself to that, while Rokossovsky advocated a pre-emptive attack against the forces facing him. Stalin, Zhukov, Vasilevsky and Antonov met on the evening of 12 April and took a preliminary decision to fight a premeditated offensive battle at Kursk; Stalin had some doubts about the troops' ability to withstand a mass tank attack, but the soldiers overcame his reservations.

Stavka and the General Staff played an even larger rôle in planning and conducting the Kursk battle than they had at Stalingrad. The basic reason for this was that the defensive battle would be followed by a much larger counter-offensive, involving more Fronts, than had been the case in the previous battle, and co-ordination could only be ensured by tight central control. In mid-May Stalin sent Vasilevsky to the Bryansk Front and the left wing of the Western Front to ensure they understood their jobs and report how their preparations were going. He returned to Moscow on 10 June, but after a few days was despatched to the Voronezh Front. In mid-June Zhukov also was in the salient, and both he and Vasilevsky had some difficulty dissuading Stalin from yielding to Vatutin's persistent entreaties to attack first rather than wait for the Germans to do so. In the first two stages of the battle (the defensive phase and the attack on the German salient around Orel) Vasilevsky controlled the two southern Fronts (Voronezh and South-western), Zhukov the three northern ones (Central, Bryansk and Western). In the third phase, the attack towards Belgorod and Kharkov, which began on 3 August, Vasilevsky co-ordinated the Southwestern and Southern Fronts, Zhukov the Voronezh and Steppe Fronts.

The pattern was repeated in the autumn, as the Red Army swept through Ukraine, Zhukov co-ordinating two or three northern and Vasilevsky two southern Fronts. Stalin did not like them to 'sit around' in Moscow, and would send them back to the Fronts they controlled as soon as their plans had been approved.

However, he required them to make daily reports, and delay in doing so on 16 August 1943 earned Vasilevsky what he claimed was the only reprimand of his career. When midnight arrived without his report, Stalin tried several times to reach him by telephone, and at 3.30 a.m. sent a message threatening to dismiss him if he offended again. He never did, and Stalin never referred to it, probably embarrassed at having revealed how much he depended on Vasilevsky.

The only variation was that as the Fronts ranged further west their names were changed to the 1st, 2nd, 3rd and 4th Ukrainian. In early March 1944, after Vatutin was mortally wounded by Ukrainian nationalist guerrillas, Zhukov had to take over his 1st Ukrainian Front, while remaining Stavka Representative. In April Vasilevsky supervised the liberation of the Crimea by the 4th Ukrainian Front, which completed the operation on 12 May. But his career almost ended there, when his car ran over a mine; he escaped with minor injuries, but was hospitalized for long enough to take a more detailed part than usual in his General Staff's planning of the largest operation of 1944, that in Belorussia which went under the codename of 'Bagration', after Alexander I's great general.

Five Fronts (from north to south the 1st Baltic, 3rd, 2nd and 1st Belorussian, 1st Ukrainian) were involved, along with partisans and the Dnieper Naval Flotilla. Stavka approved the plan on 30 May, and this time Vasilevsky controlled the two northern and Zhukov the three southern Fronts. This operation would not only clear Belorussia of German forces but carry on into the Baltic states, southern Poland and the borders of east Prussia. It would also be the final flourish of the Vasilevsky–Zhukov team as their directions diverged, Vasilevsky adding the 2nd Baltic Front to his responsibilities, then having to take command of the 3rd Belorussian when its commander, Chernyakhovsky, was killed by a shell fragment in January 1945. Zhukov had been appointed to command 1st Belorussian Front (pointing directly at Berlin) on 12 November 1944, and Stavka Representatives were abolished, Front Commanders dealing thereafter directly with Stalin.

Stalin had told Vasilevsky after the Yalta Conference to be prepared for transfer to the Far East once the European war ended, and on 17 February 1945 he ceased to be Chief of General Staff. He was replaced by Antonov, who had been the *de facto* chief for most of Vasilevsky's thirty months in the post.

Vasilevsky began planning the Far Eastern operation on 27 April. As Commander-in-Chief with headquarters in Chita he controlled three Fronts (from west to east the Transbaikal, 2nd and 1st Far Eastern). The operation entailed considerable feats of logistics because of the distances involved and the size of the forces to be supplied, but it involved relatively little actual fighting, as Japan was already on the verge of surrender. Hostilities began on 9 August 1945, and ended on 17 August when the Kwantung Army commander, General Yamada, asked for ceasefire terms.

Vasilevsky was War Minister for several years after 1945, wrote two volumes of memoirs, and died in 1977.

BIBLIOGRAPHY

Bagramyan, I. Kh. *et al.*, *Tak shli my k pobede*, Voenizdat, Moscow, 1988.

Erickson, John, *The Road to Stalingrad: Stalin's War with Germany*, vol. I, Weidenfeld & Nicolson, London, 1975.

Erickson, John, *The Road to Berlin: Stalin's War with Germany*, vol. II, Weidenfeld & Nicolson, London, 1983.

Sbytov, N. A., 'Stavka Verkhovnogo Glavnokomandovaniya', *Sovietskaya voennaya entsiklopediya*, vol. 7, Voenizdat, Moscow, 1979.

Shtemenko, S. M., *General'nyi shtab v gody voyny*, 2nd edn, 2 vols, Moscow, 1981.

Vasilevsky, A. M., *Delo vsey zhizni*, 6th edn, 2 vols, Politizdat, Moscow, 1988.

Volkogonov, D. A., *Triumf i tragediya*, 2 vols, Novosti, Moscow, 1990; in English *Stalin: Triumph and Tragedy*, ed. and trans. Harold Shukman, Weidenfeld & Nicolson, London, and Grove Weidenfeld, New York, 1991.

Zakharov, M. V., *General'nyi shtab v predvoyennyye gody*, Voenizdat, Moscow, 1989.

Zhukov, G. K., *Vospominaniya i razmyshleniya*, 10th edn, Novosti, Moscow, 1992; in English, *The Memoirs of Marshal Zhukov*, Jonathan Cape, London, 1971.

Nikolai Fedorovich
VATUTIN

DAVID GLANTZ

It is ironic perhaps that two of the Red Army's brightest and youngest Front Commanders should perish in the war which contributed so much to their notoriety. This was the case with Army General I. D. Chernyakhovsky, who was fatally wounded in February 1945 aged thirty-nine during the final stage of the East Prussian operation, and Army General N. F. Vatutin, who died at the hands of Ukrainian partisans in spring 1944. The death of both snuffed out some of the best human talent which the wartime Red Army had produced.

Unlike Chernyakhovsky, who lacked a notable pre-war record, Vatutin had already shown considerable promise during the pre-war years, when his performance had been noted by the army leadership as that of a promising General Staff officer. Also unlike Chernyakhovsky, Vatutin had already amassed considerable higher staff service. But like his counterpart, he had yet to prove himself by serving successfully in an operational command.

Vatutin was born on 16 December 1901 in the village of Chepukhino, near Valuiki, Voronezh province. One of four children (one sister and three brothers), Nikolai attended rural school and worked on his father's peasant plot from the age of ten. After attending trade school in Urozovo, 30 kilometres from Valuiki, for four years, through lack of money he was forced to return to Chepukhino. In April 1920 he joined the Red Army's 3rd Reserve Rifle Regiment, stationed in Kharkov. He was then transferred to Lugansk as a member of the 113th Reserve Rifle Battalion, where he participated in operations there and around Starobelsk against Makhno's Ukrainian partisans. He subsequently failed in his attempt to volunteer for service in the Red Army during the Polish war.

For a year from September 1921 Vatutin attended the 29th Infantry

Command Course at Poltava, which was subsequently reorganized into the 14th Infantry School. He was apparently an exemplary student, received an 'outstanding' rating and was assigned, first, to command a student squad and then to serve as assistant platoon commander. There, in 1921, he became a member of the Communist Party. He graduated on 1 October 1922 and was appointed platoon commander in the 67th Rifle Regiment, 23rd Territorial Rifle Division (of 8th Rifle Corps), located in Chuguev just south of Kharkov. By the end of the year his platoon was rated as outstanding. He later served successively as company commander and staff officer in the 7th Territorial Rifle Division (also in the 8th Rifle Corps), at Chernigov, Kiev Military District.

After attending a six-month officer-training course at the S. S. Kamenev Kiev Higher Formation Military School at Darnitsa Barracks, in late July 1924 Vatutin returned to the 67th Rifle Regiment, where he was appointed assistant company commander in the regimental school. Within six months he rose to company command, and soon raised its performance from poor to outstanding. His efficiency report read in part: 'His will-power is developed to a high degree. Authoritative. Serves as example for the regiment's command staff. Fit. Hardy. In all situations understands conditions well. Estimates situations correctly. Knows his business well. Is demanding of himself and his subordinates. Good marksman. Master of rifle tactics. Loves military service.' Armed with this glowing report, in 1926 he took the entrance exam for the Frunze Academy and was accepted.

Vatutin excelled in the three-year course. One of his early reports noted, 'Does not tolerate stereotypes. Inclined to manoeuvre battle. Capable of evaluating most complex situations and determining the optimal variant for solution.' This non-stereotypical behaviour was to become a hallmark of Vatutin's future career. He developed a talent for staff service, studied military history extensively, especially of the Russian Civil War, and developed an acute appreciation of the impact of technological change on weaponry and modern combat. He was selected as a member of his class's Party bureau and graduated with honours from the Academy in May 1929, after participating with his class in the May Day parade on Red Square.

After graduation, he was appointed assistant chief of the operations division of the 7th Territorial Rifle Division in Chernigov, where he excelled in his duties for over six months. With his first stint of divisional staff service under his belt, in November 1929 he was assigned as assistant chief of one of the staff sections of North Caucasus Military District. One of the district orders noted: 'Experimental exercises conducted under supervision of N. F. Vatutin provided rich material for organizing command and control of forces.' Dissatisfied with relatively sedentary staff service, Vatutin then requested transfer to a troop unit and became chief of staff of the 28th Regular Mountain Rifle Division (9th Rifle Corps) at Vladikavkaz.

In light of the rapid technological changes then under way and the Red Army's adoption of an intense programme of motor-mechanization, and in view of Vatutin's talents for technical innovation, in 1934 he was again sent to the Frunze Academy for a special course designed to prepare higher-level commanders. Among his classmates were future chief of the General Staff Antonov and future Front commanders Tolbukhin and Konev. Director of the Academy Shaposhnikov wrote in his assessment of Vatutin: 'In all questions has independent judgement.'

Graduating in late 1934, Vatutin returned to the 28th Mountain Rifle Division, but early the following year was transferred as chief of the 1st Department of the Siberian Military District staff, responsible for unit-readiness inspections, exercises and training. For his outstanding staff performance in that assignment, the district commander, Ya. P. Gailit, recommended Vatutin for the Voroshilov General Staff Academy, where he reported for duty on 1 September 1936 and began classes on 1 November. He did not, however, finish the course. After successfully completing the exams for his first-year's course, in summer 1937 he went on leave. While on leave, he was summoned to Moscow and given an assignment as Assistant Chief of Staff of Kiev Special Military District, ostensibly for his extraordinary performance at the Voroshilov Academy. In fact, Vatutin and his classmates were rising to higher office as a result of the purges, which began in 1937 and ultimately decimated the command cadre and staff of the Red Army. Of his 138 classmates at Voroshilov, sixty-eight received early assignments during the period August–November 1937. Among those sent to critical positions were Colonels Vasilevsky, Zakharov, Antonov, Trofimenko and Sandalov, all of whom were to play prominent parts in the coming war.

Vatutin served as Assistant Chief of Staff for more than a year, and in December 1938 became District Chief of Staff, responsible for mobilization and operational planning during the crisis preceding the outbreak of the Second World War. It was plain that he was headed for even higher service, when the Higher Examination Board of the Revolutionary Military Soviet wrote of him: 'Consider it expedient to use Vatutin, N. F. in the General Staff of the Red Army.' While serving as Chief of Staff, he was also a member of the Party bureau of the Military District staff, advisable in light of the preceding purges, and a delegate to the XV Conference of the Ukrainian Communist Party, which selected him as a member of the central revisionary Commission of the Party's Central Committee.

As District Chief of Staff and newly promoted Divisional Commander, Vatutin planned the operations in eastern Poland in September 1939. A later report noted that 'during the period of liberation of our brother Ukrainians of western Ukraine from under the oppression of the Polish papists and capitalists, he demonstrated his capability, suitability and skill in controlling large operations.' Given his 1939 performance, in late June 1940, when the Soviet government planned and conducted operations against Romania to seize Bessarabia (now Moldova), Vatutin was appointed Chief of Staff of the Southern Group of Forces (Southern Front), which was designated to conduct the operation under Zhukov's command. The operation began at 1400 hours on 28 June and ended after complete occupation of Bessarabia on 30 June. On or around that date, Vatutin was promoted to Lieutenant-General and reassigned to the prestigious position of Chief of the Operations Directorate of the Red Army General Staff.

Within a matter of months, he rose to become First Deputy Chief of the General Staff. In that position he was instrumental in formulating pre-war Soviet operational and mobilization plans. Vasilevsky, then First Deputy Chief of the General Staff's Operations Directorate, credited Vatutin with an important rôle in operation planning: 'The report [on defence of the nation] was drawn up by N. F. Vatutin, G. K. Malandin and myself, with Shaposhnikov [a Marshal since 7 May 1940] giving us guidelines.' Zhukov, who became Chief of the General Staff on 31 January 1941 and who knew Vatutin from his Kiev days, singled him out among the 'compact, friendly, close-knit team of competent and experienced men', working in the General Staff, as 'a man of exceptional industry and broad strategic thinking'.

Vatutin's capacity for understanding the nature of modern warfare propelled him to the forefront during the army's attempts to reform itself after its dismal performance in the Finnish War. In August 1940 a commission was formed to revise Red Army manuals and regulations. On 31 October it turned over its recommendations to the Main Commission on Manuals and Regulations, of which Vatutin, as First Deputy Chief of the General Staff, was an instrumental member. Vatutin also helped plan and supervise the conduct of the critical and controversial General Staff war games of January 1941. In addition, during January and February he prepared a study of rail capacity in the border military districts as a basis for the construction of fortified regions. The report angered Stalin and the Defence Commissariat, since a plan adopted the year before to improve the rail and road network had not been implemented. As an indicator of things to come, Zhukov forcefully backed up Vatutin's views.

Vatutin was then working a sixteen- to eighteen-hour day, and for weeks on end did not leave the General Staff building. In February 1941 he was awarded the Order of Lenin. He had direct responsibility for preparing and correcting mobilization and strategic deployment plans. Working closely with Malandin, Vasilevsky and Anisov of the Operations Directorate, in March 1941 he completed a plan for mobilizing industry and food production in the event of war. He also found time to supervise exercises in Leningrad Military District in April 1941. Increased tension along the western borders, and Soviet implementation of partial mobilization, meant he had to cancel taking part in another exercise planned for May in Transcaucasus Military District.

As Deputy Chief of the General Staff, on the evening of 21–22 June 1941 Vatutin received heightened warnings of German military activity from Lieutenant-General N. A. Purkayev, Chief of Staff of Kiev Special Military District, and from other major commands. With Zhukov, he drafted the warning directive transmitted to field commands at 0300 hours on 22 June, after arguing in vain with Stalin for a stronger directive, which with Zhukov he had already prepared. During the frenetic early days of the war, Vatutin stood in for Zhukov as Chief of the General Staff while Zhukov travelled to the Southwestern Front as Stavka Representative. It was Vatutin who wrote frank reports which shook Stalin from his lethargy following the German assault, and exposed the true catastrophic nature of the situation. In one exchange with Stalin, Vatutin was asked: 'What are you saying about conditions at Minsk? Are you somehow confused? Where are you getting your information?' Vatutin replied: 'No, I am not confused, Comrade Stalin . . . . The information General Staff representatives are sending to the Army and Air Force agrees. In fact, the Western Front has been penetrated.' Subsequently, Vatutin's frank assessment lent an air of realism to an otherwise stupefied Stavka. It was also Vatutin who sent 21st Mechanized Corps from Moscow to reinforce the hard-pressed Northwestern Front.

On 30 June 1941 Vatutin was appointed Chief of Staff Northwestern Front to resolve the disastrous situation in that sector and defend the approaches to Leningrad. On arriving, he found the Front staff in utter disarray with no control over combat operations. He immediately telephoned Zhukov and arranged for the assignment of a new Front Commander (P. D. Sobennikov) and Front military commissar. In the interim, Vatutin assumed command, moved Front HQ to Novgorod, and prepared a plan, which Sobennikov ultimately approved, for a more active defence against the advancing Germans. During the same period, Zhukov proposed that Vatutin be included in Stavka. Stalin rejected the proposal, perhaps thinking Vatutin more valuable at the front.

Vatutin personally took command of a Front operational group defending Novgorod and planned an active defence against General von Manstein's LVI Panzer Corps by conducting a vigorous counter-attack near Soltsy. The attack, which began on 14 July and lasted four days, halted the German advance and compelled German forces to regroup. Ultimately, it cost the Germans three precious weeks and probably contributed to their failure to take Leningrad.

Subsequently, Vatutin organized another counter-attack by his Front's 11th and 14th Armies south of Staraya Russa, which began on 14 August and which further delayed the German advance. General Chernyakhovsky's 28th Tank Division played an instrumental rôle in the counter-attack, and his and Vatutin's future close personal and professional relationship dated from this event. As a consequence of these and other counter-attacks, by late

September German forces went on the defensive in the Leningrad region. For Vatutin's performance, in September Zhukov suggested he be assigned command of the critical Central Front, defending the southern approaches to Moscow. Stalin again refused to reassign Vatutin and sent M. G. Yefremov instead.

As Northwestern Front Chief of Staff, Vatutin's main task was to block any German advance through the Valdai Hills, defend Soviet lines of communication between Moscow and Leningrad, and protect the flank of the Soviet strategic groupings defending the two cities. During October 1941, as the final German drive on Moscow commenced, Vatutin headed a special Front operational group based on Mednovo and tasked with defending against a German thrust from Kalinin northward to Torzhok. The German thrust never materialized.

During the second phase of the Soviet winter counter-offensive around Moscow, which began in early January 1942, the Northwestern Front was assigned the mission of advancing along two strategic directions towards Toropets and Smolensk to support Western Front forces operating on the Moscow–Smolensk axis towards Staraya Russa and Soltsy in support of the Leningrad grouping. Vatutin planned the ensuing Demyansk operation, which began on 7 January, but his forces failed to seize Staraya Russa. A subsequent Front attack on 29 January succeeded in encircling a German corps (XII) at Demyansk, but again failed to take Staraya Russa. (It was, however, the first Soviet encirclement of a sizeable German force.) Subsequently, in March 1942 Vatutin planned an audacious operation against the Demyansk salient by using airborne forces in a ground and air rôle, and in May yet another operation to reduce the salient with artful use of deception. Both operations, however, failed.

On 12 May 1942 Stavka recalled Vatutin to Moscow for service as Deputy Chief of the General Staff under Vasilevsky. He served in this capacity through the disastrous spring of 1942, responsible primarily for Far Eastern matters. Shortly after the new German strategic offensive, Operation 'Blau', began, on 1 July 1942 Vatutin was appointed Stavka Representative to the Bryansk Front. He had been the first to warn of the danger of an impending German offensive towards Voronezh at the critical juncture of the Bryansk and Southwestern Fronts.

On 7 July Stalin appointed Vatutin as Stavka Representative to the newly-created Voronezh Front. Several days later, however, he was recalled to Moscow to discuss command relationships between the Bryansk and Voronezh Fronts, which to that time had been particularly weak. Vatutin suggested that he himself be given command of the Voronezh Front after Stalin had rejected several other names. With Vasilevsky's consent, Stalin agreed with Vatutin's appointment to command this critical Front.

Vatutin assumed command on 14 July 1942 and was immediately tasked with the mission of defending Voronezh and the river Don line. Although the Germans subsequently succeeded in seizing the city, elsewhere Vatutin's defences held, prompting the Germans to shift the direction of their offensive southeastward towards Stalingrad. During the defence of Voronezh, Vatutin again encountered Chernyakhovsky, now the new commander of 60th Army's 18th Tank Corps. Eventually, Vatutin was instrumental in Stalin's appointing the young Chernyakhovsky to command 60th Army.

On 22 October Vatutin was once again summoned to Moscow, where he was given command of the new Southwestern Front, which had just been reformed from 1st Guards Army headquarters. As Front Commander, he played a significant rôle in planning the Stalingrad counter-offensive, launched on 19 November 1942. In his memoirs, I. M. Chistyakov, commander of his subordinate 21st Army, praised Vatutin's rapport with his subordinates: '[Vatutin] had one other notable quality. He could listen to others without losing rank or authority. We, his subordinates, felt free with him and that understandably unleashed initiative.'

After the successful encirclement of German forces at Stalingrad, in early December 1942 Vatutin planned the middle Don operation to disrupt German relief efforts at Stalingrad and to expand the Soviet winter offensive westward. He argued strenuously for the conduct of Operation 'Saturn', an ambitious operation, which was designed to destroy all German forces east of Rostov, but was forced by events and by Stalin to plan and conduct Operation 'Little Saturn', a shallower envelopment of the reinforced Italian VIII Army. Despite losing the argument, Vatutin conducted the operation with his usual vigour.

Subsequently, in late January and February 1943, Vatutin's Front launched the ambitious Donbas operation, in the course of which he pushed his forces forward relentlessly and failed to pay enough heed to the changing intelligence situation. As a consequence, his forces became over-extended and were severely defeated by von Manstein's counter-attack of 20 February 1943.

Vasilevsky justified Vatutin's failure by explaining that the German attack of February had come out of the blue, although he also admitted that 'the commanders of the Southwestern and Voronezh Fronts had assessed the strategic situation incorrectly'. In characteristic fashion, said Vasilevsky, Vatutin had asked GHQ to employ all of his forces in a 'Leap Forward Operation' to clear German forces from between the northern Donets and Dnieper rivers before the onset of the spring thaw. Stalin, on 11 February, had personally counselled against Vatutin's plan and, instead, had recommended more limited objectives. Finally, however, Stalin acquiesced in Vatutin's ardour for the more audacious plan. Thus, according to Vasilevsky, the High Command and Stalin shared with Vatutin responsibility for the failure. Despite the failure, and in recognition of his boldness, on 12 February Vatutin was rewarded for his audacity by being promoted to Army General.

S. M. Shtemenko, the Deputy Chief of the General Staff, later praised Vatutin's performance at this stage of the war, noting that his personal opinion was highly regarded at the General Staff. 'We all knew Vatutin well and not without reason considered him a gifted and original strategist with a strong dash of romanticism in his make-up.'

After the Donbas débâcle, on 28 March 1943 Stavka appointed Vatutin to command the Voronezh Front, which had experienced similar lack of success in the Kharkov operation in February. Vatutin's task was to prepare the Front either to attack or defend in the critical sector south of Kursk during the spring and summer of 1943. Vatutin responded imaginatively and forcefully. On 12 April he proposed that a pre-emptive offensive be launched on the Belgorod–Kharkov axis to disrupt any future German offensive plans and to seize Dnieper river crossings near Cherkassy and continue the attack to Nikolayev to destroy German Army Group South. Although supported by his Front commissar, Khrushchev, Stavka rejected his plan, since it did not deal adequately with the threat posed by Army Group Centre to Moscow and the right flank of the Soviet Kursk concentration. Instead, Stavka chose to implement an initial defensive phase to the approaching strategic offensive to deal with the German flank threat. Stavka chose as its principal offensive direction the axis Kharkov–Poltava–Kiev, which was, in essence, a constructive variation of Vatutin's original plan.

Vasilevsky later recalled how impatient Vatutin became, urging the need to launch a Soviet offensive during the summer. He was unmoved by Vasilevsky's argument that the enemy was about to launch his own offensive and that a Soviet one could only benefit the enemy. 'We'll miss the boat, let the moment slip,' Vatutin kept saying. 'The enemy is not going to move, soon it will be autumn and all our plans will be ruined. Let's get off our backsides and begin first. We've enough forces for it.' Stalin himself was almost convinced by Vatutin's entreaties. According to Vasilevsky, Stalin told him that Vatutin had phoned him and insisted that an offensive begin no later than the first few days of July. Stalin then said that he thought the proposal merited the most serious attention, that he had instructed Vatutin to get ready and report his ideas about the Voronezh Front to Stavka. Only after strenuous arguments by Zhukov and Vasilevsky did Stalin reject Vatutin's plan.

Subsequently, during July Vatutin's Front participated in the crucial Kursk operation, first, by conducting the tenacious defence of the southern flank of the Kursk bulge. When the attack materialized, he employed the unorthodox and controversial measure of digging in his 1st Tank Army to form a solid second-echelon defence. His post-action report to Stavka reflected his continuing audacity: 'Conclusion: At the present time,

Voronezh Front forces, having inflicted defeat on the enemy and having re-established its former position, is capable of conducting active offensive operations.' Zhukov praised his skilful defence, adding, 'General Vatutin and General Rokossovsky [Central Front] dealt with many logistical questions themselves, and this was largely the reason why our troops were so well provided with matériel by the beginning of the operation.'

Although Vatutin wanted to start the counter-offensive phase of the Kursk operation immediately after the German defeat (on 12 July), Zhukov and Stavka mandated a two-week delay to regroup and make other preparations and to permit operations, begun elsewhere on 12 July, to achieve their intended effect. On 3 August 1943, Vatutin's forces began the Belgorod-Kharkov operation and subsequently liberated the two cities. When Kharkov fell, Stalin ordered the first wartime Moscow gun-salute for a liberated city. Zhukov later dismissed criticism of Vatutin's performance at Kursk: 'As for Vatutin's ability to deal with strategic and operational questions, I must state with complete impartiality that Vatutin, the commander of the Voronezh Front, was a highly erudite and steadfast commander.'

Vasilevsky endorsed Zhukov's view, adding that Vatutin had superbly carried out this important mission, which had been one of the largest military operations. He had 'succeeded in concentrating the forces and means on the main axis decisively, strengthening the force and delivering surprise blows against the flanks and rear of the enemy grouping.' He had 'skilfully employed large masses of tanks to develop the offensive into the operational depths, organizing the close co-operation of combined forces, and reliably supporting continuous and firm control of forces.' With the Kursk operation successfully completed, on 9 September 1943 Vatutin met Antonov and Zhukov and together they worked out offensive plans for an advance on Kiev, which relied heavily on a rapid advance of 3rd Guards Tank Army to the Dnieper near Kanev. The next day Vatutin's Front broke through German defences southeast of Romny and, shortly thereafter, the tank army began its race with German forces to the Dnieper.

By 22 September 1943, 3rd Guards Tank Army and other advanced elements of the Voronezh Front had secured small bridgeheads across the Dnieper north and south of Kiev. Shortly thereafter, Vatutin talked Stavka into creating a direct line of supply to his forward forces. He also urged the conduct of the bold, but ill-fated airborne operation to seize a large bridgehead in the Veliki Bukrin area. Subsequent attempts to break out of the Bukrin bridgehead proved futile. On 20 October the Voronezh Front was renamed the 1st Ukrainian Front.

Three days later, on 23 October, Vatutin proposed to Stavka the concept of the projected Kiev operation, which involved a major secret regrouping of Front forces and the implementation of an imaginative deception plan. Vatutin is quoted as stating: 'Comrades, I am firmly convinced that we must use the Bukrin bridgehead for a secondary blow, and deliver the main blow on the right flank, on the Lyutezh bridgehead. That, I believe, will permit us to liberate the capital of Soviet Ukraine successfully and quickly.'

From 3 to 15 November 1943, Vatutin conducted the initial phases of the operation and secured Kiev and a strategic bridgehead west of the Dnieper. Thereafter, he continuously regrouped his forces to defend against a series of strong German counter-attacks, which lasted into mid-December and resulted in the defeat of von Manstein's Army Group South.

Rokossovsky, when sent as Stavka Representative to assist Vatutin when he was facing heavy German counter-attacks, wrote that Vatutin was, 'A general, highly educated in military science, always calm and collected.' He added, 'I was somewhat surprised by the way Vatutin organized his work. He personally edited all directives and orders and discussed by telephone and telegraph with the armies and headquarters. What, then, was the Chief of Staff doing?' Vatutin told him, 'It's all because I was a staff officer for so long . . . I always feel I must do everything myself.' 'Nevertheless,' Rokossovsky added, 'I must say that Vatutin coped with his task brilliantly and dealt the Nazis such blows that they quickly came to their senses and hastily assumed the defensive.' Zhukov also noted Vatutin's 'key rôle' in the recapture of Kiev.

Thereafter, in December 1943 and January 1944, Vatutin planned and conducted the Zhitomir-Berdichev and Rovno-Lutsk operations. The former involved the formulation and conduct of yet another immensely successful deception operation, of which Zhukov wrote that, when he visited Vatutin's Front to advise, he found the general in an overheated peasant hut, a warm cape over his shoulders, drawing up a directive for an attack by the major group of the Front's forces in the general direction of Vinnitsa. 'One look at him, and I realized he was obviously unwell . . . I suggested that he go to bed immediately and sweat out his illness, so that he would be completely operative by the start of the offensive. This he consented to do. After downing a glass of strong tea with dried raspberries, and swallowing a couple of pills, Vatutin went to his room.' Zhukov then set out with Vatutin's chief of staff, A. N. Bogolyubov, for Operations Division to assess the situation and check the readiness of the troops. 'Less than ten minutes after we arrived, the telephone rang. Bogolyubov picked up the receiver. It was Vatutin calling Bogolyubov to his quarters.' There Zhukov and Bogolyubov caught Vatutin poring over a map of the forthcoming offensive. Zhukov remonstrated, 'You told me you were going to bed, and here you are at your map again!' Vatutin replied that he wanted to write a dispatch to the GHQ about preparations for the offensive. Virtually dragging Vatutin back to bed, Zhukov told him he had a Chief of Staff to do precisely that.

During the Rovno-Lutsk operation, Vatutin again skilfully used enveloping manoeuvres to turn the German flank from an unexpected direction. Subsequently, in January and February 1944, Vatutin's Front participated with the 2nd Ukrainian Front in the Korsun-Shevchenkovsky operation, where he again acted in unorthodox fashion by committing his 6th Tank Army from first echelon. During the waning days of the operation, Vatutin was somewhat upset when Stavka sent Zhukov to help in the operation.

As the first phase of the Soviet winter campaign in Ukraine was ending in late February, Vatutin and the commanders of the 2nd and 3rd Ukrainian Fronts began planning for the second phase, which was to commence on 4 March and end with the expulsion of German forces from Ukraine. Vatutin, however, was not destined to see this crowning success.

On 29 February 1944, Vatutin, with his chief of staff, K. Kraynyukov, and a security detachment of ten men, travelled by car to 13th Army HQ at Rovno. There, Vatutin discussed plans for the forthcoming operation with General N. P. Pukhov and his staff. At 1640 hours Vatutin left with his chief of staff and an escort of eight men to visit 60th Army HQ in Slavata. While taking a shortcut through the town of Gosha, his car was ambushed by partisans, firing from the windows of buildings in the northern outskirts of the village of Milyatin. Vatutin was seriously wounded in the thigh, but the attackers were driven off. Vatutin was evacuated to an army field hospital in Rovno and then transported by rail to Kiev. During the night of 15 April 1944, despite the best efforts of a distinguished surgeon dispatched from Moscow to treat him, Vatutin died of his wounds aged forty-three. He was buried at Kiev on 17 April 1944.

Vatutin was one of the Red Army's finest wartime General Staff officers and Front Commanders. He managed to survive in the 1930s despite his penchant for originality and forward thinking. It was the survival of men of his ilk, the Vasilevskys, Antonovs, Katukovs and Rokossovskys, that permitted the Red Army to achieve its wartime success.

Vatutin, like others, enjoyed the support of Stalin and perhaps even could be termed one of Stalin's favourites. Stalin's biographer, Dmitri Volkogonov, has written: 'On the basis of the analysis of archival documents and memoir literature, one can say that Stalin related sympathetically to K. K. Rokossovsky, N. F. Vatutin, A. E. Golovanov, N. N. Voronov, L. A. Govorov, and A. V. Khrulev.' Stalin's attitude toward these men, and Vatutin in particular, in part explains Stalin's relative tolerance of failure. As a result, Stalin actually permitted these generals to make mistakes and to learn from them.

Vasilevsky, Vatutin's long-term associate, has rendered the most comprehensive judgement of Vatutin's skill as a staff officer and commander, noting that by his 'strategic wisdom, his knowledge and experience, and his unflagging work he made a worthy contribution to the training of the Soviet Armed Forces.' Vasilevsky especially singled out the special assignments

Vatutin had carried out for the State Defence Committee and Stavka. 'I shall never forget my meeting with him at the front where he had to do so much that was valuable to our cause.' Apart from his enormous skill in handling combined operations – a master of warfare – Vasilevsky added that Vatutin had earned universal respect and affection.

Vatutin's hallmarks were a keen appreciation of the intricacies of staff work and an audacious enthusiasm for command. Even his opponents appreciated his talents, as the German armoured specialist von Mellenthin, later wrote: 'Certainly in men like Zhukov, Konev, Vatutin and Vasilevsky, the Russians possessed army and army group commanders of a very high order.'

Unlike many commanders, Vatutin was also well thought of by his subordinates. Memoir writers at every command level speak of him often and warmly, and generally praise his attributes as a commander. It was of no little significance that, on his fatal wounding, Stavka appointed Zhukov to take his place. Later Konev would inherit Vatutin's Front and lead it to victory in 1945.

BIBLIOGRAPHY

Bragin, M. G., *Vatutin (put' generala), 1901–1944*, Voenizdat, Moscow, 1954.

Ivanov, S. P., 'Geroi Sovetskogo Soiuza General Armii N. F. Vatutin', *Voenno-istoricheskii Zhurnal*, no. 12, 1981.

Sobol', S. A. and Nikolai, I. D., *Nikolai Fedorovich Vatutin*, Tsentr-muzei vooruzhennykh sil SSSR, Moscow, 1968.

'Vatutin, Nikolai Fedorovich', *Sovetskaya voennaya entsiklopediya*, vol. 2, Voenizdat, Moscow, 1976.

Voinov, A. I., *Vatutin*, Voenizdat, Moscow, 1969.

Zakharov, Yu. D., *General Armii N. F. Vatutin*, Voenizdat, Moscow, 1985.

Andrei Andreyevich
VLASOV

CATHERINE ANDREYEV

With the passing of time interest has grown rather than diminished in Lieutenant-General Vlasov's attempt to form an anti-Stalinist Liberation Army largely from Soviet prisoners-of-war. In private conversations it is now even suggested that there might be a statue to him, at least in his birthplace, Nizhni Novgorod, if not in Prague or Moscow. Such comments would have been unthinkable a few years ago, but *glasnost*, which provided the impetus for a radical reappraisal of the Soviet past, has allowed discussion of the Russian Liberation Movement, which was previously taboo.

The history of the Russian Liberation Movement gave rise to much discussion, controversy, accusation and counter-accusation both among participants in the period 1941–5 and in the post-war Russian émigré organizations and Western literature. An article by Boris Nikolayevsky in the New York periodical *Novyi Zhurnal* in 1948 aroused such acrimony in the émigré press that he lost heart and did not complete the series. After the short notice in *Izvestiya* on 2 August 1946 that the sentence of death under Article 11 of the order of the Supreme Soviet had been carried out, the Soviet press contained no mention of Vlasov or his activities for a number of years. The amnesty for many political prisoners in 1955 meant that a few individuals began to write about their experiences, but the official history of the war mentioned Vlasov in one sentence only. However memoirs and a variety of analyses published in the West began to find some echo in the USSR, even if the assessments of the so-called Vlasov Movement were *a priori* negative. The discussion of this wartime phenomenon within the borders of what was previously the Soviet Union has not yet led either to any fundamental analysis or reassessment of the evidence and has not produced a great deal of new data from the archives. Western material, both memoirs and monographs, have been used in the exchange of views in the press. These arguments have tended to centre on the person of Vlasov himself; what kind of person was he? To what extent was he a traitor? There has also been some discussion of the situation of 2nd Shock Army, which Vlasov commanded in 1942 prior to his defeat and capture by the Germans. It was started by questions being raised in the press as to the reason why the bodies of soldiers in this area of the front had not been given a proper burial and how it was that, forty-five years after the end of the war, bones with identification tags could still be found. Some assert that the disastrous defeat of 2nd Shock Army was the result of the commander's cowardice. Some discussion of the wider conditions which produced this unprecedented movement of defeatism, when about one million Soviet citizens were to be found in the ranks of the German armed forces, has occurred, but this willingness to see Stalin's government defeated in war is still too emotive a subject to allow for wide-ranging debate. Such a discussion would involve not only an assessment of the way in which the Stalinist régime was perceived by the populace but also a re-examination of the way in which the war was conducted. From the Russian point of view, the Second World War on the Eastern Front, with its enormous losses and great heroism, cannot be easily disentangled from Stalin's policies.

Much ink has been expended on the question whether Vlasov had anti-Soviet views before the war. His early career shows no sign of this. Vlasov's father was a peasant. Andrei, born in 1900, was the youngest son of thirteen children and was, apparently, educated by his elder brother. Sent first to a church school and then to a seminary in Nizhni Novgorod, his education was cut short by the Revolution. He then entered an agricultural college but agriculture, like the Church, was in a state of disarray and uncertainty. In the spring of 1919 Vlasov was conscripted into the 27th (Privolzhsky) Rifle Regiment. He served throughout the Civil War in the Red Army, seems to have been a good soldier and to have got on well with his comrades, and his promotion was rapid. After a few weeks of service he was sent on an officer training course. Four months later he was made a platoon commander and sent to the Southern Front. Vlasov served with a regiment of the 2nd Don Division which was fighting against General Denikin on the Don and the Manych. Early in 1920, when the White armies had been driven out of Ukraine and the Caucasus, the 2nd Don Division was transferred to the Crimea to fight General Wrangel's forces. Here Vlasov commanded a company and after a few months was transferred to the divisional staff as assistant to the chief of operations. His next appointment was in command of a mounted infantry reconnaissance section in one of the regiments of the division. In November 1920, when the Red Army was in control of the Crimea, Vlasov was given command of a detachment in the Ukraine in order to combat Makhno and other anti-Bolshevik groups, as well as against armed groups of bandits. Many of those who joined the Russian Liberation

Movement during the Second World War, and particularly those who had been in the Red Army during the Civil War, were united by the idea that during the Civil War they had fought for the Bolsheviks and the Russian people, but that subsequently the Bolsheviks had betrayed their promises. Vlasov shared this experience of the Civil War, but there is no evidence that he was in any way disaffected at this period.

When the Red Army was reorganized Vlasov chose to remain a professional soldier and became a company commander. He was congratulated by the Chief of Staff, P. P. Lebedev, when the latter inspected North Caucasus Military District, on his excellent work in training his men. His record suggests that he was an able commander who was promoted and given further training so that he had a wide variety of skills. On the fifth anniversary of the formation of the Red Army, Vlasov was presented with an inscribed silver watch.

In 1930, Vlasov became a member of the Communist Party. This event has been given an unjustified degree of prominence by both Vlasov's supporters and his detractors. The former consider that he joined the Party rather late because he was not in agreement with its policies. His detractors argue that he was always unreliable and therefore was not admitted to the Party any earlier. Both these explanations are tendentious. Vlasov joined the Party at the moment when it was necessary to do so. He was unlikely to be promoted without being a member of the Party. The time when he became a member provides no clue to his political convictions.

Vlaslov's political record must have been clean as otherwise he would not have been sent to China in 1938. The USSR was pursuing a double policy in China. On the one hand it supported Chiang Kai-shek against the Japanese and on the other the Comintern supported the Chinese Communists. Vlasov, using the pseudonym Volkov, was appointed Chief of Staff to the Soviet military advisor, General Cherepanov. From February to May 1939, Vlasov served as advisor to General Yen Hsi-shan, Governor of Shansi. Vlasov had to persuade him of the necessity of joining Chiang Kai-shek's operations against the Japanese. After the recall of General Cherepanov, Vlasov performed the duties of chief military adviser to Chiang Kai-shek. In November 1939, after the arrival of the new Soviet military advisor in China, General Kachanov, Vlasov was recalled to Moscow. Chiang Kai-shek decorated Vlasov with the Golden Order of the Dragon. Apparently Madame Chiang Kai-shek gave Vlasov a watch, but both the decoration and the watch were removed from him by Soviet officials on the border. On his return, he was once again appointed to Kiev Military District, returning to Timoshenko's command under whom he had served before going to China. This suggests that his superiors found him a useful subordinate.

His service in China shows that he was well thought of as a military specialist and had been careful not to involve himself in political activity.

Some of his supporters have alleged that he escaped the Tukhachevsky purge because of his posting to China, but this, too, is not supported by the evidence.

Vlasov was appointed commander of the 99th Infantry Division which was notorious for its disarray, owing in part to being composed of a whole range of different nationalities. In 1940 he was given a gold watch and the Order of Lenin for his work in retraining and reforming this division. The division itself was awarded the Red Banner and was officially acclaimed the best in Kiev Military District. In 1940, following his work with the 99th Division, Vlasov published an article on new methods of operational training, in which he comes across as a competent and practical commander. Another article, which appeared in the army newspaper, *Krasnaya Zvezda*, praised him for his military capabilities but makes no mention of any political involvement or views.

Vlasov's military service in the early phases of the war was of an exemplary nature. When war broke out he was commanding 4th Mechanized Corps of the Ukrainian Front and came under severe pressure from Field Marshal von Rundstedt's Army Group South. Vlasov was entrusted with the defence of Lvov, and after its fall he had to fight his way out of repeated encirclement. In August and September 1941 Vlasov commanded 37th Army which was involved in the defence of Kiev. After having lost contact with the headquarters of the commander of Kiev Military District, Lieutenant-General M. P. Kirponos, the 37th Army fought its way out of encirclement.

In November 1941 Vlasov was ordered to help in the defence of Moscow. Summoned for his first meeting with Stalin on November 10th, he was asked for his views on the situation. When Vlasov said that he thought that the reserve crack troops stationed in Siberia should be called up, Stalin is supposed to have said that 'anyone can defend Moscow with reserves' but gave Vlasov fifteen tanks – all that was available. Vlasov commanded 20th Army which was part of the Northern Group defending Moscow. On 13 December 1941 the Soviet Informburo mentioned Vlasov as one of those commanders who had made an outstanding contribution to the defence of the city. In the Soviet counter-attack at the beginning of December Vlasov's troops and Rokossovsky's 16th Army fought their way to the Istra River and then to Solnechnogorsk and Volokolamsk. By January 1942 Vlasov's Army spearheaded the main attack of the Soviet counter-offensive, whose final objective was to surround the German forces in the Mozhaisk–Gzhatsk–Vyazma area. At this point Vlasov was so high in favour that he was allowed to be interviewed by an American journalist and by Eve Curie, a French journalist working for the American press. On 24 January 1942 he was awarded the Order of the Red Banner and promoted to Lieutenant-General.

In March 1942 Vlasov was made Deputy Commander of the Volkhov Front and he arrived from Stavka in an aeroplane with Voroshilov, Malenkov and the Deputy Commander of the Air Force, A. A. Novikov, which indicates that his appointment was considered important. The Volkhov Front had been created in December 1941 in order to relieve the pressure on Leningrad. 4th and 52nd Armies were assigned to it as well as 2nd Assault Army and 59th which was in the process of being formed. It appears that, from the outset, there was a difference of opinion between General Meretskov, the Commander of the Volkhov Front, and Lieutenant-General Khozin, the Military Commander of the Leningrad Front, over the deployment of troops on the Volkhov Front, notably over the question of 54th Army which remained under Leningrad command, despite Meretskov's wish to unify command in the Volkhov area. Stavka supported Khozin and A. A. Zhdanov, the political controller of the city.

Stavka ordered the troops on the Volkhov Front to continue advancing. Although officers and men were inadequately trained, 2nd Shock Army and 59th Army were fully committed to the attack. The advance was slow, and there was a lack of heavy artillery and ammunition. In a situation of great difficulty, Vlasov was appointed commander of 2nd Shock Army. Meretskov suggested that the army had to be reinforced before the thaw, or must be allowed to withdraw. The Germans pressed home their attack and on 19 March cut the lines of communication. Meretskov successfully counter-attacked, having obtained reinforcements, but much to his horrified indignation the Volkhov Front was disbanded and amalgamated with the Leningrad Front on 23 April. On 24 April Meretskov visited Stavka and in Stalin's presence warned that the position of 2nd Shock Army was critical: 'If nothing is done then a catastrophe is inevitable.'

No attention was paid to Meretskov's warnings. He was sent to join Zhukov. Meanwhile 2nd Shock Army's position worsened. On 8 June Meretskov was summoned back from the Western Front to Stavka. Stalin admitted that combining the Volkhov and Leningrad commands had been a great mistake and sent Meretskov and Vasilevsky to deal with the situation. On 10 June new attacks were ordered. After a week of heavy fighting a corridor 400 metres wide was cut from 2nd Shock Army to the railway line at Myasnoy Bor, and some of the wounded were taken out. By 23 June the area occupied by Soviet troops had greatly diminished and was subjected to heavy German fire. On the 24th a few men got out of the encirclement, but then the lines of communication were cut once more. Vlasov gave his men the order to break up into small groups and to make good their own escape.

It is not clear why Stavka did not respond to Meretskov's urgent pleas to allow 2nd Shock Army to withdraw or to provide substantial reinforcements when there was still time to do so. One might speculate that Meretskov's poor relations with Stalin may have been at the root of this failure. Meretskov's own memoirs, while mentioning Vlasov in a derogatory manner, show that Vlasov should be exonerated from blame for the situation in which the army found itself. The fate of 2nd Shock Army was one of the main elements in making Vlasov decide to take an anti-Stalinist position.

Meretskov made efforts to find Vlasov, but neither a squadron of tanks nor the partisans were successful. He was found by chance by Germans on 12 July 1942. The three-week period between the defeat of 2nd Shock Army and his capture was, he later said, very important in his appraisal of the situation. Crucial, too, in his decision to co-operate with his captors was the treatment he received and the people he met.

Vlasov was taken to General Lindemann, commander of XVIII Army, and was impressed by his courteous reception. After an interrogation at Lotzen, he was taken to Vinnitsa in Ukraine, a camp for 'Prominente'. Here Vlasov wrote a letter (Reichsführer SS records, US National Archives) to the Nazi authorities with another high-ranking Soviet prisoner-of-war, Colonel Vladimir Boyarsky, in which they tried to explain that the anti-Stalin sentiment to be found among the population at large, and prisoners-of-war in particular, should be utilized. They advocated the setting up of a Russian National Army. The letter was not understood by the Nazi authorities who read it, and it betrays the terrible naivety of the authors, who did not understand the situation in which they had become involved, and shows that they were very far from understanding the provenance of Nazi policy towards the occupied territories.

Vlasov was then visited by a series of individuals, all of whom disagreed with aspects of Nazi policy. The first of these was Gustav Hilger, a diplomat who had been with Ambassador von der Schulenberg in Moscow on the outbreak of war. Another was Lieutenant Dürksen from the Propaganda Department of the Oberkommando der Wehrmacht. His chief, Captain von Grote, was involved in producing anti-Stalinist propaganda to drop behind the Soviet lines and had been searching for an anti-Stalinist general who might be used for this purpose. Finally Vlasov met Captain Wilfred Strik-Strikfeldt who had been sent from Fremde Heere Ost, a branch of the General Staff engaged in intelligence gathering on the Soviet Union. He was a Baltic German who had been educated in St Petersburg and had served in the Russian Imperial Army. Strik-Strikfeldt had a high regard for Russia and felt that the Second World War provided the opportunity to help Russia. In this Strik-Strikfeldt was unusual. Most of the other opponents of Nazi Ostpolitik felt that Hitler's idea that Slavs were subhuman and the concomitant policies in the occupied areas of the USSR were making resistance to the German advance much fiercer and thereby making the job of the German military much more difficult.

Few people other than Strik-Strikfeldt had any interest in the future of Russia, and he became the linchpin of the 'Wlassow-Aktion' as he continued to assure Vlasov that policies could be changed and progress would be made. These meetings, it can be argued, were the critical element in Vlasov's acceptance of the proposal that he should lead an anti-Stalinist opposition movement. He met people who were adamant that Nazi policies had to be and could be altered. Vlasov's experience of the Red Army made him think that if someone of a low rank, a Captain or a Colonel, spoke of policy change, then it had been sanctioned at a high level. Individual initiatives would not have been possible. Therefore he seems to have concluded that there was a real possibility of an alteration in Nazi policies towards the USSR. It took him about a year in captivity to begin to see that Nazism, although analogous, did not operate in the same way as the Stalinist system.

The subsequent development of the Russian Liberation Movement was a product of the conflicting aims and tensions between Nazi ideology, the opponents of Ostpolitik and the aspirations of the anti-Stalinist Russians. Vlasov became caught up in a complex political situation which he did not understand and for which his previous experience had not prepared him.

The autumn of 1942 saw the production of a number of leaflets by Wehrmacht Propaganda to drop behind the Red Army lines in an attempt to encourage desertion. Vlasov's signature was used to give this greater appeal. It culminated in the first major statement of the Russian Liberation Movement: the Smolensk Declaration published on 27 December 1942. Vlasov, as chairman of the Russian Committee, supposedly in Smolensk, had signed the Declaration which announced the formation of a Russian Liberation Army and announced a thirteen-point programme. This was merely a propaganda ploy. The Committee had not been allowed to leave Berlin and no army was being formed. However, Strik-Strikfeldt had arranged for the pilot to drop the leaflet 'by mistake' on the German rather than on the Soviet side of the lines. This made the population of the occupied territories and Soviet citizens in the German armed forces think that Nazi policy was about to be altered. Smolensk was inundated with letters and people seeking the mythical Russian Committee. Soviet soldiers in the Wehrmacht began sewing badges on their uniforms to signify that they were members of the Russian Liberation Army. Vlasov had no authority whatsoever over these men except inasmuch as they regarded him as their leader.

The publication of the Smolensk Declaration justified the hopes of its sponsors. It showed that measures designed to deal with the aspirations of anti-Stalinists had substantial support, and the opponents of Ostpolitik considered that on the basis of this support they could persuade the Nazi authorities to alter their behaviour towards the population of the occupied territories of the Soviet Union. Following this, Wehrmacht Propaganda organized two tours of the occupied territories for Vlasov. At the outset Vlasov refused to co-operate, saying that he could not promise anything before the enterprise was sanctioned at the highest level. He was finally persuaded by the suggestion that the Nazi authorities would acquiesce in the enterprise once they were faced by an accomplished fact. During his two visits Vlasov put over a nationalist and down-to-earth message to which the population responded very positively.

In March 1943 Vlasov's Open Letter was published: 'Why I decided to fight Bolshevism.' This was designed to strengthen the effect created by his visits to the occupied territories. It consisted of a relatively sophisticated explanation of Vlasov's change of heart, a change which he called on his countrymen to copy. It was also a call to arms. The letter stressed that Vlasov was a typical product of Soviet society, and it emphasized how gradually he had come to the realization that the government was not acting in the best interests of the people. The composition of the Open Letter, like the Smolensk Declaration, is likely to have been influenced by M. A. Zykov. His identity remains a mystery, and although it is thought that he may have worked with Bukharin on *Izvestiya*, this hypothesis has yet to be proved. He was captured early in the war and seemed to have a very clear understanding of the situation and the possibilities facing him and his compatriots. His contribution to the evolution of the ideas expressed in the Russian Liberation Movement was considerable. He disappeared in 1944, probably murdered by the SD because of his Jewish origins, even though he was being used in propaganda against the USSR.

To judge from the Soviet propaganda directed against Vlasov, the Soviet authorities, too, feared that Nazi policy was about to change and that the Nazi authorities were going to take cognizance of anti-Soviet attitudes. The very success of Vlasov's trips, however, brought the whole enterprise to an abrupt halt. During a speech at Gatchina, he referred to the fact that the Russians were now 'guests of the Germans' but that in the future, when the war was over and the Russians were at home, then the Germans would be their 'guests'. This was reported to Himmler, who was outraged at the idea that Slav subhumans could even contemplate the idea of playing host to Germans. He then told Hitler, and an order was issued by Field Marshal Keitel to move Vlasov to a prisoner-of-war camp and that his name could only be used for propaganda purposes. Rosenberg, too, was unhappy at the prospect of supporting a Russian national movement. It seemed that Vlasov had lost all support within the Nazi hierarchy.

A further blow to the Russian Liberation Movement came from the conference at Berghof on 8 June 1943, where Hitler met Field Marshal Keitel, Chief of the High Command, and Colonel-General Zeitzler, Chief of the General Staff. Hitler made it clear that the political inferences being drawn by some of the military were erroneous and stated that there was no possibility of creating a Russian army. 'We will never build a Russian Army, that is a phantom of the first order.' Hitler sensed that Russian and Nazi aims were so disparate that there could not be real co-operation between them and that, furthermore, anyone treated hitherto as a subhuman could not be expected to be a reliable ally. Throughout this conference Keitel and Zeitzler were at pains not to reveal the full extent of the military formations composed of the national minorities of the Soviet Union and the numbers of Great Russians who were already in the Wehrmacht.

When Vlasov finally heard the results of the conference he seems to have understood that the whole 'Wlassow-Aktion' was a forlorn hope and was never going to get approval from the Nazi hierarchy. He asked if he could return to prisoner-of-war camp, but his entourage dissuaded him, saying that at least they could work to help the condition of both POWs and Ostarbeiters. Vlasov was placed under virtual house arrest in Berlin but from here he was able to visit the training camp at Dabendorf, which had been authorized by Colonel Gehlen and Count Claus von Stauffenberg in November 1942 and which became the centre of activities in the further development of the Russian Liberation Movement. Here propagandists were trained and courses were developed for them. Discussions at Dabendorf played an important rôle in the development of the programme and ideas within the Russian Liberation Movement. Vlasov was also taken on trips around Germany by Strik- Strikfeldt. In a convalescent home for SS officers in Bavaria Vlasov met Frau Heidi Bielenberg, the widow of an SS officer, whom eventually he married. This marriage has been the matter of some debate among Vlasov's supporters as Frau Bielenberg spoke no Russian, knew very little about the USSR and could hardly be imagined as providing the kind of support Vlasov would need at the head of a Russian national movement. In addition, Vlasov may have known that his first wife was still alive. Maybe Vlasov thought that he would get access to SS circles through his wife, or the SS considered that this marriage would keep Vlasov's mind off politics, and that in any case Vlasov had lost faith in a successful outcome for the Russian Liberation Movement.

Matters remained at a low ebb until the summer of 1944, when Colonel Gunther d'Alquen, who was working on the 'Skorpion' propaganda campaign on the eastern front, became convinced that Nazi policies towards the population were mistaken. He persuaded Himmler to meet Vlasov, but this was delayed owing to the 20 July plot, and Himmler finally met Vlasov on 16 September when it was agreed that Vlasov should be allowed to command divisions of Russians, and that KONR (the Committee for the Liberation of the Peoples of Russia) should be formed with the intention of producing a Manifesto of the Russian Liberation Movement.

The publication of the Manifesto on 14 November 1944 in Prague, the last major Slav city in German hands, was not the triumph for which Russians had hoped. No one from the higher echelons of the Nazi party attended the ceremony. While some of the leadership of the Russian Liberation Movement thought that they might still have a part to play in the final dénouement of the war, and that the Germans, now that they were in real difficulties, would allow the Russians to deal with their own affairs, leaving the German forces to concentrate on the western front, Vlasov had no such illusions. He thought that it was necessary to leave a record of the programme of the Russian Liberation Movement so that it should not be misrepresented in the future.

Vlasov was given command of two divisions on 28 January 1945. This caused further dispute as the Russians claimed that Himmler had promised ten divisions. Furthermore, those Soviet citizens already serving in the Wehrmacht were not allowed to join the divisions, which were recruited from among prisoners-of-war. This was unsatisfactory as these men had been less exposed to the influence of the ideas of the Russian Liberation Movement than had those who had already considered themselves as part of it. Vlasov appears to have busied himself with the minor details of these military formations in order to avoid thinking about the major insoluble issues. German commanders wanted to use the KONR divisions as cannon fodder in a last attempt to fight the advancing Red Army. The Russians had a number of nebulous plans and wanted to preserve their men as a nucleus of an anti-Stalinist force with the mistaken idea that, once the Allies had defeated Nazism, they would then begin to combat the other totalitarian power, the USSR.

Finally there occurred what George Fischer defined as 'the most dramatic single episode of the entire history of wartime Soviet opposition'. On 5 May, participants in the Prague Rising begged for help from the 1st Division. Originally General Bunyachenko, the Divisonal Commander, had not wished to become involved in Czech affairs, but later decided that fighting the remains of an SS division alongside the insurgents in Prague would help to convince the advancing American armies of the 1st Division's good faith. Vlasov did not share this view but was prepared to allow Bunyachenko to operate independently. When it became clear that the Americans were not going to liberate Prague but were waiting outside the city for the Red Army to get there, the hopes of the 1st Division were dashed, and they had to evacuate the city in the wake of the retreating Germans.

Vlasov attempted to cross the lines to the Americans, but when it became clear that he would be unable to do so he gave the order to his men to disband and work their way out individually. Vlasov was captured by a Soviet column. The circumstances are not entirely clear as the available accounts differ. At the end of July 1946 he was tried *in camera*. Apparently the Soviet authorities had originally planned a show trial for both Vlasov and the captured Cossack General Krasnov but had subsequently changed this plan. The published transcript of the trial has Vlasov admitting to cowardice as an explanation for his behaviour. He and the others captured and tried with him were judged guilty and hanged. According to General Grigorenko's memoirs, Vlasov while in prison said that he hoped that in the future his motives would be better understood by his countrymen.

Vlasov's career shows him to have been a good soldier who got caught up in an immensely complicated political situation. Once in German hands, he gave his name and support to the Russian Liberation Movement but had relatively little input into its development, which was determined more by the conflicts and contradictions within Nazism than by the views or aspirations of the anti-Stalinist Russians. These Russians considered that they were fighting for Russia but against Stalin who had betrayed them. Stalin's refusal to sign the Geneva Convention had condemned Soviet prisoners-of-war to terrible conditions. Moreover, the policies of the 1930s were a betrayal of all the freedoms which the revolution had promised. Many of the initial premises of the Russian Liberation Movement had been based on a faulty understanding of Nazism. Some Russians had hoped that the Germans came as liberators and that only through war could the Stalinist system be changed. It was their tragedy that the war was not one of liberation but of Nazi conquest, which had no thought of rational solutions to the Russian tragedy.

BIBLIOGRAPHY

Andreyev, C., *Vlasov and the Russian Liberation Movement*, Cambridge, 1987.

Ausky, S. A., *Vojska Generala Vlasova v Cechach*, Vysehrad, 1992.

Dallin, A., *German Rule in Russia 1941–45: A Study in Occupational Policies*, 2nd edn, London, 1981.

Dallin, A. and Mavrogordata, R. S., 'The Soviet Reaction to Vlasov', *World Politics*, no. 8, 1956.

Fischer, G., *Soviet Opposition to Stalin*, Cambridge, Mass., 1952.

Grigorenko, P. G., *V podpol'e mozhno vstretit' tol'ko krys*, New York, 1981.

Hoffmann, J., *Die Geschichte der Wlassow-Armee*, Freiburg im Breisgau, 1984.

Khozin, M. S., 'Ob odnoy maloissledovannoy operatsii', *Voenno-istoricheskii Zhurnal*, no. 2, 1966.

Kolesnik, A., *ROA – Vlasovskaya armiya*, Kharkov, 1990.

Kolesnik, A., *General Vlasov, predatel' ili geroi?*, Moscow, 1991.

Meretskov, K. A., *Na sluzhbe narodu*, Moscow, 1968.

Meretskov, K. A., 'Na Volkhovskikh rubezhakh', *Voenno-istoricheskii Zhurnal*, no. 1, 1965.

Pekarsky, I., 'Kak byl zakhvachen general Vlasov', in Pozdnyakov, V. V. (ed.), *A. A. Vlasov*, Syracuse, 1973.

Strik-Strikfeldt, W., *Gegen Stalin und Hitler. General Wlassow und die russische Freiheitsbewegung*, Mainz, 1970; trans. D. Footman as *Against Stalin and Hitler*, London, 1970.

US National Archives (Captured German Records).

Vlasov, A., 'Novye metody boevoy ucheby', *Krasnaya zvezda*, 3 October 1940; reprinted in *Novoe v podgotovke voisk*, izd. Krasnaya Armiya, Kiev, 1940.

Voenno-istoricheskii Zhurnal, no. 6, 1990, and nos 2, 4, 7, 9, 12, 1991.

Kliment Yefremovich
VOROSHILOV

DMITRI VOLKOGONOV

History has a way of leaving people of talent and virtue in the shade for long periods, sometimes forever. She is equally capable of raising to the pinnacle of publicity and popularity the most mediocre, faceless, intellectually dim individuals. Marshal of the Soviet Union Kliment Voroshilov belongs emphatically in this latter category. He was one of Stalin's closest comrades and he became one of the best known figures on the military, state and Party scene. For many years since his death on 2 December 1969 I have handled literally thousands of documents bearing his name – orders, articles, top secret notes – and I have yet to see a single item of evidence attesting to any intellectual power, genuine civic feeling, vision or moral stature. Historical accident, which gained a wide margin in the depths of the totalitarian system – a system which valued obedience, assidulty, ruthlessness, obsession – raised Voroshilov to the highest level of state power. It was a system that functioned by means of physical violence, but also by means of a web of myths and legends created by its vast propaganda machine. Voroshilov was one of the first of the long-lived myths of Stalinized public consciousness. His life provides a prism through which the contours of the system emerge clearly.

Kliment Yefremovich Voroshilov was born on 23 January 1881 in the village of Verkhnee in the province of Yekaterinoslav. His father was a poor railway watchman and his mother a daily help. His early life was like that of so many others at that time – early experience of work, deprivation, hopelessness. Despite his lack of education – he claimed to have had only two years of schooling – he was caught up by the revolutionary movement at the turn of the century. By the age of seventeen he had joined a Social Democratic circle where, with the help of its student members, he mastered the *Communist Manifesto* and began illegal activities. Arrests and deportations followed, of course, but it was not hard to escape under the comparatively lax conditions then prevailing.

He attended the Stockholm and London Party Congresses, in 1906 and 1907 respectively, and met Lenin and Stalin and other Social Democrats who had adopted various romantic names as 'professional revolutionaries'. He worked at intervals in factories in Lugansk,Tsaritsyn and Petrograd and thus avoided mobilization at the beginning of the First World War.

With the February and October Revolutions of 1917, the former machine operator found himself in the thick of it. He was soon noticed by the leaders, was a delegate at the VI Party Congress in August 1917, became a member of the All-Russian Central Executive of Soviets, then a member of the Cheka, and was despatched to Ukraine to help secure Soviet power there. During the Civil War, under his direction units loyal to Moscow managed with difficulty to break through the rebellious districts of the Don to Tsaritsyn – Stalingrad from 1925 to 1961, Volgograd until the present day – where his military career really begins.

Having never once worn uniform, soon after the revolution he was being described as a war leader, in official Bolshevik circles a 'proletarian war leader'. He started in Ukraine where he led a motley and badly organized mass of armed people called 5th Army which, after its transfer to Tsaritsyn, was known as 10th Army. Together with Stalin, who was responsible for food supply in the south, political commissar Ye. A. Shchadenko, and a number of former tsarist officers, he helped organize the defence of the town which was important, not only from the military standpoint, but also for the supply of food to the starving centre which was in the grip of civil war.

While Voroshilov's contemporaries testify to his personal courage and fearlessness, he displayed no leadership qualities whatsoever on the Tsaritsyn Front. Lacking the least military knowledge, he put his trust in partisan, 'proletarian' methods of warfare and was suspicious of the military experts, recruited by Trotsky from among former tsarist officers. As a member of the war council of the Southern Front and Commander of 10th Army, he clashed frequently with the Front Commander, Pavel Sytin, an experienced and knowledgeable military man. Often, with Stalin's support, Voroshilov addressed himself directly to Moscow, to Lenin and to Commander-in-ChiefVatsetis, in an effort to compromise Sytin and the other military experts.

On one occasion Vatsetis was driven to send a sharp telegram from Arzamas to the Front Revolutionary Military Committee, which among other things said: 'The present catastrophic situation in Tsaritsyn is entirely your responsibility, for it derives exclusively from your refusal to work with Front Commander Sytin. . . . I categorically order you to follow his orders and to stay in close contact with him.'

Voroshilov had long believed that the revolution must cast off the traditional methods of warfare and rely more on 'popular', partisan actions. Even Lenin, who had no military knowledge, knew that this line was deeply flawed. Speaking at the Eighth Party Congress in March 1919, he condemned the 'military opposition', of which the 'hero of Tsaritsyn' was a part, and criticized Voroshilov for eschewing military experts: 'Voroshilov said they had no military experts and suffered 60,000 losses. This is terrible. The heroism of the Tsaritsyn army lives in the popular memory, but to say we managed without military experts is hardly to defend the Party line. . . . Comrade Voroshilov's trouble is that he doesn't want to jettison this old partisan way of thinking.'

During the Civil War Voroshilov was sent to various sectors by the Party Central Committee: at the end of 1918 he was appointed Interior Commissar for Ukraine, Commander of Kharkov Military District, a member of the Revolutionary Military Committee of 1st Cavalry Army. For his part in suppressing the Kronstadt revolt he was awarded his second Order of the Red Banner, his first having been conferred for the North Caucasus campaign.

A member of the Central Committee from 1921, Voroshilov showed exemplary zeal and expeditiousness in all the tasks he was set. He was one of those military leaders who, while contributing nothing new to the field, proved himself an obedient and consistent executor of other people's wishes. On Stalin's insistence, he was appointed to the highly responsible post of Commander of Moscow Military District in place of Trotsky's friend, Nikolai Muralov. After the death of Frunze in 1925, Voroshilov – again on Stalin's recommendation – was made Commissar for War, remaining in the post (renamed Defence in 1934) until May 1940. It was during this time that the Soviet Union, feeling military pressure from all sides, and wedded as it was to the Comintern mission of world revolution, paid particular attention to its military structures. Along with collectivization and industrialization, the building of a mighty army and navy was a basic concern of the Party led by Stalin, who became omnipotent at the beginning of the 1930s, and the country now had to suffer endless deprivation in the name of a freedom which, in the conditions of the Bolshevik system was, alas, a bitter fiction. In these circumstances, Voroshilov was the perfect commissar for the 'leader of the peoples'. Maintaining friendly relations, even using the familiar form of address throughout their lives, Voroshilov turned himself into Stalin's submissive, zealous executive.

Moreover, Voroshilov was in fact the first to invoke the cult of Stalin, and he did it by referring to Stalin's experience on the battlefield. Thus, on Stalin's 50th birthday, 21 December 1929, Voroshilov wrote an article for *Pravda*, entitled 'Stalin and the Red Army'. In it he wrote:

Stalin was perhaps the only man sent by the Central Committee from one front to another, choosing places that were both most dangerous and most threatening to the revolution. Wherever things were relatively quiet and going well, you would not find Stalin. But wherever the Red Army was cracking . . . wherever the counter-revolution threatened the very existence of Soviet power, wherever disarray and panic might quickly turn into helplessness and catastrophe, Comrade Stalin would be on hand.

Ten years after the October Revolution the pretender to the post of dictator had emerged, and that was Stalin. He had great need of mass social and ideological support in order to crown himself for the unique post of 'leader of the peoples'. One of the first to assist him in his task was the head of the most influential and powerful agency, that of the Red Army.

Vast resources were thrown into creating domestic industries for the building of aircraft, tanks, ammunition and chemical weapons. For the record, it was Voroshilov who initiated the manufacture of chemical and bacteriological weapons. At the end of March 1934, he wrote to Stalin: 'I enclose the draft proposals and facts and figures for the chemo-bacterio-logical work which we asked for from Comrades Fishman, Gai, Velikanov and Demikhovsky. The proposed organization, which (with your help) we will try to staff with the proper people, should create the necessary conditions to develop this work. I request your approval of these plans.' The document bears the scrawled legend: 'In favour. Signed: I. Stalin, V. Kuibyshev, Molotov'.

The author of this frightful scheme, however, found few laurels on the field of battle. During the Soviet–Japanese conflict at Lake Khasan, Voroshilov, with Stalin's participation, sent orders of a mostly politically threatening kind which paralysed the confidence and capacity of the Far East Military Council. In the comparatively minor clashes, despite superior numbers the Red Army lost more than 3,000 killed and wounded. On 31 August 1938, however, Voroshilov convened the Main Military Soviet and cast all the blame for the Red Army's hesitant performance on Marshal Blyukher. On 4 September 1938 Voroshilov ordered the disbandment of the Far East Red Banner Front Directorate, and, with Stalin's prior agreement, Blyukher's removal as Commander and hence his tragic end. But this was a conflict of local significance. A more serious failure, and one that would cool Stalin's attitude towards the 'legendary commissar', was the inglorious 105-day Soviet–Finnish War of 1939–40.

As Commander-in-Chief of the forces ranged against Finland, Voroshilov (like all the Soviet leadership) manifestly underrated the Finns' endurance, courage and skill. Reporting to Stalin, who relied on information supplied by Beria and the Main Intelligence Directorate of the Red Army, Voroshilov wrote: 'Most of the Finnish equipment consists of pre-war models of the old tsarist army. . . . The mood of their reservists is depressed. . . . The working masses of Finland . . . are threatening to mete out justice on those who pursue a policy hostile to the Soviet Union.'

It required vast effort by a great country to break the resistance of the small Finnish army. Apart from their defence capabilities, the Finns also exposed the very poor training of the Soviet troops and especially that of their High Command. A particularly painful blow was delivered by the encirclement and destruction of 44th Rifle Division. Following this, Moscow reverted to tested methods: courts martial and executions. In his reports to Stalin, Voroshilov characteristically laid the blame for military failure on the shoulders of others: 'I regard a radical purge of the corps, divisions and regiments as essential. General Headquarters should warn Meretskov (I have already done so personally), that if he does not bring the troops to order, he will be removed and tried.'

Meanwhile, Beria was building up the pressure. In a message to Voroshilov he wrote: '139th Rifle Division is in difficulties. They have no fodder at all, they've had no fuel for three days, the regiments have been fighting for ten days; they have lost 800-900 men. 80 per cent of the officers of the 609th Regiment have been withdrawn. The troops are scattering. Morale is depressed.' Voroshilov knew that a similar report had gone to Stalin. It was only at the beginning of March that the Finnish defence was broken, to the great embarrassment of Voroshilov and Stalin. The war had cost about 70,000 Soviet soldiers' lives, plus the profound political isolation of the USSR which was condemned as the aggressor by the rest of the world. This had been no easy campaign, such as the division of Poland in 1939 had been.

Stalin learnt his lesson. A month after the end of the Finnish War, Voroshilov was replaced as Defence Commissar by Timoshenko, a military leader of the same school. Stalin tried both to humiliate Voroshilov as much as possible and to find a scapegoat, so that, while he made him Deputy Chairman of the Council of Peoples' Commissars on defence matters, everyone knew he was in serious disgrace.

The Winter War had shown to the world that the 'legendary Red Marshal' possessed neither strategic thinking, nor operational vision, nor organizational ability. A man with two seasons of schooling and military training only in the Politburo, where one had to guess the leader's wishes, had turned out to be the 'Emperor with no clothes'.

This would be demonstrated again, in full measure, during the Great Patriotic War. Stalin tried to use Voroshilov as a Stavka Representative and a member of the State Defence Committee, and as Commander-in-Chief of the Leningrad Front. In fact, Stalin kept him in this last post for all of one week. Even before this, he had sent an eloquent cipher to Leningrad addressed to Voroshilov, Malenkov, Zhdanov and Kuznetsov, which read: 'General Headquarters considers the tactics of the Leningrad Front ruinous. Leningrad Front thinks only of one thing: any way to retreat and how to find new lines to retreat to. Isn't it time you got rid of these heroes of retreat?'

The message was ominous. Voroshilov's orders and postings invariably worsened the situation. All that remained in the ageing marshal was his failing courage, and no wherewithal to alter the position.

In early February 1942 Stalin sent Voroshilov as Stavka Representative to the Volkhov Front to stiffen the efforts being made to lift the siege of Leningrad. But this effort, too, came to nothing. Stalin in a direct-line conversation then suggested to Voroshilov that he take over command of the Front. Voroshilov at once declined, citing trivial excuses, but in reality fearing the responsibility and feeling utterly unsure of himself. Enraged by this refusal, Stalin then dictated a memorandum 'On Comrade Voroshilov's work', addressed to the Central Committee and Control Commission, and later ratified as a Politburo decision of 1 April 1942, as often happened. It merits extended quotation:

> First. The war with Finland of 1939–40 exposed the poor state and backwardness of the Defence Commissariat leadership. The Red Army lacked mortars and machine guns, it had no proper inventory of aircraft and tanks, the troops had no proper winter clothing, or food-supply bases. Great neglect was revealed in the work of such Administrations as Artillery, Battle Training, Air Force. . . . This all led to the war being drawn out and to unnecessary losses. At the end of March 1940, at a CC Plenum, Comrade Voroshilov . . . had to acknowledge the bankruptcy of his leadership. The CC saw it as necessary to relieve him of his post.
>
> Second. At the beginning of the war with Germany Comrade Voroshilov was given command of the Northwestern Axis with the chief aim of defending Leningrad. He committed serious mistakes there: he issued a decree on the election of battalion commanders in the Home Guard, a decree annulled by Stavka as leading to disorganization and undermining discipline in the Red Army; he organized a Military Council for the defence of Leningrad but was not a member of it himself. This decree was similarly rescinded by Stavka as incorrect and damaging, since the workers of Leningrad might have thought Comrade Voroshilov had not joined the defence council as he did not believe in the defence of Leningrad; he was distracted by the creation of workers' battalions which were poorly armed (with shotguns, pikes, daggers, and so on), while he neglected the city's artillery defence. In view of all this, the State Defence Committee recalled Comrade Voroshilov from Leningrad.
>
> Third. In view of his request, Comrade Voroshilov was posted in February to the Volkhov Front as Stavka Representative to help command the Front. He remained there about a month. However, his stay did not produce the desired result. Wishing once more to give Comrade Voroshilov the chance to show his experience in Front operations, the Central Committee suggested he take over command of the Volkhov Front himself. Comrade Voroshilov, however, reacted negatively to this proposal and did not wish to take the responsibility, despite the fact that it had decisive importance for the defence of Leningrad, citing the fact that it was a difficult Front and he did not want to fail again.
>
> In view of the foregoing, the Central Committee decrees: First, that it be acknowledged that Comrade Voroshilov did not justify himself in the task allotted to

him at the front. Second, that Comrade Voroshilov be posted to work in the rear.

The style was typical of Stalin. By repeatedly referring to 'Comrade Voroshilov', he exposed the lack of substance in Voroshilov's title as 'First Marshal'. While it is true that Stalin gave Voroshilov another substantial post at the end of 1942, when he made him chief of the Partisan movement, it proved necessary to remove him from that position, too, after only three months. Henceforth, Stalin used him in a representative capacity, for decorative purposes, where he could do less damage.

Voroshilov could count himself very lucky. He was not shot, like General Pavlov, nor cashiered, like General Kulik, who were blamed by Stalin for the disasters of 1941 and 1942, respectively. Stalin evidently felt unable to overlook the services Voroshilov had performed in the bloody purges before the war. This separate chapter in the life of the man needs to be illuminated, not least because Voroshilov's concrete acts had a direct effect on the catastrophic opening of the war.

The chapter opens with a statement Voroshilov made at the Main Military Council in November 1938: 'In the course of the purge of the Red Army in 1937–8, we expelled more than 40,000 men,' he said. Considering that many of the 'expelled' were shot, and remembering that the purge by terror had gone on before and would continue after the years mentioned, it is not difficult to imagine the scale of the human and strategic damage wreaked on the military by this Stalinist operation, an operation actively assisted by Voroshilov, who had been elevated to Marshal of the Soviet Union in 1935 as one of the five Generals so honoured.

Voroshilov fully supported the general purge in the country that was aimed at getting rid of all potential opponents among the former Trotskyists and supporters of the various oppositions, former tsarist officers, and ideologically dubious individuals. Voroshilov gave the general directive for the rooting out of 'enemies of the people' in the Red Army carried out by brutalized minions. When things got out of control and the army was virtually without any leadership, he was obliged on 3 January 1939 to issue Order No. 001 which read: 'Permission to arrest Red Army officers of senior, higher and middle ranks may only be given by me.' He had already issued a similar order about the arrest of Trotskyists and 'double-dealers' in June 1937, and, indeed, throughout the earlier period a series of telegrams giving instructions for the execution of particular individuals bear his signature.

The consequences of this policy were not long in coming. Of five Marshals of the Soviet Union three were shot; fifteen out of sixteen army commanders; sixty out of sixty-seven corps commanders; 136 out of 169 divisional commanders; 221 out of 397 brigade commanders; all four admirals (the highest rank of flag-officers, in the contemporary parlance);

all six vice-admirals, nine out of fifteen rear-admirals. Thousands of commanders at regimental, battalion, squadron and equivalent levels were arrested. The violence continued for two years. It was surely unique in history, that the head of the army himself should organize, sanction, direct and initiate such a bloody assault on its officer corps. The man people had considered a military leader and state official was nothing more than an executioner, a henchman of the Executioner-in-Chief. He was motivated only by the desire to carry out Stalin's wishes and to be worthy of his trust. The lack of elementary human or civic decency, his dogmatic mind and false sense of duty made Voroshilov a first-hand accomplice in the great crime.

He must share with Stalin the blame for the fact that on the eve of the war regimental commanders were yesterday's company commanders, that divisional commanders were inexperienced officers, who had been elevated by several rungs at once, and that the highest echelon of the army and navy was plainly unprepared for the burden they were about to have to bear.

Thousands of arrested officers wrote to Voroshilov, asking him to sort out the 'misunderstanding'. With the exception of a few cases, he was deaf to these appeals. Before being arrested, Marshal Yegorov wrote to his former comrade-in-arms: 'Two months have passed since I was relieved of any work. I'll say nothing of the fact that it is unbearable to sit idle. The main, the most important thing is that my life has come to a complete stop, I have been cast overboard like some traitor.' Voroshilov sent the letter on to Stalin with the sole comment: 'This is the fourth such statement.' Yegorov's fate was that of Blyukher and Tukhachevsky. In fact, it was with the Tukhachevsky case that the main campaign of slaughtering the military began. It was Voroshilov who staged the farce 'to expose and discuss the counter-revolutionary military Fascist organization' that went on from 1 to 4 June 1937 at the Military Council attached to the Defence Commissariat. Voroshilov gave the report himself. The fate of the unfortunates was sealed in Order No. 072 of 7 June 1937. He knew the outcome of the case before it took place a few days later: 'The German-Japanese Fascists will not live to see the defeat of the Red Army. It has been and will remain invincible. The agent of Japanese-German Fascism, Trotsky, will know once again that his faithful accomplices, the Gamarniks and Tukhachevskys, the Yakirs and Uboreviches and the rest of the swine who are lackeys of the capitalists, will be wiped from the face of the earth and their memory will be cursed and forgotten.'

Such ferocity was not, of course, accidental. Dealing mercilessly with opponents was rewarded by the Bolsheviks as the highest revolutionary virtue. Stalin's 'comrades-in-arms' vied with each other in their implacability towards potential enemies, not that this saved many of them from a sticky end themselves. Earlier, in September 1936, Nikolai Bukharin, who was still at large, despite the ominous suspicions hanging over him, wrote a trusting, friendly letter to Voroshilov, asking how he could believe such accusations as only 'people unworthy of respect' could make. Voroshilov replied at once on 3 September 1936, sending copies of Bukharin's letter and his own reply to Stalin and other members of the Politburo. Addressing Bukharin in the familiar form, he wrote:

Comrade Bukharin,
I return your letter in which you permit yourself to make vile attacks on the Party leadership. If you were hoping by your letter to convince me of your complete innocence, all you have convinced me of is that henceforth I should distance myself from you as far as possible, regardless of the outcome of your case. And if you do not repudiate in writing your foul epithets against the Party Leadership, I shall even regard you as a scoundrel.

Preoccupied, as countless documents show, with 'cleaning up' the army, Voroshilov had little time to give to training the forces, to raising the operational skills of the officer corps, or ensuring the technological equipping of the units.

His name is associated not only with the terror against the Soviet people, however, but also against the Poles. After the division of Poland in the autumn of 1939, on Stalin's orders and the suggestion of Beria and Mekhlis, Voroshilov 'helped' to settle the fate of the Polish 'prisoners-of-war'. The resulting instructions called for 'Generals, Lieutenant-Colonels, major military and state officials and all the rest of the officers to be relocated in the south (at Starobelsk); intelligence and counter-intelligence officers, gendarmes, police and prison staff to be sent to Ostashkov concentration camp in Kalinin Oblast; soldier prisoners-of-war whose homeland is in the German part of Poland to be held in Kozelsk concentration camp, Smolensk Oblast, and in Putivl camp, Suma Oblast.' These were not internment camps, they were death camps.

Perhaps these landmarks in the Marshal's career were more impressive than his feats at the front, where he never seemed able to show himself at his best. Stalin did not want to risk putting his faithful retainer into the active army for long, even at the outbreak of war. And he had good reason. Voroshilov had barely arrived in Leningrad when he organized a series of counter-attacks in the old style of the Civil War, and on 8 September 1941 with Zhdanov composed an order to scuttle the Baltic Fleet 'in order to blockade the roadstead and harbours'. Stalin's reply came in only two days: By order of Stavka, 'Marshal of the Soviet Union Comrade Voroshilov is to be relieved of his duties as Commander of the Leningrad Front. Comrade Voroshilov is to hand over the affairs of the Front and Comrade Zhukov is to receive them within 24 hours.'

After the Volkhov Front, Voroshilov settled down in the strategic rear, where he worked on training reinforcements, and spent much of his plentiful free time trying to grasp the meaning of his military career. Before the war, he had helped to instil the notion of the easy victory over any enemy. The term 'little bloodshed' had become common parlance among the military, who had been badly prepared for full-scale modern warfare. But the Finnish war had exposed the empty arrogance of Voroshilov's words about 'little bloodshed'. He had dinned into the public the idea that 'officers had been trained to great heights', but in his written report to the Politburo of December 1939 he had had to write bitterly of matters in Karelia: 'The infantry does not exist as an organized force at the Front, a mass of people just hang around the Front (in crowds), virtually undirected. . . . Military and political commanders still think in terms of an easy, non-stop campaign in Finland.'

Such remarks could be regarded as self-critical, were it not for the fact they were followed at once by immoral accusations against Meretskov and other commanders, in fact all those lower down the hierarchy below Voroshilov. Everyone was guilty but him.

At this point, it is clearly unnecessary to dwell on the question whether or not Voroshilov was anything of a military theorist. Obviously he was not. For his part, however, he loved to address all kinds of audiences with long reports, and to put his name to long articles, all written for him. His big book, *The Defence of the USSR*, came out in 1937. Nearly 700 pages long, it contained all his speeches, articles and reports, with pride of place being given to his article 'Stalin and the Red Army', an unbridled panegyric to the 'leader of the peoples'.

The book contains such obligatory articles as 'The Union of the Red Army and the Population', 'Imperialist Slander', 'Military Chemistry', 'The Horse and the Automobile', 'For Growth in Livestock, For a Good Horse!'. There is nothing, however, on national defence, military strategy, operational skills or tactics. His superficial, agitational writings were concerned only with propaganda in the traditional Communist vein. Reading this unbearably boring material, one can say it is not only a literary monument of the epoch, but also of the plainly medicore intelligence of the 'First Marshal of the Land of the Soviets', testimony to the profound limitations of the man under whose leadership the army approached its severest test in the Great Patriotic War.

The war virtually ripped the mantle of national hero from Voroshilov's back. All the high decorations – twice Hero of the Soviet Union, Hero of Socialist Labour – he received after the war were in honour of various jubilees while occupying elevated but mainly symbolic, figurehead posts. At one time, the Politburo entrusted Soviet culture to his untutored hands. The writers, conductors, composers and artists, when they met the sclerotic old man, must have thought that it suited the system to ensure that the nation's culture should be in tune with its curator.

After the war Stalin treated this military has-been with scornful condescension, indulging him, it is true, with the post of Deputy Chairman of the Council of Ministers, which he retained until Stalin's death. When he was already past seventy, Voroshilov entered a new and political phase of his career. Stalin's comrades, even before they had laid his mummy to rest in the Mausoleum alongside Lenin, decided that, as a man who could be relied on to carry out the Politburo's wishes without demur, Voroshilov was the ideal person to be Chairman of the Presidium of the Supreme Soviet, or nominal Head of State. And so he was, at first: he supported the plot to arrest Beria and he dutifully legitimized the decrees handed down by the Party's highest instance. For example, when in 1954 Khrushchev, on his own initiative and virtually without consulting anyone, handed over the Crimea to Ukraine, Voroshilov blithely rubber-stamped this unconstitutional act by passing the appropriate decisions through the Supreme Soviet.

But soon after the XX Party Congress, as soon as genuine de-Stalinization became an issue, together with Molotov, Malenkov and Kaganovich, Voroshilov came out against Khrushchev. The decrepit Marshal clung to his office for another two years, but he was relieved of the burden of supreme power in 1960, before his eightieth birthday, giving up his place to L. I. Brezhnev, still little-known but equally lacklustre. But this was not the end of Voroshilov's humiliation. At the XXII Party Congress Khrushchev and his associates again launched an attack on the 'anti-Party group'. Voroshilov was not spared. Khrushchev declared that the Marshal bore full responsibility 'for many mass repressions against Party, soviet, economic, military and Young Communist cadres, and for other similar phenomena of the period of the cult of personality'.

Other delegates criticized Voroshilov sharply. It looked as if in his declining years one of Stalin's closest comrades was about to be thrown out of the Party in which from 1926 to 1960 he had been virtually untouchable. But he made a repentant statement to the Congress, supporting the great work the Party was doing 'to eliminate violations of revolutionary legality in the period of the cult of personality, and I deeply regret that in those circumstances I also made mistakes.'

With nothing to do, practically alone, his wife having died in 1959, although he had an adopted son and daughter, he set about trying to write his memoirs. The first part, 'Tales About Life', appeared while he was still alive, but replete as it is with his dogmatic Bolshevik outlook, it is of interest only as the testimony of one who helped bring a great country to great historic failure.

Like all the other surviving members of the Politburo, he lived out his days rather well. A special order of the Politburo of 30 July 1960 gave him a pension of 9,000 roubles a month (at a time when a doctor *earned* 80, a skilled worker 150 and a top-paid ballet dancer 3,000), he kept his state dacha, his limousines, his doctors, his servants, his bodyguards and other attributes accorded to Communist Party top brass, the 'partocracy'.

But even the longest-lived have to make the final journey from which no traveller returns. Voroshilov died on 2 December 1969. The Politburo went through its ceremonial paces in the spirit established by Kremlin tradition: the city of Lugansk was renamed Voroshilovgrad, Khoroshev District became Voroshilov District, stipends for military students were founded in his name, an academy was named after him. By this time Moscow was full of streets, districts, institutions, palaces and Metro stations bearing the 'immortal' names of dead Politburo members. The ancient capital was becoming a monument to ugliness erected by a system capable of raising to the pinnacle of power such a talentless, unattractive mediocrity, endowed with a smattering of Marxist dogmatics and mental rigidity, as Marshal Voroshilov.

BIBLIOGRAPHY

Central Archives of the Defence Ministry.
Central State Archives of the Soviet Army.
Direktivy Glavnogo komandovaniya Krasnoy Armii (1917–1920), Sbornik dokumentov, Moscow, 1969.
Leninskii sbornik, vol. XXXVII, Moscow, 1970.

Matvei Vasilievich
ZAKHAROV

RICHARD WOFF

The climb-down by the Soviet Union over the issue of missiles for Castro's Cuba in 1962 was a blow to its credibility in the eyes of its allies and clients in the Third World. That Soviet political and military clout survived Khrushchev's foreign adventures was due in great measure to one outstanding officer among those who had advised against such 'hare-brained plans' – Marshal of the Soviet Union Matvei Vasilievich Zakharov. A veteran of the storming of the Winter Palace in November 1917, despite clashes with the Party in later years Zakharov remained dedicated to the ideal of a 'socialist society', and the rôle of the Soviet Union in upholding 'world peace' in the face of the 'imperialist threat'. In challenging the United States, however, he saw that Soviet policy would have to be based on informed analysis, and a perception of both Moscow's and the West's long-term objectives, capabilities and weaknesses. There was no place for amateurish opportunism. A student of the Shaposhnikov 'school' of the late 1930s which had produced a number of outstanding wartime commanders, Zakharov's concept of the rôle of the Soviet armed forces throughout the 1960s and 1970s was rooted in the habits and experience of a lifetime as a staff officer. In the process Zakharov was to re-mould, modernize and expand Soviet military power. His legacy was to survive down to the demise of the Soviet Union in 1991. An active participant in the early revolutionary struggles in Petrograd, a Civil War combatant (1918–21), Zakharov had an impressive war record (1941–5). While many of his first comrades-in-arms perished in the purges, he survived periods of Stalin's vindictive megalomania. After Stalin's death in March 1953 he in turn survived Khrushchev's erratic meddling in military affairs, and criticism of senior officers, with a mixture of grit and compromise, dedication to his adopted profession, natural ability, pragmatism and luck. In

327

confronting successive Party leaders Zakharov could at times rely on the support of allies such as Marshals Konev and Malinovsky, comrades-in-arms from the early 1920s, whom Zakharov served successively as Chief of Staff during the Great Patriotic War. Zakharov in turn had his disciples, like Marshal Nikolai Ogarkov, who still exercises an influence over military affairs in the Russia of the post-Soviet era.

Like many outstanding Red Army commanders, Zakharov's family background was humble. Born on 17 August 1898 in Tver province, he was the youngest of six children of a peasant farmer. His hard-working father was determined to see that his children lived orderly and useful lives. Matvei attended the local school run by the village priest, intoning the rudiments of reading, writing and arithmetic. He also developed a suspicion of religion. In all other respects Zakharov was a model pupil, leaving school at fifteen, proficient in arithmetic, geography and reading. He retained a lifelong love of Russian literature. It was his elder brother, however, with tales of the hardships endured by the factory workers in St Petersburg, who aroused in Zakharov the first political sympathies and a determination to seek his own fortunes in the capital, where in late 1913 he joined his brother. The capital was the most outward token of Europeanized Russia, exuding confidence, culture and an air of elegance to compare with any other European capital. There were also glaring contrasts: an expanding labour force, impoverished migrants from the provinces employed in the growing number of industrial enterprises, many of them foreign-owned. In one of them – the 'Kreiton' (Creighton) shipyard – Zakharov first worked as an unskilled labourer. In 1915 he moved to 'Dynamo' factory, and began to take an active part in workers' agitation organized by the Bolshevik 'cell'. Ultimately dismissed, Zakharov finally found employment in the Siemens-Halske Works, thanks to the help of an underground Bolshevik. By 1916 Zakharov was a committed Bolshevik, and fifty years later would recall his early struggles 'amidst the grime, and grey mists of wartime Petrograd', developing skill as an orator in demonstrations against the Provisional Government and its programme of 'final victory' following the February Revolution of February 1917.

In March 1917 Zakharov enrolled in the Petrograd Red Guards, the start of a military career spanning over fifty years. A member of the Bolshevik Party since December 1917, he came under the influence of other Bolshevik leaders destined to play a rôle in the creation of the Red Army, such as Nikolai Podvoisky. Under Podvoisky's command Zakharov took part in the storming of the Winter Palace, 'liquidation of the Petrograd Garrison' and occupation of Tsarskoe Selo in November 1917. Having established a reputation for bravery and loyalty to the cause in the first battles of the Revolution, he was recommended for the Red Army, created by Lenin's Decree of February 1918.

In early 1918 Zakharov entered the Petrograd Artillery School, a former élite tsarist establishment. His first formal military education, the course included basic tactics, engineering, topography, administration, gunnery and rifle drill. On passing out in November 1918 the course report spoke of Zakharov's 'attention to detail, and analytical ability in any tactical situation'. A participant in the first Moscow Red Square Parade marking the October Revolution, in late November he was posted to Southern Front to command an artillery battery of 10th Army in the Donbas region. This was his 'baptismal fire', taking part in the January 1919 counter-offensive against the Whites, and earning a reputation as a disciplinarian, for quick and bold decisions. Subsequently, he commanded an independent combat group, consisting of an artillery battery, three machine-gun sections and a rifle company, his first experience of combined-arms command and control.

This was followed by a short course at the Moscow Higher School of Staff Services in July 1919, an indication that his ability as a staff officer, and potential, were already being noted. The course was an opportunity for Zakharov to meet junior commanders from other fronts, including Yepifan Kovtyukh, commander of the legendary Taman Division later in the civil war. The meeting led to Zakharov volunteering to fight under Kovtyukh as assistant to the chief of staff of a brigade, taking part throughout late 1919 and the first months of 1920 in the operations around Tsaritsyn to secure the lower Don and Volga against the White Cossack Army. There followed punitive expeditions into the North Causcasus, and the final establishment of Soviet control of the northern Black Sea littoral. While the combat experience was invaluable, it enabled Zakharov to establish links with the 'Tsaritsyn Group', a côterie of political adventurers assembled around Stalin, the nucleus of the future Red Army command, including Voroshilov and Budenny.

After the Civil War Zakharov served as a junior staff officer in the 34th Rifle Division in Tuapse on the Black Sea, before transfer in 1923 to the legendary 25th Chapayev Division, which had close links with both Trotsky and Mikhail Frunze, the outstanding Civil War commander, long regarded as the creator of the Red Army. In 1925 the commander of the Division recommended Zakharov for a course at the Frunze Military Academy. Here, Zakharov was assigned to the Military Logistics Faculty, graduating with 'distinction' in 1928. The year before he left the Academy Zakharov met Rodion Malinovsky, a 1927 entrant. It was the beginning of a close professional relationship which endured down to Malinovsky's death in 1967.

The three years in the Academy gave Zakharov the time to reflect on the experience and lessons of the first decade of his career under the guidance of the Head of the Academy, Robert Eideman (1895–1937). Towards the end of the course Zakharov delivered a lecture on his rôle in the Civil War, focusing on problems of supply in a 'campaign of mobility', an unusual honour for a student. The Academy marked the beginning of the process of metamorphosis – from the militant 'Red commander' of 1917 to supreme command in the 1940s.

On leaving the Academy in 1928 Zakharov was posted to the Belorussia Military District as Assistant Chief of the Organization-Mobilization Department of the District Staff. The District Commander was Alexander Yegorov (1883–1939), a former tsarist colonel, an officer of immense experience, but in the eyes of some observers of limited intellect. In 1929 the District Staff was the location for the All-Army manoeuvres, under Voroshilov, the Defence Commissar, assisted by Boris Shaposhnikov, Chief of the Red Army Staff, and Vladimir Triandafillov (1894–1931), Chief of Operations of the Red Army Staff. Shaposhnikov noted Zakharov's 'meticulous attention to detail, ability to organize and administer the logistics support of the opposing sides'. In 1931 Yegorov was replaced as District Commander by Ieronim Uborevich, a former tsarist NCO, and a commander of experience despite comparative youth. Two years older than Zakharov, Uborevich was erudite, a good judge of character and ability, and eager to encourage younger officers of promise. He took a special interest in Zakharov, entrusting him with a study, 'The likely strategic deployment of enemy forces on Western Front', a task which Zakharov accomplished, assisted by Malinovsky – now a junior staff officer in the Belorussia Military District – Alexander Pokrovsky and Vladimir Kurasov (1897–1973). In many respects the study foreshadowed the events of 1941–2 following the German invasion of the Soviet Union.

In 1932 Zakharov returned to the Frunze Military Academy to attend a short course at the Operations Faculty, graduating in the summer of 1933 under the direction of Shaposhnikov, appointed Head of the Academy earlier in the year. (The Operations Faculty of the Academy was instituted in 1930, and became the nucleus of the General Staff Academy when it was established in 1936.) Subsequently, Zakharov returned to his old past, renewing ties with former comrades, Kovtyukh, Malinovsky, Konev, Sokolovsky, Novikov, Kolpakchi and Zhukov. In his *Memoirs* Zhukov recorded his impressions of 'the Operations Department headed by M. V. Zakharov . . . distinguished from those in other frontier Military Districts by smooth efficiency, preparedness, and generally high operational standards'. In September 1935 Zakharov was appointed Commander 22nd Rifle Regiment of the 8th Rifle Division commanded by Kolpakchi, who was later to praise his 'outstanding qualities of leadership', combined with a deep insight into the tactics of modern warfare. None the less, this was the only independent field command Zakharov was ever to hold. Henceforth his career would be dominated by his growing reputation as a staff officer.

Although he had completed the higher operations course in the Frunze

Military Academy merely three years previously, in the summer of 1936 Colonel Zakharov was selected for the first course in the General Staff Academy, established earlier in the year to train 'suitable candidates in the art of strategy and supreme command'. He graduated in late 1937, along with a group of officers destined likewise for supreme command. At the Academy Zakharov would also become acquainted with an outstanding group of military theorists, including G. S. Isserson, an exponent of the 'deep operation' in modern warfare. In retrospect, the establishment of the General Staff Academy in 1936 emerges as a major factor in the Red Army's victory of 1945. It was one example of Shaposhnikov's ability to counter the baleful influence exercised over Stalin by his creatures – Voroshilov and Budenny. By June 1941 over 200 officers had passed through the Academy, providing the Red Army with a wartime High Command replacing the victims of Stalin's purges.

From 1937 to the outbreak of war Zakharov held a number of key posts: Chief of Staff of the Leningrad Military District 1937–8; Assistant to the Chief of the General Staff, with responsibility for Organization, Mobilization, and Matériel-Technical Supply 1938–40; and Chief of Staff of the Odessa Military District 1940–1. While he owed his appointment as Chief of Staff of the Leningrad Military District to Voroshilov, the two years in the General Staff were perhaps the most important in Zakharov's career down to 1941. Under Shaposhnikov's guidance he gained an insight into the problems afflicting the Red Army command and control, and supply. Consequently, he condemned the decision to disband the mechanized corps in 1940, which robbed the Red Army of vital 'punch' and mobility throughout the first crucial months of the war. Promoted Major-General in July 1940, after a brief period as Chief of Staff of the 12th Army during the Soviet occupation of Bessarabia and northern Bukovina (now Moldova), Zakharov was appointed Chief of Staff of the Odessa Military District on the vital southern strategic approaches to the Soviet Union, facing a powerful combined German–Hungarian–Romanian force on a 450-kilometre front. It says something of his courage and initiative that, while Stalin continued in public to dismiss the threat of a German invasion, Zakharov, having assessed local intelligence reports, in the absence of the District Commander placed all formations and units in the Odessa Military District on full combat alert two days before the German attack at dawn on 22 June 1941. His foresight and initiative subsequently minimized the losses suffered by 9th Army, one of whose corps, commanded by Major-General Malinovsky, took the full force of the German attack. It was a good start to Zakharov's war.

On 10 July 1941 Zakharov was appointed Chief of Staff of the Northwest Theatre of Operations (TVD) guarding the strategic approaches to Leningrad. The Commander-in-Chief was Voroshilov, assisted by Zhdanov, head of the Leningrad Party organization. Inevitably, given Voroshilov's moderate accomplishments, the burden, if not responsibility, fell on Zakharov. In the first months of the war, however, organizing an efficient logistics system to make good the huge initial losses in matériel suffered by the Red Army was of crucial importance. Consequently, in August 1941 Zakharov joined Shaposhnikov as Deputy Chief of the General Staff (Logistics). At Zakharov's request, however, it was a temporary arrangement. In December he was appointed Chief of Staff of Kalinin Front, commanded by Colonel-General Konev, and from November 1942 by Colonel-General Maksim Purkaev. It was the first of a series of senior Front staff posts Zakharov was to hold throughout the war. His arrival at Kalinin Front coincided with the climax in the battle for Moscow, ending with the repulse of the German assault, and the counter-offensive of the Red Army throughout 1942 and the first half of 1943. In April 1943, as the General Staff was planning the great strategic operation, the battle of Kursk, Zakharov was appointed Chief of Staff of Reserve Front (District), later re-designated Steppe Front.

Throughout the battle of Kursk, Steppe Front, operating on the Belgorod–Kharkov axis, was commanded by Konev (August–October 1943). While the two worked well together, both Konev and Zakharov at times chafed at the rigid control exercised by Supreme HQ in Moscow. The final defeat of the German Operation 'Citadel' in the summer of 1943 brought a major reorganization of the Red Army command and control structure in the field, exploiting the strategic initiative, and giving greater cohesion to the Red Army's counter-offensive westwards into the heart of occupied Europe. Steppe Front was redesignated 2nd Ukrainian Front, commanded in turn by Konev (October 1943–May 1944), and Malinovsky (May 1944–May 1945), both of whom had been promoted ahead of Zakharov, a Colonel-General since October 1943; none the less, there was no change in the warmth of their personal or working relationships.

Ahead lay the final liberation of the Ukraine in the first half of 1944; Moldavia in August 1944; and the advance into the Balkans following the successful conclusion of the Jassy-Kishenev operation in conjunction with 3rd Ukrainian Front (20–29 August 1944). With Romania liberated in September 1944 the main axis of 2nd Ukrainian Front swung north into Hungary, with the Debrecen operation (October 1944) in conjunction with 4th Ukrainian Front, and ending with the Budapest operation (29 October 1944–13 February 1945). Such were the difficulties facing the Red Army in their assault of the strongly held German position, a 'Budapest Operational Group' was created comprising formations drawn from 2nd and 3rd Ukrainian Fronts under Malinovsky, with Zakharov as Chief of Staff. The eastern part of the city, Pest, was in Red Army control by 18 January; the battle for Buda lasted until 11 February 1945. The fall of the Hungarian capital was followed by the capture of Vienna (13 April 1945) and Prague

(May 1945), a fitting end to the European phase in the wartime record of Zakharov, promoted Army General 29 May 1945.

Following Zhukov's defeat of the Japanese at Khalkin-Gol on 20–21 August 1939, the Soviet Union and Japan had maintained a precarious peace in the Far East throughout the Second World War. With the Japanese switching their military efforts to Southeast Asia from late 1941, Stalin was able to denude the Far East and Transbaikal Military Districts of valuable divisions in the desperate struggle for survival in the summer of 1941. By the end of 1944, with the end of the war in Europe in sight, the Soviet High Command could now expect the allies to step up the war in the Far East, with the prospect of defeating the Japanese some time in 1946. The Red Army, having played no part in the war against Japan – apart from maintaining a productive espionage ring in Tokyo – would inevitably play a secondary rôle in the post-war settlement of the Far East, a region of vital strategic interest to Moscow. For Stalin, a possibly greater threat was the prospect of an Anglo-US occupation of Japan, including the Kuriles and Sakhalin.

The Red Army General Staff had already foreseen the possibility of a sneak Japanese attack in the Far East. The Japanese continued to maintain a large military force in Manchuria – the Kwantung Army, established in 1919 and comprising 750,000 men, 1,150 tanks and 1,800 aircraft. As early as May 1942 a Main Directorate was formed within the General Staff, headed by a Deputy Chief of the General Staff, with responsibility for monitoring the military situation and drawing up an operational plan to meet any threat from the Kwantung Army.

With the approach of the defeat of Nazi Germany in early 1945 the first Red Army forces began to deploy east to reinforce Far East and Transbaikal Fronts in preparation for the Manchurian operation and the defeat of the Kwantung Army. It was one of the largest and most hazardous operations ever undertaken by a Russian force. With a front of some 5,000 kilometres, its depth ranging from 200 to 800 kilometres, the special geographic and climatic features presented the greatest challenges: arid desert, high mountain ranges, and formidable river obstacles. Geography and terrain also dictated the operational concept and structure of command and control: a large strategic pincer movement, enveloping the Japanese Army, and closing deep in Manchuria. 1st and 2nd Far East Fronts, the latter supported by the Pacific Fleet, formed the left-hand pincer. The Transbaikal Front, commanded by Malinovsky, provided the right-hand pincer, and was entrusted with the mission of engaging the Kwantung Army. The three Fronts were controlled by Vasilevsky's Far East High Command in Khabarovsk. Transbaikal Front operated on the main axis, with a front of some 2,300 kilometres in width. Malinovsky had one crucial asset: most of the senior commanders had served under him throughout the operations of 1944–5. In turn, Zakharov, Malinovsky's Chief of Staff, was able to rely on officers who had served with him in the past, in some cases since Kursk. This was to be a decisive factor where success depended on well co-ordinated command and control, good intelligence analysis, and an efficient supply system – especially fuel and water – to maintain the momentum of the advance. Victory hinged on High Command's ability to redeploy formations, many still refurbishing after the punishing winter and spring campaigns of 1944–5, from Europe some 6,000 miles east, over a rail and road network the first 1,000 miles of which was still suffering from the ravages of war, and with minimal air transport. Above all, while technically still at peace with Japan, secrecy and surprise were essential. This was a situation which taxed Zakharov's skill and experience in meticulous staff work and logistics.

The Soviet Union declared war on Japan on 9 August; after crossing the Hingan mountain line, and ranging over 400 kilometres into Manchuria, Malinovsky's forces had achieved their objectives by 14 August with the fall of Taonan and Taoan. The same day the Japanese government sued for an armistice. The Red Army campaign in Manchuria was characterized by speed of advance, despite the physical disadvantages; use of armoured columns advancing deep into the enemy's rear, supported from the air; use of airborne landings ahead of the main forces to unhinge local forces and seize vital objectives; deception and surprise. The Hingan-Mukden operation was a fitting climax to Zakharov's wartime career. On 8 September 1945 he was made a Hero of the Soviet Union. It was also the 'finale' of Zakharov's wartime association with Malinovsky. Since the turn of the tide in 1943 the two had established an equilibrium of minds underpinning a close working partnership, the core of the relationship of the commander and his chief of staff throughout history.

In the immediate post-war period it was Stalin's policy to split up and disperse former wartime command structures. Most of the senior officers of Transbaikal Front were redistributed soon after the end of the Manchurian campaign. Malinovsky remained in the Far East for the remainder of Stalin's rule. In September 1945 Zakharov returned to Moscow, succeeding Shaposhnikov as Head of the General Staff Academy following his death six months previously. Throughout Stalin's last years secondment to an influential post lacking prestige was, none the less, something of a 'preservation order', with a warning to be on one's guard. For Zakharov it was a challenge and opportunity to pass on his experience and operational concepts to the post-war generation of Soviet commanders. His two main concerns were to assemble an experienced teaching staff, and to organize the courses to prepare the High Command of the future. By 1948 some of the most experienced and erudite wartime commanders had been appointed to the leading Chairs, including Lieutenant-General A. I. Gastilovich, Head of the Chair of Higher Tactics, and Lieutenant-General Ye. A. Shilovsky, Head of the Faculty of Strategy. In 1946 the first of the basic two-year courses was established, and in 1948 the first group of former wartime officers graduated, the Soviet High Command of the 1960s and 1970s. In 1946, likewise, the Higher Academy Course of up to nine months' duration was introduced for special categories of officers, considered of potential but not requiring to spend a full two years at the Academy on the grounds of experience or age. In his four years as Head of the Academy Zakharov left his mark, 'restructuring the educational process and military scientific work', in line with tasks facing the Soviet High Command in the next decade. In recognition of his services he was awarded the title of Professor in 1948.

In 1949 Zakharov was replaced as Head of the Academy by his old comrade Army General Kurasov. For the next eight years he served in turn as a Deputy Chief of the General Staff with responsibility for Battle Training (1949–52), Chief Inspector of the Soviet Army (1952–3), and Commander of the Leningrad Military District (1953–7). The latter appointment was part of a major reshuffle of the Soviet High Command following Stalin's death in March 1953, an event which Zakharov marked by an article in *Krasnaya Zvezda* (13 April 1953) devoted to Stalin's 'theory of war'. The death of Stalin, followed by the eventual accession of Khrushchev, changed the nature of the relationship of the Soviet leadership with the High Command. In place of cowering acceptance of the arbitrary decisions of 'the Supreme Commander-in-Chief', masked by obsequious praise for 'the greatest leader and strategist of all time', the Soviet military were initially allowed a greater degree in decision-making, and a part in removing the worst features of Stalin's rule.

One of Khrushchev's first acts was to appoint Zhukov a First Deputy Defence Minister and Commander-in-Chief of the Ground Forces, and finally Defence Minister in February 1955. The honeymoon did not last long, and in October 1957 Zhukov was abruptly dismissed, and Malinovsky, Commander-in-Chief of the Ground Forces since March 1956, was appointed Defence Minister. The dismissal of Zhukov was symptomatic of the growing rift between Khrushchev and the senior military, none of whom, however, was prepared to defend Zhukov in public. His removal did nothing to stifle military opposition to Khrushchev's irrational military schemes. Inevitably, events were to influence Zakharov's own prospects, and ultimately his relationship with the Soviet leadership. In late November 1957 Zakharov was appointed Commander-in-Chief of Soviet Troops in Germany (GSFG) in succession to Marshal Andrei Grechko. Throughout the late 1950s a number of developments were to reshape the operational and political rôles of GSFG, the most important being the restructuring and modernizing of senior formations following the Zhukov reforms of 1955–7. To render the Soviet armed forces more mobile, compact, and able to operate in a nuclear environment, Zhukov dispensed with the rifle division and mechanized corps/division, and replaced them by the more mobile motor rifle and tank

335

division respectively. The divisions in turn were repackaged in combined arms and tank armies. There were also changes in the structure and rôle of the artillery, which now also comprised surface-to-surface tactical missile units. In turn, the logistics structure had to be reshaped, a field in which Zakharov had long experience. Finally, one GSFG Army was withdrawn, and a second split up and its formations redeployed to other Armies. The second development was the integration of the fledgling East German armed forces into the Warsaw Pact. With a wealth of experience behind him, Zakharov took a close interest in training, criticizing both East German officers and their Soviet advisors for 'shortcomings'. Many of the 'teething problems' were tackled during regular joint GSFG/East German 'brotherhood-in-arms' exercises, with a resulting improvement in training, despite the ritual propaganda. Finally, promoted Marshal of the Soviet Union 14 May 1959, Zakharov's last year in Germany was overshadowed by growing tension between the former wartime Allies stemming from Khrushchev's policy of intimidating the West over the Berlin problem and the threat to Allied rights in the city.

In April 1960 Zakharov was appointed Chief of the General Staff in succession to Marshal Sokolovsky, thus resuming the close association with Malinovsky after a lapse of fifteen years. In many respects the partnership augured well, coming at a time of reform, restructuring and modernization. The process involved the creation of the Strategic Rocket Forces in December 1959, a reduction in the overall strength of the Soviet armed forces, a fundamental reassessment of the rôle of the ground forces, and 'the manned bomber'. The programme, stemming from Khrushchev's obsession with Soviet strategic nuclear capability, was opposed by many senior Soviet officers. While Malinovsky was able to tone down the impact of the changes, pointing out in particular that victory in a nuclear war required joint action by all arms of service, and 'over-reliance' on nuclear weapons would in turn place Soviet policy in a straitjacket, the main thrust of Khrushchev's 'adventures and groundless ideas' continued to exacerbate relations with the Soviet High Command. Like Zakharov, Malinovsky was also painfully aware of the tragic social hardship facing thousands of officers and senior NCOs on their enforced discharge from the armed forces, with a bleak future in civilian life for which few were prepared.

On his arrival in Moscow in April 1960 Zakharov was immediately confronted with an entirely different problem: namely, the future of the General Staff Academy. Where Stalin could not suppress a respect for his senior staff officers – Shaposhnikov, Vasilevsky, Antonov – Khrushchev appears to have developed a deep-seated grudge against the *genshtabisty* (General Staffers), and paranoiac distrust of his generals regarding 'questions of strategic importance'. One expression of his contempt was the 1960 Decree ordering the abolition of the Academy and creation of a Faculty of Operational Art in the Frunze Military Academy – a return to the early

1930s. In Zakharov's view this would rob the Soviet High Command of the ability 'to think, evaluate, and initiate changes in strategy' at a time when strategic doctrine, thanks to 'the technological revolution', was itself being fundamentally reassessed. Moreover, the loss of the Academy would undermine professional standards. With Malinovsky's support, Zakharov initiated a move to wipe out Khrushchev's assault, and in April 1961 a Decree of the USSR Council of Ministers 'On Preserving the General Staff Academy' was adopted, and the Academy restored.

The incident did nothing to improve Zakharov's relations with Khrushchev. While he did at times praise the 'Supreme Commander-in- Chief', opposition to Khrushchev's policy of confrontation with Washington and the dispatch of missiles to Cuba in late 1962, together with the repercussions of the 'Penkovsky affair', ultimately led to his replacement in March 1963 by his wartime comrade-in-arms Marshal Sergei Biryuzov, now a leading Khrushchev supporter within the High Command. Following some months' absence, Zakharov re-emerged as Head of the General Staff Academy once more, amid renewed rumour in early 1963 of plans to disband the Academy and house the Patrice Lumumba University in the vacated building. Return to the Academy afforded Zakharov an opportunity to rethink and remould Soviet strategy. Zakharov may have been in disfavour; he was not in disgrace. He remained a member of the Party Central Committee and was among the group of senior officers who congratulated Khrushchev on his seventieth birthday (24 April 1964). He continued to publish articles, e.g. on the battle of Kursk, on command and control, on military doctrine and on the twentieth anniversary of the Jassy-Kishenev operation.

It is likely that Zakharov would have spent the rest of his career in the Academy but for the events of late 1964. On 14 October 1964 Khrushchev was unexpectedly removed while 'on holiday' following a meeting of the Politburo. Military unease with Khrushchev's brand of 'military doctrine' was a major factor in his downfall, a point not lost on Khrushchev's successors, the 'Brezhnev troika'. Meanwhile, on 19 October, a week after Khrushchev's departure, Biryuzov was killed in an air crash which, some speculated, may not have been accidental: another passenger was Nikolai Mironov, Chief of the Administrative Organs Department of the Central Committee, and a long-time associate of Khrushchev. His loyalty to Khrushchev had incurred the enmity of both Shelepin (former Chairman of the USSR KGB) and Semichastny, KGB Chairman 1961–7. It was a foregone conclusion that Zakharov, despite his sixty-six years, would be recalled for a second term as Chief of the General Staff, and that he would lose no time in putting the General Staff case regarding Khrushchev's interference in matters of military doctrine.

*

In a major article published in February 1965 Zakharov not only reviewed recent events, but set out his concern for the future. While acknowledging the leadership of the Party in military affairs, he condemned Khrushchev's dilettantism in military matters, obsessive distrust of his generals, and claims to 'so-called strategic farsightedness', lacking as he did 'even a remote relationship to military strategy'. The article went on to warn that 'with the emergence of nuclear missile weaponry, cybernetics, electronics and computers, any subjective approach to military problems, hare-brained plans, and superficiality can cause irreparable damage.' Finally, Zakharov's plea to maintain an autonomous professional military establishment, and the need to improve professional standards in all branches in an 'age of technological revolution in military affairs' was to be engraved in the minds of all senior Soviet officers down to the 1990s. On returning to the General Staff Zakharov devoted his energy to redefining its rôle, organization and structure. As a consequence, throughout the 1960s the General Staff gradually expanded the scope of its responsibilities to encompass virtual control over armaments policy, military aid to Third World states, and military doctrine.

One of the results of the Cuban Missile Crisis was an intensification of the US/USSR dialogue on a broad spectrum of issues, including strategic arms. What is now the Legal and Treaty Directorate of the General Staff was to assume a greater rôle in US/USSR negotiations on strategic nuclear weapons (SALT) by the later 1960s. In 1968 Lieutenant-General Nikolai Ogarkov, a former engineer who had served under Malinovsky in the Far East in the late 1940s and early 1950s, was appointed a First Deputy Chief of the General Staff, with responsibility for armaments control policy, reassessment of strategic command and control systems, and doctrine. Throughout SALT-I (and later SALT-II) the proportion of General Staff officers on the Soviet delegation is estimated by some US participants to have reached a third by November 1969, with Ogarkov ranking second behind the head of the delegation, Deputy Foreign Minister Vladimir Semenov. One leading US negotiator later revealed that Zakharov himself was at one point believed to have been nominated head of the Soviet SALT-I delegation.

The 1960s also witnessed renewed Soviet interest in the Third World. The General Staff was one of three agencies administering and monitoring foreign aid, along with the Foreign Ministry and Foreign Economic Aid Committee of the Council of Ministers. In all some thirty Third World states had concluded Friendship Treaties, or Mutual Aid Agreements, with Moscow by the early 1970s, including Cuba, Egypt (United Arab Republic), Syria, Iraq, North Vietnam and India. The Military Assistance Directorate of the General Staff was set up to manage the growing arms trade with the Third World, and control Military Advisor Groups (MAG) abroad. The Directorate in turn had a number of departments responsible for individual states or regions. After Cuba, the Arab world – bent on the destruction of Israel – welcomed Soviet aid and military advice.

In July 1967 Zakharov himself, despite ill-health, headed a group of senior advisors to Cairo to assess the military situation and advise the Egyptian Army in operations against the Israelis. The team included Colonel-General Petr Lashchenko (appointed by Zakharov Senior Advisor on his return to Moscow), Lieutenant-General of Aviation Vladimir Okunev (an air defence specialist, and last Senior Military Advisor in Egypt, 1970–2), specialists from all arms, legal experts, technicians, and intelligence officers. In October 1967 Army General Sergei Sokolov, Deputy Defence Minister and Commander-in-Chief of the Group Forces, headed another Soviet delegation. By November 1967 MAG Egypt comprised eight departments: command and control; air forces, air defence; navy; artillery; military intelligence (including electronic surveillance units); communications; and engineers. Soviet officers were attached to all formations and units in the field, in some cases down to battalion level. Depending on the country and mission, this was to be the standard command structure of all Soviet MAGs, including Afghanistan, down to the late 1980s.

The third area to which Zakharov devoted his attention was reassessment of Soviet strategic doctrine, based in turn on a study of political factors, the economy, the social sciences, technological advances, and the experience of the Great Patriotic War. In short, Zakharov aimed to create within the General Staff a body of experts akin to the RAND Corporation, capable of providing rational assessment of 'super-power behavioural patterns in a crisis'. Overall research and assessment remained the responsibility of the Military Science Directorate, originally established in 1942 to study current operational experience, now upgraded and tasked along with other recently established Moscow-based research institutions to monitor developments in the West. In 1966 the Military History Institute was established and Major-General Pavel Zhilin, a former Stalin Prize winner, appointed Head. Zakharov himelf made a significant contribution to the study and reassessment of wartime operations, and the problems of the Soviet Armed Forces of the 1960s and 1970s. His article 'A scientific approach to troop command and control', published in 1966 shortly after the XXIII Party Congress, was especially important, since it provided a blueprint for exploiting the latest technology, adapted to Soviet strategic defence priorities of the 1980s. In compiling the study Zakharov was assisted among others by Lieutenant-Generals Povali and Ogarkov. It was Ogarkov who ultimately implemented Zakharov's concepts as Chief of the General Staff (1977–84). Finally, in 1989 the USSR Ministry of Defence, assisted by Zakharov's daughter, published a study written in the late 1960s, 'The General Staff in the Pre-War Years'. Containing 'sensitive material', publication was delayed for two decades. In a changing Soviet Union, publication in 1989 was an expression of the abiding veneration reserved by the Soviet General Staff for both Shaposhnikov and Zakharov, with an appreciation by Army General Mikhail Moiseyev, Chief of the General Staff, dismissed following the attempted coup in August 1991. An article in a Moscow newspaper in late August 1992 revealed for the first time the existence of a seven-volume study compiled by Zakharov in the late 1960s: 'The War in Southeast Asia'. An assessment of US military involvement in Vietnam, it remains on the 'secret' list in the General Staff Archives in Moscow.

There was, however, one important field of General Staff activity over which Zakharov did not exercise absolute control: military intelligence. This was yet another legacy of the Khrushchev era, and the shake-up in the Soviet intelligence and security organs following Stalin's death and the removal of Beria in 1953. In 1958 Ivan Serov, a veteran NKVD officer, and close associate of Khrushchev from the Ukraine of the 1930s, was transferred from the KGB to make way for Shelepin, and appointed Chief of the Main Intelligence Directorate (GRU) of the General Staff. Serov continued to control General Staff intelligence throughout the first two years of Zakharov's tenure as Chief of the General Staff, and there can have been no greater contrast than between the former NKVD 'butcher' and the professional General Staff officer. The relationship between Serov and Zakharov was further impaired by the Cuban crisis, and the Penkovsky affair. With the arrest of his 'friend and former boozing companion' Penkovsky in November 1962, and the ensuing embarrassing scandal, Serov was removed. He committed suicide soon after. As surmised above, the Penkovsky affair was probably a factor in Zakharov's own dismissal in March 1963. Consequently, the Penkovsky affair strengthened the KGB's hold over GRU with the appointment in March 1963 of Petr Ivashutin, another former NKVD and KGB official, to replace Serov. Despite an unsavoury reputation, and close association with some of the most repressive NKVD operations in the first post-war decade, Ivashutin was to exercise a dominating influence over General Staff intelligence operations until retirement in 1987.

Since the late 1950s Zakharov's health had been deteriorating. A diabetic, in April 1965 he underwent an operation for cancer. In his absence the duties of the Chief of the General Staff were exercised by his senior Deputies Army General Vladimir Ivanov and Lieutenant-General Povali. Returning some months later Zakharov resumed his demanding schedule, with frequent visits to clients abroad, setting a foreign travel record for a Chief of the General Staff. The last official visit was to attend the funeral of his friend President Nasser of Egypt in September 1970. In March 1971 Zakharov was re-elected to the Central Committee. Finally, on 21 September illness forced Zakharov to retire. Next day, at his last public appearance, he was awarded his second Hero of the Soviet Union. He died on 31 January 1972.

A veteran of the October Revolution, with an outstanding military career throughout the first three decades of Soviet rule, Zakharov ranks alongside Shaposhnikov and Zhukov as a member of the 'troika' which was to influence the evolution of the Soviet Armed Forces long after Stalin's demise, throughout two decades of 'technological revolution in military affairs', and down to the demise of the Soviet Union itself.

BIBLIOGRAPHY

Akademiya General'nogo Shtaba, Moscow, 1976.

Garthoff, Raymond L., 'SALT and the Soviet Military', *Problems of Communism*, no. 1, 1975.

Gribkov, A. I., in *Voenno-istoricheskii Zhurnal*, no. 10–12, 1992, and no. 1, 1993. A critical but non-apologetic reassessment of the Cuban crisis in 1962, and Soviet military involvement, by the former chief of the Soviet Military Advisor Group to the Cuban Revolutionary Army.

Gryaznov, B. Z., *Marshal Zakharov*, Moscow, 1979.

Ogonek, no. 2, 1947.

Voenno-istoricheskii Zhurnal, no. 7, 1968, an article by Marshal Konev dedicated to Zakharov's 70th birthday.

Zakharov, M. V., *General'nyi shtab v predvoennye gody*, Moscow, 1989.

Zhukov, G. K., *Vospominaniya i razmyshleniya*, Moscow, 1974.

Georgy Konstantinovich

ZHUKOV

VIKTOR ANFILOV

Among the military leaders of the Second World War, pride of place belongs to Georgy Zhukov, for it was he who led the Soviet armed forces during the decisive operations of the main front. The path of his life, however, was neither straight nor smooth, and was strewn with as many thorns as roses.

He was born on 2 December 1896 in the village of Strelkovka in Kaluga province into the family of a poor peasant. At the age of seven he entered the local parish school which provided him with three years of instruction before he had to leave in order to help his parents. He was given into the care of a Moscow cobbler to train for the trade. Despite the difficult circumstances, he went on with his studies and in 1913 took the examination for a whole year's course at a city school.

When the First World War broke out, Zhukov was called up and posted as a private to a cavalry regiment. He later recalled that life in the cavalry was more interesting than in the infantry, if a good deal harder. In the spring of 1916 he was sent for further training. He was forever grateful to the unit commander who was to some extent responsible for the young Zhukov's future. 'You'll be at the front soon enough,' he told his pupil, 'but for now you should study military matters as thoroughly as you can. You're going to find it useful.' Zhukov was sent that autumn to the Southwestern Front. He served in reconnaissance, often going behind enemy lines. He received his first St George Cross for capturing a German officer. He was soon back behind German lines, but was seriously concussed by an enemy mine, and for this exploit was decorated with his second St George's Cross. He was now confined to convalescence and took no part in the actions of 1917. He recalled that he spent December 1917 and January 1918 at his family's village and that after this rest he decided to join the Red Guards. 'However, at the beginning of February I came down with a serious case of typhus and then again in April with a recurrence of the disease. I was able to realize my wish to serve in the Red Army only after a further six months.'

In August 1918 he entered the Red Army as a volunteer. He was posted to the 4th Regiment of the 1st Moscow Cavalry Division. He fought, first as a private, then as deputy to the unit commander, then as a unit commander himself, and finally as squadron commander. He was wounded in 1919 at Tsaritsyn and in August 1922 he was awarded his first Soviet decoration, the Order of the Red Banner. In May 1923 he was posted as commander of the 39th Buzuluk Cavalry Regiment of the 7th Samara Cavalry Division. It was a distinguished and responsible posting. Command of a regiment was always regarded as an important step in acquiring military experience.

Zhukov combined his service in the line with diligent study. In 1924 he entered the Higher Cavalry School in Leningrad. As he himself recalled, he showed remarkable endurance and fantastic tenacity in his studies. Among his fellow students were future Marshals K. K. Rokossovsky, I. Kh. Bagramyan and A. I. Yeremenko. Bagramyan recalled that Zhukov was regarded as one of the most competent of the group, while Rokossovsky wrote that Zhukov devoted himself to his work like no one else: 'If you looked into his room, you would find him crawling over a map on the floor. Even then, for him the cause and his sense of duty were above everything.' Then it was back to the concentrated work of the regimental commander. Of this time in his life Zhukov wrote in 1965: 'It was a good school. Apart from the valuable practice, I acquired considerable theoretical and tactical knowledge. Of course, it wasn't all easy, I made mistakes. The least lapse, whether in the work or the behaviour of a serviceman, used to drive me crazy. Some people could not understand this while I for my part was no doubt insufficiently sensitive to human weakness.'

From the autumn of 1929 to the spring of 1930 he was again at a desk, this time at the Moscow finishing courses for senior officers, following which he was posted as an officer to the 2nd Cavalry Brigade of the 7th Samara Division under the command of Rokossovsky, which in turn was part of the cavalry corps commanded by S. K. Timoshenko. That was the ranking of the three future Marshals. Rokossovsky characterized Zhukov in November 1930 as 'strong-willed and decisive. Has broad range of initiative and knows how to apply it in practice. He is demanding and persistent in his demands. Somewhat dry in character and insufficiently sensitive. Has a significant element of stubbornness. Pathologically vain. Well prepared on the military side. Has broad practical command experience. Likes the military life and is constantly improving himself.'

In a similar vein, Cavalry Inspector S. M. Budenny, for whom Zhukov served as deputy for two years, wrote on 31 October 1931 that Zhukov showed 'strong authoritarian signs as an officer, was extremely demanding of himself and his subordinates, revealing excessive harshness and coarseness on the last occasion.' These testimonials were fair assessments of Zhukov's character. He valued nothing as highly as the true qualities of the soldier, and by now he had developed all the hallmarks of the Russian working man: energy, stability, the capacity to appreciate the value of true friendship and soldierly comradeship.

The 1930s were the time when Zhukov became a military leader of national standing. In March 1933 he was given command of the 4th Cavalry Division with the task of correcting a 'falling off' in its military and political training. As a result of the hard work of its officers and the organizing abilities of its commander, the Division emerged as one of the best. Many of its officers were decorated with orders and medals. Zhukov was awarded the Order of Lenin, a very high award in peacetime. In July 1937 he was in command of 3rd Cavalry Corps. Recalling this period, he told me that taking part in war games and staff studies, and frequently visiting Bialystok Military District under the guidance of such figures as Yegorov and Uborevich, had broadened his horizons and helped him form his theoretical views and leadership qualities. He stressed that he had learned much in the field of military art from Uborevich. The officers' study courses, which Uborevich organized, were especially successful, and they included demonstrations of the latest technology, war games and lectures on such topics as theory and military history.

The wave of repressions which took place in 1937–8 carried off many military leaders, among them Uborevich. Some officers had written compromising testimonials on their commanding officers. At the June 1957 Plenum of the Party Central Committee, Molotov turned on Zhukov with the charge that, if one were to dig into the documents of the period, one would find such testimonials signed by Zhukov. Zhukov reacted sharply with the retort: 'No, you won't find any. Dig! You won't find my signature!'

Although he was threatened by storm clouds, they did not break over him. At the end of 1938 he was appointed Deputy Commander of Bialystok Military District. He had not wanted to leave the corps, but the prospect of working with a larger operational unit was tempting, and he accepted. On 1 June 1939, however, Defence Commissar Voroshilov summoned him urgently to Moscow. Such summonses were usually followed by arrest, as had been the case with Yakir and the others, and Zhukov was justifiably alarmed. He wrote of this episode that it was the first time in his life when he really suffered: 'Enough of the right kind of documents on me had already been prepared, I imagine, and someone was no doubt already scurrying somewhere with them in his briefcase. In a word, I could have ended up like so many others at the time. But instead I was suddenly ordered to Khalkin-Gol [in Mongolia], and I went with a feeling of joy. And I felt great satisfaction after the operation – an operation for which to this day I feel affection – not only because I carried it out successfully, but also because by my efforts I had as it were vindicated myself, I had somehow thrown off all the slanders and accusations which had been accumulated against me in the previous years and about which I had partly known and partly guessed at.'

By the time of Khalkin-Gol, Zhukov had behind him a quarter of a century of war service, and he had made his way up through the ranks from private to corps commander. But as a military leader, the Khalkin-Gol operation was to prove his touchstone. In comparison with the events of the Great Patriotic War, the scale of these operations may seem small, but their significance in Zhukov's life far outweighed their scale. Khalkin-Gol represents the point of departure for the biography of Zhukov as a military leader. It was a promising beginning. For his leadership of the troops and for his courage and audaciousness, he was awarded the title of Hero of the Soviet Union.

In May of the following year he was summoned to Moscow where he was received for the first time by Stalin who concluded their meeting by saying, 'You have now had military experience. Take Kiev Special Military District and use your experience to train the troops. Bear in mind that in a fight with the probable enemy your District is going to play the chief part.'

In June 1940 Zhukov took up command in Kiev with the title of General which had just been conferred on him. The troops under his command were taught the lessons learnt by the Red Army in the Finnish War and at Khalkin-Gol. Careful attention was also paid to the experience of the German army in the opening phases of the Second World War. In December Zhukov gave a lecture to senior officers entitled 'The character of the present-day offensive operation'. 'War,' he declared, 'must be conducted in the light of real possibilities. The German successes in the West, based on the massed use of tanks and motorized troops and aircraft, give much food for thought. Unfortunately, we do not yet have such large operational mechanized formations. Our mechanized corps are still at the embryonic stage. Yet the war could break out at any moment. We cannot make our operational plans on the basis of what we'll have in a year or two. We have to work with what our border units have at their disposal right now.'

'Zhukov's speech,' Bagramyan later recalled, 'astonished everyone.' After this meeting, war games were held in which the 'Reds', under D. G. Pavlov, were intended by the game-plan to repel an offensive by the 'Blues', standing for the German army, and were then to go over to the counter-attack. However, despite the game-plan, the 'Blues', under Zhukov's command, surrounded the 'Reds' and 'annihilated' them, as was to happen in fact in June 1941.

Zhukov's authority rose still further in Stalin's eyes. On 15 January 1941 the Politburo appointed him Chief of the General Staff, the last thing he expected, as he later claimed. Rokossovsky in his 1930 testimonial had also written that Zhukov 'should not be given either a staff or teaching post, as he has an organic detestation of this kind of work'. Zhukov asked Stalin not to make the appointment, but to no avail. With only five months to go before the German invasion, on 1 February 1941 Zhukov took up the post. 'In that short time,' he related, 'I did not even manage to acquaint myself with all the services of the gigantic mechanism that governed the Red Army.' In addition there were the vital tasks of preparing the country and the armed forces to repel aggression. The war was at the gates. Zhukov worked fifteen or sixteen hours a day at his new and demanding tasks, often staying overnight in his office. He paid particular attention to the formation of the armoured tank units which were to be the main striking force of the ground troops, and he devoted much energy to a plan for the strategic deployment of forces, and a plan for the mobilization of industry for war production, in the event of war.

During March and April concentrated work was carried out to put the fine detail on a plan to secure the western borders. According to the calculation, there were insufficient troops to hold off attacks by the German army. After repeatedly reporting to Stalin on the state of affairs, permission was finally obtained to transfer two general armies to Ukraine and Belorussia, under the guise of field-training camps. Stalin also gave permission for the call-up of 800,000 reserves for this exercise. Zhukov knew that these movements would not remain a secret from the Germans, in which case he proposed putting the troops of the border districts on battle alert. 'I reported this to Stalin,' Zhukov said, 'but after it had taken us two weeks to convince him to agree to the first two measures, he would not give his consent for the third. He replied that putting border troops on the alert could lead to war, and he was convinced that we would be able somehow to manoeuvre, and to explain even a partial mobilization and the transfer of troops in such a way as not to alarm Hitler.'

Zhukov recognized that he and Defence Commissar Timoshenko bore responsibility for failing adequately to insist that Stalin give the order in time to put the forces on a war footing. In reply to my question why they had failed in this way, bearing in mind that intelligence sources were reporting that the Germans had taken up position for an offensive, Zhukov replied: 'You have to consider exactly what it meant at that time to go against Stalin. We could all remember 1937 and 1938. To have said that he was wrong would have meant that, even before you got out of the building, you would land up in Beria's hands, and Beria was almost always present during my meetings with Stalin.' He continued: 'And yet that is only one aspect of the truth. I'll tell you another. I didn't regard myself as cleverer or more far-sighted than Stalin, or that I had a better understanding of the situation than he had. Like everyone else, I had enormous faith in him, in his ability to find a way out of the most difficult situations. I sensed the danger of a German attack, the feeling was gnawing at my vitals. But my faith in Stalin, and my belief that in the end everything would come out the way he suggested, was stronger.'

On Zhukov's faith in Stalin in 1941, it should also be noted that – as Dmitri Volkogonov has shown in his study of Stalin, *Triumph and Tragedy* – Zhukov submitted a plan to Stalin in mid-May which would have reversed the passive nature of Soviet strategy, calling as it did for an offensive while the Germans were still deploying their forces. Although there is no direct evidence of Stalin's response, the conduct of Soviet policy for the next month is evidence enough that he was not prepared to start the war with Hitler.

During the evening of 21 June 1941 the Chief of Staff of Kiev Military District reported to Zhukov that a German deserter had appeared at a border post with the news that the German army was going to attack the Soviet Union in the morning. After reporting to Stalin, Zhukov set off for the Kremlin with the Defence Commissar and his own deputy, General N. F. Vatutin. There they finalized the order for putting the border forces on full alert, with a strict proviso from Stalin 'not to give any excuse for a provocation'. At midnight this document was despatched to the head-quarters of the Military Districts, but it never reached the troops. The enemy attack took them by surprise.

The night of 21 June was a sleepless night. Talks went on with the commanders and chiefs of staff of the border districts. At 0400 came news of incursions by German aircraft over towns and districts where Soviet troops were deployed. Zhukov at once informed Stalin of this, and he and Timoshenko were summoned to the Kremlin. When they arrived, Stalin asked them, 'Could this be a provocation by the German generals?' Zhukov remarked to me with regret: 'Relying on his own wisdom, he had outwitted himself.'

Thus began the Great Patriotic War. During the course of it Zhukov would display his military talent and leadership skills to the full. He had a clear and sober mind, a razor-sharp memory, the ability to sum up the enemy's strengths and weaknesses, and these gifts together enabled him to make correct assessments of operational and strategic positions and sound predictions of the way events would unfold.

On the first day of the war Stalin sent Zhukov to the Southwestern Front, where, according to the plan, the troops, having held off the enemy attack, were to go over to a counter-attack. Owing to the unfavourable situation that had developed, however, the plan could not be put into action. On 26 June Zhukov was summoned back to Moscow to co-ordinate the actions on all fronts. On 29 June he reported to Stalin on the course of the war. As he analysed the position objectively, he drew special attention to the threat of encirclement that hung over the troops on the Central and Southwestern Fronts. To avert this, he proposed abandoning Kiev and taking up a defensive position on the east bank of the Dnieper. 'Having read my report,' Zhukov said, 'Stalin summoned me. In his study with him were Beria and Mekhlis. He cursed me in crude terms for suggesting we leave Kiev which, like Leningrad, he counted on holding at any cost. I replied, "If you think the Chief of the General Staff talks nonsense, then I request you relieve me of my post and send me to the front."' In his written report Zhukov drew attention to the need to smash an enemy bridgehead at Yelnya which greatly threatened the Moscow sector. After a pause for reflection, Stalin despatched Zhukov to deal with the problem.

On 30 July Zhukov took command of the Reserve Front. After making a correct assessment of the enemy's intentions, on 19 August as a member of the Supreme High Command he cabled Stalin, once again focusing the Supremo's attention on the possible encirclement of Soviet forces in Kiev District and proposing concrete measures to effect resistance. But this proposal was similarly ignored, leading directly to the loss of half a million men.

As a Front Commander Zhukov displayed his abilities as an organizer. Under his leadership the first Soviet offensive of the war was carried out at the end of August and early September at Yelnya. As at Khalkin-Gol, he employed a two-pronged pincer movement with the aim of encircling and annihilating an enemy grouping of ten divisions. And it was only the shortage of tanks and aeroplanes that prevented him from fully accomplishing this aim.

At the beginning of September the enemy was racing towards Leningrad and the city was in grave danger. The commander of the Leningrad Front, Voroshilov, was incapable of organizing the city's defence, and Stalin decided to send Zhukov to replace him, a task, according to A. M. Vasilevsky, which Zhukov 'accepted with alacrity', confident as he was of his own abilities. 'Before my departure for Leningrad,' he recalled, 'Stalin said the position at the Leningrad Front was extremely serious, and that if the Germans took the city our situation would become politically much more difficult. "Your task is stop the enemy from getting into Leningrad at whatever cost."' Zhukov's arrival in Leningrad on 10 September coincided with a session of the Front Military Council, where he handed Voroshilov Stalin's note stating that he, Zhukov, had been appointed Commander-in-Chief of the Front. The note ended: 'Hand over the Front to him and come back by the same plane. Stalin.'

The meeting discussed what to do should the Germans break through into the city. The naval representatives asked in what circumstances they should scuttle their ships to prevent them from falling into enemy hands, to which Zhukov retorted, 'We're not giving up Leningrad. We're going to defend her!' Addressing the commander of the Baltic Fleet, he said: 'As Front Commander, I forbid you to scuttle any ships. Clear them of mines to make sure they don't get blown up, and move them closer to the city so that they can use their heavy guns. If they have to sink, let it be only in battle, and while firing their guns.'

It took Zhukov only a few hours to acquaint himself with the situation at the front and in the city itself. By morning a plan was ready for a deep, echeloned, or staged, defence. The battles at Leningrad were extremely fierce and went on day and night. Zhukov acted with cold reason and resolution. His firmness in carrying out his decisions, and his rationality, created an atmosphere of certainty that the enemy would not break through. 'I never saw an occasion,' recalled General M. S. Khozin, 'even in the most difficult situations, when there seemed to be no way out, when Zhukov lost his head even for a second or did not find a sound solution.'

Zhukov spent only twenty-seven days in Leningrad, but in that short period he left an indelible memory. Of course, the fact that Leningrad did not fall and withstood the blockade, and the fact that the Germans were turned back at the very gates of Moscow, cannot be attributed to a few individuals. Such victories could only result from the efforts of hundreds of thousands, indeed millions of people. But if the rôle of the individual in history is to be taken into account, then the name of Zhukov is linked in the public mind with the salvation of both Leningrad and Moscow.

It should also be pointed out, however, that Zhukov treated his officers and men in the field harshly on more than one occasion. As commander of the Leningrad Front, on 17 September 1941 he signed Order No. 0064, decreeing that 'all commanders, political officers, and rank and file who leave the line of defence without prior written instruction of the Front or Military Council are to be shot on sight'. But Zhukov took no part in drafting Order No. 227 of 28 July 1942, which introduced the blocking units, penal companies and battalions that were placed as forward echelons in attack, on pain of death, on all fronts.

At the beginning of October there was a real threat that the capital might fall. The enemy had surrounded a large part of the forces of the Western and Reserve Fronts at Vyazma: the approaches to Moscow lay open. As with Leningrad in early September, so now, when the fate of the capital hung by a hair, Stalin decided to turn to Zhukov for help. On 6 October he cabled him 'to return to Moscow at once to carry out a special task'. On 7 October Zhukov was taken straight from the airport to Stalin, and was informed en route that Stalin was not well. Zhukov was brought to Stalin's apartment. As he told me, there he found Stalin in conversation with Beria: 'Ignoring me, or perhaps unaware of my arrival, he was telling Beria to use his agencies to sound out the possibilities for making a separate peace with Germany, given the critical situation. That gives you an idea of just how disoriented our head of state was at the time! Finally he noticed me and, after greeting me, said with irritation that he had no idea what was happening at the Western and Reserve Fronts. He walked slowly across to a map, and moving his finger across the Vyazma district, declared angrily: "Just like Pavlov at the beginning of the war, Konev has opened up the front to the enemy here."'

Stalin asked Zhukov to call in at the General Staff to collect a document and then to go to the relevant Front HQ in order to assess the situation and to report back by telephone. The document in question was signed by Chief of General Staff Shaposhnikov on 6 October and was an order 'to acquaint Comrade Zhukov with the situation. All future decisions by Comrade Zhukov connected with the use of troops at the front and questions of control must be carried out.'

After touring the most dangerous areas and Front HQs, Zhukov came to the conclusion that the route to Moscow was virtually open to the enemy. He told Stalin this on the telephone and requested that troops be transferred from wherever possible and as soon as possible for deployment on the Mozhaisk line of defence. On 10 October Zhukov was appointed commander of the Western Front. Stalin wanted to put Konev on trial, as he had Pavlov at the outbreak of the war, but Zhukov asked that he be left in place as his deputy. The last conversation they had on this matter ended with a threat from Stalin: 'If you surrender Moscow, *both* your heads will roll.' Zhukov was under no illusions. 'I foresaw,' he told me, 'that even without Konev I would suffer that fate if we lost the capital.'

Soon Stalin telephoned him and asked: 'Can we defend Moscow, and if so, what has to be done?' Zhukov replied affirmatively and requested only that Stalin accelerate the transfer of reserves from the hinterland. As for himself, he plunged into action. Neither sleeping by night nor resting by day, he applied his inexhaustible energy to every problem, taking urgent measures to strengthen the troops' battle-readiness and to restore a complete defence front. With his eye always on the main objective, Zhukov had the ability to make his officers carry out seemingly impossible orders. He was indeed severe, demanding and strict. These characteristics featured particularly during the defence of Moscow. Sparing neither mind nor body, and showing no fear in the face of death itself, he demanded that his troops also go to the limit of self-sacrifice.

Situations sometimes arise in war where the decision to stand to the death seems to be the only one possible to take. It is undoubtedly justified if an important end is gained which saves the majority from extinction, or if it creates conditions that ultimately secure the goal for which the soldiers' lives were sacrificed. 'Unfortunately, [Zhukov] did not always take account of this,' Marshal Rokossovsky recalled. 'Wishing alone is not enough to ensure success, but during the battle for Moscow, he often forgot this.' The rebuke was justified. But in the conditions of mortal danger which threatened the capital, and in the rapidly changing situation, it was not always possible to take carefully weighed and thought-out decisions. Zhukov was right when he said that 'in war calculation and miscalculation follow neighbouring paths.'

By late October the forces of the Western Front had succeeded in temporarily halting the German rush towards Moscow. In a cable to A. A. Zhdanov, a member of the Leningrad Front War Council, Zhukov said, 'I have cobbled together a reasonable organization and have virtually stopped the enemy's advance, and you know how I propose to go on: I will wear him out and then beat him.'

Zhukov used this method extremely successfully against a strong and experienced enemy. By this time he had faith in his own abilities, he was able to discern the genuine from the ephemeral military wisdom that Stalin had acquired, and he was defending his own ideas forcefully, as General P. A. Belov, Commander of 2nd Cavalry Corps, witnessed. On 10 November Zhukov brought him to see Stalin in the Kremlin. 'Stalin's eyes did not have their former steadiness, and his voice lacked conviction,' Belov recalled. 'But what amazed me even more was Zhukov's behaviour. He spoke sharply, in a peremptory tone. The impression was created that the senior commander here was Zhukov. And Stalin seemed to accept it as normal.'

The might of the German tank spearheads was broken on the flaming ridges above Moscow, and by early December the enemy advance had been virtually stopped. This strategic success, accomplished by troops of the Western Front with the addition of timely reserves brought up from the depths of the country, allowed the Red Army to undertake a powerful counter-offensive. After assessing the position, on 30 November Zhukov sent Deputy Chief of General Staff Vasilevsky a campaign plan for the counter-offensive, together with an explanatory note and a request that he urge Stalin to approve the operation at once, before it was too late. Stalin read the documents and wrote: 'Agreed.'

Western Front forces launched their counter-offensive on 6 December, with Zhukov spending many days and nights among them. He took minimal rest and ate only what he could snatch, but his robust constitution began to flag. The huge physical and mental strain and the sleepless nights took their toll. Some time around the middle of December, his security chief, N. Kh. Bedov, recalled, 'we just couldn't get him to wake up at the agreed hour. An hour passed, then two, but no way could we get him up. Then Stalin telephoned. Headquarters chief, General Sokolovsky, reported that we couldn't wake Zhukov up. "Don't wake him, then, let him sleep," Stalin replied.'

The Soviet counter-offensive at Moscow culminated in the destruction of the Wehrmacht's strike force which had sought at any cost to occupy the capital and win the war. The victory was of enormous political as well as strategic significance. It was undoubtedly the result of titanic efforts by the entire Soviet people and the Red Army. Zhukov's contribution was also of primary importance, and the battle for Moscow brought him popularity as a great military leader. In August 1942 he was made Deputy Supreme Commander-in-Chief and First Deputy Defence Commissar. He was not ecstatic about the appointment. 'To be quite frank,' he told me, 'I wasn't pleased with this new job. When you are in command of an Army or a Front, it's as if you have your own home, your own place, you know who you can rely on, whereas to be Stalin's deputy was very hard. Anyway, my rôle was to be where the action was hottest.'

His new job involved him in the strategic and campaign planning, all big operations in their preparation and execution. He was only rarely in Moscow, most of his time being spent at the front, where he assisted commanders in devising and carrying out the operational decisions which flowed from the general plan, and also helped with liaison. No important problem escaped his notice. He arrived at the Stalingrad Front on 29 August in order to help organize counter-attacks on the northern sector and so reduce the pressure on the city. At a meeting with the commander of 1st Guards Army, K. S. Moskalenko, Zhukov pointed out: 'We've been fighting already for two years, and now it's time we learnt to do it properly. As Suvorov said, intelligence is the eyes and ears of an army. You can't just rely on the patriotism, bravery and courage of our troops, or throw them against an enemy you don't understand with cries of "Charge!" You won't beat the Germans with your huzzahs! We don't have the right to send our men to their deaths in vain.' As already noted, Zhukov had no hand in creating the penal battalions that went in front of the attacking forces, at Stalingrad as elsewhere, but their existence should not be ignored when counting the cost of victory.

Zhukov organized the command of the counter-attack forces of 1st Guards and 24th and 66th Armies. Marshal Chuikov claimed that it was 'the firm hand and unbending will of Marshal Zhukov that helped secure these attacks during September.' And Zhukov himself wrote: 'I can state with authority that, had it not been for those strong counter-attacks by the forces of the Stalingrad Front and the systematic attacks of our aircraft, things in Stalingrad were likely to have been a lot worse.'

With Vasilevsky, he looked for ways to turn the situation around at Stalingrad, and eventually they settled on the idea of a counter-offensive. The decision was made in Stalin's office on 12 September. Once Stalin had approved the idea in principle, they worked out a plan which called for the highest degree of military skill, a plan called, with some justice, the Soviet 'Cannae'. With rough parity in manpower and weapons, the Red Army had to encircle and destroy a grouping of many thousands. 'In order to achieve the element of surprise,' Zhukov recalled, 'Stalin strictly forbade us to tell anyone about the operation, even members of the State Defence Council. We were permitted to tell each Front Commander only what he needed to know.' Rokossovsky wrote that during the campaign Zhukov displayed 'superb erudition and wide-ranging awareness of the circumstances'.

While Zhukov was almost permanently at the Don and Southwestern Fronts during the preparations, he was destined to be absent when the counter-offensive was launched on 19 November. With the object of tying down enemy reserves and preventing them from being thrown into action at Stalingrad, Stalin ordered Zhukov to prepare a diversionary operation on the Kalinin and Bryansk Fronts. 'Stalin was again worried about Moscow,' Zhukov remarked. 'This operation was therefore designed to destroy the enemy's bridgehead in the Rzhev–Ghzhatsk–Vyazma triangle, 90 miles from the capital. The aim was achieved, although it proved impossible to dislodge the enemy totally from the district at that time.'

While he was preoccupied with this task, Zhukov was also worrying about his 'baby', the battle of Stalingrad. On 24 November he cabled Vasilevsky, who was co-ordinating the Fronts: 'Further success and complete rout will depend on two factors: (1) the speed of the attack from all sides, and (2) firm security of our flanks and rear.' His advice was taken. In assessing the battle of Stalingrad he said, 'I gained greater experience in organizing that counter-offensive than I had at Moscow in 1941.'

On 18 January 1943 Zhukov was created Marshal of the Soviet Union and was the first to be decorated with the newly created Order of Suvorov, 1st Class. From January to March he co-ordinated the breaking of the Leningrad blockade, sorted out the position on the Voronezh Front, where the enemy had broken through in the Kharkov Military District, and in April successfully analysed the development of the strategic position and the course the war would take in the summer and autumn of 1943. He calculated that the enemy would not be able to create large reserves by the spring, but would try to seize the initiative and advance along a narrower front. Zhukov predicted that the enemy would make a bypass attack on Kursk. He thought it unwise for Soviet troops to go over to the offensive for the first time against a well dug-in enemy. 'It would be best,' he wrote in his report to the General Staff, 'if we exhausted the enemy on our defences, took out his tanks, and then using fresh reserves went over to general advance and finished off the enemy's main grouping.' At a General Staff meeting on 12 April, the decision was made to take up this plan of defence.

Zhukov remained with the troops of the Central and Voronezh Fronts. He studied the situation and the enemy's behaviour. He directed the training of the troops while maintaining constant contact with Stalin. On 5 July the famous battle of the Kursk Arc began. Zhukov was in the thick of it, assessing the situation, helping Front commanders, co-ordinating their actions. He gave his all for the success of the campaign, and, as one who took part in the battle, I can testify that the troops started saying, 'Where there's Zhukov, there's victory!'

By the end of 1943 the Red Army had liberated eastern Ukraine and seized a number of bridgeheads on the western bank of the Dnieper, and on 6 November they freed Kiev. In mid-December, after the Teheran Conference, Zhukov took part in a meeting of the State Defence Council and Stavka and the General Staff, where the prospects for the spring and summer of 1944 were discussed, as well as a concrete plan for the forthcoming winter campaign. Reports were given by N. A. Voznesensky, Chairman of the State Planning Committee, Vasilevsky, Chief of the Operations Directorate of GHQ, and A. I. Antonov, First Deputy Chief of the General Staff, and by Zhukov. 'This was the first time in the entire war,' Zhukov remarked, 'that such strategic planning took place.'

He then returned to his command post to co-ordinate the 1st and 2nd Ukrainian Fronts which were at that moment carrying out main strikes against the enemy. With the fatal wounding of N. F. Vatutin on 1 March 1944, Zhukov became commander of the 1st Ukrainian Front. Having completed their operation at Proskurov-Chernovitsy between 4 March and 14 April, the forces under his command advanced a distance of some 220 miles, emerging in the foothills of the Carpathians and cutting the enemy's front in two parts.

Zhukov flew to Moscow on 22 April to discuss the plans for the summer and autumn campaigns, and during dinner that evening Stalin told him he was to receive the first Order of Victory. During the discussion of the summer campaign plan, Zhukov advocated transferring troops from the southwest to the central strategic axis, where they would be in a position to effect the final operations of the war. He proposed striking the main blow in Belorussia. The German command regarded the 'Belorussian Balcony' as an important strategic bridgehead and reinforced it energetically. In early May at Zhukov's suggestion Konev was given command of the 1st Ukrainian Front. K. V. Krayukov, a member of the War Council of this Front, commented warmly on Zhukov in his report to Stalin, but added that 'at times he is short with his subordinates and displays excessive severity'. On this issue Zhukov himself said: 'I can't hide the fact that I'm no diplomat. At times I can be too sharp, if frank. When the lives of thousands of men are at stake, and it's a question of success or defeat, there isn't always time or opportunity to choose one's words with delicacy, and sometimes one has to say unpleasant things.'

In the summer of 1944 Zhukov and Vasilevsky were given wider powers by Stalin. Before the Belorussian operation they could advise or recommend a course of action to a Front Commander, but if they needed to give an order, they had to request Stalin's written permission. Now, in the Belorussian operation, which was on a massive scale, they had the power to exercise direct control over the military actions of four Fronts. In this operation, which opened on the third anniversary of the German invasion, Zhukov revealed new strengths of strategic ability. He displayed the qualities of a decisive field commander and a calculating operator, a severe instructor and thoughtful mentor, a demanding war leader and concerned guide. He used his contacts with Front, Army, Corps and Divisional commanders to great effect. The entire operation was conducted under his direct control, and when the situation became difficult and confused, he would go forward himself into the thick of it.

In the final phase of the operation Zhukov moved to the 1st Ukrainian Front in order to assist its commander in the Lvov-Sandomir operation in which four of the Red Army's six tank armies took part. As a result of this action, two German Army Groups, Centre and Northern Ukraine, were destroyed, opening the central strategic axis, to which the main Soviet forces were transferred. The Red Army's strike group was now aimed straight at Berlin, and the 1st Belorussian Front took centre stage.

Stalin summoned Zhukov to Moscow at the beginning of November. He told him that no special co-ordination of the final operation was called for, and that it could be carried out directly from Moscow by the General Staff. 'He then suggested,' said Zhukov, 'that I take command of the 1st Belorussian Front which would go straight to Berlin.' Zhukov accepted, adding that he was prepared to go to any Front. Although Rokossovsky, who until then commanded the 1st Belorussian Front, was offended by the change, it was nevertheless a natural choice: the man who had defended Moscow should be the one to take the enemy capital.

Zhukov took up his post on 16 November, becoming at the same time Deputy Supreme Commander-in-Chief. In this post he carried out two of the greatest culminating operations of the war, Vistula-Oder and Berlin. In order to stun and demoralize the enemy, Zhukov decided to launch the Berlin offensive some two hours before dawn, opening the attack by search-light and with the headlights of the leading tanks blazing. This had the desired effect. Although the operation was relatively slow to develop, this was due to the fact that Hitler threw everything he could into defending the capital. Soviet troops raised the banner of victory above the Reichstag on 1 May. On 5 May Zhukov inspected the imperial Chancellery, spinning the great globe in Hitler's study, while no doubt wondering what would have happened if he had not crushed the Nazi reptile. He was in the Reichstag next day and, like so many Soviet soldiers, scratched his name on a column.

On 7 May Stalin informed Zhukov that the act of unconditional surrender would be signed in Berlin at 0000 hours on 9 May and that he was to represent the Soviet High Command. Zhukov opened the session at the appointed hour. Alongside him sat Air Chief Marshal Sir Arthur Tedder, General Carl Spaatz and General Jean de Lattre de Tassigny, the British, American and French representatives, respectively. Defeated Germany was represented by General Wilhelm Keitel, Grand Admiral Hans Georg von Friedeburg and General Hans-Jurgen Stümpff. The act was signed, Zhukov congratulated everyone on the long-awaited victory and held a reception which ended with singing and dancing. 'I couldn't resist,' said Zhukov, 'and I danced *à la russe*, as I used to when I was a lad.'

One of the great events in Zhukov's life was the Victory Parade held in Moscow on 24 June 1945. He took the parade and Rokossovsky was the officer commanding. Zhukov rode out from the Spassky Gate of the Kremlin on a fine white horse, while Rokossovsky rode up to greet him on a black charger – it had been quite a time since they had served together in the cavalry. They both wondered if they still had a good seat and bearing and whether their fine horses would not let them down. Such an event is unforgettable and indeed Zhukov remembered it all his life.

On 12 June Zhukov received his third Hero of the Soviet Union Gold Star, in Berlin in July he was made a Knight Grand Cross of the Order of the Bath, and in August he received his second Order of Victory. From the end of the war until the spring of 1946 Zhukov was Commander-in-Chief of the Soviet zone of occupation in Germany. In March he was recalled to Moscow and made Commander-in-Chief Land Forces and Deputy Defence Minister (as Commissars were known after 1943). He remained only three months in this post.

The victor's laurels which adorned Zhukov gave Stalin no peace. He decided the time had come to discredit the war hero, to distance him from the 'court,' as the Emperor Paul had once removed Suvorov. A number of Marshals and Generals were arrested and forced to make accusations against Zhukov. In June the Chief War Council was convened with all the Marshals present. Stalin was the first to speak, and he sharply charged Zhukov with improper behaviour, with having spoken against the government, and with exaggerating his own part in the war and with giving interviews to foreign newspapers. As a result, Zhukov was removed from his post and appointed commander of Odessa Military District. He recalled: 'When Stalin . . . sent me to command Odessa, I made a firm decision that I would not reduce my demands on my subordinates one iota, nor on the troops or their training programmes. I was resolved to remain myself. I knew they would be waiting for me to change my ways, to shrug my shoulders and command the District in any old way. But I would not allow myself to do this. Of course, glory is glory. But it is also a two-edged sword and can sometimes give you a painful blow. After that blow I did everything to be myself. I saw my inner salvation in this. In endurance, in work, in not losing my strength of character even in those difficult circumstances.'

In December 1947 Zhukov was urgently summoned back to Moscow. No reason was given. Beria's web had ensnared him. People who had worked with him were being arrested. A new time of troubles had arrived. But on this occasion he had a heart attack and was hospitalized. This evidently saved him. Stalin's conscience prompted him to spare Zhukov, and in February 1948 he sent him to command Urals Military District at Sverdlovsk, deep in the interior, as he was afraid that he might escape abroad more easily from the port of Odessa. 'When I was in Sverdlovsk,' Zhukov recalled, 'Abakumov, on Beria's orders, prepared an entire case of a military conspiracy. They sank to such obscene and disgusting depths as to accuse me of masterminding a military plot against Stalin. But I was told by people who were present at the meeting that Stalin, when Beria called for my arrest, said: "No. I won't let you arrest Zhukov." It was left to me only to thank Stalin mentally for not throwing me to Beria.'

In March 1953, soon after Stalin's death, Zhukov was appointed Deputy Defence Minister. It was deeply ironic that it fell to him to arrest Beria, who had been working feverishly to seize power. Preventing this extremely dangerous development of events, which could have led to an even worse régime than Stalin's, was of fateful importance. 'I regarded it as my duty to make my own small contribution to the affair,' Zhukov concluded.

The authority which Zhukov's enemies had managed to shake was now re-established. In February 1955 he became Defence Minister and in the following year on his sixtieth birthday was awarded his fourth Hero of the Soviet Union Star. Under his leadership, the Soviet Army was restructured in accordance with the experience gained during the war and the scientific and technological revolution that was now under way.

The course adopted by the CPSU following its XX Congress in 1956, and which was aimed at correcting the mistakes and crimes committed during Stalin's rule, was not to the taste of many of the old Guard, and they determined to remove Khrushchev, that is, to stage a palace coup. On the eve of a Central Committee Plenum in June 1957, Khrushchev asked Zhukov for his support. In heated debates at the Plenum the balance seemed to be moving in favour of Khrushchev's opponents, but then at the critical moment Zhukov took the floor: 'Molotov and his supporters want to bring back the Stalinist methods of leadership. We cannot stand for that. If you continue to oppose the Party line I will be compelled to turn to the army and the people.'

The speech had a strong effect on the Central Committee members. Witnessing the rise of Zhukov's authority, which in the aftermath of the Plenum had brought him into the Politburo – or Presidium as it was then called – Khrushchev, however, decided it was time for the war hero to retire. To this end another Plenum was convened, on 29 October 1957, at which, on the pretext of improving political work in the army, and on

Khrushchev's orders, Zhukov was accused of 'Bonapartism' and of wanting to establish a military dictatorship. In his memoirs, Khrushchev wrote that Zhukov had not properly understood his rôle, so that 'we had to remove him as Minister and condemn his ideas. . . . We parted company with him on concrete political issues.' For his part, Zhukov vehemently denied that he had ever wanted to rule the country. The purpose of his whole life, he claimed, was military service for the defence of the Motherland. One can agree with Molotov's later assessment of Zhukov as 'a great military man, but a poor politician' – something Zhukov himself was prepared to admit. Khrushchev's treatment of this national hero, however, was unforgivable.

Retirement came very hard to Zhukov, even in comparison with the post in Odessa, where he had at least been closely involved with the love of his life, the army. In conversation with the writer, Konstantin Simonov, he admitted that this last crisis in his life had been especially hard to endure, even though, as he himself admitted, he may have brought it on himself, at least partly: 'There's no smoke without fire,' he said.

From autumn 1957 to May 1965 he was in total disgrace. He was now labelled a 'Bonapartist' and the slanderous articles that appeared about him in the press frightened off some of his old comrades-in-arms. It was now forbidden to hang his portrait in military establishments and his name was heard only rarely. None of this, however, affected his popular image as the national hero who had saved his country from the Nazis, and when on 8 May 1965, for the first time since being ostracized, he appeared on the podium at the Kremlin Palace of Congresses for the victory celebrations, he was greeted by a storm of applause and shouts of 'Hurrah for Zhukov!'

During his difficult retirement he wrote a remarkable book, his *Memoirs and Reflections*, a book he found it both painful and necessary to write: 'I always had the feeling that my field of knowledge was much narrower than I would have liked and that I felt I needed for my work. I suffered then and I still suffer over this.' Nevertheless, he overcame the mental barrier and wrote the book which stands as a monument of military memoirs. Shortly before his death, as it were summing up his achievements, he said: 'Time puts everything in its proper place and judges us all. The attempt to deceive and outwit history failed. One can only serve one's country properly with the truth and the struggle for the truth.'

Zhukov died on 18 June 1974 and his ashes were buried in the Kremlin wall. His old comrade, Marshal Vasilevsky, wrote: 'He was born for the military life and for large-scale warfare. One can only envy a man who so closely identified his own life with that of the people. The life and work of such a man are worthy of emulation.'

Throughout 1996, the centenary of Zhukov's birth on 1 December 1996 was celebrated in Russia and other former states of the CIS in style and with much acclaim. In Russia the event clashed with celebrations to mark the

300th anniversary of the Russian Navy. It also provided a welcome morale booster for the Russian Armed Forces, regarded by many observers as in a state of decline following the Chechen debacle, and coping with its new role, financial constraints and plummeting social status. With regard to Zhukov's wartime role, he was described as 'Marshal of Victory' and compared to the legendary Suvorov – in contrast to Kutuzov. To mark the Zhukov centenary the 'Order of Zhukov' was instituted.

BIBLIOGRAPHY

Author's personal interviews with Zhukov.
Marshal Zhukov. Kakim my ego pomnim, Moscow, 1988.
Marshal Zhukov: polkovodets i chelovek, Moscow, 1988.
Sorok besed s Molotovym. Iz dnevnika F. Chuyeva, Moscow, 1991.
Stalingrad: uroki istorii, Moscow, 1980.
Zhukov, G. K., *Vospominaniya i razmyshleniya*, Moscow, 1990.

STALIN'S GHOSTS

RICHARD WOFF

The year 1937 marked a tragic turning point in the fortunes of the Red Army High Command, as Stalin moved to settle old scores with former comrades-in-arms, wiping out virtually the whole of the former Civil War 'old Guard'. But the 'meatgrinder' did not stop there, claiming in the 1940s some of the most dedicated, if not the most outstanding, officers, whose only crime was their inexperence and inability, faced by the most powerful military machine in the world, to make amends for the wilful shortcomings of Stalin's control of military affairs.

The full truth of Stalin's purges did not begin to emerge until Khrushchev's revelations in his 'secret' Report to the XX Party Congress of 1956. Under Khrushchev's successor Leonid Brezhnev – a self-made 'Marshal of the Soviet Union' – there followed a renaissance of the 'Stalin cult'. It was only in the 1980s that public opinion in the Soviet Union was prepared to face the truth, and come to terms with Stalin's enormities and the wider implications for the future of the Soviet state. None the less, as late as 1987, in his address to the ceremonial meeting to mark the Seventieth Anniversary of the October Revolution, General Dmitri Yazov, the Soviet Defence Minister, sought to draw a veil over the Stalin period, declaring that 'Stalin after all won the War'! As Yazov's comment makes clear, while the Communist Party ruled, any outright condemnation or objective assessment of Stalin's enormities was taboo. Indeed, until the late 1980s many of Stalin's 1937–50 victims remained 'non-persons' as far as Soviet historians were concerned, their existence and achievements, and in most cases circumstances surrounding their death, subject to a veil of official silence in Soviet reference books and military publications.

The final gruesome chapter in Stalin's capricious relationship with the senior Red Army command opened on the eve of the German invasion of the Soviet Union. Paradoxically, for many senior Red Army officers at the time 1940 appeared to be a year of promise. Still basking in the glory of Khalkin-Gol, with the Finns finally pummelled into submission, morale and professional status were to be boosted by the restoration of the ranks of 'General' and 'Admiral' for the first time since 1917. Between May and June 1940 a total of 982 Generals and 74 Admirals were created. In addition, on 7 May three senior officers were promoted Marshal of the Soviet Union. Earlier the same year, the 'case' against them having been dropped, a number of senior Red Army officers were released from prison. The murderous whirlwind of the late 1930s appeared to have abated. For many this was a sad delusion.

Of the Generals and Admirals of 1940, over 100 were to be eliminated by one means or another down to 1950, mainly at the hands of Beria's execution squads. The victims fall into three groups. The first group – some thirty or more senior officers 'repressed' between 1940 and 1942, in some cases within months of promotion – form the ghostly rear guard of the victims of the 1930s purges. Many of those shot in 1941 had been under 'investigation' for some time on suspicion of 'sabotage' and 'espionage', indicating collusion between German counter-intelligence and the NKVD, as in the case of Tukhachevsky in 1937. The first disasters following the German invasion sealed their fates. Significantly, the senior Red Air Force Command was to be singled out for retribution: Lieutenant-General Pavel Rychagov (aged thirty), a Deputy Defence Commissar for the Air Force since February 1941; Colonel-General Grigoriy Shtern (forty-one), Chief of the Air Defence Directorate; Lieutenant-General Yakov Smushkevich (thirty-nine), Senior Air Assistant General Staff; Lieutenant-General Fedor Arzhenukhin (thirty-four), Head of the Air Academy for a brief five months; Lieutenant-General Ivan Proskurov (thirty-four), Chief Main Directorate of Long Range Aviation – all shot 28 October 1941; Lieutenant-General Petr Pumpur (forty-one), Commander Aviation Moscow Military District, shot 23 March 1942; Major-General Ernest Shakht (thirty-seven), Senior Assistant Commander Air Force for Educational Establishments, shot February 1942; Major-General Petr Volodin (thirty-two), Chief Red Army Air Staff, 'repressed 1941'. All were young, highly decorated officers of promise, promoted in most cases for distinguished action at Khalkin-Gol, and in the Winter War of 1939–40. One – Shakht – was a German born in Bern in 1904, and the son of close political allies of the young Lenin. All were to be 'rehabilitated' in 1954–5.

The purge of 1941 also included other senior 'scapegoats'. Colonel-General Alexander Loktionov, Chief of the Red Air Force 1937–9, Deputy People's Defence Commissar 1939–40, and Commander Special Baltic Military District since June 1940, was recalled to Moscow in January 1941 and was never heard of again. Major-General Grigory Savchenko, Deputy Chief Main Artillery Directorate, 'died' in 1941, together with Major- General Mikhail Kayukov, Chief of a Directorate in the Defence Commissariat.

The second group of generals who paid with their lives for the early disasters suffered by the Red Army in June–July 1941 were the senior field commanders and their deputies. The full force of Stalin's vengeance fell on the senior Western Front command, headed by General Dmitri Pavlov. The fate of these senior commanders has been a matter for speculation since the mid-1950s. In the late 1980s the subject surfaced again in the military press, part of the emotive debate within the High Command adapted to remind the leadership of the price to be paid for 'military cuts' and 'lack of preparedness', and the baleful results of 'the Party's concern for the Armed Forces'.

The tragedy of June 1941 on the Western and Southwestern Fronts had its roots in the purges of the late 1930s which devoured most of the senior commanders who had participated in the reforms, technical revolution, and realignment of military doctrine throughout the mid-1930s. Because of its location astride the western strategic axis, Belorussian Military District, with Kiev Military District, was the focus of General Staff concern. Redesignated Belorussian Special Military District in July 1938 and Western Special Military District in July 1940, practically the whole of the District command perished in the purges of 1937–9, being replaced on the eve of the Second World War by inexperienced officers, with little grasp of command and control higher than a division. Tragically, the new men, however dedicated and loyal to the Party, lacked initiative, and were too frightened to take full responsibility for the consequences of their actions. There were other grave shortcomings, above all in equipment, and lack of modern communications systems. Following the German invasion the District was redesignated the Western Front under General Dmitri Pavlov, District Commander since July 1940. Born of peasant stock in 1897, a Civil War veteran, 'volunteer' in the Spanish Civil War 1936–7, and subsequently a pioneering Head of the Auto-Armoured Tank Directorate 1937–40, Pavlov displayed ability and courage during the Soviet-Finnish War, but he was totally lacking in aptitude for high command, and by all accounts an understanding of modern war. In many ways, therefore, Pavlov personified the fundamental shortcomings of the 'command-administrative' system, with his imprecise, confused style of command, lack of initiative, and fatal instinct for being 'several steps behind events'. But he was not a coward, and sought to fulfil his duty to his country and those entrusted to his command. Following the disasters on the Western Front, Pavlov was arrested on 16 July and brought before a military tribunal, charged with 'disgraceful cowardice unbecoming a commander, negligence, mismanagement, breakdown in command and control, surrendering weapons to the enemy without a fight, and absenting himself from the field of battle'.

Nine other senior officers were arrested along with Pavlov, all alleged to have been implicated in the disastrous collapse of the Red Army. The victims were sentenced to be shot on 22 July. A further three were hunted down and executed in September. In 1956 a committee of enquiry, after studying General Staff records, and hearing several surviving 'witnesses', posthumously 'rehabilitated' Pavlov and the other officers as Stalin's scapegoats.

The purge did little to improve the fortunes of the Red Army, and by early October the situation on the Western Front had become even more critical, with 19th and 20th Armies facing annihilation. Bulganin, a member of Stalin's circus of military clowns and political 'supremo' on the Western Front, now tried to have the new commander, Konev, arrested for incompetence. While he had his own doubts about Konev's performance, Zhukov protested to Stalin, resenting Bulganin's unqualified interference and convinced that punishing commanders would not help the situation. Mercifully for the Soviet Union, and thanks to Zhukov, Konev did not join the ranks of Stalin's 'ghosts', although he would later be twice threatened with arrest. Following his 'reprieve' in September 1941, however, he was replaced by Zhukov and transferred to command the newly established Kalinin Front.

While the name Dmitri Pavlov stands as a memorial to July 1941 victims, Stalin also ordered the arrest of a large group of generals deemed to have been implicated in the disasters both on the Western Front and on the Leningrad Front. Among those arrested were: Lieutenant-General Nikolai Trubetskoy, Chief Red Army Transport Communications; Major-General N. I. Gopich, Chief Red Army Signals; and Lieutenant-General F. S. Ivanov, Main Personnel Directorate. As in 1937–9, the Military Academies could not remain immune to Stalin's anger, and several Heads of Chairs were also netted, including Major-General Fedor Romanov – Head of the Operations Faculty of the General Staff Academy – and Major-General F. K. Kuzmin – Head of the Chair of Tactics of the Frunze Military Academy. Of this group some officers subsequently returned to the front, others languished in labour camps, and many 'died'.

There were also cases of suicide – a tradition in the Russian Army in cases of generals *in extremis* – in order to escape being taken prisoner, or the consequences of the folly of their actions. In June–July 1941 some twenty generals took this time-honoured way out, including Mikhail Petrov and his deputy, Nikolai Kozhokhin; Ivan Konets; M. G. Yefremov; and Dmitri Lestev, Head of Political Propaganda, Western Special Military District. For a long time it was also rumoured that Colonel-General Mikhail Kirponos, Commander Southwestern Front, together with three senior officers, committed suicide in September 1941, sooner than surrender.

Other fronts also contributed to the tally of those made to answer for the disasters of June–July 1941: Major-Generals I. S. Kosobutsky, Commander

41st Rifle Corps (Northwestern Front); M. B. Salikhov (Southern Front), and his political deputy I. G. Korochkin; S. G. Galaktionov, Commander 30th Rifle Division (Southern Front), and his political deputy I. K. Yeliseyev. While a State Defence Council Order of 27 July condemning the senior Western Front command was read out to all officers and men, and Commissar Lev Mekhlis applied his own remedy to stamp on 'panic-mongers and treachery', on 16 August the Supreme High Command issued an Order commending 'the heroism of Soviet forces' under the leadership of certain senior officers: Lieutenant-General Ivan Boldin, Deputy Comman-der Western Front; N. K. Popel, political commissar 8th Mechanized Corps (Southwestern Front); T. Ya. Novikov, Commander 406th Rifle Regi-ment of 124th Rifle Corps (Southwestern Front); Lieutenant-General V. I. Kuznetsov, Commander 3rd Army (Western Front), and his political deputy N. I. Biryukov. There were also other instances of outstanding courage and sacrifice amid disasters besetting the Red Army, above all by the group of senior officers released from NKVD jails in early 1940: Lieutenant-Generals L. G. Petrovsky, Commander 63rd Rifle Corps (Western Front), killed in August attempting a break-out, and K. P. Podlas, Commander 57th Army (Southwestern Front), killed at Kharkov in May 1942; Major-General E. Ya. Magon, Commander 45th Rifle Corps, lost without trace August 1941; S. P. Zybin, Commander 37th Rifle Corps (Southwestern Front), killed August 1941; and Lieutenant-General A. I. Zygin, Commander in turn of a Rifle Division, 58th, 39th and 4th Guards Army, killed at Poltava in September 1943. In all, 421 Generals and Admirals were killed in action or died of wounds between 1941 and 1945. Of that total, 344 were Major-Generals, 295 of them killed in action. 1,065 generals were made prisoners-of-war, of whom twenty-three died in captivity, while the fate of a number of them is still unknown. Twenty Generals were executed by their own side, and have since been rehabilitated.

While the harsh retribution meted out to the Western Front command in July 1941, and to a lesser extent the Southwestern Front, remains without parallel during the war, individual commanders were subsequently to be charged with 'arrogance, complacency, backwardness, conservatism, and even arbitrariness'. While the list probably contains the names of some fifty commanders at all levels, at this stage of the war Soviet historians focus on the fate of three senior commanders in particular: Marshal Grigory Kulik, Colonel-General Vasily Gordov and Lieutenant-General Dmitri Kozlov. Born of peasant stock in 1890, a veteran of the 1st Cavalry Army, and a member of Stalin's close circle of 'military experts', Kulik was chief of the Main Artillery Directorate 1926–30 and 1937–41, and a Deputy Defence Commissar 1939–41. He is widely regarded as having been totally unqualified for the post, and responsible for many of the shortcomings in Red Army artillery organization and equipment. Promoted Marshal in May 1940 – along with

Shaposhnikov and Timoshenko – shortly after being awarded 'Hero of the Soviet Union' for 'outstanding service on command missions in the Finnish–Soviet War' – Kulik's outstanding incompetence was quickly revealed in 1941. A Stavka Representative on the outbreak of the war, his frequent visits to the stricken armies in the first disastrous months invariably degenerated into a farce; his handling of 54th Army during the defence of Leningrad September 1941 was a disaster. Placed at the disposal of the Defence Commissariat on 11 November 1941, Kulik was dispatched to control the desperate operation to hold Kerch. This was to prove his undoing; ridiculed by Zhukov for applying tactics 'of the 1920s', following the inevitable catastrophe Kulik was recalled to Moscow and demoted to Major-General in March 1942. An undistinguished 'comeback' as Commander 4th Guards Army (April–September 1943) during the Battle of Kursk was but a brief respite before final dispatch to a post where his military talents could inflict no further damage – Deputy Chief Main Mobilization Directorate (January 1944–December 1945). Ultimately, Kulik ended his career as Deputy Commander Volga Military District. According to official sources Kulik was 'retired' in June 1946, and 'died' in March 1950, suggesting a comfortable old age, a myth maintained in official Soviet literature until an article in the Russian press in July 1992 revealed the bizarre circumstances surrounding his death. Throughout his erratic career Kulik, apart from causing resentment within the Red Army, had also fallen foul of Beria. With Stalin's protecting hand removed, Kulik was arrested in early 1947 on suspicion of treason, imprisoned awaiting trial, and finally shot on 24 August 1950, along with the Commander Volga Military District, Colonel-General Gordov. He was posthumously rehabilitated and restored to the rank of Marshal of the Soviet Union in 1957.

Apart from the fateful association with Kulik, the career of Colonel-General Gordov is unique in many respects. Unlike Kulik, however, he was an officer of outstanding ability. Born in 1896, Gordov had served in the Red Army since 1918. A 'distinguished' graduate of the Frunze Military Academy in 1932, along with Kulik, during the 1930s Gordov held a number of senior staff appointments. On the outbreak of the war he was Chief of Staff Volga Military District, and subsequently commanded the Stalingrad Front July–August 1942. When Rokossovsky joined the Stalingrad Front in October 1942 Gordov, though temporarily in control, had been superseded, and Rokossovsky's first impression was of a harassed commander, upbraided by Zhukov for losing his head and 'barking too much'. None the less, Gordov was to survive, enjoying a relatively creditable war record as Commander in turn of 33rd and 3rd Guards Army on the First Ukraine Front, finally taking part in the Berlin and Prague Operations. He was awarded 'Hero of the Soviet Union' in April 1945 and returned to command Volga Military District.

The official biography gives the date of Gordov's death as 12 December 1951, which likewise has recently been revealed as incorrect. Analysis of Gordov's career suggests that he did not always enjoy the confidence and support of his superiors. Return to Volga Military District at Kuibyshev (Samara) probably sealed his fate, and that of Kulik, coinciding as it did with the first of the early post-war 'mini-purges' mounted by Stalin. The District had been a particular target during the late 1930s–1940 purge, and several of Gordov's predecessors had been removed and executed. In the early post-war period the local Party organization was under attack from Moscow, and in late 1945 Abakumov, possibly the most notorious of Beria's creatures, was ordered 'to investigate' the Volga Military District command. Headquarters communications were intercepted, offices bugged, and Gordov placed under surveillance. Finally, in a pre-emptive strike Gordov was placed on the retired list in late 1946, and in early 1947 he was arrested, together with his wife, Major-General Fedor Rybalchenko, and another Deputy Commander of the District – Kulik. They were held in prison until August 1950. Brought to 'trial' on 24 August 1950, they were shot the same day. Along with Kulik, both Gordov and Rybalchenko were rehabilitated in 1957.

The third member of the wartime trio of 'incompetents', Lieutenant-General Kozlov, was the victim of the second phase of the 1941–1942 Kerch disaster following Kulik's departure in February 1942. Born in 1896, Kozlov had served in the tsarist army as an NCO before joining the Red Army in 1918. An outstanding record during the Civil War indicated a promising career. A graduate of the Frunze Military Academy in 1928, Kozlov served in a number of commands throughout the 1930s, returning briefly to the Academy as a lecturer in tactics. During the Soviet–Finnish War 1939–40 he commanded a Rifle Corps, and subsequently served with M. V. Zakharov as a Deputy Commander of the 'front-line' Odessa Military District 1940–1. Throughout 1941–2 he held a succession of posts – Chief, Red Army Air Defence, Commander Transcaucasus Military District and Caucasus Front. In January 1942 Koslov was appointed Commander Crimean Front, created out of the Caucasus Front to control operations on the Kerch and Taman Peninsula in a desperate attempt to succour Sevastopol and retain a foothold on the Crimea. Ultimately, the operation stalled and the entire Crimean Front command was recalled to Moscow May 1942, reprimanded, and with one exception demoted. The Crimean Front staff was headed initially by Lieutenant-General Fedor Tolbukhin, and 10 March–19 May by Major-General Pavel Vechy, a capable officer, formerly Deputy Chief General Staff – Chief Southern Strategic Axis Directorate. While the Kerch operation failed due to lack of planning time, there were other factors adding to Kozlov's discomfort. On 10 January Commissar Lev Mekhlis arrived at Kozlov's headquarters in his capacity as Stavka Representative, and immediately set out to establish his pernicious influence, acting more like a political informer, attempting to supplant Kozlov, complaining of his 'inactivity' and 'incompetence' in his reports to Moscow. This in turn drew a sharp rebuke from Stalin, putting Mekhlis in his place on the one hand, while sternly reminding Kozlov that 'you are the Front Commander'. The episode, and Stalin's remark to Mekhlis that 'we have no Hindenburgs in reserve', throws an unusual light on the psychology of the 'Supreme One', and his determination where necessary to uphold the field commander's authority. The reference by Stalin to the Kaiser's summoning the aged Hindenburg out of retirement in September 1914 'to save the Fatherland' was also an indication that the purges had robbed the country of past heroes who might save the situation. The second major disruptive element was the fact that there were eventually three organs of command and control involved in the Kerch operation, all issuing conflicting orders: the Supreme High Command; the North Caucasus Axis under command of Budenny; and the Crimean Front. The unfortunate Kozlov was not helped by instructions from Moscow that orders from Budenny's headquarters should not be carried out if they conflicted with those from the Supreme High Command! The third crucial element influencing the outcome in March–May 1941 was the Commander XI German Army – the genial Colonel-General Erich von Manstcin, together with Guderian the most outstanding of Hitler's generals on the eastern front. Following the collapse of the Red Army operation Kozlov was demoted to Major-General.

None the less, Stalin appears subsequently to have turned a blind eye to Kozlov's misfortune, and in July he was appointed Commander 24th Army on the Stalingrad Front. There followed a brief spell as Deputy Commander Voronezh Front (October 1942–February 1943), reinstatement in his former rank, Stavka Representative on the Leningrad Front May–August 1943, and transfer to the Transbaikal Front as Deputy Commander. In the latter post Kozlov took part in the Far East Campaign against the Japanese Manchurian Army August–September 1945. His retirement shortly after Stalin's death possibly suggests that Kozlov was regarded within the Soviet High Command as a 'Stalin General'. With regard to the remainder of the Crimean Front Command, Mekhlis was relieved of his post of Chief Main Political Directorate, spending the rest of the war in a succession of political posts at the front. None the less, Stalin continued to protect Mekhlis, appointing him Minister of State Control in 1946. Removed in 1950, Mekhlis 'died' in February 1953 – exactly a month before Stalin himself. Major-General Vechy, while recommended to serve 'in a less responsible post', was not demoted, and subsequently served throughout the war in a succession of staff appointments. The remainder were all reduced to the rank of Colonel and transferred to 'less reponsible posts': Fedor Shamanin, Member of the Military Council; Lieutenant-General Sergei Chernyak, Commander 44th Army; Major-General K. S. Kolganov, Commander 47th

Army; and Major-General Ye. Nikolayenko, Commander Air Forces. Coming little under a year after the débâcle on the Western Front, it may be claimed that Kozlov and his associates were lucky not to have paid for the Kerch catastrophe with their lives.

The surviving members of the third group of Stalin's wartime victims were not to be reprieved. Their crime was to have spent the war years in German captivity. The sheer volume of Soviet prisoners-of-war taken by the Germans in the first months of the war came as a shock to the Soviet leadership, and Supreme Command Order No. 270 of 16 August 1941 in effect equated a prisoner of war with a 'deserter' and 'panic-monger'. It was this measure which above all provided the legal basis for trying *in absentia* those senior officers suspected of having deserted to the enemy in the first weeks following the German invasion. For their part the Germans regarded Soviet prisoners-of-war as 'subhuman'. Pictures published of Himmler gloating over the half-starved caged creatures on a visit to a camp for Soviet prisoners-of-war speak for themselves. Senior Soviet officers in general fared little better than their men. For over three decades debate in the Soviet Union, however, focused on the fate of two officers in German captivity, personifying as they do the extremes of experience: Lieutenant-General Andrei Vlasov and Lieutenant-General Dmitri Karbyshev. The case of Vlasov is dealt with by Catherine Andreyev elsewhere in this book.

The case of Karbyshev, unlike that of Vlasov, was regarded as an example of martyrdom under extreme suffering at the hands of his German captors, exemplifying 'the finest qualities of the Soviet officer'. Born in 1880, Karbyshev had a distinguished career as an engineer in the tsarist army. He joined the Red Army in 1918 and was a '1938' graduate of the General Staff Academy. In July 1941 Karbyshev was serving as a senior engineer on the Western Front, and, according to the official Soviet version, following a serious head wound was taken prisoner. In captivity he was subject to constant interrogation, pressure to join the Vlasov movement, and finally torture. Having survived Maidanek, Auschwitz and other Nazi death camps, Karbyshev died in February 1945 in Mauthausen concentration camp. He was subsequently honoured by the posthumous award of 'Hero of the Soviet Union' in August 1946.

Among others who died in captivity, all Major-Generals, were: Sergei Baranov, executed 1942 in Hammelburg for leading an underground organization together with Ivan Nikitin; Khristov Alaverdov, V. I. Prokhorov, A. D. Kuleshov, S. Ye. Danilov, in Flossenburg in 1943; S. A. Tkachenko and G. I. Tkhor, shot while in close confinement; and V. N. Sotensky, shot on 21 April 1945 in Wühlzburg fortress, together with five other fellow-prisoners, probably the last Red Army officer to die in captivity.

Since the late 1980s Soviet debate on the 'prisoner-of-war' question has become more objective, and widened to encompass the fate of the senior commanders taken prisoner in 1941–2. Among those captured in the first weeks of the war, many suffering from severe wounds, were five Army Commanders, three Deputy Army Commanders, six Corps Commanders, and fifteen Divisional Commanders. In 1945 the survivors returned to the Soviet Union. They included Generals S. V. Vishnevsky, A. S. Zotov, I. A. Kornilov, I. N. Muzychenko, P. R. Sysoyev and Ya. I. Tonkonogov. All were to suffer for the years spent in captivity. None the less, as a look at the following five cases shows, the 'system' adopted differing standards: Lieutenant-General Mikhail Potapov, 5th Army (Southwestern Front), taken prisoner following the fall of Kiev September 1941; Major-General Pavel Ponedelin, 12th Army; Major-General Nikolai Kirillov, 13th Rifle Corps; Lieutenant- General Mikhail Lukin; and Lieutenant-General Vladimir Kachalov, 28th Army.

Potapov was to suffer no recrimination, and was even fêted as the 'hero of Kiev'. Subsequently he held a number of senior appointments, including First Deputy Commander Odessa Military District 1958–65. Promoted Colonel-General in 1961, he died in 1965. Despite his 'heroism', he never became a 'Hero of the Soviet Union'. While Potapov's courage is recognized, the fate of the remaining generals became the centre of attention in the late 1980s as the Soviet Union wrestled to come to terms with the enormities of Stalin's rule, and treatment of the Red Army High Command. On his return in 1945 Ponedelin, already sentenced to death *in absentia* in July 1941, was imprisoned and subject to extreme torture by his NKVD captors, and sentenced to death for a second time. Born in 1898, Ponedelin was an officer of outstanding ability, erudition, and courage. A former Chief of Staff Leningrad Military District, it is possible that, but for the years spent as Head of the Chair of Tactics at the Frunze Military Academy in the late 1920s and early 1930s, Ponedelin might have advanced further up the chain of command. While at the Academy he was one of a group of officers, together with Tukhachevsky and Antonov, who worked on the draft 1936 Field Manual. Indeed, his contribution to the evolution of Red Army doctrine in the pre-war years was recognized in 1980 in the official history of the Academy. While serving in Kiev Special Military District on the eve of the German invasion he was described by Bagramyan, Head of the Operations Department, as 'one of our most erudite commanders', an 'expert in tactics at a higher level'. Equally significant was the praise of the District Commander, Georgy Zhukov. In July 1941, while commanding 12th Army, Ponedelin was surrounded by superior forces, and although 'the last bullet and last shell' had long been expended, attempted to fight his way out. Severely wounded, he was captured and spent the rest of the war in Germany. Throughout he steadfastly refused to co-operate with his captors, and is reported to have spat in the face of Vlasov when the latter attempted to 'turn' him. None the less, this did not save him from being shot on 24 August 1950 after five years in a

NKVD jail. A similar fate overtook Kirillov, executed the same day. Indeed, 24 August 1950 deserves to be remembered as 'Bloody Thursday', the day on which, after five years of 'cat and mouse', Beria finally executed what remained of Stalin's 'ghosts'.

Another commander who had tried desperately to resist capture in July 1941 when facing overwhelming odds was Lukin. He had served in the Red Army since 1918 and had a distinguished Civil War record. A former Commandant of Moscow (1935–7), in 1940 he was promoted Lieutenant-General and appointed Commander 16th Army. Taken prisoner near Vyazma in July 1941, Lukin spent the rest of the war in Germany, and at times was tortured for resisting interrogation. He was also one of the generals contacted by Vlasov, to no avail. On his return to the Soviet Union his bravery was recognised by the award of the 'Order of Lenin'. It is likely that captivity had taken a toll of his health, and in 1946 he was placed on the retired list. He died in 1970.

The case of Kachalov was unusual. Killed in action 4 August 1941 near Smolensk while resisting capture, when V. I. Kolesnikov reported to Mekhlis that Kachalov had 'met an heroic end' trying to fight his way out in a tank, the latter's response was that Kachalov was 'politically immature', and in reality was attempting to surrender. It was not until December 1953 that Kachalov was finally rehabilitated and his honour restored. In May 1965 he was posthumously awarded the 'Order of the Fatherland War' First Class, and a plaque erected on the site where he and five other Generals were killed in action.

Among the great war leaders Stalin was not unique in taking a close interest in the fortunes and misfortunes of his commanders in the field. In their turn Churchill, Roosevelt and Truman, not to mention de Gaulle, all clashed with their generals. None the less, backed up by the NKVD and the political commissars in the field, Stalin's policy of 'shoot in order to encourage the others' was effective, enabling him to pounce with ferocious precision on 'the loafers' and 'panic-mongers'. Sadly, the 'liquidation machine' created a momentum of its own. At the first sign of a wink from the head gamekeeper the beaters would spring to action flushing out the hapless game; on a good day's shoot, a couple of brace of Generals was not un-usual. As the fate of Marshals Novikov and Khudyakov, Admirals N. G. Kuznetsov, V. A. Alafuzov, L. M. Galler and G. A. Stepanov, bear witness, the NKVD penal brigade continued to stalk its prey long after the victory over Nazi Germany. With Stalin's death in March 1953 the 'ghosts' finally had their revenge. The scourge of the Red Army officer corps, Mekhlis, had already 'died' in February 1953. In December 1953 it was the turn of Beria, summarily shot, after a perfunctory trial, not before attempting to escape through the window of a Kremlin toilet.

Inevitably, Stalin's legacy influenced the relationship of successive Soviet leaders with their senior military. In his turn Khrushchev was capable of mustering his Generals and imposing his quack schemes on them very much in the style of the deranged Emperor Paul I, at times rubbishing any general likely to oppose his will like an ill-tempered mongrel. The wartime commissar Marshal Leonid Brezhnev settled for cosy cohabitation with his generals. It was left to President Gorbachev to come to terms with the enormities and injustices of Stalin's régime, and placate an increasingly disgruntled High Command as he attempted to roll back seventy years of Soviet history, while defending Communist rule. The task was left unfinished when he relinquished office in December 1991.

BIBLIOGRAPHY

Izvestiya, 16 July 1992.

Maltsev, Lieutenant-General P. V., 'Kto vinovat?', *Voenno-istoricheskii Zhurnal*, no. 10, 1988.

ViZh, nos 6, 9–12, 1991, nos 6–7, 8, 9, 10, 11, 12, 1992, and nos 1–4, 1993. 'They gave their lives for the Homeland': list in alphabetical order of senior Red Army officers killed in action or reported 'missing'.

ViZh, no. 12, 1991, for complete figures of generals killed in action or taken prisoner since 1941.

INDEX